TRAILBLAZERS
Rediscovering the Pioneers of Business

Bernard M. Baruch: The Adventures of a Wall Street Legend
James Grant

An Autobiography
David Ogilvy

Bernard M. Baruch

THE ADVENTURES OF A
WALL STREET LEGEND

James Grant

JOHN WILEY & SONS, INC.

New York • Chichester • Weinheim • Brisbane • Singapore • Toronto

Grateful acknowledgment is made to the following for permission to quote excerpts:

Eugene Meyer, Jr., memoir (copyright © 1975) and Frances Perkins memoir
(copyright © 1976) in the Columbia University Oral History Project. By
permission of the Trustees of Columbia University in the City of New York.
Kent correspondence, the Frank R. Kent Papers, Manuscripts Division, courtesy of
the Maryland Historical Society.
Fred Schwed, Jr., *Where Are the Customers' Yachts? or, A Good Hard Look at Wall
Street*, copyright 1940, by permission of Simon and Schuster.
Swope correspondence, the Herbert Bayard Swope archive, Mugar Memorial
Library, by permission of Boston University.
Michael Teague, ed., *Mrs. L.: Conversations with Alice Roosevelt Longworth*,
copyright © 1981, by permission of Doubleday.

This text is printed on acid-free paper.

This publication is designed to provide accurate and
authoritative information in regard to the subject
matter covered. It is sold with the understanding that
the publisher is not engaged in rendering legal, accounting,
or other professional services. If legal advice or other
expert assistance is required, the services of a competent
professional person should be sought.

Library of Congress Cataloging in Publication Data:

Grant, James, 1946–
    Bernard M. Baruch : the adventures of a Wall Street legend /
J. G. Grant.
       p.   cm.
    Originally published: Bernard M. Baruch. New York : Simon and
Schuster, c1983.
    Includes bibliographical references and index.
    ISBN 0-471-17075-5 (alk. paper)
    1. Baruch, Bernard M. (Bernard Mannes), 1870–1965. 2. Statesmen—
United States—Biography. 3. Capitalists and financiers—United
States—Biography. 4. United States—Politics and government—20th
century. I. Grant, James, 1946-. Bernard M. Baruch. II. Title.
E748.B32G7 1997
973.91'3'092—dc20
[B]   96-34635

Printed in the United States of America

10 9 8 7 6 5 4 3 2 1

For Patricia

Preface

Bernard M. Baruch and I were at each other's sides for four years, he in posthumous, archival form. We had our ups and downs together. I began work on his biography with the hypothesis that there was less to the legendary investor and mythical Adviser to Presidents than met the eye. Bringing out the truth, I hoped to put a famous American life in the context of almost a century of American financial history.

I was successful in one thing, at least. I was able to show conclusively that Baruch, as a moneymaker, was only human. Thus, he did not sell out at the top in 1929—he was, indeed, bullish—a fact that may prove to be of more than academic interest in the highly speculative market environment of 1996. However, what I quickly came to understand was that this fallibility was worthy and appealing. Certainly, the success that the mortal Baruch enjoyed through trial and error was harder won than any that the legendary Baruch might have achieved through pure clairvoyance. My skepticism turned to admiration.

And presently, admiration was mingled with affection. As I read Baruch's correspondence and talked to some of his surviving friends, I began to like him. ("I nearly laughed myself sick at the idea of your looking dignified at the time the degree was conferred upon you," Baruch wrote to his old friend Frank Kent, star political columnist of the Baltimore *Sun*, on the occasion of Kent's receiving an honorary degree for which Baruch had nominated him. "Your poor wife! Your poor wife!") I, too, became his friend. And then, as the years passed and as my research moved into the public phase of his career, all previous feelings gave way to an overwhelming sense of exasperation. By the time the first book was published, in 1983, I was glad to see the back of him. Then, again, I have no doubt, Baruch would have been delighted to be done with me.

The differences in our lifestyles were unbridgeable. Baruch, who was born in 1870 and died in 1965, lived in a Fifth Avenue mansion, a South Carolina plantation and a Scottish castle, among other splendid addresses. He loved hunting, racing, boxing, motoring, speculating and passing the time of day with his boon companions. He would travel to Saratoga for the racing season and to Europe to take the waters. He was a man's man and a ladies' man all at the same time. The circle of his friends naturally tended to exclude biographers, harmless, bookish people who are always writing (or preparing to write or pretending to write) and who tend to talk about little except their subjects. Baruch loved to talk about himself, but even for him there were limits.

The paucity of sex in this book (with which I was taxed by some readers after its first publication in 1983) can be put down to my determination to hold to the same high evidentiary standards in romance and adultery as in speculation. The unintended consequence of this scruple is the impression conveyed through omission that Baruch was not very interested in the opposite sex, that his marriage was a success, or both. Neither was true, in fact. The evidence on this score, although circumstantial, is strong and convincing. Baruch's marriage having become a formality, he ardently sought female companionship outside of it. He loved women and they him.

As for the financial side of things, previously untapped primary sources helped to shed new light on Baruch's speculative and investment methods. These sources included the documents in which Baruch carried out some stock market-related litigation, the minutes of the New York Stock Exchange deliberations in which he participated and—a particular gold mine—the correspondence that traced his venture-capital investment in what was to become the Texas Gulf Sulfur Company. I studied his brokerage house records from the late 1920s and early 1930s and old documents, interesting and otherwise, from the State Department and the Federal Bureau of Investigation. None of these, I think, had been cited before.

Rereading my record of Baruch's life, I thought that the speculator particularly distinguished himself at the Versailles Peace Conference. In service of his hero Woodrow Wilson, Baruch brought a rare and valuable common sense to the economic negotiations, in the process crossing swords with John Maynard Keynes. As a rule, Baruch's pronouncements on public issues were oracular or platitudinous, and he was a tireless defender of the institution of the garrison state, from which the end of the Cold War has delivered us. At Versailles, however, his special Wall Street intelligence—intuitive, incisive, down-to-earth, impatient for results, focused on future outcomes—was just what the historical moment seemed to need.

My politics are libertarian, whereas Baruch's were not. Or, more correctly, his were usually not. Sometimes, he was the epitome of the Grover Cleveland Democrat, a proponent of limited government, hard money and individual liberty. More often, he seemed to profess something else. In the political arena, he seemed to have no clear purpose, except patriotically to advance the interests of the United States as he understood them. Once he condensed his ideological contradictions into a single sentence of moderate length: "I have unlimited faith in the American people taking care of themselves—if they are told what to do and why."

In finance, in clear distinction, his life was purposeful, artful and even inspirational. In the stock market, he realized harrowing losses as well as fabulous gains. In venture capital, he sometimes miscalculated (as with his attempted rehabilitation of the Wabash Pittsburgh Terminal Railway Company); or, calculating correctly, he sometimes committed himself too timidly (as in Texas Gulf). He did not buy the market at the 1932 bottom any more than he sold it at the 1929 top. Still, he made his millions, and, more impressively, he kept them. If he bought too little, sold too soon, or seemed on occasion to be otherwise risk-averse, it was perhaps because he was mainly risking his own money. He was a freelance capitalist, a type rarely seen in the institutionalized financial markets of the late twentieth century.

At this writing, the stock market is higher and more popular than it has ever been before, and the idea that a mutual fund is little riskier than an insured savings account has gained credence.* Baruch would

---

*Higher as measured by the ratio of stock-market capitalization to gross domestic product; for example, more accessible as measured by unprecedented, $20 billion-per-month inflows into equity mutual funds.

have disagreed, I suspect, although there can be no telling how he might have been positioned in this, the greatest bull market ever. Possibly, he would be even more bullish than the next fellow, as, indeed, he was in the terminal phase of the Coolidge boom. Baruch's speculative genius was his trader's flexibility. What he said (or was quoted as saying) was less important than how he acted. That he was able to regain his bearings and salvage the greater part of his fortune during the long bear market of the early 1930s was a feat of discipline that every investor must admire.

Baruch was an old-fashioned millionaire who had less money than the public imagined but more than enough to live as the public imagined that every millionaire should live. Was his a happy life? He was a poor father, he presided over no railroad (a lifelong ambition) and he spent the last several decades of his political career on the outside looking in. However, he was exceptionally happy in his own skin. His vanity was pure and innocent. "What a fine figure of a man I am," he would say, meaning every word of it. Walking down Madison Avenue in New York, he would beam at passersby, trusting that they would beam back at him, which they often did.

In the special cutting department of the Brooks Brothers store on Madison Avenue and 43rd Street today is an unidentified portrait of an elderly gentleman, luminous, elegant, well-tailored and quite clearly pleased with himself. It is none other than Bernard Mannes Baruch, my friend.

JAMES GRANT

New York, New York
December 1996

holder. As a literal matter he preferred the sunshine to any office, and the familiar photographs of him cogitating on a park bench across the street from the White House somehow reassured millions of Americans that the nation's leaders were being sensibly advised. Following his stint at the United Nations (which followed years of wartime advisory work) there was an outpouring of public affection for Baruch the likes of which few elected officials have ever enjoyed. For years, honorary degrees, testimonials, commissions, resolutions, awards and citations poured in on him, not excluding a framed membership certificate from the Society of Yogurt Eaters in 1955 and, in 1956, a certificate of Honorary Membership in the Class of 1918 at West Point.

After his death in 1965 at the ripe age of ninety-four, *National Review* perceptively described him as a "good citizen" in the Stoic tradition, someone "not passionately committed to party, faction or cause . . . but . . . firm in his belief that lawful government is a part of the reasoned order of nature. When lawful government [was] in danger from domestic or external enemies, he [was] ready to do his part in defending it."

It might fairly be asked what more can be said about a man whom four biographers have already tackled and whose autobiography runs to two volumes. My answer is that Baruch's financial career has been largely unexplored, except by Baruch himself, whose recollections on the subject were perhaps understandably selective. From time to time he would bemoan the myth of his trading infallibility, but he could bring himself to deflate only so much of it. He was, in fact, a gifted trader, but the details of his career as a New York Stock Exchange governor, as an unlucky railroad bondholder and as a temporarily bewildered investor during the 1929 Crash have never been told before. Through most of this book my emphasis is on money and markets.

Anyone who made $1 million in the stock market, then put that first million at risk to earn a second, less important million, and so on until he accumulated roughly $25 million, as Baruch did, obviously was willing to climb out on a limb. "The very contemplation of it," wrote Fred Schwed, Jr., of that speculative cast of mind, "makes my bourgeois soul shudder." Baruch amazed his middle-class friends with his proclivity to gamble—he told Harold Ickes that he had put $10,000 on Roosevelt to win a third term in 1940, and that the President, not unreasonably feeling a proprietary interest in the outcome, had asked to be cut in on the winnings, and was—but by his forties he had put his plunging days behind him. In his middle and late years he conserved and husbanded his fortune. So careful a venture capitalist was he in what proved his grand coup, the founding of the Gulf Sulphur (later Texas Gulf Sulphur and still later Texasgulf) Company, that he declined repeated offers by his fellow investors to take the property off their hands for a song.

By necessity, a successful stock trader holds no brief with lost causes. If he's wrong on the market, he must cut losses or risk financial extinction. Baruch brought this trader's flexibility to national politics. In general he believed in the old-time Democratic tenets of hard money, low tariffs and individual liberty, but when the political trend changed during the New Deal he bowed to the new age. In public life he was the least audacious, most risk-averse of men. As a young man he grew rich by taking chances, but as an old man he became famous by playing it safe.

Besides his autobiography, Baruch left behind an extensive and magnificently accessible archive at the Seeley G. Mudd Library of Princeton University, a lifetime's trail of legal and corporate and public documents and a small army of friends, admirers and detractors. The years have thinned the ranks of that army, but a number of people whose lives touched Baruch's were kind enough to share their reminiscences with me or in other ways to lend assistance. I am beholden, then, in strictly alphabetical order, to: Adele J. Busch, Benjamin J. Buttenweiser, John Chamberlain, Margaret Coit, Thomas G. Corcoran, Stanley T. Crossland, John Davenport, Harold Epstein, Virginia Epstein, Mae Fitzsimmons, Kathleen Gilmore, Eric Gordon, Luther H. Gulick, W. Averell Harriman, J. Victor Herd, W. J. Hirsch, Jr., Ira Langsan, Samuel Lubell, Clare Boothe Luce, Marcia Kendrick McCue, John F. McHugh, Robert G. Merrick, Sr., Robert Moses, James Myers, Elizabeth Navarro, Joseph Orecchio, Dorothy Rosenman, Vermont Connecticut Royster, Paul Sarnoff, Dorothy Schiff, Ella A. Severin, Oscar Straus, Henry J. Taylor, Blanche Higgins Van Ess, Dr. Henry Viscardi, Jr., Irving Weiss, Dr. Martin Zweig.

As far as possible I have tried to work from original sources and documents, but without the assistance of numerous experts, researchers, scholars and archivists, that ambitious undertaking would have been impossible. I would therefore like to thank (also in alphabetical order): Katherine K. Baran, Florence Bartoshesky, John P. Boland, Nancy Bressler, Franklyn J. Carr, Mary Cope, Cindy Crowley, Ruth

Dennis, Josephine C. Dzikowicz, Robert H. Ferrell, Deborah Gardner, Stephen P. Gietschier, Benjamin Greenberger, Gary Gunderson, Henry R. Hecht, Sim Johnston, John C. Kavanagh, Maria K. Kavanagh, Frank R. Levstik, Carol K. McGinley, Nicholas X. Rizopoulos, Michael Sandroni, Darnall C. Steuart, Harold Swarthout, Kenneth W. Thornton, Jr., Eliot B. Weathers, Dianne Yaeger and Peter Yaeger. Special thanks go to Mark Fury, an indefatigable reporter, and to a scholar whom I have never had the pleasure of meeting, Jordan A. Schwarz, author of the rich political and economic study of Baruch titled *The Speculator: Bernard M. Baruch in Washington, 1917–1965* (Chapel Hill, North Carolina, 1981). And my appreciation of the scrupulous checking and editing of Patricia Miller is very great indeed.

My thanks, too, to my editor at Simon and Schuster, Alice Mayhew, and to my editors at *Barron's*, Alan Abelson and Robert M. Bleiberg, for their repeated gifts of that most precious commodity, time.

JAMES GRANT

Brooklyn, New York
August 1983

Contents

Bernard M. Baruch

ONE

A Doctor's Son

Even when he was old and very deaf, Bernard Baruch liked to pass the time of day on the telephone with his stockbrokers. After the market closed he would stretch out in an easy chair, shut his eyes and listen to the reading of long lists of quotations. Often he would talk about the menace of inflation (to the point of boring the party at the other end of the phone, because very few people were as worried about that problem as he was in the 1950s) or reminisce about himself.

"I guess that you've met a lot of important people in your time," he said one day, out of the blue, to his favorite broker.

The man agreed. "Most of them thanks to you," he said.

"Well, of all those people, how important would you say that I am?"

"Number two."

The answer jarred Baruch. In his Ptolemaic universe, he was the earth and other mortals were the lesser planets and moons. His vanity was pure and rarefied, and it hadn't occurred to him that his own broker would fail to understand what he himself saw so clearly. He tried to coax an amplification from the man, but none was given. Some time passed before Baruch's curiosity overcame his pride.

"A while ago," he ventured again, to the same broker, "you said that I was the second-most-important man you ever knew. Who was the most important?"

"Why, my father."

Baruch was delighted and relieved.

"You know," he said, "my father was the most important guy I ever met too."

Dr. Simon Baruch, the father of four sons of whom Bernard Mannes was the second, was born in the Prussian village of Schwersenz in 1840. In 1855, dodging the Prussian draft, he made his way to a seaport and sailed to America. He settled in Camden, South Carolina, where another emigrant from Schwersenz, Mannes Baum, owned a general store. Baum made the boy his bookkeeper, helped to teach him English and generously financed his education at the South Carolina Medical College and the Medical College of Virginia. By the time Baruch graduated the Civil War was on, and the erstwhile fugitive from the Prussian draft decided to volunteer his services to the Confederacy. He was commissioned an assistant surgeon in the Third Battalion, South Carolina Infantry, in April 1862.

Without having so much as lanced a boil, as Dr. Baruch said, he was thrown into active service. He attended the sick and wounded at the Second Battle of Manassas, South Mountain, Fredericksburg, Chancellorsville, Gettysburg, Wilderness, Spotsylvania, Cold Harbor, Cedar Creek and Petersburg. Twice he was captured by Union forces, occasions he remembered as the most agreeable of his Confederate service. A sense of his battlefield practice is conveyed by the title of an essay he drafted during a restful detention at Fort McHenry, in Baltimore: "Two Penetrating Bayonet Wounds of the Chest." His advice to his younger brother Herman, who had followed him from Germany to South Carolina and was seventeen when war broke out, was to stay out of the army. When the brothers next met, however, each was in uniform, Herman in the garb of a Confederate cavalryman. The younger man explained that he had enlisted because he could no longer stand the reproach in the eyes of the ladies.

Family lore has it that Dr. Baruch fell in love with his future wife during a wartime furlough at her father's plantation in Winnsboro, South Carolina. Perhaps it was late in the war: Isabelle Wolfe, eldest daughter of thirteen children, was eleven when the fighting started. Her father, Sailing Wolfe, owned twenty-six slaves, and it was Belle's luxurious lot never to have to dress herself. The war was the family's financial ruin. Union troops burned its home, crops and outbuildings, drove off its livestock and freed its slaves. Many years later a friend of the Wolfes wrote to Baruch with her memories of that time: "My first recollection I have of your family was the night your home in Winnsboro was burned by Sherman's army; and my father, Dr. Robinson, was returning to his home after one of his long country visits, found your grandfather and grandmother with all their little children gathered around them offering up prayers in Hebrew." After the war the family home was rebuilt, but the Wolfe fortune (put by the census taken in 1860 at $13,000 in real estate and $67,750 in "personal estate") was denominated irretrievably in Confederate money. Sailing Wolfe died, a poor man, at eighty-four, when the chair in which he was sitting to warm himself tipped forward into a fire.

As the war ended, Dr. Baruch was penniless and weakened by typhoid but eager to build a country practice in Camden. He came home on crutches to discover that not only had the Yankees borne off his surgical tools (he had been presented with an initialed set by a Confederate sympathizer in Baltimore) but also that a Union officer had insinuated himself into the good graces of Belle. This Yankee, a Captain Cantine, had performed some act of chivalry for Belle's sake, but Dr. Baruch was six feet tall and had blue eyes and claimed the advantage of proximity. On November 28, 1867, he and Belle were married. (Fifty-one years later, a visitor asked Bernard Baruch, then chairman of the War Industries Board under President Wilson, to help him get to the fighting in France. He bore a letter from Baruch's mother which said: "The bearer of this is a son of Captain Cantine. I know you will do what you can for him.")

Baruch put small store in genealogy but was pleased to repeat the family history that he was descended from priests and kings. In Germany his namesake and paternal grandfather, Bernhard Baruch (our Baruch came by his middle name from Mannes Baum), stated that the Baruchs were a rabbinical tribe of Portuguese-Spanish origin that was augmented by Polish or Russian blood. "Grandfather," wrote Baruch, "also claimed descent from Baruch the Scribe, who edited the prophecies of Jeremiah and whose name is given to one of the Books of the Apocrypha. On this claim Father himself was silent." After repeatedly being mistaken for Senator William E. Borah on a trip to Poland in 1931, Baruch lightheartedly offered the Idaho Republican an honorary membership in the Baruch clan, observing that among the advantages thereof was a presumptive link to King David.

Bernhard Baruch, who stood six feet tall and wore thick spectacles, was an amateur student of Sanskrit who loved to sit dreaming in beer gardens. Baruch's grandmother was a very different type, short, blue-eyed, and (as her grandson found her on a visit to his father's German home) matriarchally thrifty and hardworking. Her maiden name was Theresa Gruen, and she was, Baruch thought, a Pole.

Never a hostage to the literal truth in matters involving himself, Baruch implied that he was descended half from immigrants and half from early Americans. This was literally a half-truth. On Baruch's mother's side, Sailing Wolfe was a first-generation American: he was born in Prussia. Sailing's wife's family, however, was indeed established early in the New World. Its first colonial forebear, a shipowner named Isaac Rodriguez Marques, made landfall in New York in the 1690s. His vessel, the *Dolphin*, sailed between New York and England and also bore slaves to the New World from Africa. This commercial blot was disclosed by Baruch in his autobiography without apology but with the ameliorating fact that, on one voyage, the *Dolphin* was known to have carried a surgeon. Furthermore, in Baruch's view, Marques's sins were amply expiated by his descendants through their suffering in the Civil War. As Baruch was later to do, Marques bought a large house in a fashionable Manhattan neighborhood. His family was of Spanish and Portuguese descent, the Jewish strain known as Sephardic. A genealogical joke that was told at the expense of Baruch's vanity was that he (Baruch) was the only Sephardic Jew, ever.

The first of Baruch's maternal ancestors to turn up in South Carolina was Samuel Marks (as he spelled his name), who arrived about 1800. A daughter of his, Deborah Marks, married Rabbi Hartwig Cohen. It was *their* daughter Sarah who married the immigrant Sailing Wolfe. On the birth of Isabelle Wolfe, on March 4, 1850, it was written in the family Bible, "God grant her a blessing." When, in short order, she married Simon Baruch, whose surname is the Hebrew word for "blessed," the union was seen to be propitious. Hartwig, the first of their four sons, was born in 1868. Our Baruch followed on August 19, 1870. Herman was born in 1872 and Sailing in 1874.

The most elegant of men, Bernard Baruch was a chubby little boy called "Bunch." He had blue eyes, black hair and freckles, and was prone to tantrums. Once in a fury he reached across the breakfast table and spitefully stuffed a piece of meat down his throat. He recalled losing fights. A favorite of his mother's, he insisted on sitting at her right hand at meals (a domestic custom he continued in marriage by stationing himself at his wife's right hand). A childhood ordeal he recalled with special clarity was an evening at the home of his father's old benefactor, Mannes Baum. His mother, who held high forensic hopes for her sons, led him to the center of the room.

"Now say something, dear," she said.

In a singsong voice Baruch began to recite the first few lines of "Hohenlinden" by Thomas Campbell:

> *On Linden when the sun was low,*
> *All bloodless lay the untrodden snow;*
> *And dark as winter was the flow*
> *Of Iser, rolling rapidly.*

His father, squirming with embarrassment, raised a finger to the side of his nose and made a derisive noise. The boy ran out of the house and all the way home and cried himself to sleep.

The Baruchs lived in the town of Camden in a spacious three-story house with tall windows and a pillared balcony. At first they made do without much cash. The doctor's patients, as hard hit by the war as he was, sometimes paid in kind—some chickens or cotton, a day's work in the experimental garden behind the Baruch home, or a dog. Mrs. Baruch taught piano and voice and sold butter and milk. However, the family fared no worse than most in postwar South Carolina and in fact, one gathers, considerably better. The doctor's means increased and he accumulated some land and livestock. A black nanny, Minerva, attended the boys. Baruch recalled that she was simple, superstitious and loving, and that she was the exclusive administrator of household spankings. When Dr. Baruch grew severe, his wife admonished him, "Now, Doctor, don't be hard on the boys or they won't love you."

The impression that Camden made on Baruch was profound and disproportionate to the ten years he spent there as a boy. He was a derivative southerner, taking his loyalty from his mother and father (she with her membership in the Daughters of the Confederacy, he with his rebel yell) and from the state of South Carolina, to which he returned as a millionaire to buy a barony. Seventy years after he came to New York he still hadn't relinquished a trace of a southern accent.

In his reminiscences of boyhood, Camden appears as a fair copy of Mark Twain's Hannibal. In the springtime the Wateree River obliged young raftsmen by flooding its banks. There was everyday swimming at Factory Pond and a regular baseball game between the uptown and downtown gangs. The Baruch boys, doctor's sons, belonged to the affluent uptown side. In his autobiography Baruch wrote little about his younger brothers, Herman and Sailing, but a great deal about Hartwig. Harty fought and won, swam distances, recited coolly before adults and had a dog, a white mastiff named Sharp, in his own sporting image. When Baruch started school, attending a kind of kindergarten with the schoolteacher's wife, Sharp escorted him to the schoolhouse door and obediently went home again. "I have the most distinct impression of my sitting on the floor deciphering such things as 'I see the cat,' and 'I see the dog,' while she had her baby on her knee feeding it porridge," wrote Baruch of that time to the journalist Mark Sullivan. "And how the lessons were interrupted by the squalls of the children!"

The Camden of Baruch's boyhood was a tiny county seat in the north-central, or pine belt, region of South Carolina. In the year of his birth its population was 1,007. By 1880, it had grown to 1,780. The local economy was supported by a backward agriculture (in which, for example, crop rotation was largely unpracticed). An eclectic and public-spirited man, Dr. Baruch interested himself in the improvement of farming. He raised experimental crops of cotton, corn and sugar cane in a three-acre plot behind the house and subscribed to farm journals that accumulated in yellow piles in his medical office.

Mrs. Baruch, who suggested that this agricultural energy might be profitably rechanneled into his medical practice, was a force for domestic gentility. Her religious appetites were prodigious, and she tried to imbue a sense of art and religion in her sons. She herself worshiped impartially among Christians and Jews, and she asked that her sons observe the Sabbath on both Saturday and Sunday. Baruch, more than his brothers, indulged his mother in her religiosity, but at last he followed his father into agnosticism. He was unable to carry a tune, refused to study piano, and liked to steal birds' eggs and shoot rabbits (he picked cotton in order to earn the money with which to buy powder and shot). He had one other boyhood interest. At his grandfather's house in Winnsboro, he was enchanted by the passing trains of the old Charlotte, Columbia & Augusta line. Watching the cars rumble by, and throwing rocks at them, he imagined the glory of actually owning a railroad—an acquisitive daydream for a child rising ten.

In the early 1870s South Carolina was conquered territory. It was a mark of the violence of the politics of the day that Dr. Baruch, who disliked firearms and had no truck with slavery, was moved to the idea of insurrection against Reconstruction rule. "There is one recourse when all is lost," he wrote to a former Confederate colleague in a moment of despair or romanticism. "I mean the sword. What boots it to live under such tyranny, such moral and physical oppression when we can be much happier in the consciousness of dying for such a cause?"

Evidence of their father's convictions was uncovered one day by Baruch and Harty in the family attic. Rummaging through a horsehair trunk, they turned up a Confederate uniform and, beneath it, a white hood and a robe with a crimson cross—the regalia of the Knights of the Ku Klux Klan. In its heyday in the 1920s the Klan filled its ranks with lost souls from the Middle West. In Reconstruction days it was led by former Confederate officers, landed gentry and professional men (even if louts and ruffians helped to fill out its ranks). In Kershaw County, of which Camden was the county seat, blacks outnumbered whites by two to one; this electoral imbalance the Klan sought to redress by terrorizing black militias, black voters, northern schoolteachers, Union Leaguers, Republican candidates and others allied to the cause of equal rights (as it was known to one camp) or carpetbag rule (as it was known by the other). When Mrs. Baruch discovered the boys, bug-eyed, in the attic, she swore them to secrecy, for the Klan was outlawed and its members were wanted men. Harty and Baruch felt very grown up and extravagantly proud of their father.

Baruch saw something of the violence of the Reconstruction era with his own eyes. On an election night when his father was away, his mother became alarmed at ugly noises from the street. He wrote in his autobiography:

> . . . She told Harty and me to get our guns.
>
> We got them—one a single-barreled and one a double-barreled muzzle-loader. Mother told us to load them and to take a position on the second-floor porch.
>
> "But do not shoot," she cautioned, "unless I tell you to shoot."
>
> We stood there, our hearts pounding, each with a gun almost as tall

as himself, watching the crowd of colored people milling about the street. Drunk on cheap whiskey, they were on their way to the polls or to a rally.

I have a blurred memory of what happened next. I recalled seeing a Negro fall from behind a tree. Suddenly everyone fled. We ran down to where the man lay to see what had happened. His head had been split as with an ax. Mother brought a basin of water and dressed the wound. I do not know what became of him, but he could not have lived long with his head as it was. . . .

Understandably, Mrs. Baruch wanted to raise her boys in a more peaceful setting, but for one reason or another Dr. Baruch had resisted the idea of a move. His mind was changed, according to Baruch, by the death of a friend, Colonel William M. Shannon, an attorney and father of thirteen, in a duel. The shooting occurred in July 1880, when Baruch was still young enough to be impressed with the marksmanship of the victor's son, Boggan Cash, of the notorious dueling Cashes of Chesterfield County. Although no evidence has been found to support Baruch's recollection that his father played a part in trying to head off the killing, and later a role in defusing a movement to lynch Cash, it is likely that the episode shocked him. Camden was a mecca for dueling in that day, and with Shannon's death, perhaps, Dr. Baruch decided that he had had enough of it. At all events the family made ready to leave. Late in 1880, the doctor sold his practice and house and amateur farm, the total, with his savings, yielding the tidy sum of $18,000. Minerva was to stay behind, and Sharp was given away to friends. Mrs. Baruch, asked what she was going to do in New York, said she meant to find her boys the best overcoats that money could buy.

Bernard M. Baruch's first appearance in the city of New York occurred on an unknown date in the dead of winter 1881. It is safe to assume that he found the city too cold, because as a grown man he wore an overcoat, and sometimes long underwear, in order to ward off summertime drafts. Also, probably, he found the city too big and the pair of rooms that his father had rented in a boardinghouse at 144 West 57th Street too small.

New York City at the census of 1880 was more populous than the state of South Carolina. In one teeming square mile there were 222,000 souls, ten times the number in the entire county of Kershaw. The city's black population numbered 20,000, or 1.7 percent of the total. Foreign-born New Yorkers, on the other hand, amounted to 479,000, or 40 percent of the whole. In Kershaw County it had been the other way around. Blacks had been greatly in the majority. The foreign-born element (presumably including Dr. Baruch) numbered exactly 74.

Everything in New York, by Baruch's lights, was unfamiliar, or upside down, or both. Water ran from taps, everyone wore shoes all the time and steam locomotives rumbled overhead on elevated tracks (ladies emerged from the smoky cars with the outline of their veils etched on their faces in ash). Baruch, not yet eleven, was awestruck and frightened but more than ever buoyed by the courage of Harty.

The Baruchs lived near the northernmost populous fringe of Manhattan. The future site of the Plaza Hotel, at Fifth Avenue and 59th Street, was occupied by a squatter and a mean little dog. There was a blacksmith nearby whom Baruch envied for his muscles. Except for the village of Yorkville, at 86th Street, the Upper East Side was sparsely settled. In 1884, a new apartment building at Central Park West and 72nd Street was called the Dakota, for its inaccessibility. Harlem was known as Goatville, for a still common Manhattan quadruped. The Bronx was exurbia; the Brooklyn Bridge had opened just the year before.

The family's first northern winter was cold, cramped and anxiety-ridden. At the boardinghouse Baruch remembered huddling against a wall for the sake of the warmth that radiated from a chimney behind it. Sleeping quarters were allocated one room to Harty and Baruch and another to Sailing and Herman and their parents. Baruch remarked on the kindness of their landlady, a Miss or Mrs. Jacobs, who gave his brothers and him sweets.* Not long after their arrival the doctor took

---

*Their austere domestic arrangements suggest that the Baruchs were prepared to go to some lengths before they stooped to live on capital. They had brought $18,000 from South Carolina, which at the prevailing savings rate of 4 percent would have yielded $720 a year. Seven hundred twenty dollars was a reasonable sum of money, but rents in New York were characteristically unreasonable. Apartments that had been let for $600 to $1,000 a year in 1880 fetched $660 to $1,100 in 1881. Furnished houses commanded $2,500 to $5,000. Rents in 1881 were the highest since the Civil War, a fact explained by a real-estate agent in *The New York Times*: "You see the great majority of newcomers in this City have plenty of money and their willingness to pay liberally for comfortable accommodations has helped to advance prices." However, overcoat prices, thanks to improved manufacturing techniques, had fallen. Mrs. Baruch probably outfitted her sons for less than $100.

sick. He consulted a colleague who diagnosed a heart condition and warned him that his days were probably numbered. For a while there was sad talk of a return to South Carolina. Then a second opinion was sought. The welcome (and accurate) diagnosis was indigestion.

Soon the family found its urban bearings. Baruch was entered in Public School 69, on 54th Street between Sixth and Seventh Avenues. He recalled vividly being led to class the first day by the principal; being introduced to his teacher, Katherine Devereux Blake; and being shown the way home by Clarence Housman, a fat boy who was to become Baruch's senior partner in Wall Street fourteen years later. At the end of the term he received a gift copy of *Oliver Twist* from Miss Blake in which she had written the inscription, "Awarded to Bernard Baruch for Gentlemanly Deportment and Excellence." (Baruch later did his best to reciprocate. In 1923, when Miss Blake's name came up for promotion to district superintendent, he put in a good word with Mayor John F. Hylan.) Harty gained new stature by facing down a gang that had taunted him and Baruch with the name "sheenie," challenging any two of its members to a fight and whipping the boy who did step forward.

As Baruch and Harty distinguished themselves, each in his own way, their father advanced professionally. In 1884 he was named physician in chief of Montefiore Home for Chronic Invalids, and he played an advisory role in the development of the appendectomy. A consummately general practitioner who attended lectures and clinics on subjects ranging from gynecology to ophthalmology, he developed a special interest in the curative power of water. He wrote the first English-language text on the subject, *The Uses of Water in Modern Medicine*, in 1892, taught hydrotherapy at the Columbia University College of Physicians and Surgeons, became a chronic writer of letters to newspaper editors and was the chief exponent of public baths in the United States.

For the would-be reformer in health and sanitation, Manhattan of the 1880s was so much unformed clay. Dr. Baruch appositely described the city as a "body of land surrounded by sewage." The Census Office commented in 1886: "The method of disposal of sewage in New York is to conduct it by the most convenient course to the bulkhead of the nearest river, and to leave the rest of the operations to nature." Every year fifteen thousand beasts, mostly horses, were hauled, dead, from city streets. There was a great manure pile surrounded by breweries at the foot of East 46th Street, and the East Forties were lined with slaughterhouses. (In June 1881 a thousand-pound steer escaped from a pen near First Avenue and 47th Street. Before a brave butcher dispatched it near First Avenue and 30th Street, the animal had knocked down two pedestrians and gored a black mare.) The city's medical establishment, which soon included Dr. Baruch, pleaded for reform. Early in 1881, the president of the New York Academy of Medicine warned that the streets, come the thaw, would yield enough filth to start an epidemic. The Police Department, which was responsible for the cleanliness of the streets, countered that they were not nearly so vile as the drinking water, and within a month, in fact, in an area south of the Baruchs' boardinghouse, the water tasted strongly of fish. The autumn brought a drought.

Appalled by these conditions, Dr. Baruch began to apply himself to the propagation of municipal baths. He made some headway in 1891 when the New York Association for Improving the Condition of the Poor opened the People's Baths on the Lower East Side, but he wanted action by government, not charity. As progressive ideas and politicians gained sway in the 1890s, the bath forces made strides in Albany and Tammany Hall, but the increase in public bath and shower facilities coincided with improvements in apartment-house plumbing. According to a historian of the movement, the baths so ardently championed in the event enjoyed only a limited patronage. However, declared Dr. Baruch, "I consider that I have done more to save life and prevent the spread of disease in my work for public baths than in all my work as a physician." Under his father's influence Baruch became a lifelong patron and advocate of spas and water cures. Late in the 1920s, when the governor of New York, Alfred E. Smith, wanted to enlist Baruch's help in restoring the spa at Saratoga, he knew that his surest talking point was to invoke the memory of Simon Baruch.

In New York Mrs. Baruch found a feast of ladies' clubs and churches and synagogues. On Sundays she made the trip to Brooklyn Heights to hear the sermons of the evangelist Henry Ward Beecher. At the top of her form she belonged to thirty-two different organizations, including the Daughters of the American Revolution, Daughters of the Confederacy, Drama Comedy Club, Eclectic Club, Washington Headquarters Association and Widowed Mothers Association. In 1914, lightening up, she resigned from seven simultaneously.

As her sons grew up (to anticipate our story), and as her husband's practice improved and her second son struck it rich in Wall Street, she accumulated some servants. In the past she had received her boys in the morning for inspection and instruction. Now she saw her laundress, chauffeur, maid and cook. After the turn of the century, at the family's spacious home at 51 West 70th Street, she entertained in a living room done all in red. Her clubs and charitable work brought her a large correspondence for which she retained a secretary, a favorite niece from Chicago, Virginia Wolfe (later Epstein). One day Virginia confessed that she was a socialist. "Yes," said her aunt without rancor, "and you're not nearly as sweet and lovely as you used to be."

Mrs. Baruch, who had a vast Wagnerian bust and who regarded the camera lens imperiously, held definite opinions. She repudiated women's suffrage, feminism and socialism, as her husband did, and she made speeches in favor of domesticity. Once she was hissed by suffragists. In 1914 she gave her views on sex and the family, as follows:

> Not long ago, out of the purest curiosity, I looked in at an afternoon dance at one of the big hotels. There I saw several melancholy sights.
>
> Among them was that of a lovely young woman whom I know smoking a cigarette in a public room filled with strange men. I may be an old fogy, but I feel sure that if that was a possibility, almost anything is a possibility.
>
> It was half after 6. Presently I saw the mother of another young lady whom I know, evidently unescorted, but dancing now and then.
>
> It troubled me. I might take more privileges than many women might because my life and age would warrant it, but I would not remain unescorted in the public room of a hotel after 6 o'clock at night, much less there participate in the prevailing gayeties. . . .
>
> There is too little chaperonage. . . .
>
> Of the widely criticized dances I have seen nothing. My objection to the dance craze is that it is too absorbing. I have seen the tango and found it beautiful. Some steps in the maxixe seem questionable to me. Of course I have never visited second-rate places. . . .
>
> I believe the modern woman's aim in life should be to bring the modern man back home. To do that she must stay at home herself.

Mrs. Baruch deplored the New Woman in the abstract but made no enemies of individuals. On social matters her advice was always to remember names. When her husband let pass an occasional ad hominem remark, she chided him gently, "Now, Doctor, we all have our faults."

Her educational hopes for her second son were ambitious but limited by geography. She wanted him home with her. In the days before public high schools were established, it was customary for college-bound youth to get an early start in higher education. Baruch announced that he had his heart set on Yale and that he was prepared to wait on tables to help pay his way. But his mother pronounced him too young, and in the fall of 1884, at the age of fourteen, he enrolled in the College of the City of New York.

In the 1880s, City College was a small municipal meritocracy. It had no playing fields, no dormitories, no fraternity houses and no extra pedagogical baggage. The faculty totaled thirteen professors and thirty-seven instructors. The campus comprised a single turreted building at the corner of Lexington Avenue and 23rd Street (site of the present Bernard M. Baruch College of the City University). Students were plentiful in the first, or sub-freshman, year, but scarce at the collegiate finish line five years later. Several hundred were entered with Baruch in the fall of 1884; fifty were graduated with him in June 1889. "When we first came here we were large in number but small in intelligence," said the class history; "now—behold us—we are small in number but large in intelligence." Baruch's classmates were young, boisterous, optimistic and patriotic. In its yearbook the Class of '89 identified the nation's centenary "under our noble flag and glorious constitution" as the foremost event of the year. However, in another respect it was not so different from the more cynical classes that followed it late in the twentieth century. The yearbook also contained a facetious essay on "cribology," or the science of cheating.

Baruch put down the high rate of attrition among his classmates to financial as much as to scholastic causes. Tuition was free, but many students fell by the wayside under the burden of working to feed and clothe themselves. According to Baruch his own finances were straitened. He said that he worked part time as a collection agent and medical bookkeeper for his father and that he walked to school to save the dime he would have spent on the elevated. His allowance was twenty-five cents a week until his senior year, when it was munificently doubled. Possibly this raise reflected the family's improved economic circumstances. Their address at the time of

Baruch's graduation from grammar school was 158 West 54th Street. By the spring of 1885, they had moved to 43 East 59th Street. By the spring of his junior year in college they had pushed to 47 East 60th Street. It was perhaps from this address that Baruch set out for school on foot on the morning of the blizzard of 1888. He made it, half frozen, only to find that there was hardly anyone there to appreciate his zeal.

In the 1880s, under its president, General Alexander Stewart Webb, City College stood aloof from the elective-system "nonsense" that was fashionable at Harvard. Only one important choice was available to Baruch and his classmates, the Scientific Course or the Classical Course. After a false start in science, Baruch took up the classics. In his autobiography he made himself out to be a rather poor student, but this was either faulty memory or the dissembling of a man who had little use for eggheads and college professors. Out of a class of fifty, he was graduated thirteenth, and his strongest grades were in Greek, Latin, English and French. As a grown man Baruch was famously fluent with numbers but inarticulate. In college, however, he did better with languages than he did with mathematics. He had four years of math (which took him into calculus), five years of Latin, four of English and Greek, three of history, two of chemistry and not quite two of physics. He struggled with drawing and what was called "aesthetics."

He did worse than he remembered in political economy, which he studied in the second semester of his junior year under Professor George Benton Newcomb. For the full year's course, which included a semester of philosophy, he finished thirty-fifth out of fifty-four students (his only worse showing that year was in applied math, in which he ranked thirty-seventh), but at least one lesson sank in. He recited it later, quoting Newcomb: "When prices go up, two processes will set in—an increased production and a decreased consumption. The effect will be a gradual fall in prices. If prices get too low, two processes will set in—decreased production, because a man will not continue to produce at a loss, and, second, increased consumption. These two forces will tend to establish the normal balance."

Newcomb was no believer in the sanctity of natural processes, and if his lectures followed the lines of his writing, he condoned an interventionist role for government in the economy. For instance, he wrote in 1885: "[T]he economic end is ever subordinate to the higher social ends, notably the ethical end, and wherever the pursuit of the former prevents the attainment of the latter and superior ends, the social conscience and will may and does interfere . . ." Although he might have put it in different words, Baruch too believed that society had a will and a conscience and that the individual owed fealty to the mass of his fellows. There is no telling whether he got that from Newcomb, or what impression the economic textbook that he was assigned to read might have made. On the one hand, *Political Economy*, by Francis A. Walker, was defensive about moneymaking and cool to slightly hostile toward Baruch's future vocation, stock trading. On the other hand, it stated some things that Baruch might have advocated himself a few decades later. Thus, concerning capital: "It arises solely out of saving. It stands always for self-denial and abstinence." Many years later, when John Maynard Keynes floated the idea that the way out of a depression was through spending instead of self-denial and abstinence, Baruch rejected both the idea and the economist.

In college Baruch was as thin as he had once been fat, and he recalled being among the last of his friends to get a date. At six feet three inches (an inch short of his final topping out), he was the tallest man in school his senior year. He weighed only 170 pounds, had beanpole legs and was slow afoot. In May of his senior year there was an ambiguous note in *The College Journal*: "Baruch is greatly improved in his lacrosse playing." His being a Jew debarred him from college fraternities, but he was president of the senior class for a term and chaired the Class Day Committee. He belonged to the Senior Secret Society and was one of a three-man body to represent CCNY at a convention of the Intercollegiate Athletic Association in 1889. His deportment was flawless except in his sophomore year, when he took a swing at a classmate who called his mother "a vile name." Baruch related this episode colorfully. President Webb suspended him, he said, but softened the blow by suggesting that a boy as likely as he ought to apply to West Point. Webb was a West Point man himself, and he had won the Congressional Medal of Honor at Gettysburg by repulsing Pickett's charge at Bloody Angle. Unfortunately, Baruch's application got no further than the discovery that he was almost deaf in his left ear—the result, he said, of a whack he sustained across the side of his head with a bat in a college baseball game. (Furthermore, said Baruch, he won the game with a ninth-inning home run.) Except for that blow, he liked to say in the company of military men, he would have been a general, as indeed he probably would have been.

Baruch was graduated without academic honor, but his practical credentials—budding good looks, amiability, a calculating intelligence and a sharp memory for faces and names—were impeccable. *The College Journal* reported that on Class Day, 1889, he received a special gift from his classmates: "As an evidence of the survival of the fittest, 'Shorty' Baruch was given a pair of knee trousers suitable for a small eight-year-old. . . ." Thus equipped and accoutered, Bernard M. Baruch set out into the world.

Three Dollars a Week

From *The College Journal*, September 23, 1889—" '89—Baruch is in Wall Street."

In college Baruch entertained medical ambitions, but after graduation followed them no further than to haunt some dissecting rooms and dip into a few textbooks. His father was noncommittal on the subject of a career, but his mother actively steered him toward business. Among other things, she invoked phrenological evidence.

Phrenology, a pseudoscience then in vogue, was the practice of deducing human aptitudes by an examination of the bumps and ridges of the skull. Shortly after they arrived in New York, Baruch and his mother had paid a call on a practitioner named Fowler. The phrenologist asked Mrs. Baruch what she intended to do with her son.

"I am thinking of making him a doctor."

"He will make a good doctor," Fowler agreed, passing his hands appraisingly over the boy's glabella, "but my advice to you is to take him where they are doing big things—finance or politics."

In the spring or summer of 1889, Baruch began his career in the small way of answering help-wanted advertisements. Nothing happened. Then he began to call on his father's patients, among whom was Daniel Guggenheim, second son of a family that was getting out of the lace trade and into metals and mining. Baruch was a foot taller than his would-be employer, but the awkwardness of their meeting was dispelled by a smile of Guggenheim's. The applicant must have made a favorable impression, because Guggenheim offered him a job as an ore buyer in Mexico. To this Baruch said yes, but his mother, decisively, said no.

Next Charles A. Tatum, another patient of Baruch's father and a Quaker from an old Philadelphia family, offered an apprenticeship in his wholesale glassware firm. As the business was situated in Manhattan, no maternal objections were raised, and Baruch took the job at $3 a week. This was in the summer of 1889. Dr. Baruch was then resident physician at the West End Hotel in the seaside resort of Long Branch, New Jersey. Sometimes his older sons came out on the train from New York for the weekend and put up on cots in his office. On Saturday nights, in defiance of standing family orders, Baruch would slip off to a local gambling hall, or "hell," as it was known to reforming elements. Once he was a couple of dollars ahead at roulette when the doctor appeared at the casino door. On recollection, Baruch stated that the room fell silent when his father entered, as if his goodness cast a beatific spell on the patrons. The doctor made his way to his son's table, drew up next to him and said gently, "Son, when you are ready, we will go home." Baruch was ready right away. He followed his father out the door and back to the hotel. The office in which Baruch slowly began to undress adjoined the bedroom in which his parents slept; soon the door opened and his father reappeared. "To think that at my age," he said (he was forty-nine), "I should have to take my son from a gambling house." Forty years later, Baruch said that the memory still troubled him. (The distinction that Dr. Baruch drew between racing and roulette was unexplained but deeply felt. A few years earlier he had given his son two silver dollars to bet on a horse named Pasha. The horse, Baruch's first racetrack selection, lost.)

When at last Baruch had drifted off to sleep he was awakened by the presence of his mother on the edge of his cot. As he opened his eyes, she whispered consolingly and gathered him up in her arms. Now thoroughly rattled, he lay awake long after she had gone. At 5 A.M., he got up, dressed, crept out, breakfasted at a saloon near the railroad station with some coachmen and horse handlers, and caught the first train back to New York. The day was still young when he fell in with a cousin and some friends of his cousin's in Manhattan. When somebody suggested an all-day poker game, Baruch hospitably offered the use of his own home, his parents being in Long Branch. The game was going strong in the basement when the cousin sprang from his chair, announcing, "Good Lord, there's Aunt Belle!"

She was just mounting the steps. Baruch had failed to reckon that his guilt would induce a counter, maternal guilt, and that his mother would be off in pursuit of him. As she walked in the door, a file of young men, nonchalantly putting on vests and coats, passed her on their way out. Apparently seeing nothing but her son, she threw her arms around him and said: "I am so glad to see you! You have such a sensitive nature that I was afraid something serious might have happened."

She told him that she had met a man on the train. After some talking he said he was a banker in need of an apprentice, and that he wanted someone dependable, bright and upstanding. Mrs. Baruch instinctively replied that she knew just the boy—"My son, Bernard."

Mrs. Baruch's new banking friend was a Stock Exchange member and fellow East Sixties resident named Julius A. Kohn. Mr. Kohn's approach to apprenticeship was the Frankfurt method in which a young man did a clerk's job in return for the opportunity to learn. To start with no money changed hands. Banking sounded better than glassware, and Baruch served notice on Whitall, Tatum & Company and began work at Kohn's, 46 Exchange Place. Soon he was learning about speculation, arbitrage and foreign exchange, and was making $3 a week again.

His education was interrupted, or redirected, in the summer of 1890 by a casual suggestion of his Uncle Herman's. Dr. Baruch was about to leave for Europe to see his parents, and the Baruch clan, including Uncle Herman, had gathered at dockside to wish him bon voyage. A few hours before sailing time, Herman asked his brother whether Bernie couldn't go too. The answer was yes, if he could get home, pack and get back to the ship before lines were cast off. This Baruch managed to do but soon profoundly wished he hadn't. He and the three strangers who shared his cabin, all Cubans, got sick and stayed sick. Once on dry land, father and son traveled to the Prussian city of Posen, where Dr. Baruch was reunited with his mother and father for the first time since he emigrated thirty-five years before. The doctor introduced the handsome towering boy to his grandfather and namesake, Bernhard, and the three generations drove off together to Schwersenz.

Meanwhile Mrs. Baruch patched things up with Kohn on behalf of her absent son. Kohn did take him back that fall on his return from Europe, but Baruch again grew restless, and late in 1890 he resigned and set out with Dick Lydon, his college pal, to strike it rich in the Colorado gold and silver mines. The adventurers journeyed west by day coach to Denver and then by stage to Cripple Creek. In the daytime they worked underground as "muckers," clearing up the rock left behind by blasting. At night they gambled, Baruch having noticed that the house always seemed to win the big pots and laying his own small bets accordingly. They slept at the Palace Hotel in a large open room to the accompaniment of barrack noises.

By his own account, Baruch rubbed shoulders with the foremost speculator of the day (James R. Keene) and was complimented on his physique by the fairest beauty (Lillie Langtry, who caught sight of him shirtless aboard a sailboat). Furthermore, he was encouraged in his boxing by one of the greatest fighters, Bob Fitzsimmons, who had happened to be watching on the day he stepped into the ring with a big redheaded policeman. For a while the fight was all one way, the redhead's. Then Baruch collected himself and dropped his man with a left to the stomach and a right to the chin.

Quoting Baruch:

. . . I felt a slap on my back and turned to face freckled, grinning Bob Fitzsimmons.

"The prize ring lost a good man in you," he said, laughing. "You were getting a licking but you hung on. That's what you always want to do. You know how you feel and maybe you feel pretty bad. But you don't know how the other fellow feels. Maybe he is worse off than you are.

"A fight is never over until one man is out," he emphasized. "As long as you ain't that man you have a chance. *To be a champion you have to learn to take it or you can't give it.*"

Baruch never lost interest in boxing, and he never stopped quoting Fitzsimmons; he dusted off the champion remark in a telegram congratulating Franklin D. Roosevelt on his fourth-term victory in 1944. A favorite memento of his days at Woods' and as a gym instructor at the West 69th Street Boys' Club was a picture of himself in fighting trim, his arms folded across a bare chest with biceps bulging under his fists.

His hair is thick and parted down the middle, his nose is straight, his face is unmarked and his mustache is well tended. Quite obviously he is afraid of nothing.

At the time Baruch was still unemployed, but his mother kept her eyes open. In her charitable work she had met Abram B. deFrece, a well-to-do New York businessman and philanthropist, and deFrece put her in touch with Arthur A. Housman. Housman, who had just bought a "seat," or membership, on the New York Stock Exchange, met Baruch, and he hired him.

Housman was a big man, standing six feet tall and weighing more than two hundred pounds, and an optimistic one. He was some fifteen years older than Baruch, was unmarried and was the principal breadwinner for many or all of his five sisters. The son of a New York wholesale dry-goods merchant, he entered Wall Street in 1876 and made a name for himself as a bull even in the professionally optimistic circles of brokers and customers' men. In 1898, he demonstrated his versatility by citing peace as a reason to buy stocks in January and war as a reason to buy them in July (hostilities between Spain and the United States having intervened in April). "It seems to me absolutely certain," he declared that summer, "that we are entering upon a period of wonderful prosperity," as, indeed, we were. The McKinley bull market vindicated Housman and made him rich. By the end of the 1890s he had become known is the Street as "Morgan's broker," meaning Morgan's representative on the floor of the New York Stock Exchange. "While Housman never said he was," a newspaper report commented, "Wall Street found ample confirmation for the report in the almost daily conferences he had at the office of the banker." (Interestingly, Baruch failed to mention any such connection with the great firm; as for himself, he believed that the Morgan partners systematically thwarted him.) A pen-and-ink sketch around the turn of the century shows Housman sitting in the bar of the old Waldorf-Astoria with James R. Keene, master speculator, and the broker Jake Field. Of Field the story was told that once, when asked at a dinner party whether he liked Balzac, he answered, "I never deal in dem outside stocks." Housman, who amply fills a carved wooden chair, rests his right hand on an upright cane. He wears a bowler and a pair of pince-nez.

Baruch began in early 1891 as a clerk, runner and office boy. He bore securities here and there, called for checks, copied and filed letters, copied transactions in Mr. Housman's record book, and fetched sandwiches for the Housman brothers, Clarence and Fred. This last menial errand grated on him and sometimes brought him the jeers of other young men, but, as Baruch recalled, "I was paid to do whatever I was told and I did it. I got into a fight with another runner and after that they didn't jeer at me very much."

Baruch envied the Ivy League men who started out on the ladder a rung or two higher and had more pocket money than he did. They lunched at Delmonico's or Fred Eberlins and drove carriages on Sundays while he ate at sandwich counters and took the air on foot. Thanks both to creative envy and a lack of funds for dissipation, he applied himself to study. He attended night classes in bookkeeping and business law and memorized facts and figures about railroads and industrial corporations. He became a close reader of the *Commercial & Financial Chronicle* and *Poor's Manual*. He learned to draw a workmanlike map of the Union and superimpose the routes of the important railroads and the names of the principal products they carried so that he could grasp the financial significance of the news without time-consuming research. He gained a reputation as a bright and encyclopedic young man.

His rise from runner to junior financial analyst was completed as early as 1895, because that was the year that James Keene commissioned him to investigate the Brooklyn Union Gas Company and its new securities. As Baruch, aged twenty-five, was preparing his report, someone from the underwriting syndicate offered him a $1,500 "commission" to accentuate the positive; this fact too was disclosed to Keene.

To scout for Keene was an honor—it was he whom Morgan would ask to make a market in the new shares of the United States Steel Corporation in 1901. The trader had begun his career in California in the 1850s as a miner, newspaperman, mule puncher and speculator in mining stocks and had run his bank account from nothing to $150,000 and all the way back down again. Heavily in debt, he hit upon the idea of becoming a broker rather than a customer. The change was revolutionary, and soon he was a millionaire and president of the Mining Exchange. He made a fortune by selling railroad stocks short in 1876 but lost all that and more in the wheat market in the 1880s. Again he began to rebuild his affairs, and again he succeeded, leading one admirer to praise his life as a "symphony of gamble." Asked why he persisted in putting his fortune at risk, Keene replied: "Why does a dog chase his thousandth rabbit? All life is speculation. The spirit of speculation is born with men." When provoked he swore colorfully in a penetrating high voice, and when the spirit moved him he quoted at length from his favorite poets. To "Deacon" S. V. White, another trader who went from boom to bust and back, and who announced grandly that he was the king of a certain speculative situation, Keene cautioned: "Uneasy lies the head that wears the crown. . . . Fierce is the light that beats around the throne."

Baruch's introduction to Keene was provided by a friend of Housman's, the lawyer Middleton Schoolbred Burrill. In the early 1890s, when A. A. Housman & Company did mainly a wholesale business with other brokers, Burrill was the rare retail customer. The son of a lawyer who represented some Vanderbilt interests, he practiced in his father's office and speculated in stocks, first as an amateur and later, frequently teamed with Baruch, as a professional. In the 1890s he rode a commuter train with Keene and drank highballs with Housman. Keene, Housman and Burrill each preferred the optimistic, or bull, side of the market, buying for the rise rather than selling for the fall. It was Keene who coined the saying: "You don't see any Fifth Avenue mansions built by bears." Of Burrill, Baruch said: "He had the most tremendous belief in the future of America and in the ability of his fellowmen to function and conquer anything, and I got that from him also. I learned to feel that there were no ills from which humans suffered that could not be overcome by human ingenuity. . . ." Burrill drank socially until the day his doctor prescribed abstention, at which point he instantly quit. According to Baruch, the same self-control stood the lawyer well in the market.

Baruch was an up-and-coming office boy when he was introduced to Burrill. The older man, who had lost two daughters and a son of his own, was impressed by the younger; and the younger was flattered by the attention of the older. When a question of fact arose, Burrill got in the habit of asking Baruch before consulting a reference book. Sometimes the two ate lunch together at a counter in the basement of the Consolidated Stock Exchange, ordering roast beef and mashed potatoes and talking about stocks. Burrill was struck by Baruch's trustworthiness, a quality he called to the attention of Keene.

Keene was an ardent turfman—he donated the skeleton of his own champion Sysonby to the Museum of Natural History and called on it there from time to time as a man might visit the grave of a crony—and he liked to back his racing judgment with money. One day a Keene horse was entered to run at Coney Island, and the owner wished to place a big bet on him; so as not to queer the odds unnecessarily, he wanted to bet anonymously. Burrill suggested that Baruch could be trusted for the job, and the young man was called to the speculator's office for an interview. Satisfied of his character, experience and brawn, Keene gave him several thousand dollars in cash with the instructions that he was to bet it all silently.

> Keene's horse won in a canter [Baruch related]. I returned to the city on the 34th Street ferry with my pockets literally bulging. I kept worrying that someone might hit me on the head and take all the money away.
>
> When some swelling waves struck the front of the ferryboat, I remember thinking that we were about to capsize. Buttoning my coat tightly, I decided that if the ship went down I would strike out to get far away from the crowd so that no one would be able to pull me down.

He landed safely, of course, won Keene's confidence and came to perform such services for him as investigating Brooklyn Union Gas.

Baruch's gift for making friends was natural, but a certain part of his fluency in financial markets was acquired. In time the two capacities enhanced one another. His friends helped him to speculate; as he grew richer, his circle of acquaintances widened, and the more people he knew, the better his information became. He befriended Richard Limburger, head of the arbitrage department of what at the time was one of the leading arbitrage firms, Ladenburg, Thalmann & Company. Fred Edey, an important customer of Housman's, was a fast enough friend to become godfather to Belle, Baruch's first child, at her confirmation in the Episcopal Church. When he was an old man, Baruch told a broker friend that, early in his career, a big-time operator had given him a "free ride," meaning a free share in a stock-market profit. If Baruch weren't good-looking and companionable, he might never have met his benefactor, but if he hadn't also been smart and quick, the rich man might never have paid attention to him.

Since he traded too much with too little money, Baruch made a slow start in the market. He dealt in ten-share lots on the Consolidated Stock Exchange through the firm of Honigman & Prince, of whom

Prince was a distant relation. He tapped closer relatives for funds, including an uncle, Harry C. Lytton, a Chicago haberdasher; evidently his uncle and he lost money together. In reminiscing, Baruch said that he sometimes bet a dollar on whether the next Stock Exchange trade would be up, down or unchanged from the previous price on the tape, and it isn't unthinkable that he patronized the bucket shops in which such low-budget speculation was carried on. One of his first losing family investments was to help finance an out-of-town production of the melodrama *East Lynne*. In 1890 Harty was an aspiring actor, and he had fallen under the influence of an older would-be actress. Baruch, in turn, was under his brother's spell, and when Harty and his friend presented their plan to mount a production of *East Lynne* at the opera house in Centerville, New Jersey, Baruch agreed that the idea was foolproof. Again to quote Baruch:

> Perhaps the actors were artists, as represented. If so, they were not artists who knew the lines of *East Lynne*. During Act One, the audience was alternately angry and amused. During the second act it was only angry.
>
> Although small, this audience outnumbered the performers, so I asked the fellow at the box office to give the patrons their money back. Like the Duke in *Huckleberry Finn*, I went backstage and told the troupe that fortunately I had bought round-trip tickets and it was only a short walk through a dark street to the depot.
>
> I think we were at the railroad station before the audience realized there would be no third act. A train had just pulled in. We climbed aboard without even noticing which way it was going. Luckily it was headed for New York.

Later, to his father, Baruch proposed a scheme that he had heard from a man whom they both had met on their voyage home from Europe. The idea was to build a tramway to a hotel at Put-in-Bay on an island in Lake Erie. Baruch was enchanted by the scheme, and he talked his father into investing $8,000 in it. All the money was lost, and although his father never upbraided him, Baruch suffered enormously. When subsequently he mentioned to his mother that Tennessee Coal & Iron was cheap, and with $500 he could make some money in the stock, his father unexpectedly appeared with a check in that amount. The gesture of confidence touched him.

The challenge to every stockbroker in the wake of the Panic of 1893 was to find enough solvent customers. Just starting out, Baruch had no customers of any description. His name was unknown to the public, the firm for which he worked was obscure and the bonds that he sold were often in default. In an attempt to drum up business he wrote research bulletins and knocked on office doors. Once he called on James Talcott, a prominent dry-goods merchant. Turned away by Talcott's secretary, Baruch waited outside until the merchant appeared, then hurriedly introduced himself and followed his man up the street, saying, approximately, that the spate of railroad bankruptcies afforded opportunity because mergers and consolidations were inevitable and values would be reclaimed, if only one knew where to look, which he, Baruch, having made a study of the situation, did. Talcott, who was tall and wore a gray beard and was descended from seventeenth-century Connecticut settlers, finally yielded, giving Baruch an order to buy a single 6 percent Oregon & Trans-Continental bond, which then was quoted at about 78 cents on the dollar. The issue in fact went up, as Baruch said it would, and Talcott became a steady customer. The commission on this, the first bond that he sold, was $1.25.

Although he husbanded his customers' money, Baruch played fast and loose with his own. He usually bought stocks on credit, or margin, and when he was especially sure of himself he committed every cent he had. The advantage of margin trading is that a small down payment controls a large investment. The drawback is the ever-present risk of being wiped out. In Baruch's day the required margin was as low as 10 percent of the price of a stock, the broker lending the remaining 90 percent. The collateral for the loan was the stock itself. As long as the price went up or stood still, the collateral was safe. If, however, the price fell, the collateral was impaired, and the broker took steps to protect his loan. Time permitting, he issued his customer a dunning telegram, or margin call. The customer's choice was to put up more money or not. If not, the broker sold the stock, salvaging what he could of the value of the loan and billing the customer for the deficiency, if any. The down payment was lost. If losing on margin was spectacular, so was winning. For the investor who bought a share of stock for $100, and actually paid cash, a rise in price to $105 meant a gain of 5 percent. For the margin trader, who had bought the same stock with only $10, a $5 profit represented a gain of 50 percent. Baruch was drawn to margin.

Until 1897 or so the attraction was ill-fated. For every large profit, there was an offsetting loss. Losses, in fact, predominated, because he invested too much and held back too little in reserve.

This manic-depressive financial life was discouraging to Baruch and deeply frustrating to his fiancée, Annie Griffen. They had met about the time he was graduated from college, a formal introduction following an unsuccessful overture by Baruch near the Griffen brownstone at 41 West 58th Street. He had seen her coming down the street: "Raising my hat, I asked if I were addressing Miss Annie Griffen. 'No indeed!' she retorted with a toss of her head and walked up the steps."

Annie was nearly as tall as he was—years later, after their three children attained their own lofty adult heights, the five Baruchs out walking were said to resemble a basketball team—and she had a long face, thin lips and a corseted hourglass figure. Her father, Benjamin Griffen, was a Phi Beta Kappa graduate of City College and a principal in the glass-importing firm of Van Horne, Griffen & Company. He and his wife had some money (she was the daughter of a lard merchant, W. J. Wilcox); the family kept horses and a carriage.

Mr. Griffen, the grandson of an Episcopal minister, opposed the intermarriage of Christians and Jews. He had nothing against him personally, he assured Baruch, quite the contrary, but religious differences would certainly spoil the chance of his being happy with Annie. His advice had the predictable result of uniting the lovers in a conspiracy against him. A kind of semaphore was devised to signal whether the coast was clear for calling: shades drawn meant no—Mr. Griffen was home; shades raised meant proceed. Happily for Baruch, Mrs. Griffen took his part. She welcomed him as a weekend guest in Pittsfield, Massachusetts, where she and her daughter spent their summers. He and Annie went to dances and disappeared together on long bicycle rides.

Another matrimonial hurdle was money. No sooner did Baruch accumulate some capital than it disappeared into the maw of the market. In 1895, seeking a surer source of funds than speculation, he asked Mr. Housman for a raise to $50 a week from $25. This was refused, but an even better counteroffer was made: one eighth of the firm's annual profits. If business was no better than it had been the year before, the arrangement would yield about $35 a week. However, we may be sure Housman added that 1894 had been a quiet year in Wall Street and the times were bound to get better and better—which, in the event, they did.

"Being a junior partner in a brokerage house, I decided, called for some expansion of my personal budget," Baruch wrote. "I acquired a Prince Albert coat, a silk hat, and all the accessories that went with them." In 1895, his first year in the partnership, A. A. Housman & Company earned $48,000, of which he kept $6,000, or about $115 a week. But there was no wedding that year or the year after.

The outlook brightened in 1897. In the spring Baruch took an interest in the American Sugar Refining Company, the fortunes of which hung on the tariff. As long as cheap foreign sugar was barred from this country, American Sugar stood to gain. If foreign sugar was not kept out, the company's profits, and therefore the price of its stock, would fall. In the Senate, a bill was pending to lower the sugar duty. Similar legislation had been passed in the House. The question before the market, then, was whether or not the Senate bill would pass. Baruch, reasoning that western sugar-beet growers had as much to gain from tariff protection as Wall Street did, thought not. He backed this educated guess with $300. If he bought on 10 percent margin, as seems likely, he would have controlled $3,000 in stock. He related only that he bought in the spring. In April and May, Sugar changed hands at about $115 a share. By the end of July it had reached $139. As the price rose, Baruch bought more, using the paper profits he had earned on earlier purchases as credit. He kept buying, or parlaying, as the price went higher, all the while protecting his position with a precautionary order to sell in case the market suddenly fell. This progressively higher "stop loss" order was never touched off, however, and Baruch's profits mounted wonderfully. The Senate bill was defeated, and the stock kept climbing. On August 31, the price leaped by $8 a share, to $156.25, the largest daily rise of the advance, on the strength of a story that the Treasury Department was about to bar Dutch sugar from the United States. It evidently was about this time that Baruch sold. His profit totaled $60,000, an astonishing return on an investment of $300. It bears mention that at the time he was buying, Washington insiders were selling and Wall Street was mainly pessimistic.*

James Keene was a long-standing bull on the company, but whether

---

*Thus The Wall Street Journal on July 3: "Washington correspondents of various newspapers are taking extremely bearish views and nearly all Washington houses are short of the stock . . . The street [i.e., Wall Street] impression certainly is that the Sugar Co. has been defeated." And on July 24: "Never in the history of Sugar manipulation have so few people been right on the stock."

or not Baruch joined forces with him is unknown. "The Standard Oil people" were rumored to be buyers. Harry Content, a favorite broker of Baruch's, and Arthur Housman both were heavy buyers on the day that the stock jumped to $156.25, which proved its high price for the year. "The move in Sugar," said the *Journal* next day, "was generally attributed to [Housman] by the room [i.e., by professional traders], and there is reason to believe that he had a good deal to do with it."

When Baruch told Annie that he had taken $60,000 from the market and at last they could marry, she was incredulous. They had spoken on the telephone:

"You'll lose it as quickly as you made it."

"This time I'll keep it."

Each was mistaken—Baruch didn't lose the money; he gave most of it away. But she was persuaded and her father was overruled (evidently Dr. and Mrs. Baruch gave their blessings), and the wedding took place at her home on October 20. An Episcopal service was presided over by Dr. Richard Van Horne, a Griffen relative, who beforehand had taken Baruch aside and mentioned that he planned to dispense with reference to the Father, the Son and the Holy Ghost, in deference to him. Baruch thanked him but encouraged a traditional reading.

The newlyweds honeymooned in Washington, D.C., and at Old Point Comfort, on Chesapeake Bay, the groom becoming seasick en route. They paid a visit to the Baruch birthplace in Camden, South Carolina, and returned to New York to live in the Baruch home at 51 West 70th Street where the household already comprised the groom's parents and three brothers. There Annie and he remained for two years or more.

It was common enough at the time for a man to bring home his wife to live with his parents. Probably not everyone relished this arrangement, and perhaps Annie had her qualms. Baruch's mother, a dominating woman, had always enjoyed the sole command of her home and the undivided attention of her sons. For Annie, who was seeing more of her mother-in-law than of her hardworking husband, the first few months of domesticity were a difficult prelude to a marriage that turned out more or less as her father had predicted, though not necessarily for the reason he gave.

For Baruch the fall of 1897 marked a coming of age. Between his coup in American Sugar Refining and his wedding, he bought a seat on the New York Stock Exchange. ("Yes," said his mother when he gave her the news, "and you will go further.") Harty, who had graduated from *East Lynne* productions to become leading man to the vamp Olga Nethersole, returned from the theater one night to report that contractual trouble had developed between his costar and him. As Harty came in, Baruch and his mother were winding up one of their regular collaborative solitaire games. Looking up from the cards, Baruch impulsively offered his brother his new seat if he would leave the stage and settle down. Harty accepted. Baruch exulted but presently despaired. Many sleepless hours later he decided that there was nothing to do but to buy another seat for himself. Then, late in November, he made his father the staggering anniversary gift of $20,000. He wanted to give $30,000, one thousand gold dollars for each of his father's married years, but he had already settled $19,000 (the cost of the seat) on Harty. Thus in the course of a few months, Baruch had earned $60,000, distributed two-thirds to the men he idolized and married the woman he loved. All together, his standing at home had never been higher.

THREE

Baruch's Wall Street

Considered as matters of timing, Baruch's apprenticeship in Wall Street was unlucky but his journeyman years there were heaven-sent. The signal event of his early career at A. A. Housman & Company was the Panic of 1893 and the long depression that followed it. Railroads failed (William H. Vanderbilt had assessed the prospects of that basic industry a decade before: "In a year or so we may have no Government. We must have railroads."), violent strikes erupted and the nation passionately chose up sides over the currency. In 1894 a seat on the New York Stock Exchange was sold for what would prove the lowest price from that day to this: $14,000. In Chicago, soup kitchens were thrown up to accommodate the casual travelers who had drifted to town for the Columbian Exposition of 1893 and who had been stranded by the panic as if by a blizzard.

Not until after the defeat of William Jennings Bryan and the silver movement in the 1896 presidential election did the depression run its course. The ensuing boom smiled on Baruch's stockbroking years. In 1896 a wave of corporate mergers began that would culminate in 1901 with the capitalization of the United States Steel Corporation at $1.4 billion, a sum a third again as large as the public debt. Industrial companies were organized, railroads were reorganized and new securities poured from Wall Street. The stock market, which in the early 1890s had been in the hands of professionals, increasingly engaged the public. At the turn of the century more people traded more common stock than ever before. Endowed with what a later generation would call "glamour," the shares of a trolley line, Brooklyn Rapid Transit Company, in 1899 leaped from 61 to 137, much to the delight of the waiters and clerks who had had no idea that money was so easily gotten. Late in the 1890s, 400,000 shares was considered a good day's business on the Stock Exchange. In 1901, a single session brought 3,000,000 shares and a seat changed hands for $80,000. "Everybody was making money," a fictional but authentic account of those days related.

The steel crowd came to town, a horde of millionaires with no more regard for money than drunken sailors. The only game that satisfied them was the stock market. We had some of the biggest high rollers the street ever saw: John W. Gates, of "Bet-you-a-million" fame, and his friends, like John A. Drake, Loyal Smith, and the rest; the Reid-Leeds-Moore crowd, who sold part of their steel holdings and with the proceeds bought in the open market the actual majority of the stock of the great Rock Island system; and Schwab and Frick and Phipps and the Pittsburgh coterie; to say nothing of scores of men who were lost in the shuffle but would have been called great plungers at any other time. A fellow could buy and sell all the stock there was. Keene made a market for the U. S. Steel shares. A broker sold one hundred thousand shares in a few minutes. A wonderful time! And there were some wonderful winnings. And no taxes to pay on stock sales! And no day of reckoning in sight.*

---

*Gates, famous as a barbed-wire salesman, stock-market speculator and gambler, organized the American Steel & Wire Company, one of the components of the U.S. Steel consolidation. Drake was a financial and racing associate of Gates's, and Smith was a real estate operator. Once in a baccarat game at the Waldorf, Baruch recounted, Gates drained the blood from the faces of Smith and Drake by betting them $1 million. Baruch was in the game too, but Gates was betting with him, not against him. (Bet-a-Million, as Gates was fittingly known, won and lost a half million on that game—a heart-pounding draw.)

The Reid and Moore in the "Reid-Leeds-Moore" crowd were Daniel G. Reid and William H. Moore, important stockholders in the National Steel Company, American Tin Plate Company, American Steel Sheet Company and American Steel Hoop Company. To each man's enormous profit, the businesses were merged into U.S. Steel. Before the consolidation, William B. Leeds was president of Tin Plate. Charles Schwab, Henry C. Frick and Henry Phipps, of course, were also leading steel executives.

So intimately bound up with Wall Street is Baruch's story that a so-cial, financial and geographical digression on that place as he first knew it might now be in order. To begin with appearances: the financial cen-ter, of which the epicenter was the New York Stock Exchange, at Broad and Wall Streets, was small, sunlit and equine. The Trinity Building, up Broadway from Wall and just north of the Trinity churchyard, was six stories high, not the twenty-one stories of the current successor Trinity Building. Across Broadway, the Equitable Building rose eight stories rather than the current thirty-eight (a mass which at its construction in 1915 constituted the highest office structure in the world). The streets downtown were thronged with horse-drawn transport: wagons, han-som cabs and streetcars; also with pushcarts and with men who invari-ably wore hats. To venture outdoors bareheaded or in shirtsleeves was to risk the open derision of passersby. (Wall Street was very much a man's world. In 1900 the census counted exactly 240 women brokers and bankers in all of New York State as against 11,293 men, of whom 7 were black.) Before the arrival of subways in 1904, the main locomotive transportation downtown from the Upper West Side was the Sixth Av-enue Elevated. For a nickel the El bore passengers down past Central Park and the Plaza Hotel, past the reservoir at 40th Street and by Macy's and Union Square, down to Chambers Street and around the steepest railroad bend in the world, past Newspaper Square and City Hall and the old Post Office (a magnificent granite neo-Renaissance pile, razed in 1938–1939), by the churchyard at St. Paul's and the Jer-sey City ferry slips to Rector Street; all in all, from Baruch's first house at 245 West End Avenue near 72nd Street, a trip of about forty min-utes. Baruch's first year as a clerk in 1891 was the last year before the advent of the Stock Exchange Clearing House. Every share that was bought or sold was received or delivered by hand even if a subsequent offsetting transaction made the receipt or delivery redundant. A few blocks east of this old-fashioned clerical swirl, longshoremen drove horse carts to the sailing ships that were moored along the East River and boys swam nude, in season, from the docks at the Fulton Fish Mar-ket. In all seasons at the Curb market, antecedent to the American Stock Exchange, brokers traded stocks in the open air.

Among the many latter-day landmarks not then built or conceived was the New York Federal Reserve Bank's Florentine structure on Lib-erty Street. Until 1914 no Federal Reserve System existed. There was no Securities and Exchange Commission, no federal insurance of bank deposits, and no federal law to segregate commercial and investment banking. Most important, there was no federal income tax, except for the short-lived statute that was struck down by the Supreme Court in 1895. Limited government was as fixed and obvious a condition of finance in Baruch's youth and middle years as a regime of federal regulation was to become in his old age.

In the early 1890s, life on the Stock Exchange was clubbable, sometimes lighthearted and, by the later standards of the McKinley bull market, dull. Trading began at 10 A.M. and ended at 3 P.M., except on Saturdays, when the closing bell was at noon. On Mondays in the summer the opening was civilly put back until 11 A.M. (an amenity dispensed with in the crush of bull-market business in 1902). Baedeker's *United States*, in 1893, described the trading floor as a "strange scene of business, tumult, and excitement, a wilder scene probably than that presented in any European exchange," but on a sleepy day in July 1892 only 30,000 shares were bought and sold. The amount of commission income thereby produced, according to an estimate that discounted sleight-of-hand transactions in which little commission was paid, was less than $1 per member, or barely enough for sandwiches for two. Earlier the same month, on another dull day, the brokers honored the visit to the galleries of several hundred members of the Christian Endeavor Societies with a spontaneous chorus of "Shall we gather at the river?" Business, such as it was, was disrupted for half an hour.

Trading on the floor, then as now, was done at a high pitch by high-spirited people. The Governing Committee, a forty-man council elected by the members (and to which Baruch, at the unusually tender age of thirty-three, was elected in December 1903), was charged with upholding decorum against difficult odds. One long-standing fugitive rite was the hazing of new members. On his first day on the floor, a member might expect to be stripped of his buttons, to have his hat pulled down over his eyes and to have his suit ripped from his back. The governors, who officially deplored this roughhouse in 1894, were obliged to condemn it again in 1900 and 1912. Another worry was gambling, a subject on which the constitution was silent except to prohibit the laying of bets on stock prices. (That is, betting without buying or selling the shares.) Voting 18–12, the governors in 1897 outlawed all wagering, and in 1900 they went so far as to forbid the playing of bridge-whist in the library.

At the turn of the century, the Stock Exchange was a private association very much like a club. It was unincorporated and therefore, as its lawyers argued, beyond the reach of the laws that regulated corporations. Its object was to provide a market (as the constitution was made to read in 1902): ". . . to furnish exchange rooms and other facilities for the convenient transaction of business by its members; to maintain high standards of commercial honor and integrity among its members; and to promote and inculcate just and equitable principles of trade and business." The attitude of the governors was that prices on the floor were set by buyers and sellers and that the Exchange, as an institution, should be as little involved in that process as possible. They reasoned that nobody was forced to trade or to buy a seat, and that those who chose to join had necessarily agreed to abide by the constitution.*

Although committed to free and fluctuating prices, the Exchange believed in certain fixed standards of conduct. Regarding speech, for instance, it demanded clean talk (in 1902, in keeping with the bull market, the fine for cursing was lifted from $10 to a maximum of $50) and judiciousness in advertising. It also insisted that corporations begin to divulge more of their own affairs. It forbade the members to have truck with bucket shops, where bets were laid on the prices of stocks without the formality of the shares themselves changing hands. It prohibited arbitrage between domestic exchanges (the esoteric practice of buying and selling the same security in different markets in order to exploit the differences in price that sometimes prevailed in different cities). In fact, rarely were objectionable practices banned outright. The custom was rather to declare them "detrimental to the interest and welfare of the exchange," a phrase which it fell to the governors both to define and to apply. The most egregious sin in the eyes of the Exchange was a breach of the rule that fixed the basic rate of commission at $12\frac{1}{2}$ cents a share. For the first offense a member was liable to suspension for up to five years; for the second, to expulsion. The reporting of fictitious, or "wash," sales was also outlawed but under milder penalty. Maximum sentence was suspension for a year. A man who was tried by the gover-

---

*One ancillary reason for joining was the $10 death duty that the members customarily assessed themselves upon the passing of a colleague. If the mourning family had nothing else to show for the deceased's career in the stock market, it at least had $10,000 from the Stock Exchange Gratuity Fund.

nors had the right to confront his accuser but not to retain a lawyer to defend himself at the hearing.

The start of the new century found the Exchange not only richer than ever before but also more influential. W. H. Granberry, a member of the Governing Committee, illustrated the point with some fellow members in 1906. Many years before, he said, the New York Central Railroad had announced it was moving its securities transfer offices from Pine Street, which was downtown, to 42nd Street, which was all the way uptown. The Exchange protested that the remoteness of the address would complicate dealings in the company's securities. Cornelius Vanderbilt weighed the governors' position and said: "It is not convenient for the New York Central to have a down-town transfer office." And, as Granberry noted, that was that. In 1904, the transfer-office situation was again thrown into confusion by a law that was seemingly at odds with the Stock Exchange rule that every listed company maintain an office in Manhattan. The Exchange insisted that the companies take steps (inconvenient but not extralegal) to comply with *its* rules. Every company but the largest grudgingly submitted. At length, U.S. Steel, which had threatened to withdraw its shares from listing, also gave way. ". . . [T]he Stock Exchange," said Granberry, "was superior to the corporation; and I believe the Stock Exchange is superior to every corporation today."

The Exchange's new quarters, which were opened in the spring of 1903 (and which are still in service), were capacious enough to accommodate a growing volume of business and sufficiently imposing to satisfy the members' rising sense of place. The building was designed by the architect George B. Post and was to be finished in 1902 at a cost of $1 million. Construction dragged on for an extra year, and costs ballooned to $4 million or so, however, owing in part to Broad Street's watery subsoil, in part to an old stone safe that could not be gotten around and in part to an extensive series of alterations in the original plans. In one of the changes the Building Committee asked that the trading-floor telephones be installed at the New Street entrance and not, as Post had them, at Broad Street. The New Street variation would save five feet of floor space, the committee said, and not incidentally make it unnecessary for the telephone clerks to clutter up the members' entrance. Post agreed. Earlier in the planning, the Exchange had played with the idea of making the second floor the trading floor and of renting the first to banks. When it was pointed out that a crush for the elevators might develop in a financial panic, trading was restored to terra firma. (As a writer at the time put it: "Accessibility to the street and generous egress thereto from the Board Room [trading floor] was emphatically demanded.") Bearing in mind the anarchist bombing of the French Chamber of Deputies in 1893, the Exchange decided it could do with less space in the visitors' gallery.

The trading floor was expanded by 60 percent, however, more light and ventilation were provided, a new safe of 776 tons was built and on Broad Street, above six Corinthian columns, a group of marble statuary was mounted of which the central figure symbolized Integrity. For the members' convenience a complete emergency hospital was established on the fourth floor and baths were provided in the basement. On the day of the grand opening, April 22, 1903, confetti and ticker tape fluttered from the windows of the buildings nearby. At the Stock Exchange, the new boardroom was decked in palms and floral pieces and American flags. Just after 11 A.M., to general applause, J. P. Morgan made his way through the crowd to the speakers' platform. The Reverend Dr. Morgan Dix of Trinity Church offered the invocation—"The silver is Thine and the gold is Thine, O Lord of Hosts . . ."—and Rudolph Keppler, president of the Exchange, described the construction as a feature of the national destiny. It was, he said, ". . . but one of the many astounding changes that typify our onward march toward supremacy, and give lasting and monumental expression to the unexampled progress and prosperity with which our beloved country has been blessed." A congratulatory statement from the oldest member was read, and with that, three cheers were given, Morgan being in especially strong voice.

It was easy enough for progressive critics to point up the inevitable lapses between what the Exchange professed and what it did: for example, the occasional blatant manipulations or such self-serving practices as that which gave the members first call on the proceeds of the sale of a bankrupt member's seat. However, what distinguished the Stock Exchange was not so much its laxness as its honor. At least in professional matters, a member was expected to be as good as his word.

A public-relations disaster but a financial boon to Wall Street in the 1890s was the rise of the large industrial company, or "trust." At the start of the decade the stock market was mainly involved in railroads, and as late as 1900 the bellwether New York Stock Exchange trading issue was the Missouri Pacific Railroad; the industrial company was an odd fish. In the early 1890s the most actively traded industrial was the National Cordage Company, a would-be rope monopoly that hanged itself (as everybody said) on the eve of the Panic of 1893. Public feeling against the trusts ran high, and the Cordage collapse shook even professional Wall Street. The day after the announcement of the Cordage failure, the shares of General Electric Company, suffering in sympathy, dropped to $58 a share from $84. In the long depression, merger activity—the consolidation of small companies to exploit the economies of large-scale production and ultimately, the promoters hoped, to monopolize—declined. It resumed again in the McKinley bull market, which served as a greater incentive to merge and to issue new securities than the Sherman Act proved a deterrent. In 1894 *The Wall Street Journal* had deemed only two industrial securities important enough to include in its twelve-stock average: American Sugar and Western Union. By 1896, it had compiled an average entirely of industrials, as follows: American Cotton Oil, American Sugar Refining, American Tobacco, Chicago Gas, Distilling & Cattle Feeding, General Electric, Laclede Gas, National Lead, North American, Tennessee Coal & Iron, U.S. Leather (preferred) and U.S. Rubber. Beginning its career at 40.94 on May 26, 1896, the Dow Jones Industrial Average slumped by August 8 of that year to 24.48, its all-time low, but three years later, in the summer of 1899, it had more than tripled, to 77. "Every conceivable line of manufacturing had its trust," a historian of the period wrote. "Conservative bankers, shrewd business men, and doctrinaire economists became infected with the virus of large-scale production. People condemned the trusts one moment and bought their securities the next. It was the harvest time of promoters."

There were amalgamations in copper, glue, hay, steel, flour, needles, thread, elevators and envelopes, among other lines of business. Some redeemed the hopes of investors. Thus in 1898 came Otis Elevator and International Paper; in 1899, American Smelting & Refining and United Shoe Machinery. Others fell flat, vindicating only the axiom that business involves risk. The American Bicycle Company, for example, which had won a commanding position in two-wheeled transportation, failed in 1902 in an attempt to manufacture automobiles. A study of thirteen major consolidations of the period found that, over the course of nine years, seven of the companies returned something to the stockholders in dividends and capital gains (standout performer: United Shoe Machinery, up 22.7 percent a year) while six did not (including, unexpectedly, Allis-Chalmers and American Can). One curious flash in the pan was the United States Flour & Milling Trust. The stock was offered to the public on September 11, 1899, at $51 a share. On September 20, it broke 32 points, from $56 to $24 a share, on negligible trading volume. By February 1900 the corporation was bankrupt.

In railroads too the 1890s were a time of consolidation, but the mergers were typically the result of distress, not prosperity. In 1894, at the end of the panic, the Interstate Commerce Commission reported that 192 railroad corporations were bankrupt, representing a combined capitalization of $2.5 billion, no less than a quarter of the par, or face, value of all outstanding railroad bonds and stock. "This, as a record of insolvency," the commission said, "is without parallel in the previous history of American railways, except it be in the period from 1838 to 1842."

Among the causes of failure was always and by definition an unsustainable burden of debt. The Union Pacific, for example, which succumbed as a result of overall bad management, and the Norfolk & Western, which suffered from overexpansion, had scarcely made ends meet before the depression. In 1892, each earned just 5 percent more than what it owed its creditors. When income slipped below that slender margin each was a bankrupt. The failed lines all needed new financing and lower fixed charges, which meant that the security holders, many of whom were British and understandably out of sorts over the turn of events in America, had to agree to make do with less. To devise a satisfactory plan and make it stand up was typically the work of J. P. Morgan and his detail-minded staff. Not until 1897 did another up-and-coming railroad man, Edward H. Harriman, make a serious bid for the Morgan reorganization business. From the point of view of corporate finance, the 1890s were very much the Morgan epoch.

What was new in the railroad debacle was its scale and the correspondingly greater size of the corporate units into which the surviving lines were merged. In 1887, only twenty-eight railroads controlled one thousand or more miles of track; by 1896, there were forty-four. The proportion of the nation's track miles held by thousand-mile roads climbed to 57 percent from 44 percent. The wave of industrial consolidation that had broken at the turn of the century found its counterpart in railroading: between July 1, 1899, and November 1, 1900, more than an eighth of the country's railroad mileage was "absorbed in various ways," as the ICC noted. "At the beginning of the decade," a chronicler of railroads wrote, "there had been innumerable great independent systems, each with its own group of subsidiaries, but each competing against rival systems in the same regions. At the end of the decade there were practically no independent systems; the various systems had been drawn into a few huge combinations which were dominated by a single man or a small group of men working in harmony with each other." Thus in the South, the Atlantic Coast Line, the Southern and the Seaboard Air Line had emerged under the domination of Morgan. Before the depression, five transcontinental lines had vied for business; as the new century opened there were two, the northwestern roads under Hill's control and those to the south under Harriman's. By 1902, the ICC was worrying about monopoly instead of ruinous competition, while the surviving lines were beginning to have cause to worry about the ICC.

As new lines succeeded old, brokers like Baruch applied themselves to the complicated study of which securities should be bought and sold. It was easy to believe that railroads were so deeply mired in law and reorganization that nothing of value would ever come out of them again. Construction, by late in the decade, had almost stopped; some 70 percent of railroad common stock paid no dividends. In the event, however, reorganizations were effected, railroad vital signs, by 1900, began to return to normal and the optimism of those who saw opportunity in distress was amply rewarded. Railroad bonds, declared Henry Clay Frick, in this happier time, were the "Rembrandts" of investments.

The railroad reorganizations bore the stamp of a long-running trend in American finance: a decline in long-term rates of interest. In the last quarter of the nineteenth century, rates paid to depositors at savings banks, for example, fell from 6 percent to $3\frac{1}{2}$ percent. The prices of bonds that paid a relatively high rate of interest accordingly rose. Chicago & Northwest Railroad 7 percent bonds, for instance, appreciated in value from $830 to $1,450 in about twenty-five years. At the lower price, the issue yielded about $8\frac{1}{2}$ percent; at the higher price, less than $3\frac{1}{2}$ percent. In the 1890s it could be reasonable assumed that interest rates would continue to fall, and that, according to the mathematics of bond prices, long-term issues would appreciate more than short-term ones. The hapless holders of defaulted railroad debt, having had no choice but to settle for lower annual interest payments, asked for, and often received, as a kind of consolation, longer maturities. Until the reorganizations of the 1890s, bonds of forty years or more were comparatively rare in America. Now they became commonplace. Hundred-year bonds were forthcoming from the Reading & Atchison and 150-year bonds from the Northern Pacific.

The bond market in those days was almost a perfect inversion of what it was later to become. At the turn of the century the risk to bondholders was default—that the railroad in which they had invested would fail—or the early redemption of sound securities, and not, as in the 1970s, the risk of a general destruction of values by inflation. Even amidst the currency turmoil of the middle 1890s the trend to lower long-term rates continued. Nowadays all maturity classes are volatile; then, only the market for short-term money. The currency was, as the phrase went, "inelastic." When the demand for funds increased at crop-moving season, no Federal Reserve System was on hand to lend to hard-pressed banks. By the same token, no Federal Reserve was available to buy the Treasury's debt with money it had created out of thin air just for that purpose. The price of short-term money, therefore, varied with supply and demand, occasionally shooting up to 100 percent and even higher on the Stock Exchange in a panic and receding to 1 percent or 2 percent in quiet times.

The strength of the long-term bond market was a mirror image of the health of the dollar. At the turn of the century the currency was sturdy to a fault. Between 1893 and 1896, farm prices fell by 22 percent, indicating a proportional rise in the value of money in terms of commodities. This was the inflationary arrangement reversed. In the South and West a cry went up for silver, a cheaper and more plentiful monetary metal than gold and one calculated to bring higher prices. In the East, sentiment opposed inflation and favored gold, the existing standard of money. Since 1879 the dollar had been convertible into gold at a fixed price: $20.67 an ounce. A tribute to the Republic's finances under the gold standard was that this right of redemption had been largely unexercised. Between 1879 and 1893 just $34 million of Treasury notes had been turned in for gold. Paper was preferred on simple grounds of convenience. In March and April of 1893, however, the public began to demand gold itself. What caused this shift were two laws, one of which was Gresham's. It held that bad money drives good out of circulation. The other law, passed by Congress, directed the Treasury to buy silver, which was depreciating in value, with paper, and to offer to redeem the paper with gold. Accordingly the public descended on the Treasury. In 1888 the government's gold reserve had exceeded $200 million. In 1895, it briefly sank to $41 million.

Although the act to require silver purchases was repealed in the fall of 1893, the run on the Treasury's gold continued. Not only was more gold going out; as the depression deepened, less was coming in. The silver agitation was not quelled. Foreigners, appalled by the mismanagement of the Atchison, Topeka & Santa Fe, among other large railroads, exchanged American securities for gold. Twice in 1894 the Administration sold bonds to restore the Treasury's gold reserve, but no sooner was more paper issued than it too was redeemed in an "endless chain." In 1895 the Administration enlisted Morgan and August Belmont to obtain gold from abroad. In 1896 more bonds were sold, a total, in three years, of nearly $300 million. (A vast sum: in the 1890s the federal government's annual outlays ran in the neighborhood of $350 million; in 1899, when bills for the Spanish-American War were falling due, spending barely topped $600 million.) The Democrats in 1896 contentiously produced the champions of both sides of the silver issue. President Cleveland, who had saved the gold standard, was repudiated by his party for Bryan, the arch silverite. But Bryan, in his turn, was defeated by William McKinley, a Republican, and the gold standard was saved again.

From a quite unexpected quarter, however, the inflationists also got their way. In Australia, in the Klondike and in the South African Rand, enormous new veins of gold were opened up. In 1896–1900, twice as much bullion was produced in the world as in the comparable period a decade before. Money grew plentiful, prices and interest rates began to rise, and the Republic's anxiety was redirected from deflation to inflation. Between 1900 and 1910, an index of general prices rose by an average of not quite 3 percent a year; between 1890 and 1899, the same index was hardly changed. Baruch, a lifelong gold partisan, in later years could marshal the sensible defense of the gold standard that it had worked.

Gold was an international money, and Wall Street was a cosmopolitan market. The New Yorkers kept an eye on gold shipments, world agricultural news and especially developments on the London Stock Exchange. In the boom summer of 1897 some three hundred British dealers made markets in U.S. stocks and bonds. On both sides of the Atlantic, arbitrageurs kept odd hours (rising before dawn in New York and working into the evening in London) in hopes of buying stocks cheap in one market and selling them dear in the other. The first thing that Baruch and his colleagues asked when they walked into the office was "What's London?"

In New York, if not yet in the world, the Stock Exchange was the first market among many. Besides the aforementioned Curb, the city's roster of exchanges included the Coal & Iron, Coffee, Cotton, Maritime, Metal, New York Fire Insurance, Produce and the Consolidated Stock & Petroleum. The Consolidated dealt in speculative mining issues, in contracts for the future delivery of oil and in "odd lots" of fewer than 100 shares of stock. The odd-lot business was important because the cost to an investor who bought a round lot of a $100 stock outright, not on margin, was $10,000 gold dollars before commissions, a small fortune. Of the three stock markets, the New York Stock Exchange was the longest established, charged the highest commissions and demanded the greatest concessions from corporate applicants for listing. On the Curb no commission rate was fixed, while the Consolidated charged half the posted Stock Exchange rate of 12½ cents a share. Alone among the three, the Stock Exchange developed a procedure to require that listed companies divulge their profits and revenues and balance sheets to the public.

At the turn of the century, financial reporting was spotty. Railroad companies, then still the premier investment, regularly published their results, but industrial companies often did not. American Sugar Refining Company, for example, one of the most actively traded stocks of the 1890s and the one in which Baruch scored his first coup, disclosed nothing of its profits until 1909. (In 1890, in a master stroke of reticence, it refused to talk to the Census Bureau.) The annual report of the United States Leather Company in 1900 consisted of a simple balance sheet on a single piece of paper. When the Amalgamated Copper Company went public in 1899, the information it revealed about itself was contained in the following newspaper advertisement:

Amalgamated Copper Co. Capital, $75,000,000. This company is organized under the laws of the State of New Jersey for the purpose of purchasing and operating copper-producing properties. Its capital is $75 million divided into 750,000 shares of common stock on a par value of $100 each. It has no bonds or mortgage debts. This company has already purchased large interests in Anaconda Copper Co., Parrot Silver & Copper Co., Washoe Copper Co., Colorado Smelter and Mining Co., and other companies and properties. (Signed)

> Marcus Daly, President
> H. H. Rogers, Vice President
> William G. Rockefeller, Secretary and Treasurer

The offering was oversubscribed.

"As a general thing," complained *The Wall Street Journal* about industrial management in 1899, "very few figures are published and those figures are usually in such a form that it is impossible to canvass the integrity of net earnings. In fact the figures necessary for this process are the very figures which are most jealously guarded from competitors. Consequently in ninety-five cases out of a hundred the stockholder in an industrial company is obliged to take the word of the managers—with all that that implies—for the company's net earnings."

A question sometimes before the courts in those years was whether an insider, knowing what he did, was bound to divulge it before buying or selling his company's stock in the open market. Out of some sixteen cases that dealt with the issue from the mid-nineteenth century until 1909, the verdict in eleven was no. Fraud and "active or intentional" concealment of information were illegal, but directors and other insiders could generally trade as they liked with the knowledge uniquely at their disposal. (Baruch later described his objections to this doctrine, but he too traded often and profitably on the basis of inside information.) Henry O. Havemeyer, president of American Sugar, was especially successful in his own company's stock. "It has been a saying on Wall Street," a New York *Herald* reporter wrote in 1897, "that each up and down movement in 'sugar' provided profits for Mr. Havemeyer to put up a new 'skyscraper.'"

Long before the Securities and Exchange Commission came on the scene the Stock Exchange had taken steps to increase the amount of information available to the public (and thus to decrease, if only infinitesimally, the trading advantage of the insider over the outsider). By 1906, for instance, Sears, Roebuck & Company, in application for listing, was obliged to supply the following to the Committee on Stock List: certificate of incorporation; copy of bylaws; legal opinion as to proper organization; income statements and balance sheets signed by a public accountant; samples of stock certificates; list of real estate owned (and mortgages and encumbrances, if any). Sears promised to publish its financial results once a year and also to refrain from speculating in its own stock, ". . . except in the regular course of the legitimate business of said company, or for the purpose of retirement." In the year of the Sears application, a member of the stock-list committee remarked to his colleagues that "to deal in any security without such duly certified information would be a gambling proposition of the extreme ultra type."*

If the Stock Exchange aspired to self-regulation, the Curb attained spontaneity. Its rules were unwritten, it had no standing committees, no listing procedure and no roof over its head. These raffish circumstances stemmed from both the Curb members' independence and from a Stock Exchange rule that barred *its* members from dealing with another organized exchange in New York. The Consolidated, which was organized and which had rashly tried to compete with the Stock Exchange in its own securities, was officially off limits. The Curb, in its disorganization, enjoyed the senior exchange's sufferance. Rain or shine, the brokers collected outdoors on Broad Street to trade in a list that incongruously encompassed Standard Oil, U.S. Pneumatic Horsecollar and United Copper (the latter, between 1904 and 1907, going from 70 cents a share to $77 and nearly all the way back down again).

On busy days the brokers spilled off the sidewalk and into the street. They were diamonds in the rough, these all-weather traders, and for merriment they sometimes exchanged exploding cigars and squirted each other with water pistols. According to the historian Robert Sobel, their weird dress and sudden gesticulations (they communicated in a kind of semaphore with clerks perched on the window

---

*The Exchange took considerable pride in its pioneering work in investment disclosure. Among the documents it selected for immortal filing in the cornerstone of the new building in 1901 were the requirements for listing of new corporate securities laid out by the Committee on Stock List.

ledges of nearby office buildings) spooked horses and snarled the traffic on Broad Street. Clerical standards outdoors were predictably casual. Not every legitimate transaction was noted by the official reporter, and phony ones sometimes were. In 1906 a New York Stock Exchange member, William H. Burger, told some fellow members that he wouldn't have a ticker of Curb prices in his office, ". . . because I do not believe that 25 percent of the transactions out there are legitimate." If this was an invidious opinion, the Hughes Commission, investigating stock-market practices in New York in 1909, apparently shared it. Said the commission of the Curb: "Quotations frequently represent 'wash sales,' thus facilitating swindling enterprises."*

Another source of competition for the Stock Exchange was the bucket shop, in which the house offered to bet the public on the short-term movement of stock prices. No actual securities changed hands, a condition that satisfied the Stock Exchange's definition of gambling. Furthermore, the shops pirated Stock Exchange quotations, which were copyrighted, and deprived the members of commission revenue, which was unforgivable. Despite occasional legal action against them, however, the shops managed to flourish, and in 1905 the Stock Exchange heard complaints that sixty such dens of iniquity did a lively business in Pittsburgh. In Milwaukee the bucketing clientele included some of the city's leading bankers.

At the turn of the century the Stock Exchange opposed gambling but condoned certain forms of price manipulation. Nowadays the Securities and Exchange Commission, principal arbiter in such matters, condones gambling but prohibits manipulation; a speculator may lay a bet on prices in the options market but he may not willfully jiggle them. In its day the Stock Exchange drew a subtle distinction. It banned fictitious transactions, so-called wash sales. However, it permitted another manipulative device called "matched orders" in which

---

*The New York Stock Exchange's low assessment of the Curb was exactly the view that many reformers took of the senior exchange itself. Thus the Pujo Committee, investigating the alleged Money Trust, concluded acidly in 1913: "In other words, the facilities of the New York Stock Exchange are employed largely for transactions producing moral and economic waste and corruption; and it is fair to assume that in lesser and varying degree this is true or may come to be true of other institutions throughout the country similarly organized and conducted."

an order to buy a stock was given to one broker and an order to sell the same stock was given to another. The purpose of the feint was to create the illusion of market activity where none really existed, and so to entice the public. To the governors of the Exchange the practice had the redeeming feature that commissions were paid both coming and going. Moreover, the manipulator was at some risk, since the rules forbade him from telling his brokers that they were working at cross-purposes; thus he might buy too high through broker A and sell too low through broker B. No rules checked short selling, however, and stocks could be hammered just as they could be bulled, by brokers acting singly or in pools. Operations on either side of the market were facilitated by margin requirements (as noted) of as little as 10 percent.

A master of the arts of trading and manipulation was Baruch's favorite broker, Harry Content, a polished and soft-spoken man who in 1905 bought control of the National Lead Company in a single session without unduly disturbing the price of its stock. To put that coup in relief, National Lead was at the time a component of the Dow Jones Industrial Average. Content's prowess was described by an eyewitness on the Stock Exchange floor in the fall of 1899:

> I stood at the [Brooklyn Rapid Transit Company] crowd at the close and saw the tactics of the brokers to mark down the price of that stock. If one wanted evidence of professional skill in manipulation he could see it then. The stock was $83\frac{3}{4}$ bid. Mr. Content suddenly received a message which made him act furiously for about ten minutes. Nobody had time to bid for the stock before it was offered below what they intended to bid. The broker threw the stock at anyone who tried to buy it with the evident intention of creating as low a price as could possibly be made in the limited time before the close. The market recovered very rapidly and in fact would have closed quite strong which would have led to bullish articles in the press this morning. The bear party studies such a situation and naturally tried to work against any such condition and therefore all the professional skill to counteract the bullish effect of a strong closing was utilized.

Many years later, when public suspicion of Wall Street had reached a pitch that prompted the Money Trust hearings, the first federal inquiry into stock-market practices, Content was among the brokers called to testify. To a question about manipulative technique, the magician (whom one client described as "thunderless lightning") replied blandly: "I cannot describe any from my personal knowledge."

At all events, market rigging was a practice more easily condemned by moralists than brought off by speculators. No less a trader than James R. Keene went broke in the mid-1880s in a failed attempt to corner the wheat market. Content himself was wiped out in the Northern Pacific corner of 1901, and Jay Gould, the consummate Gilded Age railroad baron, was, according to his biographer, a failure at stock trading.

One of the oddest of failed manipulations had a literary inspiration. *Friday the Thirteenth*, a novel by Thomas W. Lawson that was published early in 1907, was about a man who managed to sell so many shares of stock short that he brought down the market. Lawson did more than dream up this fanciful yarn; he also declared it a foolproof formula for real-life success. Either the book or the author's guarantee impressed a Philadelphia broker and accused bank wrecker named Albert E. Appleyard. On June 12, 1907, Appleyard, imitating art, sold short thousands of shares of stock, but there was no collapse except of his own finances. "Appleyard has disappeared," *The New York Times* reported on the fourteenth from Philadelphia, "but it is not believed that he has gone to Boston to claim the $5,000 reward offered by Lawson for a practical demonstration that his theory would not work, although it is considered here that his demonstration was clear and convincing."

Such was the neighborhood in which Bernard Baruch made his fortune.

FOUR

"Wealth Commenced to Pour In on Me"

Even if Baruch had burned to fight in the "splendid little war" with Spain (and nothing suggests that he did or wished that he had), there was Annie to consider. They had been married only six months when hostilities broke out in April 1898. Furthermore, there were his bad left ear, his partnership in A. A. Housman & Company and his mother. (He was a demonstrably loving son; he greeted his mother with an enveloping hug and his father with a filial kiss in the middle of the forehead.) In any case, Baruch sat out the war on Wall Street.

Business was good in 1898—stock prices fell with the threat of war in the spring but rallied as victory drew near in the summer—and both the firm and its senior partner were coming into their own. Baruch at the age of twenty-seven was a broker, or "customer's man," with neither wealth nor public reputation, but Arthur Housman, in the estimation of *The New York Times*, was "the recognized representative of some of the most prominent and most powerful millionaires credited with having swung the biggest lines in the activity [of 1897]." This tribute accompanied the text of Housman's New Year's financial outlook, which the *Times* saw fit to print alongside the views of such business luminaries as James J. Hill, the railroad builder, and Jacob H. Schiff, the investment banker. Fortunately for Baruch's career and for his subsequent reputation for decisive action, Housman and the financial editor of *The New York Times*, Henry Alloway, stayed in touch with each other.

It was Alloway who tipped off Housman to news of the American naval victory at Santiago on Sunday, July 3, hours before it was officially confirmed in Washington; and Housman called Baruch, reaching him in Long Branch, New Jersey, where he and Annie and his family were weekending. Housman and Baruch agreed that the news meant a quick end to the war and a strong market. The New York Stock Exchange would be closed the next day, Monday, the Fourth of July, but London would be open as usual. The thing to do was to buy at the opening in London and to sell in New York for a trading profit. The difficulty was getting to the office in time for the opening bell in London, which was 5 A.M., New York time.

As no scheduled train was running to New York on Sunday before a national holiday, Baruch chartered his own. The special, consisting of locomotive, tender and coach, pulled into the station at Long Branch about 2 A.M. Three men climbed aboard: Sailing, Baruch's youngest brother and a Housman employee; Clarence Housman, the senior partner's brother; and Baruch himself. As they sped to New York, Baruch reflected expansively on America's gathering empire and on the looming imperial bull market. In the excitement, one workaday detail had slipped his mind—the key to the office door.

Before first light, the three brokers left their train on the Jersey side of the Hudson. They boarded a ferry for Manhattan and made their way on foot to the financial district. Across the river, in Brooklyn, Fourth of July fireworks began to pop. Before dawn the temperature was 80 degrees.

At the locked Housman door, the men stopped short. Suddenly Baruch remembered the key and somebody noticed the transom. Sailing, the lightest, hopped on his brother's shoulders, climbed through, dropped to the floor and opened the door from the inside. Baruch got busy on the cable to London with orders to buy. Presently, Housman himself arrived and began to rouse his sleeping customers on the telephone, which he cranked. Baruch overheard him in top bull-market form: "Great American victory . . . New markets . . . Empire rivaling England's . . . Biggest stock boom in years . . ." Orders poured in.

In New York next day, stocks opened higher but faded before lunchtime. In Europe, Spanish bonds advanced on the theory that peace would benefit the vanquished too. A. A. Housman & Company took its profits Tuesday morning. Although it was far from alone in buying in London on Monday, it revealed itself as a resourceful and wide-awake firm.*

When he first got to Wall Street, Baruch believed that $6,000 a year was all that he needed because that would be all that he could reasonably spend. As the 1890s wore on and as his vistas widened, $1 million seemed a reasonable sum to possess. On the available evidence, his fortune rose from next to nothing to $1 million in about three years, from 1897 to 1900. As striking as the speed with which he made it is the variety of means employed. Nowadays on Wall Street nearly everybody is a specialist: broker or venture capitalist; floor trader or investment banker. Baruch was all those things at once.

One particularly eclectic episode of moneymaking involved the acquisition of the Liggett & Myers Tobacco Company in 1898 and 1899. It began with a visit to the Housman offices of an Annapolis man named Hazeltine. Hazeltine had resigned his Navy commission before the Spanish war to enter business but had returned to the colors that spring. In the fall, he was again demobilized and, back in business, he had come to see Housman with some information. He said that it was his understanding that the Union Tobacco Company wanted to buy Liggett & Myers, of St. Louis. He happened to know the Liggett people intimately and could help bring them and Union's management together.

The reason for Union's interest was that Liggett & Myers was one of a few large tobacco companies outside the realm of the American Tobacco Company. American was king of the trade, commanding most of the cigarette market and much of the larger chewing-tobacco, or "plug," business. This was the heyday of trusts, and James B. Duke, president of American, had it in mind to monopolize. Union, behind which stood some prominent moneyed men and a top American defector named William Butler, was formed to stand in Duke's way. Both Union and American sought Liggett & Myers.

What American had in market share, it lacked in public relations. It was hated and feared by growers and rival manufacturers. It was hated,

---

* *The New York Times* seemed to describe Baruch without naming him. "In one important instance," it reported on July 5, "a Stock Exchange man, summering at Long Branch, chartered a special train at 2 o'clock in the morning in time to cable instructions abroad for the execution of orders said to be beyond 25,000 shares."

but also tolerated, by many of its customers, for in seeking to absorb the competition it first cut prices. At great cost to Duke, it pitted Battle Axe, its fighting plug brand, against Liggett & Myers' Scalping Knife. (In the stock market, American also had its enemies. "The stock," *The Wall Street Journal* commented, "has been more or less boycotted in Wall Street, because of its manipulation by one of the officers of the company, and probably no dividend payer on the list has been more persistently ignored by commission houses and other interests in Wall Street which believe in open and above-board methods in the management of a company, and its stock interests.") By late 1898, it might have seemed to American that the plug war was well on its way to being won. Just then appeared Union.

In short order in the fall of 1898, Union bought two of the three major independents, National Cigarette & Tobacco Company and Durham Tobacco Company. Liggett & Myers, the third and greatest prize, remained. It was agreed by Housman, Baruch and Hazeltine that they would pool their resources in order to bring about a merger.

Baruch, for his part, labored under the drawbacks of relative youth, of knowing none of the principals and of having no experience to speak of in corporate finance. Furthermore, chewing tobacco, of which Liggett & Myers was the leading manufacturer, made him sick. On the asset side, there was his considerable personal equipment as well as the fact that he knew whatever Hazeltine knew. His first step was to meet and sound out Thomas Fortune Ryan, a chief stockholder of Union, and George Butler, a brother of William Butler, Union's president. This was duly arranged: "Their conversation was guarded at first," Baruch wrote, "but I gathered that Hazeltine was correct about their wanting to purchase Liggett & Myers. Moreover, with the information Hazeltine had given me, I was able to convince these gentlemen that I might be useful to them in the matter." Before long, Baruch and a lawyer named William H. Page had been retained by Ryan to proceed to St. Louis and help negotiate an option for Union to buy Liggett & Myers. Baruch kissed Annie goodbye and boarded a train west.

In St. Louis the lie of the land appeared to favor Union. One substantial minority stockholder was believed to be ready to sell to Duke at the drop of a hat. But Colonel Moses Wetmore, the Liggett & Myers president, disliked the trust, had vowed never to sell out to it and, together with a united band of heirs and corporate officers, evidently controlled the majority of stock. Talks on the Union side were conducted mainly by George Butler, who happened to be an old friend of Wetmore's. (Just what Hazeltine knew that Butler didn't know, or couldn't have found out from Wetmore, is something of a mystery.) Baruch and Hazeltine were relegated to the ancillary duty of ingratiating themselves with the heirs. After weeks of amiability and low-key southern salesmanship, Baruch was recalled by Ryan on special assignment.

The job that Ryan had for Baruch was to harass the American forces in the stock market by a campaign of short selling. The obvious target was American Tobacco itself, but every short seller must sooner or later buy, and there were relatively few American shares in the market. Ryan thus chose Continental Tobacco Company, an American subsidiary, which traded actively outdoors on the Curb Exchange. Baruch's instructions were to drive down the price of the stock and generally to "hang on the flank" of the company and its management. Ryan turned over $200,000 as market ammunition.

Baruch began his operations in the iron cold of January 1899 with the assistance of two floor (literally street) traders, men named Lavino and Tobey. His tactics were to sell Continental when it was strong and to buy it when it was weak; to sell short when the stock was rising and to "cover" his shorts, or purchase the stock he needed to deliver, when the price was falling. Each morning he left Annie, now pregnant with their first child, and dropped in on Ryan at his house on West 72nd Street, which teemed with little boys. Ryan received Baruch in his bedroom and listened to his reports while he shaved. In January the damage to Continental amounted to a fall from 43 to 37. On February 18, the price hit 30½. Although the weakness in Continental was ascribed publicly to the tobacco wars, it bears mention that the drop in that stock was far more severe than the drop in American. One day when Continental was especially hard hit, Ryan demanded to know how much Baruch was costing him. As a matter of fact, Baruch said, he was making his $200,000 grow. "I want you to annoy them," said Ryan, with mock severity, "but I don't want you to ruin them."

Meanwhile, newspapers in New York and St. Louis were quoting anonymous sources to the effect that the great Union–American Tobacco war was a hoax. It was argued that although Wetmore would refuse to sell to American, he would nonetheless sell to another company if he could be duped into believing that it opposed the trust. Thus

Union was formed, in league with Duke, to furnish the pretense of rivalry. It would buy Liggett & Myers, and American and Union would come to terms. And so it proved that February (although Baruch, for one, and Duke's biographer, for another, doubted the existence of conspiracy). With the plug war settled at last, by whatever means, shares in American and Continental climbed.

When it came time to negotiate a fee with Ryan for the services of A. A. Housman & Company, Baruch tried to enlist the sympathies of Ryan's lawyer. He offered William Page $10,000 if he could help him get more money from Ryan. Properly taken aback, Page replied that he would do what he could but, as he was Ryan's lawyer, he could hardly accept money for working against his client's interest. The fee turned out to be $150,000, "ridiculously small" in the light of the deal, Baruch reflected later on, but Housman hadn't conceived the business and it was a choice between that or nothing. The fee brought Housman's earnings in 1899 to $501,000. Baruch's share of the profits, which Arthur Housman by that time had raised to one-third, amounted to $167,000. This was exactly $161,000 more than the $6,000 that Baruch once thought was big money.

In keeping with the Wall Street maxim that money is more easily got than kept, Baruch next managed to lose most of what he had gained. The vehicle of his losses was the American Spirits Manufacturing Company, the nation's largest distiller of whiskey. Common shares of the company changed hands inactively on the New York Stock Exchange. In 1898, they had been as high as $15\frac{3}{8}$ and as low as $6\frac{1}{2}$. In the spring of 1899, when Baruch sank most of his spare money into the stock, the price was about 10.

Tips to buy had been noised around and had surfaced in the press early in June. The story was simply that insiders thought well of whiskey stocks. It developed that the reason for the optimistic talk was a planned merger of four major distilleries, including American, into a trust. The consolidation was disclosed late that month.

At the turn of the century, "trust" appealed to the imaginations of investors as "growth" or "Internet" were to do some ninety-odd years later. The Street's thinking was that the whiskey merger would benefit all parties, particularly investors in American Spirits. (Later came reservations about the quality of financial information that the promoters provided.) Baruch bought for that reason and for one other, namely, that Ryan had bought. Or so he was told by a man who presumably knew. It was a plausible notion, because it had been reported that the "Whitney syndicate" was involved in the deal. William C. Whitney, whose Fifth Avenue mansion had once inspired Mrs. Baruch to tell her son, "You will be living there some day," had been in on the Union Tobacco venture so happily ended. Thus, Baruch loaded up with American Spirits.

The result is told by two quotations. On June 13, the price of the stock was 10¼. On June 29, it was 6¼. Baruch called the loss the quickest and proportionately the greatest of his career. When he explained the details to Annie, he added that, as an economy measure, she would have to give up the black cabriolet, complete with plate-glass lamps and liveried footmen, that he had bought her. At the time she was seven months pregnant.

> Rather sheepishly [Baruch related] I admitted to Mr. Ryan the cause of my comedown in the world.
> "Did I tell you to buy that whiskey stock?" he asked.
> No, I said, I had never asked him about it, but I had heard a man close to him who liked me say that Ryan thought well of it. [Someone, said Baruch, whom he had met through Ryan in the tobacco operation.]
> "Never pay any attention to what I am reported to have said to anybody else," Ryan replied in his quiet voice. "A lot of people who ask me questions have no right to answers. But you have the right."

Among the facts not uncovered by Baruch about American Spirits before he invested was that some of the officers were so crooked that, in Keene's words, "they could meet themselves coming around a corner."

To lose money in a bear market is regrettable. The sinking of American Spirits was intolerable because the broad market was rising and most of Baruch's friends were probably getting richer. (Arthur Housman had just returned from a ten-thousand-mile observation-car tour of the American West with the report that silos were full, railroads prosperous, money plentiful and politics tranquil. "I have come back a greater bull on railroad and industrial securities than ever before in my life . . . ," he declared.) Unwilling to take a loss, Baruch sold his good stocks to shore up his stake in whiskey. His loss deepened. By the time he extricated himself, he had upset Annie and jarred his own self-confidence. All this within weeks of the tobacco coup.

Fortunately his misery was short-lived. In May, as he was blundering into whiskey, a powerful Wall Street figure, former New York governor Roswell Pettibone Flower, unexpectedly died. Flower was the bull market incarnate. In early 1898, when the bears, or "croakers," as Housman contemptuously called them, were sitting in the driver's seat, Flower announced that he was a bull. "I am a believer in American stocks and a buyer of American stocks because I am a believer in our country," he said a year later. For a time he was opposed in the market by Russell Sage, among other rich bears, but optimism carried the day. So great did Flower's influence become that, at the top of his form, he could put up a stock market merely by saying that it was due for a rise. One of his favorite issues was Brooklyn Rapid Transit Company, the country's largest trolley line at a time when Brooklyn was a kind of national Sunbelt. In 1897, when the stock was at 20, Flower invited the city's workingmen to invest their savings for a rise to 75. When the price reached 50, he forecast a move to 125. Thanks to management that he personally helped to invigorate and to the growth of traffic to Manhattan and Coney Island, the stock that spring touched 135.

Flower was born on a farm in upstate New York, taught school in the country and remained countryman enough so that, in his term as governor of New York, he could deliver convincing talks to rural audiences on "Hop Culture" and "Insect Pests." Flower & Company was a leading Wall Street firm, but Flower himself presented an unbankerly appearance, shaving irregularly, filling his left cheek with plug tobacco and generally dressing down, all the while exuding optimism. "The ex-governor preached Americanism and confidence," wrote Henry Clews, "until everybody believed that if a stock was only grounded, and the property located in America, you could buy it at any price and still be on the safe side."

On Thursday evening, May 11, 1899, Flower repaired to a country club in Eastport, Long Island, for a long weekend's fishing. On Friday morning, he complained of indigestion; that evening he was stricken by a heart attack. His death orphaned a half-dozen "Flower stocks," so named for the governor's attention and sponsorship, including BRT, People's Gas, Federal Steel, Rock Island Railroad and New York Air Brake. On Saturday the market broke badly. Only the action of a pool comprising Morgan, Keene, Darius Mills and the Rockefeller interest, among others, averted a full-blown panic on Monday. BRT, which had slipped to 100, rebounded to 115.

In a feeble way stocks rallied that summer, but something was wrong with BRT. In Albany there was talk of a new streetcar franchise tax, and in New York City of a law to require that the line's above-ground wires be buried. The company's annual report, which was published late in August, showed lower profits and strangely disclosed no balance sheet. Again the stock worked lower. Baruch had profited by the rise in BRT. Now he decided to share in the fruits of the fall. Early in September, the price struck 100, a point deemed to be a key line of support. "To hold the price there," wrote Baruch, "Allie Wormser, the sportsman son of one of the partners of I. & S. Wormser, bid par [i.e., 100] for two or three thousand shares. In a flash, I sold them to him." Baruch sold short, that is, without actually owning the shares he was bound to deliver to Wormser. Those he would borrow. He planned to return the borrowed stock with shares that he would buy at a profitably lower price.

His timing was flawless. On September 5, which was just about the time he sold, the rail and industrial averages began a short, sharp break. Moreover, a well-financed bear pool, including Keene and the brokers Harry Content and Jules S. Bache, had begun to sell BRT. They did so in the face of predictions of a "squeeze" of the shorts, meaning a campaign to ruin them. Baruch, who only three months before had been skinned in the market, sold too. His profits totaled $60,000 and his self-confidence was restored.*

In his seventies Baruch sat for a portrait by Yousuf Karsh, the eminent Canadian photographer who had recently snapped the then Princess Elizabeth of England. In the sitting Karsh happened to remark on Elizabeth's charm, to which Baruch replied with a smile, "As you get older you will realize that every Princess and every wealthy man is charming. I am so much more charming than when I was a mere twenty." He had, indeed, by that rule, made enormous strides in personality even between the ages of twenty-eight and thirty. "Wealth commenced to pour in on me," he said of the turn of the century, and he shared that swift untaxed stream with his father, just as he had shared an earlier windfall with Harty. They were an extraordinarily close-knit family. It was no accident, for instance, that his and Annie's

---

*By year's end, BRT had sunk to 60. In December the company posted a $25,000 reward for information leading to the discovery and conviction of persons who had spread false and malicious rumors about its stock.

first child, Belle, was named for his mother and delivered by his father at his father's summer cottage. (Not until he was twenty-eight or twenty-nine and an expectant or actual father did he leave his father's home on West 70th Street, and his three brothers were still there when he moved.) For years Dr. Baruch had worried about losing his livelihood to younger and better-trained men when he was no longer able to climb his patients' stairs. On his father's sixtieth birthday, in July 1900, Baruch was able to present him with a $75,000 retirement trust fund and thereby erase his financial worries. According to Baruch this was the first time that his money had ever engaged the doctor's interest.

Such was Baruch's reputation, or charm, that investment proposals were increasingly coming to him. Late in April 1901 a stockbroker named Harry Weil paid a call to court his interest in a new, and as yet unincorporated, retail chain called United Cigar Stores. After Weil laid out the possibilities of sensible pricing and economies of scale, Baruch called Ryan to run the idea past him. Ryan said that he couldn't see the money in it. Deferring to Ryan, his mentor, Baruch declined to invest. (An ironic miscalculation, as it turned out. Before the end of the year, American Tobacco, of which Ryan was now a director, bought a majority interest in United; within five years the chain had accumulated 150 stores.)

Weil incidentally mentioned that he happened to own 5,000 shares of Northern Pacific. Baruch, who had seen the stock sell for 2½ in 1895 and at 19 as recently as 1898, ventured the view that it was too high at 100. With that, he called the president of the railroad, Charles S. Mellen, to ask his presumably authoritative opinion. Mellen not only accepted the call and talked to Baruch and agreed with him, but he also put in an order to sell 2,500 of his own shares. His confidence rattled, Weil sold *his* Northern Pacific, at a price of about 102. Within two weeks, Northern Pacific, capping one of the most astonishing runs in Stock Exchange history, briefly touched 1,000. Weil subsequently computed the cost of Baruch's advice at $2.5 million.

It might be noted here that the possibilities for error in the stock market are vast, and that the trail of every Wall Street fortune is crossed with wrong turns. One can buy and sell too early and too late. One can be right but unlucky. Baruch, in the spring of 1901, had the good fortune to be wrong but lucky.

This was the boom time of the McKinley market and the idea had gained currency that prices would go up forever. It was true in the past that bull markets had ended, but this was (as it was said) a New Era. U.S. Steel had been capitalized for $1 billion or more, the gold standard was secure and general prosperity was inevitable. In the stock market, the alliance of James J. Hill and J. P. Morgan had bought up a majority interest in the Chicago, Burlington & Quincy Railroad, thus sowing the hope that other lines might similarly catch the eye of a wealthy syndicate. Alexander Dana Noyes wrote of that self-confident age:

> Probably 1901 was the first of such speculative demonstrations in history which based its ideas and conduct on the assumption that we were living in a New Era; that old rules and principles and precedent of finance were obsolete; that things could safely be done to-day which had been dangerous or impossible in the past. This illusion seized on the public mind in 1901 (in New York at any rate) quite as firmly as it did in 1929. It differed only in the fact that there were no college professors in 1901 who preached the popular illusion as their new political economy.

James J. Hill, in the ordinary run of events, had small use for New Eras, Wall Street or perpetual bull markets. He was the builder and steward of railroads, notably of the Great Northern and the Northern Pacific, and he boasted that he had never bought a share of stock for "gambling purposes" in his life. But it was he, not his bankers at J. P. Morgan (nor the hired president of the NP, Mr. Mellen), who first spotted the telltale market action in Northern Pacific. Through April the stock had been rising. On Friday, the twenty-sixth, it spurted by 3 points on the startling volume of 106,500 shares. Hearing the news the same day in St. Paul, Hill set out Saturday evening for New York to investigate personally. It was obvious to him that somebody was accumulating the stock and that the logical buyer was E. H. Harriman.

Hill and Harriman got along tolerably well as neighboring railroad geniuses, but Harriman had no use for Hill's banker, Morgan. Their enmity dated to 1887, when Harriman outmaneuvered Morgan to acquire the Dubuque & Sioux City Railroad. Next, in 1894, Harriman mounted a noisy campaign to block a Morgan plan to reorganize the bankrupt Erie, on which Harriman commuted to work. Morgan won the fight in court, but Harriman was vindicated by events: the plan failed just as he had predicted. Most galling to Morgan was the colossal success that Harriman had made of the Union Pacific Railroad in the late 1890s after he, Morgan, had given up the line as a lost cause in 1895. One day on the floor of the Stock Exchange, Baruch's attention was drawn to a slight man, bespectacled and bowlegged, at the Union Pacific post. "Who's that damn fellow buying all the UP?" he demanded. It was E. H. Harriman, making his fortune.

The first shot in the greatest struggle between Harriman and Morgan was the aforementioned acquisition of the Burlington by the Northern Pacific. The strategic value of the Burlington to the NP was that it provided a sorely needed link to Chicago. Harriman too needed a Chicago terminus for the Union Pacific, and he asked the NP interests, Hill and Morgan, to sell one-third of the Burlington. They refused. Harriman's answer was audacity itself: he began to buy up the Northern Pacific. It was this stroke that Hill read between the lines of the April stock listings and which put Baruch accidentally in the way of a market killing.

When Hill stepped off the train in New York on Monday morning, April 29, he made his way downtown to his office and to a frank proposition. On hand to meet him were Harriman himself and his banker, Jacob Schiff, of the firm of Kuhn, Loeb. The two men announced that their holdings, added to Hill's, would constitute clear control of the Northern Pacific. Would Hill throw over Morgan and join them? Hill most definitely would not. Thus were battle lines drawn in the famous Northern Pacific corner.

While Harriman, backed by the millions of the Standard Oil interests, continued to buy NP, Hill marshaled his bankers. On investigation it turned out that the house of Morgan had been selling Northern Pacific to Harriman because it thought that the price was too high. Morgan himself was in Europe. Not until Saturday did a cable reach him at the Grand Hotel in Aix les Bains, in the French Alps. Not until after the close of the market that day was his answering directive—buy all necessary stock—received in New York.

The same Saturday found Harriman ill and uneasy. On paper his control of the Northern Pacific was perfected. He owned a majority of the voting stock, common and preferred together, although not of the common alone. What he did or did not realize that day was that the directors could vote to retire the preferred on January 1, 1902. If the Hill and Morgan interests could postpone the annual election of directors until after that date, Harriman's preferred, and a block of his votes, could be erased. For whatever reason, Harriman was moved to put in a call to Schiff's office. He left an order to purchase enough stock to give him undisputed control of the common. Schiff was at synagogue. When the message was relayed to him there, he declined to interrupt his Sabbath, directing that the matter be held until Monday. But Monday proved too late.

Baruch, an early bird, customarily began his day at the arbitrage rail of the Stock Exchange, comparing prices in New York and London. Sometimes, especially on Mondays, the two markets fell out of step, so that the same stock could be quoted at widely different prices on either side of the Atlantic. In that case, Baruch would buy in London and sell in New York or vice versa, restoring order to the quotations as a curator might tidy up a gallery by straightening the pictures.

Bright and early on Monday, May 6, Baruch was perusing the London list at the old Produce Exchange, where the New York Stock Exchange had found makeshift quarters during the construction of its new building. Beside him stood Talbot Taylor, a Stock Exchange member and son-in-law of James Keene's. In his friendly way, Baruch remarked to Taylor that, on the basis of its London price, Northern Pacific looked a little high in New York. Often, when Taylor was executing an order in New York and the stock was also listed in London, Baruch would handle the transatlantic end, buying or selling in London at a small arbitrage profit. On this occasion, Taylor regarded him evenly. Baruch related the following conversation:

> "Bernie," he said, tapping his lips with the butt end of his pencil, "are you doing anything in Northern Pacific?"
>
> "Yes," I replied, "and I'll tell you how to make some money out of it. Buy London, sell here, and take an arbitrage profit."
>
> Taylor went on tapping his lips, then his forehead, with the pencil. At length he said, "I would not arbitrage if I were you."
>
> I did not ask why. If Taylor wanted me to know he would tell me. I offered to let him have some of my previous London purchases if they would help him any.
>
> "All right," he agreed, "you can buy N.P. in London, but if I need the stock I want you to sell it to me at a price and a profit that I will fix."

To this I agreed. Taylor stood there for an instant. Then, taking my arm, he led me out of earshot of anyone else.

"Bernie," he said in almost a whisper, "I know you will do nothing to interfere with the execution of the order. There is a terrific contest for control and Mr. Keene is acting for J. P. Morgan.

"Be careful," concluded Taylor, "and don't be short of this stock. What I buy must be delivered now. Stock bought in London will not do."

For the second time in a month, Baruch was made privy to nonpublic information concerning Northern Pacific. Mellen had an opinion, which backfired. Taylor, however, had facts, and Baruch proceeded to act on them. He resolved (a) to do nothing in Northern Pacific except to hold the stock that he had already bought in London and (b) to sell other stocks short in anticipation of a general collapse. He reasoned that traders who were mistakenly short of NP would be driven to raise cash to buy themselves out, and to raise cash they must sell stock. The list would plunge but rise again. What Baruch knew and deduced was known only to the inner councils of the warring camps. Asked on Monday by a St. Paul newspaperman what had gotten into NP, Hill replied blandly that he didn't know but that he deplored speculation.

On Monday the stock opened at 114. More than 400,000 shares later, it closed at 127½. Harriman, unwilling to chase the price higher and convinced that his preferred was as good as his common (a point on which legal counsel subsequently reassured him), stepped aside. Hill and Morgan waded into the market for 150,000 shares. When, on Tuesday, the price reached 146, they stopped buying, convinced that *they* had control. But the rise in NP ("Nipper," to traders) had scarcely begun.

The source of the new buying was short sellers. They believed, as Baruch did before Taylor had filled him in, that NP was unnaturally high, that it couldn't stay up and that it deserved to be sold. So widespread was this view that, by Wednesday, when the corner became common knowledge, 100,000 more shares had been sold than were ever engraved. For the shorts, the arithmetic meant ruin. Under the rules, a seller had only one day to deliver what he had sold. If he failed to deliver, the buyer was permitted to bid any price for what was owed him and to send the bill to the hapless seller.

In an ordinary corner a squeeze of the shorts is the object desired.

In the Northern Pacific corner, it happened by accident. The buyers wanted stock to own, not the blood of bears. But in the end it was the plight of the sellers that overshadowed the struggle of the buyers and that brought Hill and Harriman together in settlement.

After the close of the market on Wednesday (after Nipper had put on another 16½ points, to 160, up 50-odd points since Saturday), desperate shorts gathered at the Northern Pacific post to beg or borrow some stock certificates. It was announced that none could be lent because each side was taking final inventory. To someone who buys a security the ultimate risk is known: a price of zero. For a cornered short seller, the ultimate risk is limitless and unknown, because the price of a stock or bond might go up indefinitely. To the panicked brokers who filled the public rooms of the Waldorf-Astoria that evening and waited in vain for news (bull-market affability gone, evening dress dispensed with), calamity loomed for Thursday. Baruch, a very solvent bystander, remembered:

> Only the stoutest could maintain outward signs of composure. I saw Arthur Housman in the company of John W. Gates of "Bet a Million" fame. The bluff, breezy Chicagoan kept up his old bravado. He denied all rumors connecting him with a short interest in Northern Pacific, saying that he had not lost a cent and that if he had, he wouldn't squeal. The latter part of this statement was true, if the first part was not.

On Thursday morning, NP opened at 170, traded at 400 before 11 A.M. and at 700 before noon. The market had become a series of spasms, successive trades at midmorning, for example, occurring at the prices of 300, 230, 300, 400 and 320. Money was lent to brokers overnight at the rate of 60 percent. There was a rumor that Arthur Housman had dropped dead. Before he could show his face on the floor of the Exchange in rebuttal, the lie was cabled to London. In Albany, Bache & Company hired a special train to rush some odd unsold Northern Pacific certificates to New York. (*The Wall Street Journal* reported a dilemma in brokerage-house ethics: "A broker had 100 shares of Northern Pacific owned by a man on his way to Europe. He knew that the customer would sell at 500, but he felt that he could not sell without an order to do so. Was he right?") Just before 2 P.M., 300 shares changed hands at 1,000, cash.

The mirror image of the panicked rise in NP was the rout in the rest of the list. U.S. Steel gave up 6¾ points, American Sugar 8⅜ and Amalgamated Copper 10. Then, late in the session, hope dawned: an announcement that delinquent short sellers would not be "bought in" that day. The market rallied and NP sank. By the closing bell, Nipper had settled back to 300, having traded as low as 190 and as high as 1,000. Another announcement followed: Hill and Harriman would settle accounts with short sellers at the unexpectedly lenient price of 150. The panic was over.

Forewarned, Baruch emerged richer. He sold short before the collapse and bought at the lows on Wednesday and Thursday. He bought Northern Pacific in London at a cost of $112 to $115 and sold it at a huge profit. He related that he cleared the biggest day's profit of his career on Wednesday, which sum, however, he did not mention.*

As for Hill and Morgan, Schiff and Harriman, the battle ended anticlimactically. It was agreed that Morgan would name the next Northern Pacific board and that among the directors would be Harriman. Harriman, furthermore, would gain representation on the board of the Burlington, which would remain strictly neutral in competitive matters between the Union Pacific (the Harriman line) and the Northern Pacific.

Concerning Talbot Taylor, Baruch's benefactor, he was divorced from Keene's daughter, Jessica, in 1908. He ended his days in the south of France, devoting himself to his garden and regularly winning first prizes at the Riviera flower shows.

Shortly after his serendipitous turn in Northern Pacific, Baruch happened to pass an afternoon in the Waldorf with Herman Sielcken, a well-to-do coffee merchant. Sielcken was a customer of Housman's, an occasional speculator in stocks and an all-around student of markets. That day he talked about copper, fixing Baruch with his sharp black eyes and sometimes animatedly watering his speech with saliva.

---

*Baruch was short of stocks outright and also short against call options. A call grants the holder the right to buy a stock at a particular price over a certain period of time. For example, an option on U.S. Steel might have granted the option holder the right to buy 100 shares at 50 until June 30. If the price of Steel had happened to run to 100, the option holder could have merely exercised his right to buy at 50. A call option, therefore, served (and still serves) as a kind of insurance policy for short sellers.

There was too much copper and the price was too high, he said. Inventories were building and exports falling. If the price fell, as it must, the price of the stock of Amalgamated Copper Company must also fall. Amalgamated was incorporated in 1899 with the aim of monopolizing the world's copper market, which, said Sielcken, was impossible.

Baruch investigated Amalgamated for himself, and his findings corroborated Sielcken's. Through the early summer, the price of the stock fell, from 130 in mid-June to 111 in mid-July. (Baruch took enough time out from research to buy a new Panhard horseless carriage and to have his picture taken behind the wheel by a photographer from the New York *Herald*. "Mr. Baruch is an Expert Chauffeur," the caption under the newspaper picture said, "and His Handsome Motor Carriage is Much Admired along the Ocean Drive.") When President McKinley was shot on September 6, stock prices broke. They rallied and gave way again. The sensational and entertaining disclosures about the birth of Amalgamated by Thomas W. Lawson—of which the nut was that the company was grossly overcapitalized—lay three years in the future. What led Baruch to sell was the imbalance of supply and demand. Not long after the assassination, when Amalgamated was in the neighborhood of 105 to 115 and sinking, he sold.

Two autumns before, when he had gone short of BRT, he was one short seller among many. This time circumstances were different. Amalgamated had been organized under the auspices of the Standard Oil interests (notably of William Rockefeller and Henry H. Rogers), and some of the ablest operators in the Street stood beside it. Keene owned the stock. When it got around that Baruch was bearish, Thomas F. Ryan took him aside. "Bernie," he said, "I hear you are short of Amalgamated Copper. I just want to let you know that the big fellows in it are going to twist your tail."

Coming in the wake of the Northern Pacific corner, such a warning was calculated to cause restless nights. Furthermore, the Wall Street establishment was rallying around the list in the aftermath of the McKinley assassination, and J. P. Morgan pronounced himself bullish. Baruch held his ground. Some of his recollections of that time, dictated later without autobiographical touch-up, are as follows: "I became heavily short of it—heavy [*sic*] for me. All kinds of names were hurled at me and rumors spread about my integrity and ability and all the slimy stuff . . . but I listened to no one but the merchant Herman Sielcken." And regarding his day-to-day routine on the Stock Exchange floor: "I never left the [Amalgamated] crowd but round and round I would walk, with brokers like Harry Content, Eddie Norton and Charlie de Witt who were my brokers and would act for me. I was making the biggest play of my life. I was sure of certain facts and was looking for that bubble to burst."

Baruch took the occasion of the death of the convalescing President on September 14 to sell a little more stock. On the nineteenth the market was closed for McKinley's funeral. On Friday, the twentieth, the Amalgamated directors were expected to meet to consider the future of the $8 common dividend. Although newspaper reports were optimistic, selling on Wednesday indicated that insiders were not. Then, late Friday, Amalgamated rose, as if the dividend were secure after all. In fact, it had been cut to $6. Baruch was transported. In Saturday's half session, the stock lost almost $7 a share. A decisive market verdict would come down on Monday.

Just then Baruch's mother called to remind him that Monday was Yom Kippur. Now he fretted. Observance of this holiest of Jewish days would mean isolation from all temporal matters, in particular from the hammering of Amalgamated Copper. Baruch was not a religious man. Everything except filial devotion argued against a literal observance of the Day of Atonement. Devotion to his mother prevailed, however, and he laid plans in preparation for his absence from the floor. Eddie Norton, who in the Northern Pacific corner had sold short the famous 300 shares at 1,000, had been doing Baruch's selling. He was instructed to continue bear operations, specifically, to hold some "hammer stock" over the market in order to discourage buyers. In case the price of the stock went the wrong way, Harry Content was instructed to buy, thus covering Baruch's short sales. In this way each speculative flank was guarded.

Baruch passed Monday in South Elberon, New Jersey, with Annie, the baby and his mother. Although he had left word that nobody was to call on business, he spent the day distractedly listening to the ringing of the telephone. Baruch is his own witness to the fact that not once did he yield to temptation and answer. Only after sundown, when the secular world was again permitted to intrude, did he learn that Amalgamated had crumpled. It had opened at 100 and dropped to 97⅞ before coming back to 98½ just after 11 A.M. Then if fell more or less steadily to 93¾ by the 3 P.M. bell. It continued in that direction for the rest of the year, closing on New Year's Eve 1901 at 69½. By the time Baruch got around to taking his profits, they amounted to some $700,000.

(He was quick to put down his triumph to his reluctant observance of Yom Kippur. Had he been on the floor, he said, he would probably have taken his profits when the price of the stock ticketed up to 98½. Perhaps, but he might plausibly have sold more stock on the resumption of the decline that day.)

Baruch's prowess on the short side won him some commission business from sellers who wanted to leave the impression that the character of their selling was speculative, not the respectable investment kind. So large had his personal operations become that anything he did on behalf of a customer of the firm might conceivably have been done on his own hook. His desirability as a broker was therefore enhanced. Another dividend of the copper episode was a news clipping, one of his first, that celebrated his career, as follows:

> The substantial decline in Amalgamated Copper has brought into prominence a man who, though he had been well known to the inner circles of Wall street for some time, has not hitherto been generally conspicuous because of an abhorrence of self-advertisement that is not often found among Wall street men. The man is Bernard M. Baruch, a partner in the big house of A. A. Houseman [*sic*]. Anyone who gives attention to Wall street matters hears much of Wormser, Field, Oliver, Content, etc., but he hears nothing of Baruch. Yet Baruch has done wonderful things in the relatively few years he has been in Wall street, and in the opinion of the men who know he has attained a position and reputation for shrewdness, foresight and nerve in combination that is only second to that of the veteran Keene. From the beginning of the Amalgamated Copper downfall Baruch, of all the big men, has been the only one who has had the proper idea of what was going on, and instead of suffering, as other wise ones have done, he and his friends have profited wonderfully. He has never missed a move in the copper game, and he has frustrated every attempt to twist him. What he has done in Amalgamated reminds one of what Keene used to do in Sugar in the old days. It will be well to watch Baruch. He will be heard from in many ways in the future.

Baruch had arrived.

FIVE

His Own Man

In the mid-1930s, when Baruch was momentarily fed up with the
New Deal, he confessed to an impulse to get rid of his money and go
out and fight for the rights of the people. The impulse passed. In 1902,
with fewer millions to feel guilty over, he had had similar musings. One
cause of his dissatisfaction was the irritant of having to deal with other
people's money. It was becoming Baruch's view that a speculator
should not be a stockbroker, bank director or any other kind of fiduciary. He should be his own man, exclusively. For another thing, now
that he had made a lot of money, he began to wonder what it meant.
His brother Herman had studied medicine, and his own faint medical
ambitions stirred again. For a while he toyed with the idea of becoming
a lawyer and of championing the poor, but the prospect of law school
dismayed him. Wanting some time to think, he gathered up Annie, his
father and a business friend, Henry C. Davis, and packed them off to
Europe with him in the summer of 1902.

Davis, who was Housman's authority on the American West, declined to venture beyond London, because across the Channel they
spoke foreign languages. The three Baruchs (Belle and her infant
brother and their governesses and grandmother apparently stayed behind) pushed as far east as Constantinople before Dr. Baruch left the
party to pay professional calls. Baruch and Annie made their way to the
Ritz Hotel in Paris. It was there, late one night, that Baruch was roused

from a sound sleep by a cable from New York. The message, which was signed by his brother Sailing, was that Housman was in financial straits. Reading it, Baruch almost fell to his "knees from shock." If Housman was in trouble it followed that the firm was also imperiled. Baruch, as a partner of A. A. Housman & Company, had pledged his own assets, which included $3.2 million in cash, to the solvency of the firm. Arthur Housman and he, therefore, were potentially in trouble together. Baruch cabled a transfer of funds to his partner's account and boarded the next ship home.

In New York, he found Housman pacing at dockside, ready to relate more or less the following. He had, said Housman, fallen in with Edwin Hawley, the railroad man, to buy stock in the Minneapolis & St. Paul and the Colorado & Southern railroads. Hawley, a member of the board of the Colorado road, was authoritatively bullish, but the price of the stocks dropped nonetheless. Housman had bought on margin, so he hadn't the luxury of waiting for the market to turn. He had to put up more money at once or lose what he already had invested.

Baruch, taking charge, advanced the money himself. The market finally rebounded and Housman was able to sell at a profit. Secure again in his fortune, he continued to support his several unmarried sisters and to maintain some sixty head of cattle at his estate in Babylon, New York, in what a newspaper called "luxurious sanitary quarters." His distress escaped the official notice of the New York Stock Exchange.

Baruch was happy to help a man who had done so much for him, but notwithstanding his affection for the Housman brothers he decided to quit the firm. In the first place he wanted to be independent of any firm. A second reason might be conjectured. It is that Baruch was worried that Housman's uncritical market judgment might one day be the ruin of them all. (It wasn't. The firm was the forerunner of Housman-Gwathmey & Company in 1926 and of E. A. Pierce & Company in 1927. In 1930, it absorbed most of Merrill Lynch & Company and in 1940 was merged with that large and fated organization.) Although Baruch was by no means always bearish, Housman was nearly always bullish. Baruch told a story of how they had once characteristically disagreed on the market. He wrote:

> After a particularly bad drop [in the market] I was sitting at a table in the Waldorf bar listening to some of the traders comfort themselves. Jake Field, who was also on the bear side of the market, was doing the

talking for both of us. I never would argue about what was going to take place but tried to let the results speak for themselves. Pretty soon James Keene came up.

"Gentlemen, what do you think of the great firm of A. A. Housman & Company?" he asked in his high-pitched voice. "At the head of it you have a roaring bull, and at the other end, a snarling, scratching bear!"

By August 1903 Baruch had moved into an office of his own,* which he furnished with three parental oddments: a congratulatory telegram from his mother, mounted and hung; a green china cat, speckled with red, also from his mother; and a photograph of his father, framed and inscribed with the motto: "Let unswerving integrity always be your watchword." (He listed these things only; if Annie sent anything he failed to mention it.) Thus the result of months of introspection was a decision to stay in Wall Street but to leave A. A. Housman & Company. Baruch continued to trade for his own account on the floor of the New York Stock Exchange; he devoted more of his time to venture capital, especially to mining ventures, and he reluctantly took on an occasional client. One day a woman whom he had never met walked into his office to ask him to invest a quarter million dollars that she had inherited from an aunt. She said that she found him smart, cool and "funny looking."† If there was something odd in his face (and he certainly didn't think there was; nor did many women), it was his long nose, atop which was perched a pair of pince-nez, and his wide, thin

---

*In his autobiography Baruch indicates an immediate move from the Housman offices at 20 Broad Street to new quarters in the Trinity Building, 111 Broadway, but the city directory reports no change of address until 1906. The directory appears the better source. In 1906, a new Trinity Building, rising twenty-one stories on the site of the old one, was opened. Baruch's office was on the seventh floor; the original Trinity Building had only six. In court documents Baruch gave the date of his leaving Housman as August 10, 1903, but he apparently made his first new office in the same old building.

†Marcia Kendrick McCue, granddaughter of Baruch's caller, Sarah Kendrick-Strahan, writes:

> How she got an appointment, I do not know but she did and went to his office.
> He must have been very impressed by this very dainty British lady and started to give her a few tips when she interrupted him and said, "I do not know anything about what you are saying—I want you to do it." Then she pulled these drafts out and turned them over to him. He must have been surprised but said, "I'll get you a receipt." She said, "Sir, a hand shake will be my receipt," and left. After two–three months dividends etc. started arriving. . . . [at] 72 [I] am still receiving dividends.

lips. He had shaved his moustache, and his hair was streaked with a bankerly silver. (In 1903, his first year as an independent operator, Baruch turned up in the city directory as a "banker" instead of a "broker." Evidently somebody found that persona unsatisfactory, however, because in 1904 he became a "broker" again. His brothers Sailing and Harty joined him in this occupational round trip.)

"Unswerving integrity" is no easy standard to uphold, no matter what one's father adjures, and Baruch apparently did veer from it. Once he was led into temptation by some Baltimore men who somehow had met him when he was still a partner at A. A. Housman and described an accountant's report that they had at their disposal. The report concerned the Metropolitan Street Railway Company, a giant Manhattan streetcar line that was then in the formative stages of crookedness. Early in 1902, Harry Content, Baruch's favorite broker, filed a stockholder's suit alleging that a certain Metropolitan leasing scheme was "born in iniquity." Eventually the directors, including Thomas Fortune Ryan, were accused (though never indicted or convicted) of looting, and the belief gained currency that the company trafficked in jurors and politicians. In the fall of 1902, before most of this dirty laundry had been aired, the Baltimoreans brought their inside information to Baruch. The accountant's report must have been negative, because it was supposedly understood that Baruch would sell the stock short: selling first and buying later, it was hoped at a lower price. He would risk his capital and take half the profits. His informants—by name, Barreda Turner, Frank G. Turner and Motz Prag—would share the other half. Nothing was written down and no deadline was set, but it was agreed that Baruch would deal in at least 10,000 shares of stock. Such were the Baltimoreans' recollections.

In October 1902, when the deal was allegedly struck, the price of a share of Metropolitan was $142. A year later it was $105 (a decline almost exactly in line with the fall of the Dow Jones Rail index). At the end of September 1903 Prag sued Baruch, charging that he had held back huge profits. Just $4,271 had been accounted for, the complaint charged, although Baruch had earned half a million. Baruch denied even trading on the basis of an "expert accountant's report," much less hiding his profits. However, he agreed to settle out of court for $9,000, "as a matter of compromise," he later explained, "and to avoid the personal inconvenience of being made a party to an unfounded litigation." This was in 1904. Probably if Prag had been cheated to the extent he claimed he wouldn't have settled for $9,000 (which, in point of fact, was a pretty good sum in 1904). On the other hand if Baruch were absolutely innocent he probably wouldn't have paid any tribute. In 1901 he had litigated a suit that had been brought against him on account of his chauffeur and appealed a $1,000 verdict, a record that suggests a certain legal pugnaciousness. In any case, neither Baruch nor Prag breathed a word of the suit to the Turners, the other alleged partners. (Frank G. Turner was the son of a Lutheran minister, a lawyer and the treasurer of the Maryland State Bar Association; Barreda, who may or may not have been related, was a court clerk; and Prag was apparently an insurance and stock broker.) But nine years later they did find out, cried foul, filed suit and settled too.

Baruch's fellow Stock Exchange members overlooked (or never heard about or perhaps wrote off as small potatoes) the Metropolitan contretemps. On December 9, 1903, they honored the defendant Baruch with election to the forty-man Governing Committee, and in 1904, he began a long tenure on the Committee on Unlisted Securities, which he used as a forum to advance the acceptance of mining issues by the rest of the governors. As mentioned, the Stock Exchange elicited a certain amount of information from listed companies years before the Securities and Exchange Commission was in business to demand it. Corporations seeking the privilege of full-fledged listing after the turn of the century were obliged to conform with the disclosure requirements of the Committee on Stock List. The job of the Committee on Unlisted Securities, which numbered three, was to admit worthy companies that were unwilling or unable to comply immediately but which had it in mind to do so eventually.

On the evidence of the minutes, Baruch was a diligent Unlisted committeeman. He examined the quality of engraving on stock certificates, attended to various administrative matters and worked to hustle companies as quickly as possible into the light of full listing. The record shows, for instance, that on January 24, 1906, he urged that the American Smelters Securities Company move faster on an issue of preferred that it had promised to submit to the Committee on Stock List. Smelters Securities was sponsored by his friends the Guggenheims.

The turn of the century had brought a boom in mining finance, and copper issues in particular had attracted enormous speculative attention on the Curb and Boston exchanges. The New York Stock Exchange was suspicious of mines and their stocks and bonds but fascinated by the commission income they produced for brokers. Early in 1906, the Unlisted Committee, augmented by the president of the Exchange, Frank K. Sturgis, took up the matter of the admission of mine securities. More fundamentally, it weighed the question of whether the Exchange should deal in Curb issues, in effect annexing the best of the outdoor market. The argument for bringing the Curb under the Stock Exchange roof was that the arrangement would yield more income to the members. The argument against was that the Curb was crooked and infra dig, and that to admit even its more popular issues, like United Copper and Greene Consolidated, would constitute a lowering of standards. (A compromise proposal that Curb issues be traded in-house but only in the subbasement was phrased as a question: "Shall a separate room be provided for trading in promiscuous securities, where members of the Exchange only shall be allowed?") Baruch spoke before the committee regarding the annexation of the Curb in March 1906. The force of his personality is inevitably lost in transcription, leaving only the slightly disjointed sentences, thus:

I am like Mr. Thomas, if I had to declare myself right now, I would be against it, for the following reasons. I believe first that we could get around this matter much easier than by giving a market for these outside securities. I believe if we give them a market, whether they are listed or not, quoted on the ticker or not, they would have the same standing in the public eyes as the securities at present traded in. I believe it would be giving them the same standing unquestionably in the eyes of the public and the money lenders. How are you going to decide that a security is reputable. You leave the disreputable ones on the outside [i.e., on the Curb] and that would still make a market there. I have made a list of the securities dealt in on the Curb and this brings up another point. If this Department would take action in the when, as and if issued securities there would be very little left of the market out there. ["When, as and if" securities, nowadays better known as "when issued" securities, were stocks and bonds that hadn't been offered but which were scheduled for imminent public sale. They were dealt in on the Curb.] I think this brings us to still another question that I have studied over a good deal but have no solution of it as yet—that is, we will sooner or later have to have a mining department. Nearly all the

stocks traded in out there are mining stocks. No matter what the prejudice of the New York Stock Exchange members may be it has got to
come.

Baruch, whose name had just been admitted for listing in the Social
Register, got off a final shaft at the Curb: "I think we ought to brand it
as much as possible that it is the outside market, and that the securities
are not as high on the social scale as securities traded in on the Floor."
In the end, the Curb Exchange, which grew up to become the American Stock Exchange, was not annexed, and the Big Board adopted a
more lenient attitude toward mining securities. It was perhaps owing
the Baruch's influence that the Unlisted Committee received a mandate
to look into such "Mining Corporations as in their judgment are surrounded by the proper protection of reputable people and whose securities are legally issued. . . ."

In carrying out its charge the committee heard from some of the
brightest lights in mine finance. In January 1907 came John Hays
Hammond, principal engineer to the Guggenheim family, and his assistant, A. Chester Beatty. February brought Eugene Meyer, Jr., the investment banker, and Daniel Jackling, the strip-mining pioneer.
Jackling, who was born on a farm in Missouri and whose boyhood
dream was to own 108 acres free and clear, believed in one great idea. It
was that a meager copper ore could be profitably mined if there were
enough steam shovels to scrape it from the surface and enough mill capacity to refine it. The site he favored was a desolate canyon in Utah.
"It's in Bingham," explained Colonel Enos Wall, Jackling's partner,
"and it's a mile wide and as long as a railroad. . . ." Jackling, a big,
ruddy man, laid out his theory to Baruch in about 1903. Baruch was
impressed by the idea, or the man, or both, and he bought "a good
many shares" of Utah Copper Company. He was the exception. Without success, Jackling had solicited capital from the Amalgamated Copper Company, Ben Guggenheim and John Hays Hammond. In the
summer of 1904 he presented the idea to the General Electric Company, which wanted a copper mine, but which, as one director put it,
didn't believe the "damn figures." At last, in 1906, Utah won over the
Guggenheims, who invested and sold some convertible bonds to the
public. Thus it happened in early 1907 that Baruch, Jackling and
Charles MacNeill, president of Utah, were seated around a table at the
New York Stock Exchange discussing the merits of admitting the secu-

rities of Utah Copper to trading on the Big Board.* Over the next decade, Utah would yield 617,785 tons of copper, pay $76 million in dividends, accumulate $48 million of working capital and establish itself as the greatest copper mine in the world.

Baruch's professional acquaintance with the Guggenheim family began when Daniel, failing to reckon with the applicant's mother, invited him to go to Mexico to buy ore in 1889. (Once Baruch asked Thomas F. Ryan for his opinion of Daniel. "He's a big man," said Ryan approvingly; "he bores with a big auger.") Meyer Guggenheim, the patriarch, was a patient of Dr. Baruch's and an occasional patron of the gaming tables in Long Branch, New Jersey. Some time after Meyer and his seven sons gained control of the American Smelting & Refining Company in 1901, Solomon, the No. 4 son, favored Baruch with some pertinent facts and figures on the company. Baruch bought the stock and recommended it to his friends.

The first sizable joint undertaking of Baruch and the Guggenheims was a mission in which Baruch negotiated for the purchase of a pair of West Coast smelting companies on behalf of American Smelting & Refining Company. He left for Everett, Washington, site of the Tacoma Smelting Company offices, early in January 1905 with the trusted Henry Davis and a lawyer from the office of William H. Page, the same Page with whom Baruch had had truck in the Liggett & Myers acquisition in 1898. A measure of Baruch's growth in the intervening years was his rise from the station of agreeable young man on the St. Louis trip to chief negotiator and tactician for the Guggenheim brothers.

The first stockholder to be courted by Baruch was Darius Mills, a multimillionaire who kept an office in his own building on Broad Street in New York. Mills wore muttonchop whiskers, visited English country homes and told charming stories of having slept under a wagon during the California gold rush. Such was his business perspicacity that a chain of low-price hotels that he founded as a philanthropic enterprise managed to return a small profit to the philanthropist. Mills owned most of the stock of the Tacoma smelter as well as a smaller interest in the Selby Smelting & Lead Company, in San Francisco, which was the Guggen-

*No declaration by Baruch of his interest in the company appears in the Unlisted Securities Committee minutes. It is possible that none was made, that something was said in private or that his holdings were common knowledge. Perhaps he thought that they were nobody's business.

heims' second objective. When Baruch asked him for an option on his stock, the old man declined, but he left the door open and promised not to talk to the Rockefeller interests, who were also knocking.

Out in Washington, Baruch began talks with the president of the Tacoma smelter, William R. Rust, who happened to be a friend of Davis'. Baruch ventured a bid of $800 a share for his stock, Rust shook hands and the rest of the stockholders, Mills included, fell in behind him. Negotiations for the Selby company proceeded more slowly, word having leaked out that Baruch represent the Guggenheims. But thanks to Rust's help and to the influence of Darius Mills, the Selby holders too appeared well disposed to a sale. Confident of a deal, Baruch climbed aboard the *Overland* for New York in early March. Shortly after his return, the Selby matter was closed, but the Tacoma deal was unexpectedly reopened. Three more weeks of talks ensued, Baruch participating from New York via telegraph. By late March, Rust and Davis had gotten the deal done, and Baruch opened negotiations of his own with the Guggenheims.

Baruch's understanding with the brothers was that the Selby and Tacoma companies would be merged and recapitalized and that a block of the new stock, worth perhaps $1 million, would be his commission. Instead, Dan decided to absorb both organizations into the American Smelting & Refining Company. He invited Baruch to discuss his fee with the gifted and high-handed family lawyer, Samuel Untermyer. Baruch's recollection of their meeting was as follows:

> . . . I told Mr. Untermeyer [*sic*] that was what I was asking for [$1 million, which he felt he had been promised] and declined to debate the matter. Mr. Untermeyer inquired if I intended to "hold up" the American Smelting & Refining Company.
>
> Leaning across the table that stood between us, I replied, "No, Mr. Untermeyer, I had not thought of that until now."
>
> Then I said good day and left the room.
>
> The question was referred to Daniel Guggenheim, who settled it characteristically. "If Bernie says he ought to get $1,000,000, that is what he will get."

The check was made out in the sum of exactly $1,106,456.00. Baruch in turn wrote checks to Rust and Davis, each for $300,000 in thanks for their help. They were flabbergasted.

An obvious question is whether the Guggenheims offered Baruch his commission in the shares of the American Smelting & Refining Company. It is reasonable to suppose that they did and equally probable that he declined. At the start of the year, Smelters was quoted at 82. By mid-April, in part as the result of a bull pool that Baruch directed for the Guggenheims on the floor of the Stock Exchange, the price had cleared 120. Then, suddenly, the pool disbanded, or "realized," and the price of the stock slipped. An explanation for the withdrawal of support was provided later. It was that Baruch had decided the price was high enough, and that no pool had the right to bid up a stock only to sell it to an unsuspecting public. He served notice on the Guggenheims that he planned to sell his investment holdings and to suggest to his friends that they sell too.

The brothers took umbrage at this information, perhaps because, as Baruch maintained, they were stock-market amateurs, or perhaps because they felt it rank ingratitude for the recipient of a seven-figure check to be anything but bullish on the parties who had signed it. At all events, the price of the stock resumed its climb, hitting 174 by January 1906. But just then the market gave way and Smelters sold off with the rest of the list. In the spring it touched 138½.

On Wall Street a rumor was hatched that the fall in the stock was caused by Baruch selling short. The story was untrue—Baruch, who saw nothing wrong with short selling in general, perhaps inconsistently drew the line at hammering the securities of his friends—and when it was credulously repeated by Solomon Guggenheim, Baruch called on him to set the record straight. When Solomon heard from *his* source that the rumor was unfounded, he apologized to Baruch.

It was Baruch's settled opinion that nobody could know all investments thoroughly and that it was best to stick to what one knew best. For himself, he said that he had never understood commodities. "My self-confidence," he confessed, "suffers a very real shock when I contemplate the sum total of my operations in coffee, sugar, cotton and other commodities. . . . It always seemed to me, in fact it never failed where I was concerned, that what I bought suddenly became something else again when I paid for it, especially when I wanted to deliver it." His most searing early experience in commodities was in coffee. He bought heavily in early 1905, just about the time he was headed west on the Guggenheim smelter mission.

He entered the market on the advice of Herman Sielcken, his wise counselor in the Amalgamated Copper affair. Sielcken was the largest importer of Brazilian coffee in the United States, and the authority with which he spoke on that commodity was absolute. He predicted short Brazilian crops in 1906 and 1907, in the first year on account of nature and in the second owing to a government scheme to curtail production. But there was a curse of abundance instead, and prices fell, from 7.65 cents a pound at the start of 1905 to 6.65 cents in December. Baruch, who had bought on margin, was bound to put up more earnest money with each drop of a fraction of a cent. To raise cash, he sacrificed a profitable position in the Canadian Pacific Railroad. Sielcken continued to express confidence.

Definitely, the market needed help, and the Brazilian authorities, in consultation with Sielcken, dreamed up a "valorization" scheme to finance the storage of surplus coffee. Loans were floated and warehouses filled but still the price fell. By early December it was less than 6 cents. When at last Baruch came to sell, his loss had mounted to $700,000 or $800,000. More galling, he was forced to admit that he had been misled by a man who had once shown him the immutability of the laws of supply and demand, that he had let his losses run, failed to face facts and sent good money after bad. The experience literally turned his stomach.

Around Christmastime 1906 Baruch was distracted from the vicissitudes of the coffee market by the unexpected arrival of two visitors in his office. One of the men, well known to him, was William Crocker, the San Francisco banker. Crocker introduced his companion, Senator George Nixon of Nevada, president of Goldfield Consolidated Mines in Goldfield, Nevada. Nixon was an incumbent United States senator but he was burdened with private business. "Nixon," said Crocker, by way of introduction, "needs a million dollars and he's good for it."

The Goldfield property had been organized in November and promptly hailed a bonanza. It was the result of the merger of four mines, but Nixon decided that he needed a fifth, the Combination, right away. The price was $1 million down, in cash, and $1.6 million payable in a few months, in cash or Goldfield stock, as the sellers chose. Knowledge of the fact that Nixon needed money had depressed the price of Goldfield shares, which in turn exacerbated the senator's financial predicament.

Baruch liked Crocker and he decided that he liked Nixon too. He talked to some friends, organized a syndicate and raised $1 million. (Baruch's warmth was fully requited by Nixon. "I haven't a closer friend on earth than Baruch, and he is a good man to have on the property," declared the senator in June.) A cashier's check in that amount was drawn up for Nixon, who agreed to repay it by February 1908. As a further emolument, Baruch and his friends received an option to buy 1,000,000 Goldfield Consolidated shares.

Baruch next dealt with the psychological factor. He told Nixon to put the check in his pocket and take a table at the Men's Café at the Waldorf. If somebody asked him about his money troubles he was to produce the check and drop the Baruch name. The senator complied. As expected the question was solicitously raised, and Nixon flashed the six zeros. Heads turned.

The senator's next stop was Chicago to meet with the sellers of the Combination Mines. It was naturally in Nixon's interest that they choose stock in payment for the final installments. It was in their interest too, if they could be led to believe that the price was going up. For reasons not entirely explained, they obliged, choosing stock then and there.*

The Nixon stratagem was endorsed by the Goldfield board and was duly ratified by the stockholders. Nixon was well pleased. Baruch, anticipating a bull market in the stock and a profit on his option, was also pleased. The main dissatisfied element was the miners. The Industrial Workers of the World, or Wobblies, which spoke for some of the Goldfield men, deplored the wage system and, indeed, capitalism. In particular, they opposed a rule that was instituted by management to halt the theft of high-grade ore. The rule held that miners must strip naked at the end of their shift and hop over a bar in order to dislodge any rock that might be adhering to their persons.

All together, 1907 was an unrepaying year. Earnings were a disappointment. The annual report was derided by the authoritative *Mining*

---

*The reason advanced by Baruch is unsubstantiated. It is that the Combination men, wanting to test the strength of the Goldfield market, entered a large sell order on the Curb Exchange. Expecting it, Baruch forehandedly entered a large buy order. Purchase met sale and the price held firm. Impressed by the market action, the Combination men elected stock. However, for the period in question, there is no record of any Curb transaction in Goldfield.

& Scientific Journal as a "confused and inconsistent jumble of figures."
Ninety-one days of work were lost to strikes, and "labor relations" had
deteriorated into pitched battles between armed men. Late in the year,
the governor of Nevada appealed to President Roosevelt to send troops
to Goldfield to quell, among other things, "the unlawful dynamiting of
property." Nine companies were bivouacked by Christmas.

In early August, before the U.S. Army encamped, Baruch traveled
to Goldfield to consult with the board of directors. He took some
friends along, including his brother Harty and Count Roger de Perigny,
a Parisian nobleman who had joined the Baruch syndicate and was curious about life in the American West. George Wingfield, vice president
of the mine, was on hand when the contingent arrived at the station.
Baruch, a fastidious dresser, noticed that Wingfield wore no jacket.

> It being a warm evening, a man did not need a coat [he remem-
> bered]. Also, this made it easier for Wingfield to get at the five re-
> volvers he carried, two in front, two behind and one on his left breast.
> George explained that the four serious-looking men who accompanied
> him were Pinkerton detectives, and said something about labor trou-
> bles. One of the Pinkertons rode with us to the company's building.
> There Wingfield explained that everything would be all right if we kept
> the lights off in our rooms.

One of the items on the business agenda in Goldfield was Baruch's
stock option, which had caused some indignation in the press and second thoughts among stockholders. In the *Nevada Mining News*, Nixon
was portrayed as a kind of financial nitwit and Baruch as an evil genius.
It was said that Baruch, in league with powerful interests, was insinuat-
ing himself into control of the mine. ("There is a rumor that the Roth-
schilds, Belmont, Ryan, and I don't know but what the King of
England and others have sent experts here and are about to secure control of the Consolidated Mines," said Nixon in May. "There is no truth
to the rumor whatsoever.") As for the stockholders, the longer that
some of them thought about Baruch's option, the madder it made
them. On account of the strikes, all-around mismanagement and unlawful dynamiting, however, the price of the stock failed decisively to
clear the $7.75 mark, at which Baruch could have cashed in. By late
September a compromise was struck. Baruch agreed to forgo the option for the consideration of 100,000 shares. It was further agreed that

the $1 million loan would be repaid mainly by stock. By 1908 Baruch reportedly owned more shares than Nixon, Wingfield or Henry C. Frick, the last named an important Goldfield investor who was better known for his exploits in steel. Gradually labor peace was won, production increased and the mine came into its own. Stock that had paid a dividend of 20 cents a share in 1907 yielded 90 cents in 1909.

The notion that Baruch was panic-proof—that he unfailingly profited from market breaks—is disproved by his own records of the one episode in which his records survive, 1929. For the rest, what remains is recollection. In his autobiography he wrote that he had sold stocks in advance of the so-called Rich Man's Panic of 1903. And also in 1907: "Like many other people I had made preparations, not for a panic but for a financial stringency. I had increased my cash balances at the Manhattan Company. Moreover, I had told Stephen Baker [president of the bank] that I might want my money in cash at any time."*

The 1907 Panic affected Baruch intimately because it struck both the stock and copper markets. The price of the red metal, which began the year at 25 cents a pound, by early autumn had sunk to 15 cents. Mines were closed in Butte, Montana, by the Amalgamated Copper Company and in Mexico by the Guggenheims. Even the banking news was copper-bottomed. Preceding the Knickerbocker Trust Company into trouble that October was the Mercantile National Bank, the officers of which were prominent in a failed attempt to corner the shares of United Copper Company. Utah Copper, which had raised $9 million in the capital market (some of it from Baruch) but had only started production, was making heavy weather of it. Late in October, Baruch

---

*In 1911, the Boston News Bureau published a literary interpretation of Baruch's market operations about this time:

At the height of the Harriman bull market in 1906, Baruch was carrying a big line of Union Pacific expecting to see it sell for $250 a share. One day he received from a friend a copy of a book printed in London in 1851 and written . . . by Charles Mackay. . . . Its title was *Extraordinary Popular Delusions and the Madness of Crowds.* It told in detail the story of the South Sea Bubble, John Law's Mississippi Bubble, the Darien Expedition, the famous alchemists of the Middle Ages, the Crusades and other historical "madnesses." Baruch was so impressed by the similarity between the speculative orgies of history, as related by Mackay, and the Wall Street enthusiasm for railroad securities selling at sky-high prices that he unloaded his whole line of stocks and sat back to wait for the crash.

received a telegram from Charles MacNeill, the president. The message was, send cash.

MacNeill, according to Baruch, wanted $500,000, which by everyday working-capital standards was the earth and sky. On June 30, the company had kept a bank balance of only $35,803. Its customers owed it $90,580. It owed *its* suppliers $18,887. (One of the larger balance-sheet items was an inventory entry called "copper in transit": $425,597.97.) Furthermore, half a million dollars was a vast sum for that particular time. On October 24, money was lent on the Stock Exchange at the distress rate of 100 percent. J. P. Morgan was hard pressed to round up a bankers' pool of $25 million.

Even so, Baruch was able to oblige MacNeill. He wrote that he had the money boxed and shipped express to Salt Lake City, and that he charged the nominal rate of 6 percent, which MacNeill insisted on bumping up to 20 percent. With some leftover cash, Baruch bought Utah Copper cheap in the market.*

In that tumultuous autumn—when Morgan, aged seventy, assisted by the United States Treasury, virtually saved the banking system—Baruch was moved by a sense of duty. As a rising financial personage, he felt it incumbent on himself to fall in with Morgan to check the tide of liquidation. One night he lay awake rehearsing what he would tell the great man. He would appear at his door and announce that he wished to lend some money to the pool he was raising. Morgan, flashing his beacon eyes, would ask how much. Baruch—Baruch the Stock Exchange governor and investor, not the young man in the Waldorf crowd who had done all the short selling—would say, a million and a half, cash. It would be a very large loan: some banks had put up less. But in the light of morning Baruch's native caution asserted itself and he made his contribution anonymously, through the Manhattan Bank. (Arthur Housman, the chronic bull who had helped do Morgan's dealing on the floor of the Stock Exchange, was spared the ordeal. He died, after a brief illness at his country home in Babylon, Long Island, on August 21, at the age of about fifty-two. Baruch and Sailing were among his pallbearers.)

A stock that Baruch had accumulated in the preceding panic year of

---

*It is difficult either to prove or disprove Baruch's account on the basis of independent sources. For example, no news of Utah Copper's alleged distress appeared in the Salt Lake City *Tribune, Deseret News, The Mining Review* (Salt Lake City) or, for that matter, in the company's annual report for 1907.

1903 was the Rubber Goods Manufacturing Company. It was also in 1903 that Middleton S. Burrill, Baruch's mentor from his Housman days, joined the Rubber Goods board. It is possible that (a) Burrill joined the board because Baruch owned the stock or (b) Baruch invested because Burrill was on the board. Baruch liked to keep posted on companies in which he'd put his money, and Burrill was in a position to brief him authoritatively on Rubber Goods. In any case, rubber appealed to Baruch's imagination. One day he proposed to Daniel Guggenheim that they pool resources, buy control of Rubber Goods and turn it into something along the lines of the Standard Oil Company. Guggenheim said he'd think about it, but he thought too long, and Baruch, who saw a trading profit in his stock, took it.

Meanwhile, an inventor named William A. Lawrence had discovered a technique to extract rubber from a bush called guayule. Late in 1905 he invited Thomas Fortune Ryan and Senator Nelson Aldrich, a moneyed Republican from Rhode Island, to back him. They brought the proposition to Daniel Guggenheim, and Guggenheim, recalling that Baruch had had an interest in rubber, took it up with him. The result, in December 1905, was the incorporation of the Continental Rubber Company under the impressive aegis of Aldrich, Baruch, the Guggenheims, Ryan and (among other subsidiary stockholders) John D. Rockefeller, Jr. The company was capitalized at $30 million.

Now that he was back in the rubber business, Baruch set out for Mexico via railcar with Annie, Sailing and the broker Eddie Norton, of Northern Pacific corner fame, to investigate the prospects for guayule. He found them so promising that, on behalf of the company, he negotiated for the purchase of several million acres of rangeland on which to raise it. Guayule grew wild in northern Mexico. Continental proposed to bring the bush under cultivation and to build a factory at Torreon to extract the rubber under the Lawrence process. The Rubber Goods Manufacturing Company contracted to buy the raw rubber when production would begin three years hence. When production did begin, however, Rubber Goods pronounced the merchandise substandard and abrogated its contract with Continental. Rather, U.S. Rubber abrogated its contract with Intercontinental Rubber, both companies by that time having changed their names.

Usually not the litigious kind, Baruch wanted to sue the U.S. Rubber people because, as he insisted, the Torreon rubber was in fact up to par. But, he related, J. P. Morgan and George F. Baker, president of the

First National Bank, "pulled us off the suit." Next Baruch urged that his company, Intercontinental, buy up U.S. Rubber stock in the open market, turn out management and reinstitute the contract themselves. This plan was rejected. He made an attempt to secure a contract with another rubber company, Baruch wrote, but the deal was ruined by the greed of his associates.

Now impartially disgusted with friend and foe, Baruch again retired from rubber. By a happy turn, he sold his stock before the start of the Mexican revolution of 1910, which trampled the corporate guayule bushes and closed the Torreon plant (which did, ultimately, find a taker for its rubber). Moreover, as he was selling, one of the firms that had stood in the way of his lawsuit was buying. A news account of the time reported: "The wisdom of Bernard M. Baruch in getting out of Intercontinental Rubber just as the Morgan people went into it at around $30 a share is demonstrated by the recent shutdown of the plant because it is the center of the revolutionary troubles in Mexico. The stock is now under $15."

As a freelance venture capitalist and occasional investment banker, Baruch traded chiefly on his judgment, tenacity and salesmanship. A big-picture man, he left as many of the details as possible to somebody else. One such detail-minded associate was Eugene Meyer, Jr., the head of his own investment-banking firm, a specialist in copper securities and a pioneer in what has come to be called investment research.

In his old age Meyer remembered a bond underwriting that Baruch and he had jointly tackled for the Guggenheims in 1909. The issuing company was Braden Copper Mines Company, which drew its ore from the western slope of the Andes Mountains in Chile some eight thousand feet above sea level. Production had been under way for a year or two when Baruch and Meyer agreed to buy $1.5 million worth of Braden convertible bonds in order to resell them to investors.

> [Baruch] didn't do the work on it—I did the work—but he was friendly with the Guggenheims [said Meyer]. He was a good man to have as a partner because he'd go out and do the selling job. He had a following and people he'd recommend. He didn't know anything about them. He never did any work on the legal papers. We had to do all that legal work and all that engineering. He just signed his name to anything I sent—he wouldn't even read it.

Baruch was less disposed than usual to read the fine print on the Braden deal because he was in Paris with Annie when the bonds were offered. Meyer, who had sent him a prospectus and invited him to do some selling if he had the time, reported late in July 1909 that the issue had flopped and that the reason was entirely the failure of the Guggenheim name to inspire investor confidence. Meyer wanted the details to be kept confidential—sales of bonds to the public had amounted to only $150,000—"as a knowledge of the facts would reflect great discredit on the Guggenheims and also interfere with our own marketing in the securities."* From London about a week later Baruch cabled that the bonds and the Guggenheims were a hard sell on that side of the Atlantic too: "AFRAID IMPOSSIBLE HERE PEOPLE UN-POPULAR BARUCH."

If Baruch was discouraged with the Guggenheims, he still believed in Meyer. While the Braden bonds were going unsold, Meyer wired him in Paris with a bullish prognosis on the United States Steel Corporation. The cable had more than ordinary effect, because Meyer, in the opinion of no less an observer than J. P. Morgan, had written the seminal Wall Street research report on the company. Meyer's communiqué followed news of an increase in the Steel Corporation's dividend. The wire reported that earnings in June had been unusually strong, that orders were heavy and that another rise in the dividend was likely in October or January, probably October. From Paris, on July 30, came the answering cable: "BARUCH LENDS YOU 920000 MON-DAY OPINION STEEL." By October 26, the date on which the second dividend boost was duly declared, the price of the stock had climbed by 18 percent.

An interesting feature of the Braden underwriting is that Baruch and Meyer expected to make most of their money in an option in Braden stock. After Baruch got back to New York, in August, the two decided not to proceed without some change in contractual arrangements. Wrote Baruch: "Under no conditions do I think it advisable for us to take over the Braden stock at present nor attempt to make a market until we have a modified option." On the face of it, Baruch and Meyer had agreed with the Guggenheims to manipulate, support or

---

*Baruch, in fact, was more than a supernumerary. When the bonds met with public rejection, he arranged for a $1 million loan to finance them in inventory until such time as they could be sold.

otherwise to take charge of the market in Braden, an arrangement then unexceptional but subsequently illegal under the Securities Exchange Act of 1934.

Braden was a short-term nuisance for Baruch (the mine quickly redeemed itself), but another Chilean venture repaid him handsomely almost at once. This was the Chuquicamata mine of the Chile Copper Company, which was bigger, more desolate and even richer than the Utah Copper works in Bingham. Chuquicamata had been mined by the Incas before 1536 and was incorporated under the laws of Delaware in 1913. In 1915, when the price of copper was 20 cents a pound, the mine began to produce at a cost of about 6 cents a pound. Eugene Meyer, who had foreseen this bonanza, negotiated with the Guggenheims for the privilege of underwriting a $15 million convertible bond issue (the Guggenheim name by then having been restored to its former luster). Baruch again joined him for what proved one of the most lucrative operations of his career.

Baruch often sold out of his venture-capital projects before they reached the dividend-paying stage, but some never got that far. One of his more obscure investments was something called the New York Orient Mines Company, founded by Daniel Jackling, William Boyce Thompson and himself in the early 1900s. It was Thompson's idea to send a mining man to China to delve into old records for clues about forgotten by exploitable mineral deposits. Evidently nothing came of this archival enterprise. In 1910, the Intercontinental Fertilizer Company was incorporated on a shoestring to engage in fertilizer manufacturing in Charleston, South Carolina, and points south. Baruch was identified as vice president of the company (a rare instance of his accepting any corporate title, honorific or not); Allan A. Ryan, son of Thomas Fortune, was treasurer; and W. B. Chisolm, a former officer of the Virginia Carolina Chemical Company, was president. In 1915 Baruch wrote the senior Ryan that, contrary to the stockholders' high hopes, there were no profits to distribute. He blamed Chisolm.

Perhaps the longest-running disappointment of Baruch's venture-capital experience was the Alaska Juneau Gold Mining Company. The company's claim, which had been staked out in 1899, was situated along the Gastineau Channel outside the city limits of Juneau. Fred W. Bradley, the distinguished engineer, believed in it. Its ore was thin, but it lay adjacent to the claim of the Alaska Gold Mine Company, in which Dan Jackling himself was interested. On the subject of meager ore, what Jackling said, went. In 1915 Alaska Juneau drew up plans to offer 400,000 shares of stock, and it invited Baruch to underwrite the deal. Baruch accepted, and he engaged Eugene Meyer, Jr., to help.

Before an announcement of the deal could be made, Wall Street got wind of it, and Baruch was importuned for stock. "Dear Mr. Baruch," wrote a broker with a Baltimore firm, "Can you take care of your poor friends from the provinces to the extent of a few hundred shares of the Alaska matter?" Baruch could not. All the stock was gone. Before the issue was priced—indeed, Baruch protested, before it could be priced—trading was under way on the Curb Exchange. *The Wall Street Journal* termed the anticipatory demand "unique." In the end, five times as much stock was demanded as was engraved and put into circulation.

Baruch and Meyer each took 100,000 shares to sell at a price of $10. Their commission was $1.75 a share. Also, Baruch was granted an option on 75,000 shares at $8 each through June. That is, Baruch could buy at $8 regardless of the market price. On April 15, just three weeks after the offering, Alaska Juneau was quoted at $15. By the end of July it was down to $9.50.

Thus began the slide that was to take the stock closer to zero than anyone had dreamed possible. An early disappointment was Jackling's decision to suspend operations at neighboring Alaska Gold Mine. At Alaska Juneau, there was what mining historian T. A. Rickard called a "serious blunder" in the design of the mill, which caused a significant reduction in its capacity. By the close of 1916, the stock was quoted at $7.75. It slipped to $2 in 1917. By 1920, Fred Bradley, the president, was inviting the stockholders to subscribe to a bond issue to rebuild the mine's depleted working capital. Eugene Meyer, Jr., answered him drily: "My relation to Juneau up to the present time has been that I have a very large interest in the shares in which I have a very large loss. My ownership of the stock does not, at first glance, make me feel that I would care to take $425,000 worth of the bonds at 6 percent interest, of which a liberal part of all the interest would go to the United States Government."

Eliciting only two orders for $500 each, Bradley committed substantial funds of his own. His example inspired other important stockholders, including Baruch, to ante up, and in time $1.9 million was raised. Bradley had refused to quit because his name had been used to sell the stock to the public, and Baruch, for the same reason, had refused to quit before Bradley. Not until 1931 did the mine yield its first dividend. In 1934, when the dollar was devalued against gold, the mine and its stockholders enjoyed a windfall. Baruch reaped an especially large profit, for he had been buying stock and gold bullion in expectation of some such monetary depreciation. It was as well-earned as any in his long investment career.

SIX

The Baron of Hobcaw

Baruch was a peripatetic millionaire, and he came and went conspicuously. He had his own private railroad car in the days when everybody traveled by rail, and he was an early enthusiast of motoring. His first automobile, an eight- or ten-cylinder Panhard, frightened horses and set up a racket along the Jersey Shore and irritated at least one of his summertime neighbors, Eugene Meyer, father of the investment banker. His second car, a yellow Mercedes, had forty horsepower and cost $22,000. Once he raced it at an exhibition in Long Branch, New Jersey, clocking more than sixty miles an hour against an American car driven by a Standard Oil heir named A. C. Bostwick. Baruch's taste for speed was keen enough to overcome his dread of seasickness, and together with his brother Harty he bought and raced a 190-horsepower boat, the *Skeedaddle*. In 1906 they won—by a nose—the National trophy at the Motor Boat Club of America races on the Hudson River.

Behind the wheel Baruch was at least as accomplished as his paid help, perhaps more so. In 1908 a chauffeured automobile of his jumped the curb on West 55th Street and allegedly struck a pedestrian. A similar episode was set in motion in 1901 by a telephone call from Baruch to his driver. "You be off to-day," the driver, in sworn testimony, later quoted him as saying. "I go to New Haven." The chauffeur was forbidden to use the car without permission, but he took a chance and drove to Brooklyn to watch an auto race. On the way home he bumped a pedestrian who was crossing Eighth Avenue at 42nd Street. In a subsequent lawsuit Baruch lost a $1,000 verdict at trial but successfully appealed. Probably the chauffeur was Heinrich Hilgenbach, who had come with the car and who turned out to be, in Baruch's laconic words, a "good man when sober." Whoever he was, the court records show, he kept his job. (In 1913 Baruch's mother disapproved of such indulgent employment practices. She declared that, "If your chauffeur knows that he will be dismissed if he goes too fast and if pedestrians will exercise more care there will be fewer accidents." She said that her personal speed limit was twelve miles an hour.) On summertime excursions to Europe, Baruch sometimes took an automobile along with him for the pleasure of driving it himself.

It wasn't always easy to reach Baruch or to do business with him because he was so often on the move. He tried to tour the United States once a year to get the lay of the land for business and stock-market purposes. He was in Europe in the summertime and at his barony in South Carolina for a part of every winter. Hobcaw, as the barony was called after an Indian word meaning "between the waters," was his second home (Belle, his daughter, always thought of it as her first home) and the tangible link to his mother's and father's South. The first baron of Hobcaw, John, Lord Carteret, was presented with 12,000 acres of what was called Hobcaw Point by King Charles II. The Point was a neck of land between the Waccamaw River and the Atlantic Ocean, and it turned out to hold 13,970 acres, not 12,000. Carteret and Baruch had at least two important things in common. Each was alive to the possibilities of precious-metals mining, and each was a charming companion (Carteret was described as an "ardent convivialist," which was also Baruch to a T). Carteret, however, never laid eyes on the place, and he sold it in 1730 to one John Roberts, of Dean's Court, Middlesex, England, for £500. The transfer included timber rights, "Sightwood Pitchings, Lakes, Ponds, Fishings, Waters, Water Courses, Pastures, Feedings, Marshes, Swamps, Ways, Easments, Profits, Commodities, Advantages, Emoluments, Hereditaments and Appurtenances," and also "Hunting, Hawking, Fishing and Fowling," but not the gold and silver rights, which Carteret wanted to keep mainly for himself. Alas, there turned out to be no precious metals.

By late in the nineteenth century the Barony had been divided and subdivided, and the river swamps on its western side (the one facing Winyah Bay to the south and the Waccamaw River farther north) had been turned to rice cultivation. In 1875, Robert James Donaldson, a Scotsman, bought a good part of the place; and in 1904 his sons, John Henry and Sidney T., decided to sell. Baruch by then was an available buyer. At the time a local newspaper paid him the compliments of being "of fine address" and "widely traveled," and of having "brains, youth and genius." The Donaldsons made good crops but were plagued by poaching and for that reason or another were prepared to let go of about three quarters of the original barony. In the negotiations to buy, Baruch bided his time. He took out an option to buy in Christmas week 1904 and had the option extended in February 1905. At last, in May, he bought the tract called Friendfield Plantation and a handful of enticingly named specks of land in Winyah Bay and Muddy Bay, including Big Marsh Island, My Lady Bush and Pumpkin Seed; all in all, 10,000 acres for $20,000. In 1906 he added 2,522 acres just to the north of Friendfield (including the land known as Bellefield and Crab Hall) for $25,000; and in 1907 the next northerly tract (Alderly), which amounted to another 2,500 acres or so, for $10,000. When he was through he owned about 15,000 acres as well as the planter's house and four tiny villages inhabited by former Hobcaw slaves or their descendants. The cost was $55,000, or less than the equivalent of about 1,200 shares of U.S. Steel. In 1912 or 1913, Harry Payne Whitney, an awestruck guest of Baruch's, bid $1 million for the place, which the host gracefully declined. Eventually he turned it over to Belle, who in turn established a foundation and willed the land for marine and biological research.

One of Hobcaw's charms for Baruch was its inaccessibility. The route from New York was by train to Georgetown, South Carolina, via Lane, South Carolina, then by boat across Winyah Bay. The boat discharged Baruch and his guests on a pier near the house that the Donaldsons had lived in, Friendfield House, which was of wood and had white columns, shuttered tall windows and a wide porch. The house was framed by moss-draped live oak, and in the spring there were palettes of azalea and magnolia. At length there was a road, and guests arrived overland, but the trip still took time and determination. King's Highway, the unpaved lane that connected Friendfield House and the public road, wound four and a half miles, all Baruch's, through stands of virgin timber along a bleak cypress swamp. Mail and telegrams were delivered twice a day from Georgetown, but Baruch allowed no telephone lines to be strung. "How I miss the telephone!!!?" Annie once wrote in the guest book.

The salt tidal marsh, fallow rice fields, forest and creeks harbored a rich assortment of game and marine life. In early years Baruch trapped otters and saw bears and wildcats. There were deer (a guest book entry by Bernard M. Baruch, Jr., in child's hand: "I love my ducks but oh you, deer"), wild pigs, jacksnipe, quail and woodcock. So profuse were the wild turkeys that they sometimes snarled traffic on King's Highway. Offshore or in the creeks and inlets there were clams, oysters, terrapin, shrimp, sea bass, sheepshead, whiting, bluefish, shad, mullet and crabs. An ecological complication was the litter of oyster shells on the floor of the marsh, which cut the paws of bird dogs. Once Belle shot an alligator. When, at the age of twelve, she killed her first deer, the New York *Herald* reported the news in connection with the account of the sentencing of a trio of poachers on the Baruch property to jail terms of eight months each.

For outdoorsmen, the chief attraction of Hobcaw was its hunting, although not every friend of Baruch's was an outdoorsman. (Heywood Broun, the newspaperman, declined a sporting invitation of Baruch's explaining, "I do my hunting in bed.") Hunters rose early and finished early. They set out the evening before the hunt by buckboard for shacks by Clambank marsh and awoke before dawn,* ate a breakfast of hot stew, grits and coffee, were shown to boats and rowed to blinds in the salt marsh. Presently black Vs appeared in the pink sky. Guides called, the birds dropped to the decoys and shotguns blasted. Ducks flew in by the thousand and fell by the score. So big were the bags that they strained the credibility of nonguests, or of guests who arrived after the quarry thinned out in the 1920s. (Ducks became thinner at

---

*Sometimes Baruch visited the barony's black church for an evening service. On one such occasion, the presiding minister, a "broadax" preacher not formally ordained, spoke along the following lines:

"And Moses divided the Red Sea, and they had air rifles and shotguns, and the guns was all apoppin' all over the place, and the water was divided, and all the people went over and no harm, and then Moses commanded that the waters go back together, and now I've got to close the sermon 'cause the Boss has got to go hunt early in the morn and we got to go to bed."

roughly the same time as the stock market became more efficient and the income tax began to take an appreciable bite out of one's income; all together, Baruch's opportunities contracted.) Once Thomas W. Gregory, Wilson's Attorney General, remarked skeptically to Jesse Jones, the future head of the Reconstruction Finance Corporation, in Baruch's presence: "Jesse, keep quiet. Let's sit back and hear Bernie lie about the ducks."

Hobcaw was very much Baruch's, and he went so far as to remind a friend that it was he who issued invitations and that the status of his wife at the barony was that of guest. In general, Baruch took a sphere-of-influence approach to marriage. Hobcaw was his, as was the castle that he rented in Scotland for summer shooting later on. The four-story brownstone at 6 West 52nd Street at which they lived after 1905 was evidently Annie's turf, except the top floor, which was his. Annie was apparently as detached from financial markets, ducks and bridge (which he played seriously) as he was from the antique English silver and furniture that she collected. In one of the rare references to his wife in his correspondence, Baruch described her as "level headed." Dorothy Schiff came away from a dinner party at which the Baruchs were present in the 1930s with the impression that she wasn't his type. Certainly after her death, in 1938, he chose the company of very different women, and the weight of the circumstantial evidence in the years before her death is that he was unfaithful to her. The only known record of his amorous exploits was left by Helen Lawrenson, whose famous *Esquire* essay "Latins Are Lousy Lovers" was written with his encouragement. He was ten years dead when she wrote that he was a lousy lover too.

Two more children came along after the birth of Belle in 1899: Bernard, Jr., in 1903 and Renée in 1905. Baruch always accounted himself a parental failure, and his advice was to enjoy one's children while they are young, as the trouble starts later on. He was an absentee father—besides business travel, golf and nights out, he sailed to Europe in the summer with his wife but sometimes without a full complement of children—but the sorrow he expressed at his children's bruises suggests that he loved them even if from a distance. The genesis of one such hard knock was the friendship of a daughter of Howard Page's with Belle. Page was president of the Intercontinental Rubber Company and one of Baruch's closest friends. The Page girl had attended the Brearley School in Manhattan, and she encouraged Belle to apply there. Belle did so in 1912, passed the entrance examination, but encountered resistance. According to Baruch, who reflected on it many years later, the trouble was that he was a Jew:

> That really was the bitterest blow of my life because it hurt my child and embittered my whole life for many years afterwards. The man and woman who were the cause of it were keeping the school pure from being injured by the presence of my daughter, because she was the daughter of B. M. Baruch. There was only one reason and that was the religious reason. While it was true that two other girls had gone through the school, they said they didn't want any more. The man who was the cause of keeping her out rose to have a considerable position, and his wife was identified with Democratic politics. I had an opportunity to take my revenge but I never did. I am sure the man expected it, in fact I know he did. When he was being asked to consider a position in the Federal Bank [probably the Federal Reserve Bank] a man said to me, "You have a chance to be even with the _____ _____." My first desire was to do so. He said, "All you have to do is to tell McAdoo [William G. McAdoo, Secretary of the Treasury under Woodrow Wilson] you don't want his appointment," but I felt I had no right to take revenge upon the man and abuse the use of public office, so I did nothing. His wife was connected with many political movements, but I never mentioned the matter to a single person, though I always refused to contribute to any committee of which I saw she was a member. The bitterness and hurt has [*sic*] lessened but will never entirely be removed. I will forgive any man anything he does to me, but why make little children suffer?

So little was Baruch a Jew except by birth, so disinclined was he to pick a fight if it could possibly be avoided and so much did he want to please, that he was never entirely alienated from Gentile society. To a notable degree, he was, in fact, in it. For one thing he moved freely in the downtown meritocracy. He belonged to the Recess Club, for instance, where Kuhn, Loeb partners, who were Jewish, lunched with Morgan men, who were not. For another thing, he had a share in Annie's Protestant social credentials. It was on the strength of her name that the Baruchs were admitted to the *Social Register* in 1905, a book which in the first two decades of the century contained no Warburgs,

Schiffs, Seligmans or Guggenheims. From time to time the names of the Baruch daughters turned up in the papers on horsey topics (Belle became a champion equestrienne), and in the summer of 1911 the whole family, Baruch's parents included, vacationed at the WASPy Adirondack colony of Kamp Kill Kare. As late as 1920 Baruch was the only Jewish trustee of City College, and in the 1930s, Frances Perkins, Franklin D. Roosevelt's Secretary of Labor, didn't think of him as Jewish at all. (What eventually changed her mind, she said, was the interest he displayed in spas and water cures.)

It was equally true that socially Baruch could go so far but no farther. For a while he belonged to the Whist and Author's clubs but not to the University and Metropolitan, of which his father-in-law, Benjamin Griffen, was a member. Thus he was wary when John Black, a business friend and golf partner, invited him to stand for membership at the patently restricted Oakland Golf Club, in Bayside, Queens. Baruch knew the Oakland, having played there in a foursome that was regular to the point of compulsion, and he knew the homogeneous cast of the membership. The quartet, besides Black and him, included Dick Lydon, Baruch's college pal, and James Travers, who appears to have been a partner of Baruch Brothers, the brokerage firm that Harty and Herman set up with the help of their rich brother in 1903. According to Baruch, the foursome played eighteen holes in the morning and eighteen in the afternoon on Saturdays, Sundays and holidays, in season, until the deaths of Travers and Black in the 1920s. It was about 1909 when Black offered to put up Baruch's name for membership.

Black assured him that religious bigotry was the furthest thing from the members' minds. H. J. Pomroy, a former president of the New York Stock Exchange, repeated the assurances and offered to second him. Baruch agreed, but there was opposition after all. Embarrassed, he offered to withdraw, but Black and Pomroy said they wouldn't hear of it. The nomination became a cause célèbre. Allies were marshaled—James Mabon, Baruch's colleague on the Unlisted Committee, lined up on his side—and at last he was voted in.

More than a decade later, much the same set-to was fought in another arena. In the early 1920s it went without saying that Jews were unwelcome at the Turf and Field Club and that only members were admitted to the track enclosure at Belmont Park. Baruch, a serious breeder and horseplayer, kept his counsel on this arrangement until August Belmont, the racing grandee, asked his opinion. Baruch answered that it was a destructive policy, that it was bound to throw racing into disrepute, and that, in an expression he was fond of, all men should be equal "above the turf as well as below it." Belmont countered by asking why, if he felt as he did, he had anything to do with racing, to which Baruch rejoined, "I won't as long as such men as you are in it." For a while Baruch boycotted the Belmont track and turned over his stable to his racing friend Cary Grayson. In the long ensuing row he was elected to the club, declined membership, but was persuaded to accept when promises were made of a general lowering of discriminatory bars.

By his forty-first year, Baruch was important enough and the stock market still small enough so that his whereabouts became a subject of speculation in the financial press. Now and then his itinerary was reported as if his mere absence from the floor would be the cause of some significant realignment of market forces. Thus on June 23, 1911: "The belief prevailed in some usually well-informed quarters that the heavy selling of stocks in the forenoon was for Baruch, who intends to leave for a prolonged vacation Saturday next." And on March 6, 1912: "One of the things which made many of the room traders bearish was a rumor that B. M. Baruch was about to go away on a short vacation— those operators apparently thought the market was a part of Mr. Baruch's personal belongings and that he would take it away with him." On the tenth of March, the New York *World*, noting the departure of Baruch for Hobcaw, called him the "recognized leader in all great speculative movements in Wall Street." On the twenty-sixth, the *Herald* related a lighthearted conversation ostensibly overheard downtown:

"'Barney Baruch is buying Reading,' said one trader to another.

"'Don't believe it,' said the other. 'He's now South in his shooting box.'

"'Can't help that,' said the first. 'Barney has a stock ticker in his match box.'"

In the fall of 1912, when Baruch was probably worth less than $10 million, the tall tale was published that he had just "cleaned up" $20 million. Baruch, basking in the attention, uncharacteristically climbed out on a limb to make a projection. "The good features are so overpowering that they compel recognition," he declared on October 8, 1912. The truth was that the good features were just then at their best. Not until the war boom of 1915 did the Dow Jones Industrial Average match its peak of October 8, 1912, which was 94.12. Not until 1927 did the Rails top *their* peak of October 5, which was 124.35. But Baruch's reputation was unharmed by that errant judgment, and as he left for vacation in the summer of 1913, the New York *Morning Telegraph* wondered what the market would do without him:

> "Barney" Baruch has gone to Europe—having sailed yesterday. This more or less commonplace notice would, under ordinary conditions, attract little more than passing attention, except among his immediate relatives and intimate friends, but in the present instance it possesses more real significance, perhaps, than would appear at first blush.
>
> Baruch, as has been frequently pointed out of late in these columns, has been way in the forefront in the work of rejuvenating the stock market and bringing it out of the slough of despond into which it had drifted.
>
> Backed by the millions of several of the "big men" of the Street, that astute operator was selected for this task, and how well he performed the duties entrusted to him is amply attested by the fact that since he took hold of the market and started to move prices up, Union Pacific has risen about 14 points. Steel around 10 points, and all the other recognized leaders of the list in proportion.*
>
> Now that the "ablest and largest trader on the floor of the Stock Exchange" has gone abroad to enjoy a well-earned vacation, and in consideration of the very conspicuous part he has played during the past month or so in shaping the destinies of share speculation in general, the Street is very naturally asking itself the question: "Is the bull movement in stocks over?"†

The adulation of Baruch as a speculator seemed to get under the skin of Paul Warburg and Jacob Schiff, bankers at Kuhn, Loeb & Com-

---

*Most of this may be doubted. Baruch seems to have made markets discreetly, in individual stocks, not wholesale, for the "big men," whoever they were.

†Almost, as it turned out. Baruch left on August 7, 1913. The upturn that had begun on June 11 ended on September 13.

pany who found some of his market operations distasteful. (James P. Warburg, quoting his father, inaccurately insisted that Baruch was chronically short of stocks. In fact, he was long or short as circumstances required.) Baruch himself was of two views about his place in the financial world. On the one hand he maintained that speculation was necessary and honorable. On the other, he was partial to the word "constructive" to distinguish the creation of wealth, particularly in mining and agriculture, from its manipulation in the form of stock certificates. His place in that world was at all events hard to pinpoint. He worked for himself, kept his own office, picked and chose deals as they appealed to him and corresponded on a letterhead that said simply "Bernard M. Baruch." He was close to the Guggenheims and to Eugene Meyer, Jr., and others, but he was not in the position of having to take business because he was under obligation to a large financial institution. In 1912, when Congress was taking a hard look at Wall Street, a man sounding very much like Baruch unburdened himself to the journalist Garet Garrett, who happened to be one of Baruch's close friends. The unnamed market operator was asked how the alleged concentration of financial power in the hands of a few rich men and large institutions affected him:

> "It doesn't affect me at all. Do you know why? . . . Well, in the first place, I never borrow any money from them, and, in the second place, I'm never as deeply committed in the stock market as they think I am. That is to say, I don't trade as heavily as they believe I do. They have tried many times to get me. They think they have me in a corner, and I'm not there. One of them once said to a friend who told me: 'Just when we think we've got him he's loose again.' The man who said that holds it against me that I upset him once in a stack market campaign. Then they have tried to get me in with them on various things, and to take up sides with them, but I'm too cagey for any of that. I like to sit up here on my own crag and fly down when I please."

If "they" were the financial establishment, Baruch was a member at least to the extent of his station as a governor of the Stock Exchange. There he was the diligent organization man, upholding tradition, serving on committees and falling in with policy with which he happened to disagree.* He was a "progressive" governor, holding the view that there was too much funny business on the floor and that it wouldn't be such a bad thing if the Exchange were incorporated under the laws of New York State. The official line was there was very little funny business and the incorporation would dilute the disciplinary authority of the governors and bring the members under the regulatory thumb of the legislature. "Baruch," said the Boston News Bureau, "is something of a philosopher, and he has what the Street regards as advanced views of the ethics and morals of business. He believes that the doctrine of 'caveat emptor' has been carried too far in finance, and that another generation will scorn to do the things that Wall Street gentlemen now consider fair in the struggle for gold."

Baruch was not so progressive that he welcomed governmental intrusion in the market, and in 1913 he helped to compile a book for the Stock Exchange that laid out the case against unreasonable intervention. *Short Sales and Manipulation of Securities*, his anonymous contribution to the Money Trust debate (although it was common knowledge that Baruch had had the booklet privately published, he declined to sign his name to it), was a sixty-seven-page collection of documents on financial regulation. The gist of it was that short sales were salutary, and that government meddling in the speculative arena usually did more harm than good, but that there was room for improvement in self-regulation. A distinction was drawn between honest and dishonest manipulation of prices. If, for example, a man gave a buy order to one broker and a sell order to another, both in the same stock, and if neither broker knew what the other was doing, then the manipulation was aboveboard. (The point of the exercise would be to attract public participation by creating the appearance, or indeed, for the moment, the reality, of trading activity. Such a feint, wrote Baruch, was recognized as "a necessary and useful part of the machinery of speculation.") If, however, the brokers

---

*In keeping with Stock Exchange custom, for instance, Baruch rallied to the side of Mrs. William Laimbeer, whose husband was killed in an automobile accident in 1913. It came out that Laimbeer, a friend of Baruch's and member of the Exchange, had never recovered from the Panic of 1907, and that, unless his debts to fellow members were expunged, the proceeds of the sale of his seat would be lost to his widow. Baruch liked widows, as indeed he liked most women, and along with some other members he helped to assure her the income from $75,000.

arranged the trade in advance, then the manipulation was fraudulent and punishable under both common law and the rules of the exchange.

Altogether Baruch's public-policy vistas were widening. In 1909, he became interested in the New York mayoral candidacy of William Gaynor. Victorious, Gaynor appointed Baruch a trustee of City College in 1910. The mayor was a Tammany Democrat of an eccentric, Jeffersonian stripe—Albert Jay Nock called him "by far the ablest man in our public life"—although Baruch, in national politics, was a progressive Republican. He cast his first presidential ballot for a Democrat, Grover Cleveland, in 1892, but in 1896 oddly lacked a conviction on the monetary question and was unable to recall on which side he had ended up. (Never an ideological person, Baruch came around to the gold standard later in life but made no public protest when President Roosevelt embraced a quasi–paper standard.) He said that he had probably voted for McKinley, a Republican, in 1900 over the admonition of his great-uncle Fischel Cohen, a Confederate veteran, who said that the marking of a GOP ballot would cause a southern arm to wither. He was all for Theodore Roosevelt in 1904 and for William Howard Taft in 1908. However, when Mayor Gaynor, who wanted to be President, allowed a delegation to travel to the Democratic National Convention in Baltimore in June 1912 to put up his name for the candidacy, Baruch was in the entourage.* He was settled in a chair in the Fifth Regiment Armory on the night that William Jennings Bryan, champion of silver money and foe of Wall Street, offered a startling resolution:

> Resolved, That in this crisis in our party's career and in our country's history this convention sends greetings to the people of the United States, and assures them that the party of Jefferson and of Jackson is still the champion of popular government and equality before the law. As proof of our fidelity to the people, we hereby declare ourselves opposed to the nomination of any candidate for President who is

---

*His expedition was promptly invested with stock-market significance. ". . . Bernard Baruch ought to have 300,000 shares that he hasn't got," a broker was quoted as saying. "In fact I know that Bernie when he was at the Baltimore convention did not have a share of stock, either in his box or in the 'Street.' Therefore, I figure that he has got to buy 200,000 or 300,000 shares on the present good times, for he cannot keep out of the market."

the representative of or under obligation to J. Pierpont Morgan, Thomas F. Ryan, August Belmont, or any other member of the privilege-hunting and favor-seeking class.

Be it further resolved, That we demand the withdrawal from this convention of any delegate or delegates constituting or representing the above-named interests.

The house dissolved in a roar. Baruch cast an anxious glance at Ryan, who rose defiantly from his seat in the Virginia delegation. Fistfights erupted. One man cursed at Bryan until he actually frothed at the mouth. The money changers in fact remained in the temple, but the party's nominee, Woodrow Wilson, took the sanitary precaution of refusing to accept campaign contributions from "three wealthy Democrats," presumably the trio excoriated by Bryan.

It was late in the campaign before Baruch met Wilson. The introduction took place at the Plaza Hotel through the offices of William McCombs, a fellow trustee of Baruch's at City College and chairman of the Democratic National Committee. Baruch, who was summoned at the Oakland Golf Club, proceeded to the Plaza where he was met by James Gerard, the future ambassador to Germany, and Edward Mandell House, Wilson's right-hand man. Sensitive to the political risks of meeting alone with a Wall Street man, Wilson summoned aides to sit in as witnesses.

Insofar as one virile man can be said to fall in love with another, Baruch that day fell for Wilson. He was smitten by his bearing, by the beam of his gray eyes and by the fact of his southern birth. He admired the fight he made at Princeton against the eating clubs (an admiration undiminished by his own success in scaling the walls of the Oakland). Wilson was a low-tariff man, and Baruch had, or recently had had, a vested interest in protection by reason of his holdings in the American Beet Sugar Company. But Baruch was in broad sympathy with reform and he heard out Wilson approvingly. Regarding competition and monopoly, the candidate pointed to a telephone, "Here you have a monopoly," he said. "But it is a reasonable monopoly. It represents a necessary concentration of capital under private control. But just the same, I believe it should be regulated." Whatever the abstract merits of the New Freedom for Baruch, the program first and foremost was something that Woodrow Wilson expounded.

Baruch was far from the only moneyed man to appear in the progressive camp in 1912, but he was one of the few Wall Street men to give handsomely. He gave $12,500. Ryan, who had supported Wilson's gubernatorial run in New Jersey in 1910, was, as noted, persona non grata. Jacob H. Schiff, the Kuhn, Loeb partner, also gave $12,500; Cleveland H. Dodge gave $35,000, and Henry Morgenthau, the banker and father of the Treasury Secretary under Franklin D. Roosevelt, gave $30,000. William R. Rust, the Tacoma smelter man whom Baruch had surprised with a big check in 1905, contributed $7,500. Samuel Untermyer, the Guggenheim lawyer turned chief inquisitor at the Money Trust hearings, gave $10,000.

A curiosity of party finances that year is that Baruch's money was found palatable while Morgan's, Belmont's and Ryan's was not. Baruch took umbrage neither at the ostracism of Ryan nor at his party's professed hostility toward Wall Street. Out of fear that the presence of a prominent speculator in Wilson's ranks might embarrass the party, he hung back in the shadows of the campaign, giving only his money.

When Baruch alighted from his crag on the seventh floor of the Trinity Building, it was sometimes in the company of his old friend Middleton Schoolbred Burrill. A Wall Street lawyer by profession, Burrill remained an active stock trader, and he comprised, along with the broker Harry Content and the Housman firm, the heart of what was sometimes identified in newspaper stories as the "Baruch interests." In 1911 the attention of that body turned to the American Beet Sugar Company.

Beet Sugar, which had farmland or factories or both in Colorado, California and Nebraska, was a prototypical agribusiness. It raised enough beets and refined enough sugar in 1910* to generate profits of $1.7 million and sales of $7 million, a record little changed from the showing in 1909 and 1908 but double the results of 1905. The shares, of which only 150,000 were outstanding, were listed on the New York Stock Exchange. No common dividend was paid and there was no long-term debt.

In 1910 Burrill was elected to the board of directors. The next year came reports that Baruch headed a "pool" in Beet Sugar or was at least a substantial holder of the shares. In July 1911 an apparently well-briefed financial columnist speculated on the company's prospects:

---

*The company's fiscal year, which ended March 31.

Some of the keenest operators in Wall Street continue to predict big things for a little stock—American Beet Sugar. They are even prophesying that in the course of the next year or so this issue will cross the old Havemeyer specialty—American Sugar. I understand announcement will soon be made of the passing of the control of the American Beet Sugar Co. into new up-to-date hands. The quiet absorption of the common and preferred shares of this company during the past six months has embraced, I am informed, the old family holdings of two of the original interests in the property whose stocks have been purchased in the open market and much to the surprise of the family interests in question have not been for sale again. The Burrill-Baruch-Housman interests together with two large banking houses, now control this company and dividends at the rate of 4 percent payable quarterly, are to be commenced at no distant day on American Beet Sugar common. Middleton S. Burrill and Bernard M. Baruch, two of the largest operators in the Street are extensively interested.

In fact that fall a maiden dividend was declared at the rate of 5 percent, not 4 percent, and the price of the stock, which in January was below 40, by November had vaulted to 55. Talk of a Baruch-Burrill pool, with the implication of insider trading (as a director Burrill heard corporate news first), persisted into 1912. The story was discounted by the Boston News Bureau, which stated on what sounds like the authority of Baruch or Burrill: "Both B. M. Baruch and M. S. Burrill have long held Beet Sugar, but have no pool in it. The earnings of this company are public property and together with dividends prospects account for the advance in its shares." With or without manipulation, the stock continued to climb, reaching 77 in September 1912. It weakened on news of Wilson's election and the prospect of lower sugar duties. By year's end it broke 50. Unexpectedly, on January 3, 1913, it fell below 42 on the announcement that the directors, citing burdensome inventories, had voted to suspend the dividend. The collapse led to a lone demand in Congress for an investigation of the company and to a run of suspicious comment in the financial press, of which a sample from *The Wall Street Journal*:

Conservative Wall Street interests would like to see an investigation of the operations in Beet Sugar. A year ago the stock was placed on a 5 percent basis. A pool carried the price up to 77 in September, and the

Street was filled with rumors of an increase in the dividend to 6 percent, or even more. Then came the selling movement, and now the climax in the passing of the dividend. The whole thing may be all right; and if so, Wall Street would like to see that fact established. In the other event, it is felt that something should be done to restore public confidence in Wall Street.

The "other event" alluded to was the possibility of the wrong kind of manipulation. A Wall Street maxim has it that the reason for sudden market movement is duly furnished after the fact. In the case of Beet Sugar the 1913 annual report disclosed, too late, a 54 percent drop in profits. The violence of the break on January 3 was proof that the public had been caught unawares. The preceding decline in the stock suggested that the insiders had not been. Baruch was closely identified with the rise. What part, if any, he played in the fall was unmentioned. (Burrill left the board between April 1, 1912, and March 31, 1913, in circumstances unknown. In the same twelve months two other directors stepped down; the board numbered eleven.) Evidence that Baruch retained the respect of the Stock Exchange elders was the fact of his appointment to the prestigious Law Committee later that January. Equally convincing evidence that somebody held a grudge against him surfaced the next summer. The grudge was brought to light in the course of the impeachment of the governor of New York.

William "Plain Bull" Sulzer, eighty-first chief executive of the Empire State, was elected in 1912 and set to work at once on a scheme to uplift Wall Street. A regular machine Democrat, he had done Tammany's bidding in the State Assembly but went to Congress in 1895 as a boomer of good causes. In Washington, he caught the satirical eye of Finley Peter Dunne, whose Mr. Dooley remarked: "It's always been a great relief to me whin bowed undher th' yoke of opressyon to know that ol' Bill was weepin' and runnin' f'r office or makin' someother sacrifice f'r me." With the watchword "No honest broker has anything to fear," the new governor introduced measures to outlaw fraud and manipulation, to set a 15 percent ceiling on call-loan rates and to incorporate the New York Stock Exchange under state law.

The brokers, who had had their fill of reform, closed ranks. The Law Committee, reinforced by Baruch, began the drafting of counterproposals, and a ten-man delegation was named to treat with Sulzer. Among the ten were Baruch, Eugene Meyer, Jr., James Mabon and

Melville B. Fuller, of whom more was to be heard. In Albany the brokers told Sulzer that they had nothing against reasonable laws, but that the level of interest rates was beyond their control and that incorporation would do more harm than good. Baruch happened to see the incorporation question more or less Sulzer's way, but kept his opinion to himself.

The delegation and the governor amicably parted company. The milder reforms were passed into law, and the usury and incorporation bills died. Sulzer, meantime, had broken with the Tammany regulars who had helped to elect him, damning them for grafters and endorsing a bill to inaugurate direct primary elections. Charles F. Murphy, Tammany chief and the incarnation of all that progressive democracy reviled, answered by causing an investigation to be started into Sulzer's finances. A working hypothesis was that the governor had failed to report all funds received, but the truth proved unexpectedly richer. It developed that the candidate had diverted some contributions for the purpose of taking a flyer on Wall Street. Among his brokers, it turned out, was M. B. Fuller, one of the Stock Exchange governors with whom Sulzer had discussed the ethics of the marketplace. Fuller was later to testify that the governor kept a chronically impaired margin account, that the account was identified by number only, and that, late in 1912, the governor-elect had paid $10,000 of the deficit in currency.

In the course of the investigation charges were inevitably bandied and reputations besmirched. One day, early in August, Baruch's name turned up in the columns of the New York *World*. The suspicion was reported that Sulzer, while a congressman, had dealt in American Beet Sugar stock when the sugar tariff was under consideration. He was alleged to have dealt through two brokerage houses, A. A. Housman & Company and Baruch Brothers. The *World*'s story wound up: "Bernard M. Baruch, who now has offices at No. 111 Broadway, was formerly a member of the firm of A. A. Housman & Co., and has been prominent in the affairs of the American Beet Sugar Company, whose stocks have moved in most irregular ways from time to time."

Harty Baruch and Clarence Housman each protested that he had never had truck with Sulzer and knew of no trading of his in Beet Sugar. Furthermore, the record showed that Sulzer, as a congressman, had opposed the tariff, whereas the company's interest lay in protection. Transparently false, the charge was forgotten, but others bore up, and Sulzer was impeached, found guilty and removed from office. The diehard progressive view was that the governor had been framed, and Baruch, believing it, contributed to his unsuccessful legal defense. The significance of the affair to Baruch was trifling except to remind him of the vigilance of his enemies and also of the love of his older brother. It happened that, when his name was leaked by the investigating committee, Baruch was aboard ship for a vacation in Europe, which prompted malicious gossip. Harty commented: "It is not true that Bernard M. Baruch, who by the way, is not a member of this firm, went to Europe on Saturday to avoid this committee. He is not the kind to run away from any one or anything." Harty, in his brother's eyes, had always been a hero. Coming from him, the words might have given Baruch goose bumps.

SEVEN

Striking It Rich
Reluctantly

In the spring of 1911, a dull time in the stock market, Baruch accepted one proposition and refused another. The one he took was a block of bonds of an insolvent short-line railroad. That, in turn, led him to another investment in the bonds of a second indigent road. The opportunity he turned down was control of a majority of stock in an undeveloped sulphur mine. In retrospect (in the clarity of which he is second-guessed) it was just the time to have done the opposite. His railroads went from bad to worse. The sulphur mine struck it rich on a plateau forty feet above sea level in Matagorda County, Texas. Eventually Baruch extricated himself from his railroads and bought heavily in sulphur, but the false start cost him millions.

The story of why and how he erred begins with the fact that he was a railroad buff. As a boy in South Carolina he was delighted by the passing trains of the Charlotte, Columbia & Augusta line. As a grown speculator in 1902, he had bought stock in the Louisville & Nashville Railroad with an eye to acquiring control of the company, but was obliged to settle for a $1 million trading profit instead. In 1911 or 1912 he committed a large sum to the Wabash Railroad to the end of securing a voice in *its* management. In his single-mindedness, he overestimated both the Wabash and the prospects for railroads in general, which were slipping.*

The news, on March 30, 1911, of his purchase of $3,128,000 of the 4 percent, first mortgage, fifty-year bonds of the Wabash Pittsburgh Terminal Railway Company was met with expressions of hope and bafflement. The Terminal Company, to shorten its name, was insolvent, money-losing and lawyer-bound. It was not entirely clear that the company would be around when its bonds fell due in 1954, much less have the money to redeem them, or even, in the meantime, to resume the annual payment of 4 percent interest which it had suspended in 1908. Bonds that would ostensibly mature at 100 cents on the dollar changed hands about the time when Baruch bought at about 46 cents.† The difference between the two figures was roughly the measure of the market's doubts about the Terminal Company. It was also a measure of the potential profit to Baruch if the road were restored to financial health. As prospects for payments improved, so would the price of the bonds. The fact that a trader as shrewd as he had seen something of value in the company was a hopeful sign. The question was, what had he seen?

What anybody could see was that the road was in trouble. In 1908 the bondholders went to court to complain that they hadn't been paid and to ask the judge to install a management that would try to pay them. He did so. This is the legal state known as receivership, in which management is vested in people whom a court appoints rather than in directors whom the stockholders elect. Since the Terminal Company earned too little and owed too much, the goal of the receivers was to enhance earnings and to reduce the fixed charges that had to be met year in and year out. The most important of these was interest on its bonds. The company's trains ran and its mines yielded coal, but its bondholders went unpaid, which was the symptom of the trouble.

The impetus for building the Terminal Company was the fact that the Pennsylvania Railroad had the great Pittsburgh market almost to itself.

---

*Baruch's reputation as a powerful figure around railroads, if not actually in them, became sufficiently well established that in 1935 a Nazi propagandist fell into the error of describing him as the "president of various railroad corporations." Baruch could only have wished it were so.

†A price of 46 meant that a $1,000 bond cost $460. Thus Baruch's overall investment would have amounted to $1,438,880, which is 46 percent of the face, or par, amount of his purchase, namely, $3,128,000.

The plan of the entrepreneurs was to contract a line sixty-three miles to the west of Pittsburgh to connect with Toledo. In advance the backers booked business with the Carnegie Steel Company and formed an alliance with two Midwestern lines. The first of these allied roads was the Wheeling & Lake Erie, which ran to Toledo from the Terminal Company's westernmost point at Pittsburgh Junction, Ohio. At Toledo, the Wheeling & Lake Erie connected with the second friendly road, the Wabash, which described short loops around the Midwest. The entente gave the Wabash and the Wheeling & Lake Erie the right to run trains into Pittsburgh. In return the Terminal Company gained access to Toledo and from there to the dozens of points served by the Wabash, including St. Louis and Chicago. The Terminal Company got the better of the deal because the Wheeling & Lake Erie and the Wabash pledged to turn over a portion of their earnings to the Terminal Company's bondholders. The alliance was sealed in common ownership and by a shared strategic design. The Terminal Company was to own a majority of shares in the Wheeling & Lake Erie, and the Wabash was to own all of the stock of the Terminal Company. When Jay Gould, the unregulated capitalist, died in 1892, he left an estate well furnished in the stock of the Wabash and Missouri Pacific railroads. George Gould, his son, had an ambition to build a transcontinental line, pushing east and west from St. Louis, in which both the Terminal Company and Wheeling & Lake Erie would be vital spurs. Although the Gould dream dissolved in the Panic of 1907, the bonds of the Terminal Company had earlier seemed a safe investment. Savings banks and life insurance companies bought them confidently.

As much as any other single cause, topography was the bane of the Terminal Company. So rugged was its right-of-way that ninety-five bridges, three trestles and seventeen tunnels had to be built or acquired, representing a distance of 6.9 miles spanned or bored through, fully 10 percent of the 67 miles under ownership. Earnings fell short of the sums that were needed to pay interest on the capital that was borrowed to build it all. The company had 15,000 acres of first-class coal land but only 1,500 freight cars. It lost $936,972 in its first year of operation and continued to lose money in 1906, 1907 and 1908. On May 28, 1908, on complaint of the holders of its bonds and notes, it was declared insolvent, making the elapsed time between organization and failure four years and twenty-three days, flat. The Wheeling & Lake Erie failed eleven days later.

The striking feature of the Terminal Company's career in the courts is how long it lasted and how little came of it. The point of receivership is to bring about a reorganization. A bondholders' protective committee was appointed to draw up a plan, but the committee slumbered. In 1910, a rival committee was organized, but it too was ineffectual, and beseeching letters from investors began to reach President Taft. To anticipate slightly, the committees were merged under the leadership of the lawyer Samuel Untermyer, who dunned the bondholders for a large assessment. When he was asked what the money was for, he replied that the joint committee's expenses had run to $3 million. By that time, the market value of the company's bonds had been slashed to less than $5 million, compared to some $30 million at the start in 1904, and letters from aggrieved bondholders began to reach President Wilson. Meantime, upon *its* fall into receivership in 1908, the Wheeling & Lake Erie had gone to court to ask that its contracts with the Terminal Company be set aside. The harmonious exchange of traffic ceased, and the price of Terminal Company bonds sank. In 1910, they were quoted at 54 cents on the dollar, down from 95½ cents in 1905. The Kennebunk Savings Bank of Kennebunk, Maine, which had bought some bonds at a high price, was asked what it thought of them at a low price. "Thoroughly disgusted with the whole situation," wrote an officer in 1910. "Sold out some time ago." By March 1911, when Baruch, paying a price of 46 or so, became the largest individual holder of that issue, gloom was thick.

The best speculators seem to buy when everybody else wants to sell. Sizing up the situation in 1911, Baruch perhaps decided that the bad news was out, that a reorganization plan would emerge sooner rather than later and that the Terminal Company would one day become a vital link in a refurbished Wabash system. E. H. Harriman, his idol, had invested in the Wheeling & Lake Erie in 1908, when the bad news was only starting to come out.

It was the system in which Baruch believed and he began to accumulate the 4 percent bonds of the Wabash proper. To the casual observer the Wabash Railroad had as much or as little to commend it as the Terminal Company did. In the fiscal year ended June 30, 1911, it lost $403,421. The loss was significant because it occurred despite a $1 million rise in gross receipts. The company was short of boxcars and was incidentally burdened by its investments in the Terminal Company and in the Wheeling & Lake Erie. In September 1911, the president of the Wabash, Frederic A. Delano, wrote the stockholders frankly:

Speaking in general terms of the Company's present condition and future prospects, it is gratifying to point out that it has reached an earning capacity of practically thirty million dollars gross [i. e., $30 million of revenues], or, approximately $12,000 per mile—being about double the figures of twelve years ago—and this has been accomplished with only a moderate increase in facilities. At the same time this very lack of facilities, such, for example, as insufficient double track and car and locomotive equipment, in large measure accounts for the higher ratio of operating expenses. Every investigation of Wabash conditions, and there have been many by both interested and disinterested parties, confirms the statement that the property as it stands has been well maintained but that it might, if cash were available for needed betterments and improvements, greatly increase its earning capacity and decrease its operating ratio. The Wabash, with its short lines between St. Louis and Kansas City, St. Louis and Omaha, St. Louis and Chicago, St. Louis and Detroit, Chicago and Detroit, Chicago and Toledo, Kansas City and Toledo, Kansas City and Detroit, lags behind its competitors both in volume of business and in the cost of doing it, because it has not the adequate facilities. The difficulty is a financial one and has been beyond the power of the management to remedy.

Shortly thereafter, the Wabash found that it too was unable to meet the payments due to its creditors. At Christmastime 1911, it was haled into court, found insolvent and consigned to receivers. Although insolvency connotes ruin and upheaval, the Wabash proceedings began in a forgiving way. Two of the three men whom a judge in the U.S. Circuit Court in St. Louis appointed to help the company catch its breath were drawn from incumbent management. One of them was Mr. Delano, the president, who had just confessed that the financial problems were out of management's control. As in the Terminal Company receivership, rival bondholders' protective committees were formed, the insurgents charging that the proceedings were a little too friendly. The irony there was that the chief of the Wabash insurgents was James N. Wallace, who had headed up a determinedly inert committee of the Terminal Company. The personnel of the established Wabash committee included Edwin Hawley, the railroad man with whom Arthur Housman had almost come to grief in the stock market. It was Hawley's death in February 1912 that drew Baruch into the thicket of the Wabash.

Baruch's first step in that direction was the purchase of a large block of the railroad's 4 percent, fifty-year first refunding and extension bonds. The size of his investment was not reported, but it was described (as the Terminal Company block had been) as the largest held by any one man. Next, on April 4, he was named to fill the place on the bondholders' committee left vacant by Hawley's death. News of his appointment raised hopes for an expeditious reorganization, caused a rally in the company's low-priced stock and prompted good press. The Hearst papers predicted that Baruch's railroad career would rival Harriman's. There was talk that he meant to retire from Wall Street to devote himself to railroad matters, which the New York *Herald* doubted: "Those who know him best declare that he has no intention of retiring, and, so far as wishing to become another Harriman, he is perfectly willing to remain B. M. Baruch, the only and original." (However, citing the press of business, he did step down as a governor of the Stock Exchange, in November 1913.) *The Wall Street Journal*, ordinarily not given to personality pieces, let itself go:

> The announcement by Dow Jones & Co. that B. M. Baruch would be elected to the Wabash bondholders' committee was received with mingled feelings. Most people seem to regard Mr. Baruch as a speculator, or stock market operator, and nothing more. They can hardly be blamed for this, as it is only in such capacity that the newspapers have mentioned his name. Yet that view does him an injustice. He is a man who has shown remarkable ability in selecting investments, and sizing up the business situation. He would be an addition to any board of directors, and the prospects of the Wabash will be brightened when his voice is heard in the councils of its management.

Besides Baruch the committee included Thomas H. Hubbard, who had helped to reorganize the Wabash when it got into trouble back in 1889; Winslow S. Pierce, a lawyer who specialized in railroad bankruptcies and who had once been chairman of the Union Pacific; Robert Goelet, a New York City real estate investor; Alvin W. Krech, president of the Equitable Trust Company, and a Mr. Robert Flemming. Their job was to serve as a kind of board of directors in extremis. The work was difficult technically because of the complexity of an enterprise spanning 2,514 miles, and also morally, because the committeemen represented different interests but were charged with serving the good of all.

The question was by how much fixed charges, in particular interest payments, would have to be reduced, and which class of securities would bear the brunt of the reduction. To the annoyance of the people who thought they were running things, Baruch threw himself into the job. That May, Jacob Schiff, whose firm was banker to the reorganization proceedings, dashed off a stiff note to Baruch to remind him who was who.

> Though we have among ourselves discussed the lines of a reorganization plan very frequently, we have sought to avoid getting our ideas fixed too firmly, preferring to keep an open mind until we shall very thoroughly understand the full possibilities of the property, when properly reorganized . . . We are large bondholders ourselves, and we want to see full justice done to the holders of the 4 per cent. bonds, but at the same time we feel responsibility for the reorganization will attach vastly more to ourselves than to the individual members of the committee, except perhaps its chairman, and because of this, I am sure, you will cooperate with us in the framing of a plan which shall do credit alike to ourselves and the committee.

The committee kept an open mind for what struck Baruch as an unconscionably long time. In 1912, consultants' reports were received, inspection tours were embarked upon and improvements were effected, but no plan of reorganization was produced. Although the Pierce and Wallace committees agreed to join forces, they produced no plan in 1913. In 1914, a federal judge in Cleveland held that the traffic exchange agreements among the Terminal Company, Wheeling & Lake Erie and Wabash were in fact null and void. The Terminal Company bonds for which Baruch had paid 46, and which he may or may not still have owned, changed hands around 12. Moreover, the Wabash continued to founder. Its annual deficit, which had been cut to $376,332 in 1913, in 1914 opened to $2.7 million. The inability of the bondholders' committees to produce a reorganization plan became a small Wall Street joke, of which *The New York Times* took note in April 1914: "The reorganization plan for the Wabash Railroad, originally ready for the underwriters a year ago, and subsequently ready every few weeks, has not been materially changed now since April 1, which leads security holders to think perhaps it is in its final form."

On May 21, two years after Schiff had admonished Baruch to be patient, a plan was floated. It proposed various reductions in the railroad's capital and in the annual burden of its fixed charges. Holders of the 4 percent bonds were invited to exchange those securities for a more junior (but, it was thought, safer) type in a new Wabash; stockholders were asked to pay $20 a share in cash in exchange for new stock and a small bond. But just then the earnings of the road took a turn for the worse. On July 31, 1914, the New York Stock Exchange was indefinitely closed on account of the imminence of war in Europe. On October 15, the Wabash plan was withdrawn. The failure, Baruch and his associates hastened to note, was owing not to the war but instead to onerous taxes and to the unwise regulation of railroad rates. The *Commercial & Financial Chronicle* quoted them:

> Passenger rates have been broken down and freight rates have been held stationary or reduced in an era of rapid advance in the cost of everything entering into the requirements of a railway operation. During the last few years, one-third of the space between revenue and cost has been closed. Briefly, passengers are now carried on the Wabash RR. at the rate of one-tenth of a cent per mile less than it costs the railroad to run its passenger service; freight is carried at a revenue of only a little over one-tenth of a cent per ton mile over the cost of carrying it. Under these conditions, no increase in the volume of either class of business will offset the proportions of cost. Economies have been carried to a limit where they have become more than doubtful, and costs cannot be materially or permanently reduced. Improvement and equipment programs have been necessarily discontinued: Credit has been definitely terminated. The situation of the Wabash is not unique. Its position is in the path which all the railways of this country are following in varying stages of progress.

The committee's bleak appraisal was confirmed by the market. On January 19, 1915, the Wabash 4 percent bonds slipped to 19, their lowest price ever. Baruch, who had paid something on the order of 50 or 60 for his bonds (which he probably still owned), was sick at heart and rumored to be impaired in finances. One day at lunch, Thomas F. Ryan, who was his usual solvent self, approached him and said in a stage whisper: "You know I am with you half on that Wabash deal." In other words, if necessary, he would take half of Baruch's bonds at the price he had paid for them. It wasn't necessary, but the gesture was welcome.

Late in January, thanks to a regulatory and financial thaw, the committee got back to work again, and a final plan was presented in April 1915. In keeping with the railroad's decline, it was more austere than the first. Instead of $20 a share, stockholders were asked to pay $30. The railroad's capital was reduced by $17 million as compared to the $10 million proposed in 1914. The bondholders were assessed for cash to the extent that the stockholders refused to pay. It turned out that the toll per $1,000 bond was $654.82. The bondholders could pay, in which case they received securities in the new Wabash, or not. If not, they received the munificent sum of $33.15 per bond.

For Baruch, the plan, the talk and the years of delay constituted a personal defeat. There had been speculative huzzahs when he was elected to the bondholders' committee: the price of Wabash common had jumped by ⅝ of a point, to 7⅞. Three years later, it changed hands at 1¼. The bonds, which traded at 61 in the spring of 1912, were quoted at 29. Baruch blamed management for its "gross misrepresentation of earnings" and his fellow committeemen for their selfishness and all around bullheadedness. But the truth was that the Wabash was only one railroad wreck among scores and that the Midwest was more prolific of failure than any other part of the country. In 1907–1917 the crisis of the 1890s was replayed: 59,846 miles of railroad fell into receivership, representing invested capital of $3.7 billion, or an amount three times greater than the national debt prior to the First World War. Baruch had chosen the wrong industry, the wrong region and the wrong company. (As a generous contributor to progressive political candidates, he had helped, in a roundabout way, to foster the regulatory climate that pushed the railroads down.) It was announced in the spring of 1915 that the members of the reorganization committee would be paid for their work. Baruch, on principle, would accept nothing. Six months later, he stood at the head of a syndicate that wanted to buy a large interest in the Southern Pacific Railroad. For better or worse, he failed in this too.

As Baruch grew older, caution naturally tended to assert itself against audacity, and once, in a reflective mood, he imagined himself as a turtle. He wrote to Frank Kent how, in this transfiguration, he would climb out on a rock to sun himself and roll off into deep water at the first sign of trouble. He could stick his head out with impunity, he explained, because "no one was able to cut a turtle's head off when he stuck his neck out." Herbert Bayard Swope, after close observation, preferred the image of the elephant, and one day he elaborated on his theory to Baruch in the company of President Wilson. Baruch, he said, resembled

> . . . the Asiatic elephant, which has five toes, as against his African brother, which has only three, it being agreed that Baruch would have all the toes that nature permitted. The Baruch elephant, representing the embodiment of all animal wisdom, would be walking along a narrow path and come to a deep river, across which was thrown a flimsy bamboo bridge. First the elephant would try it with his trunk; then with his right foreleg; then with his left foreleg and, backing up to it, repeat the process with both hind legs. Having completed the inspection, the elephant, turning to his followers, would announce: "This bridge is perfectly safe and will carry my weight—but I guess I'll let some other sucker cross first!"

In the Wabash episode, Baruch had bravely bought bonds, but cautiously, or loyally, declined to break ranks with the bondholders' committee. In sulphur, he was undividedly pachydermatous. He stood for years at the bridge, testing it. Had he ventured out first, he might have become as rich as the public always imagined him to be.

In 1909 Baruch received an unexpected invitation. It came from J. P. Morgan & Company, the nonpareil Wall Street bank, and it concerned what appeared a promising sulphur deposit outside of Galveston, Texas. A proposition was put to him (Baruch by that time having made a name for himself in mine finance): he would mobilize some engineering talent; reconnoiter Bryanmound, as the site was called; make a report; and, if all went well, take 40 percent of the profits. Morgan would furnish the capital and take 60 percent of the profits. Baruch said yes, and he put in a call to Seeley W. Mudd, the mining engineer who in 1905 had staked his professional reputation on the future success of the Bingham Canyon copper mine, to ask him to go along. Mudd said yes to Baruch.

At length, the Baruch party rendezvoused in the hamlet of Brazoria, which lay within striking distance of Bryanmound. The suspected sulphur had long been confirmed to the satisfaction of a handful of local prospectors, who predicted big things from it. By day, Mudd and his assistant, Spencer Browne, conducted their own tests, and by night painstakingly analyzed the results with the implements at hand. Mudd dried cores of earth in a homely double boiler while Baruch occupied himself with a study of the world sulphur trade. Everybody slapped mosquitoes.

Despite the lack of amenities, it was an ideal time to be prospecting in Brazoria. For one thing, the demand for sulphur, a mainstay of industrial chemicals, notably of sulphuric acid, was on the rise. For another, the basic patents on the Frasch process for mining sulphur deep underground had expired in 1908. The Frasch idea was to ram a ring of concentric pipes into the ground. When sulphur was struck, superheated water was pumped down the first pipe to melt the sulphur. Compressed air was forced down a second pipe. The air pushed the molten sulphur up a third pipe. Above ground, the liquid was dried in giant yellow slabs, blocked and shipped.

The conclusion drawn by Mudd was that the chances of reaching sulphur in recoverable quantities were no better than 50–50. Back in New York, Baruch relayed this to J. P. Morgan in person. He added that the property could be bought for $500,000, of which he, Baruch, would "gamble" half.

Perhaps it was merely the word, or perhaps the way it lay on Baruch's lips. Harriman, for example, bet. Morgan did not. "I never gamble," the banker said, gesturing that their business was done. With as much dignity as the circumstances allowed, Baruch rose from his chair and left the room.

By coincidence, just about the time Baruch offered to put up $250,000 for a sulphur venture, another Texas company as capitalized in that amount. The Gulf Sulphur Company was chartered in Matagorda, near Beaumont, on December 23, 1909, under the auspices of four St. Louis men and five Texans. The application for charter stated that the company owned land situated

at or near Big Hill in Matagorda County, Texas, and comprising part of the William Simpson and Ira Ingram Leagues of land in said County; said tracts of land being, according to our best information and belief based upon repeated and successful tests; underlaid with a strata of Sul-

phur from 40 to 60 feet in depth, and which it is proposed to develop
and produce, and the cash value of which is $250,000.00, that being
the price at which it was received from J. M. Allen, one of the incorpo-
rators hereof, . . .

In the summer of 1909, before the incorporation of the Gulf Sulphur Company, word of the goings-on at Big Hill had attracted the
attention of Spencer Browne, of the Baruch party, who called to investigate. The Big Hill men, who had heard of the New York money
over at Bryanmound, were happy to see him, and he was impressed
by what he saw there. Reporting to Mudd and Baruch, Browne said
that Big Hill was at least as promising as Bryanmound, probably
more so.

Following his rebuke by Morgan, Baruch for a while did nothing in
sulphur. Early in 1911, his interest was stirred by a follow-up report on
Big Hill by Mudd, who was hopeful but cool. He called the property
unproved, but "worthy of further work." A man who thought he knew
it to be proved was Alfred C. Einstein, a St. Louis electrical engineer,
quondam prospector and an original stockholder of the Gulf Sulphur
Company. Einstein and his associates needed money, which they
thought Baruch could provide. In the spring of 1911, just as Baruch
was pouring more than $1 million into Terminal Company bonds, it
was proposed that he purchase an option on two-thirds of the stock of
an expanded Gulf Sulphur Company. He would advance $25,000 at
once to buy more land, another $25,000 for drilling and prospecting
and $100,000 for a boiler plant. For the next three years, he could buy
a controlling interest at $12 a share, making the entire outlay some-
thing in the neighborhood of $600,000. The proposal fell through.
Next, in June, Einstein wondered whether Baruch would care to buy
control of the existing Gulf Sulphur Company. There were 25,000
shares outstanding. Einstein's friends were willing to sell 17,000 shares
for $10 each for a total of $170,000. Capital necessary to begin operations, which Einstein judged to be $150,000 or so, would be furnished
by Baruch and him equally. Baruch called the proposal "entirely out of
the question."

Baruch didn't buy but he kept listening. In January 1912 Einstein offered him the same 17,000 shares on an installment plan.
Again he demurred, which exasperated Einstein. The son of a mining
engineer, Einstein was four years older than Baruch and a successful

builder and manager of utility enterprises. He was bald and wore a mustache and chain-smoked cigars. He erected electrical signs extolling the advantages of St. Louis for the benefit of incoming travelers and held office in numerous local clubs and civic organizations. "Personally and frankly speaking," he wrote Baruch, "I cannot reason out what you seem to be afraid of in this Gulf Sulphur deal. The proposition made you by my associates appeals to me as certainly most liberal, and is only brought about by certain conditions in the affairs of some of these men, which I would not feel at liberty to elaborate on in detail."

Baruch might have decided that it was foolish to negotiate with the stockholders when they were content to negotiate against themselves. In June 1912 he signed an option under which he might buy control at a fixed price for the next eighteen months. He also agreed to put up $25,000 for the purchase of land. Without exercising the option in full, he began to accumulate some stock. By 1913, he had 4,500 shares, which made him the third-largest stockholder.

As preparation for the start of production moved forward at Bryan-mound (it began in November 1913 under the aegis of the Freeport Sulphur Company), Big Hill lay fallow. For his part, Einstein wanted to mine sulphur. J. W. Harrison, J. M. Allen and Theodore F. Meyer, his fellow stockholders from St. Louis, were ready to sell. Baruch too was inclined to settle for a fast profit. Einstein was the visionary, but Baruch held the option, and prospective buyers were directed to him. Baruch found the lot of them unimpressive, as he wrote to Einstein:

> The man supposed to be from the Berlin Mills never showed up after the first call. The other man, Lattarulo, who was sent here by some lawyers, brought a lot of men around here to see me who looked like fakirs and who certainly acted like it, with whom I felt that I could have no dealings, and, in fact, they did not want to do anything except apparently use my good name to make some money for themselves. So far the inquirers who have been desirous of purchasing Matagorda have turned out to be merely fakirs.

Or commission hunters: "All these men who have been supposed to want a sulphur proposition want to get options and have the property financed for them and they want a large interest in it for standing around and looking pretty."

By the spring of 1913, the company needed money. Its technical man, Hugo Spitzer, had gone unpaid, at $150 a month, since January. There was also a watchman at Matagorda to be paid. Einstein, on his own hook, had lent about $2,500 for working capital. In the past Baruch had offered to lend such amounts as might be needed for corporate subsistence. Now Einstein asked for $3,500, which Baruch grudgingly agreed to put up: "I am willing to lend the Company $3,500 if you will send me the note properly endorsed, the understanding being that it shall be a prior claim against everything. I am doing this in order to assist you gentlemen and do not want you to take it in any way as a willingness on my part to lend further money or in any way committing me to do so." On June 7, another period of Baruch's stock option expired, unexercised. Einstein, who was losing patience with him and with Mudd, his adviser, wrote to try to stir up some action: "I am becoming more satisfied every day we are losing a splendid opportunity to bring about some most satisfactory results at Matagorda. The amount involved to a man like yourself is within the most reasonable limits for the possibilities it offers for most reasonable returns."*

The cost to bring the Big Hill into production was put between $109,000 and $240,000, the low estimate being the company's and the high one Mudd's. Hugo Spitzer said that $109,000 would pay for a steam plant and for the miscellaneous expenses of starting up a well. By his reckoning, the first pumping plant would be able to turn out 20,000 tons of sulphur a year (or 4 percent of the average annual production in the United States in 1911–1913). Even by Mudd's figures, the cost per ton delivered in New York ran to no more than $14, or $4 less than the market price.

Spitzer estimated, on the basis of exploration already carried out, that there were 750,000 tons of sulphur underground, but he correctly suspected more. By the time Big Hill was exhausted, in 1936, production had totaled 12,350,000 tons. Bryanmound had yielded only 5,000,000.

Lacking either clairvoyance or Einstein's faith, Baruch listened to Mudd, who was skeptical. (So was the International Paper Company,

---

*By June 1913, the Terminal Company bonds for which Baruch had paid about 46 were quoted at less than 15. He might have felt a poor millionaire.

which nibbled at Big Hill in 1913 but refused to bite.) Presently Baruch and the St. Louis men changed places, Baruch giving *them* an option on *his* stock. No change of ownership resulted. In St. Louis, Allen grumbled to Einstein about a clerical oversight of Baruch's and added, acidly: "I don't believe that Mr. Baruch has any thought of playing anything but a 'sure thing.'"

A year passed. At the start of 1915, ownership of the company was still distributed mainly among Baruch, Einstein, Allen, Meyer and Harrison. Einstein, hoping to move matters off dead center, wired Baruch on March 1, 1915:

WOULD YOU BE INTERESTED TO BUY OUT J. W. HARRISON GULF SULPHUR COMPANY AT PRACTICALLY HIS COST. THE OLD GENTLEMAN TALKS AS THOUGH HE NEEDS FUNDS BADLY. THINK THIS OPPORTUNITY FOR PROMPT ACTION.

Baruch answered directly:

WHAT IS PRICE.

Einstein wired:

HARRISON ASKS THIRTY-FIVE THOUSAND DOLLARS IMMEDIATE ACCEPTANCE FOR FORTY-FIVE HUNDRED SHARES AND APPROXIMATELY SIX THOUSAND BONDS. HE IS NOT SURE EXACT AMOUNT LATTER HAS A FEW LESS THAN OTHER PARTNERS. I BELIEVE TWENTY-FIVE THOUSAND CASH IN MY HANDS WILL BUY.

Baruch parried:

DO NOT CARE FOR IT MUCH OBLIGED.

Persisting, Einstein wrote to explain a few things about Harrison. He was, he said, old, sick and illiquid. He needed money and there was family trouble over his holdings in Gulf Sulphur: "I am telling you these things confidentially to give you all the side lights on my agency in the matter, which is in the interest and behalf of both Mr. Harrison and yourself and without any moti[v]e on my part for

profit." On the fourth of March, Einstein forwarded to Baruch a letter from Harrison in which the old man asked Einstein to ask Baruch
to make his best offer. Einstein asked Baruch to keep the letter under
his hat.

Called to St. Louis on some Wabash business, Baruch saw Einstein a
few days later. (He'd alerted him of his impending arrival by a commanding telegram: "PLEASE ENGAGE FOR ME PARLOR BEDROOM AND
BATH AT BEST HOTEL FOR MONDAY NIGHT . . .") The two talked over the
sulphur matter, as Einstein subsequently reported to Harrison. Baruch,
wrote Einstein, could take the stock or leave it: "Mr. Baruch said to me
frankly he was not in the market buying anything at the present time,
but if, however, you practically wanted to give your holdings away I
should make you an offer of $10,000 for your holdings." They had cost
Harrison between $25,000 and $30,000. Baruch himself would sell below cost if he were going to sell at all, which he wasn't eager to do, Einstein went on. "I do not think Mr. Baruch is very anxious either way, he
seemed to be very sincere in his discussion with me on the subject of
the purchase of your stock, and frankly told me he did not really care
[for] it, but if you desired to sell it cheap and make a sacrifice he would
gamble on it, and that's what he thought he would be doing in buying
at this time."

Even if he were as mortified as Morgan at the use of the word
"gamble," Harrison was in no position to foreclose commercial relations on account of it. On March 11, he sold 4,695 shares of stock and
$4,000 worth of bonds for a net price, after deducting odds and ends,
of $11,800. If the price of the stock alone is taken to be $10,000, the
price per share amounted to $2.13. In 1929, a share fetched as much
as $341. Baruch kept half of the Harrison interest. He sold the other
half to Einstein to show his gratitude for services rendered. Not in
funds at the moment, Einstein financed the purchase on Baruch's
credit.

Now that Harrison was out of the way, Einstein urged Baruch to
buy out Allen and Meyer. He reasoned that the way to bring Big Hill
into production was to consolidate its ownership in strong hands,
namely, Baruch's and his own. Baruch agreed, but only to the extent of
seeking an option to buy, not an outright purchase. His nonchalance in
the matter began to grate on Einstein again, and the bid that Einstein
made on Baruch's behalf to Allen and Meyer roused suspicions in them.

Reports of the mistrust reached Baruch, who answered that he would rather drop the entire affair if they felt that way.

In what had become a characteristic state of exasperation, Einstein again called for action, reassuring Baruch that his friends really didn't think he wanted to "squeeze them out," and observing that, if Baruch and he didn't buy their stock, someone else would. Why let a few thousand dollars more or less stand in the way of a good thing? He went into details on June 14, 1915:

> I recognize [he wrote Baruch] your investment in the Gulf Sulphur Company is merely an incident and that you are willing to bide your time, in the meanwhile fellows like myself who have to work for results get impatient, and frankly speaking I have about reached the point that I feel it incumbent upon myself to make an individual effort to see what I can do regardless of Mr. Mudd or your associates if you are willing to go the route with me to the extent of your holdings in which I may be able to get started. I have never really made an effort in that direction, to the contrary I have rather been the stumbling block to my associates deferring the outcome of our previous plans from time to time. I know that you have taken a "longer shot" on many other things than is involved in financing the Matagorda proposition and with possibly less hope and promise of success, and also possibly not offering an outcome as promising as that which I believe the Gulf Sulphur Company holds in store for its owners.

Still hurt by the suggestion that Meyer and Allen didn't trust him, Baruch answered that he was perfectly willing to proceed, on the right terms, and that the first step was to see that the company's bonds were converted into stock. (One cause of the Wabash's troubles was that there had been too many bonds.) In the fall of 1915 came an optimistic geological report and a recommendation that $50,000 more be spent for exploration. Baruch agreed to furnish the money and dispatched an engineer of his own to the scene. Early in 1916 he wrote Einstein in a proprietary way: "I wish you would get the financial situation of this Company straightened out and have every bondholder convert into stock, as I have suggested before. The first thing you know we will find ourselves in trouble."

Sarcastically, Einstein begged to remind him that the Gulf Sulphur Company was a corporation with bylaws, a board of directors and voting stockholders. Furthermore, Spitzer, who owned some stock, had been stranded in Vienna since the start of the war, and Allen, one of the St. Louis stockholders, was touring Hawaii. Nothing could be done without their consent. Meanwhile, Baruch redoubled his efforts to obtain the Meyer and Allen stock, which totaled 9,380 shares, or 38 percent of the 25,000 shares in existence. An option was offered, which Allen spurned by telegraph:

> NO MORE OPTIONS. IF MEYER WILLING WILL ACCEPT PROPOSITION. ALL CASH IMMEDIATE ACCEPTANCE.

Einstein answered:

> ALL CASH IMPOSSIBLE. PARTIES WILLING OPTION CONTINGENT ON RAISING CAPITAL SUFFICIENT OPERATE PROPERTY.

In the next exchange Allen gave way, offering his and Meyer's stock and bonds for $70,000, of which $30,000 was to be paid in cash. The rest of the securities would be Baruch's to buy or not in the following fifteen months for a price of $40,000. (Poor Harrison had sold for a fraction of that.)

Baruch's counteroffer was for $15,000 in cash and a two-year option. Allen declined, and Baruch raised the ante. He wired new negotiating instructions, which struck the recipient, Einstein, as peculiarly phrased:

> IN VIEW OF YOUR PERSONAL POSITION AND TO AVOID ANY COMPLICATIONS FOR YOU IN ACCORDANCE WITH RECENT OFFER OF MEYER AND ALLEN WILL AGREE TO PAY $30000 CASH FOR THREE SEVENTHS OF THEIR SECURITIES WITH AN OPTION FOR TWO YEARS ON BALANCE FOR $40000 THEY AGREEING TO CONVERT ALL INTO COMMON STOCK AS OUTLINED.

Allen and Meyer said yes, but now it was Einstein's turn to take umbrage. The "personal position" remark of Baruch's offended him. He had thought that they were partners.

Baruch now owned, or held an option to buy, the majority of stock in Gulf Sulphur Company, and he faced a conundrum. He could risk his own capital to try to bring the property into production. Alternatively, at the cost of a loss of control, he could seek outside capital. Baruch made the second choice and looked up J. P. Morgan & Company. Inasmuch as the elder Morgan was three years dead and because the firm had approached him about sulphur in the first place, it seemed the unexceptional thing to Baruch to call on the Morgans now. He talked to Henry P. Davison, a Morgan partner, who referred him to Thomas W. Lamont, another partner, who in turn called in William Boyce Thompson, a successful mining entrepreneur. Thompson, on commission, looked into the prospects at Big Hill and reported favorably. On the basis of his report, the firm agreed to buy 60 percent of the stock, which Baruch allotted at the price of $10 a share. He sold some of his own to friends and acquaintances, including Dan Jackling, John Black, Eugene Meyer and Daniel G. Reid, who was chief of the American Can Company. Presently Morgan sold to Thompson for a small profit. The sale infuriated Baruch because he thought that the stock should have been offered to him first. His outrage prompts the question of why he had sold the stock at all. The capital that had to be raised was about $500,000. In 1910, he had offered to gamble $250,000. In 1916, when the gambling element was substantially diminished, he thought nothing of throwing $3 million into the stock market in a single day on a speculative hunch. His net income that year topped $2 million (a feat duplicated by only sixty-six other Americans).

Probably the first reason for his reluctance in sulphur is that he continued to underestimate it. For another thing, he was an investor and speculator by temperament and long experience, not an operating man. Moreover, on a practical level, he had reason to believe that the Union Sulphur Company would file suit over some contested property and that the suit would stand up. (It was, in fact, lodged, and settled, in 1921, at a cost to Texas Gulf of $700,000.) There is one last, speculative hypothesis. The Morgan partners, as a class, were at the center of the establishment from which Baruch had been largely excluded. When he brought them a good thing, it was perhaps with the hope that they would come closer to accepting him as one of them. Their selling, in his eyes, was tantamount to a rejection of him.

Before he entered public service in 1917 Baruch sold such stocks as he could and patriotically invested the proceeds in Treasury bonds. ("Three and one half per cent tax free is good enough for me," he told Clarence Barron in 1918, which in normal peacetime circumstances it patently was not.) Happily, there was no ready market for his stock in the Gulf Sulphur Company, and he kept it. By the time he returned from the Paris Peace Conference in 1919, the company had changed its name to Texas Gulf Sulphur Company and had enlarged its capital to $5 million from the original $250,000. In 1919 it mined its first sulphur. In 1921, it mined one million tons and sold stock to public investors. It was just about then—while its shares were listed on the New York Stock Exchange—that Baruch began to sell.*

As Texas Gulf had issued more stock, he had occasionally bought, so that by late 1921 his holdings had grown to 61,963 shares with a market value of more than $2 million. By late 1925, he had pruned his position to 19,000 shares. Einstein, the guiding spirit of Texas Gulf, had died unexpectedly, of a heart attack, in November 1916, just after Baruch had sold to the Morgans. In November 1921, Einstein's widow, Blanch Bloom, owned 2,094 shares while Mary Boyle, Baruch's secretary, owned 10,000.

Baruch's selling coincided with a spectacular rise in the company's fortunes. In 1921 the dividend per share was $1. In 1925, it was $8.75. Between those years, the price of a share of Texas Gulf had vaulted from a low of 32⅝ to a high of 121⅞. In a self-congratulatory mood, the stockholders, in September 1926, voted to split the stock four for one, that is, to multiply everybody's holdings by four and to reduce the price per new share proportionately. Baruch read the vote as a sign that optimism had been carried too far; in the fall of 1926 he sold his last share. Although other Baruchs turned up on the stockholder rolls later in the 1920s—Herman, a director of the company since 1919, owned a good bit of it—Baruch himself stayed off.

While in he had done famously. His earnings from dividends alone were on the order of $1 million. A reasonable guess is that his profits on the sale of his stock amounted to $6 to $8 million. The campaign, his most lucrative, was until the end a characteristically cautious one. After he sold, the price of the stock continued to rise, reaching a 1929 high, on the old, pre-split basis, of $341 a share. At that ebullient instant, the company that he could have bought for $250,000 was valued in the market at $216,535,000.

---

*Baruch left the impression that his affairs were dormant during his government stint, but in fact he didn't entirely rest on his oars. In July 1918, for example, he exercised his right as a stockholder to subscribe $89,910 to a new issue of Texas Gulf common. In late 1918 and early 1919, he let it be known through his secretary, Mary Boyle, that he was unhappy with the amount of stock that was allotted him in another closely held venture, Cyprus Mines Corporation. His fellow stockholders obligingly contributed some more.

EIGHT

Poison-Pen Letter

Little by little, Baruch assimilated his money until it seemed not so much a possession as a trait, like his blue eyes. As far as he was concerned, he was an American, a southerner and a Democrat, in that order, but others saw him first as a millionaire, and it was as a rich man that he entered public life, writing checks. He warmed up with a $12,500 contribution to the Wilson campaign in 1912. In 1914, when the Administration was trying to raise $135 million to lend to cotton farmers—a bumper crop was unmarketable in Europe on account of the war—Baruch offered, if necessary, to subscribe $3.5 million. As a native South Carolinian he meant the offer sincerely but was relieved to find that it wasn't necessary after all. One of his favorite public causes was the drive to foster military and industrial preparedness for war, and he pledged $10,000 to Major General Leonard Wood one day because the general mentioned that he needed that much to finish building roads at the reserve officers' camp he was founding at Plattsburgh, New York. Out of sympathy rather than financial conviction, he subscribed to the Anglo-French war loan in the fall of 1915, held his bonds for a decent interval and sold them at a loss. In 1916 he gave $35,000 to the second Wilson campaign and another $15,000 to help meet the party's postelection deficit. After the United States entered the war, in 1917, he obliged another uprooted southerner, William G. McAdoo, the Secretary of the Treasury, by subscribing $5 million to help put the first Liberty Loan over the top.

Baruch dealt not only in money but also in the alternative political coin of favors. Once he prevailed on Charles F. Murphy, the boss of Tammany Hall, to secure a place for his friend Dick Lydon on the New York ballot as a candidate for a state judgeship. Murphy agreed, and he asked Baruch for a reciprocal good turn. A close friend of *his*, said Murphy, wanted a job in customs court, a federal bailiwick. He asked Baruch to find it for him, which, Baruch recalled, he did. Baruch was happy to oblige Colonel House, President Wilson's adviser, in another help-wanted situation. In 1914, House's brother-in-law, Sidney Edward Mezes, had his eye on the presidency of City College, which had become available the year before. Baruch, a trustee of the college, was on the board's presidential search committee, and he did what he could for Mezes, then president of the University of Texas. In November it was duly announced (not by Baruch but by the chairman of the search committee, Frederick Bellamy) that Mezes had been hired.* In 1916, when Baruch wanted to resign from the board, House asked him to stay, "on Mezes' account." By that time, William McCombs, the trustee who had led Baruch into the Wilson camp in the first place, had had a falling-out with the Administration, and House feared reprisals on Mezes. A few years later the colonel hoped that Baruch would push the board to grant Mezes a leave of absence so that he might be free to head up what became known as the "Inquiry," a secret postwar planning body. The leave, which was unpaid, was approved, although what part Baruch played in the deliberations is unrecorded.

Besides contributing money and favors, Baruch made a name for himself in politics by booming the idea of preparedness. He liked what he saw of the Wilson Administration in regulatory policy and praised the Federal Reserve System, which had just been founded, but his influence in economic matters was small. Starting in 1915 he devoted his

---

*Besides being related by marriage to House, Mezes was also a friend of David F. Houston, who had preceded him as president of the University of Texas. Houston went on to become Wilson's Secretary of Agriculture, and he praised Mezes lavishly. A historian of City College writes of Mezes' appointment: "He had been strongly recommended for the City College post by a group of influential educators [including Charles W. Eliot, president emeritus of Harvard University]. And, most important, he had powerful friends with political influence."

public energy to preparing the United States for war and especially for industrial mobilization. That summer he issued a defense dictum from the point of view of the stock trader: "The only thing that prevents a bull market is our unpreparedness. The most important thing before us financially, commercially and economically is the immediate organization of an adequate military and naval defense. . . ." Unluckily for the letter of that statement, nothing at all, least of all unpreparedness, was standing in the way of a bull market. On July 9, which was the day after his remarks appeared in the *Journal of Commerce*, the Dow Jones Industrial Average made a low that was not to be seen again for almost two and a half years. But nobody knew it at the time, least of all the editors of the New York *Call*, a socialist newspaper, who took offense at what seemed the bald connection between blood and property. "Boiled down to a few words," they wrote, concerning Baruch's *Journal of Commerce* prediction, "Mr. Baruch plainly states that capitalism is the cause of war; that if one nation gets any 'possessions,' the rest regard it as immoral and illegitimate appropriation, and will fight to replevin it. . . ." (The year before, the *Call* had taken nonideological note of Baruch in the course of reporting another accident involving his chauffeur. A sixty-seven-year-old carpenter was run down, the paper said, and Baruch himself had gone to the hospital to look in on the man and to insist that he get the best medical care available.) Undeterred, Baruch continued to call for more ships, guns and troops and also for a plan to organize industry in case of war. Returning from vacation in 1915, he laid out his ideas to McAdoo, who relayed them to the President, who in turn asked to see Baruch. An appointment was set up, and Baruch dropped in at the White House on September 8. It was his first look inside the place. According to one newspaper account, he stayed for an hour and talked about a "Businessman's Commission" that would synchronize plans for industrial mobilization. He elaborated on his ideas in a letter to House that fall, adding a proposal to raise a reserve army of college graduates.

After his meeting with Wilson, Baruch became, or appeared to become, an Administration insider, and when Hugo Spitzer, Gulf Sulphur's occasionally unpaid superintendent, was waylaid in Austria and needed diplomatic help to return to America, it naturally fell to Baruch to see what could be done for him. Whether he got action is unknown, but his colleagues at least believed him capable of it. (Einstein wrote to Allen, one Gulf Sulphur stockholder to another, "Mr. Baruch happens to be in close touch with the present administration on several matters which he mentioned to me, which I do not care to repeat in correspondence.")

Early the next spring, Baruch was campaigning again, and he wrote to House in April to press for the creation of a Mobilization Committee. His heart leaped at the reply, which was signed by President Wilson: "Mr. House has handed me your letter to him of April twenty-fourth about what I may briefly call industrial efficiency in case of need to mobilize all the resources of the nation. I remember the stimulation I received from our conversation about the matter and it has ever since been at the front of my thoughts. We are now trying to give shape to the matter and I heartily value your generous interest and cooperation." Baruch was back at the White House in June. The President and he discussed mobilization and also politics and the loyalty of certain Cabinet officers, which Baruch made brave to question. He suggested, for one thing, that Wilson get rid of his outspoken Secretary of the Navy, Josephus Daniels, and replace him with John D. Ryan, the copper man, who happened to be a friend of Baruch's. (Daniels, when asked a year later by the President what he thought of Baruch, answered that he found him "somewhat vain." According to Daniels, Wilson fired back: "Did you ever see a Jew who was not?") In August 1916 a pale copy of what Baruch and others had been urging was passed into law. A Council of National Defense, consisting of the Secretaries of War, Navy, Interior, Commerce, Labor and Agriculture, was provided to direct the home front in time of war. An Advisory Commission was established to help out the Council. Baruch read the news impassively. His main concern was a case of rheumatism, which racked him. (He was suffering on Long Island that summer. He'd been in Europe when the war broke out, in August 1914, had sailed for home in September and hadn't been back in Europe since.) On October 12, he opened a paper to read that he was a member of the Advisory Commission. The news took him aback.

His fellow commissioners comprised the van of the preparedness movement: Howard E. Coffin, an engineer who preached standardization and efficiency and who was vice president of the Hudson Motor Car Company; Dr. Hollis Godfrey, a like-minded engineer who was president of Drexel Institute; Daniel Willard, president of the Baltimore & Ohio Railroad; Julius Rosenwald, president of Sears, Roebuck & Company; Dr. Franklin H. Martin, director general of the American

College of Surgeons; and Samuel Gompers, president of the American Federation of Labor. Baruch was identified as "the New York banker." He was concerned about the euphemism and worried about what the public would think when his true speculative credentials came to light. In a self-effacing way he called on House to say that he was sorry he'd been named. In the privacy of his diary, House waspishly wondered about it too: "I doubt his sorrow as much as I doubt the wisdom of the President's making the appointment. He might have chosen a more representative business man." The response from Wilson via House to Baruch was that it was time to put up or shut up. Baruch, as he himself wrote, put up. To ensure his timely arrival at the first meeting of the Advisory Commission on December 6, he chartered a special locomotive to speed his private railway car to Washington from Hobcaw.

No sooner had Baruch tasted some of the pleasures of public life than he suffered its worst torment. All in the space of a few weeks he was attacked by rumor and by poison-pen letter and was called on to defend himself before a congressional investigating committee. In the anxiety of waiting to testify, he lost twelve pounds.

What caused the crisis of Baruch's reputation was the collapse of the bull market that had taken him by surprise in 1915. The economic consequences of the carnage in Europe smiled on America. In 1915, International Mercantile Marine Company, a shipping line, earned a profit ten times greater than the annual average of its profits in the prior decade; in 1914 it had been insolvent. In 1916 U.S. Steel Corporation earned more than it ever had before, and crude oil was quoted at $2.75 a barrel, its highest price in twenty years. The Dow Jones Industrial Average, which on July 9, 1915, made a low of 67.88, by the autumn of 1916 cleared 100.

Because the market was so high and the public so bullish, a few professional operators were nervous. Jesse Livermore sold stocks short in November. Eugene Meyer recalled that, in December, he didn't like the market and had told Baruch so. "All the women in town, at every house you went to, were talking stocks," said Harry Content. On November 21, the Dow Industrials reached what proved their apex for the time being, 110.15 (an advance of no less than 62 percent from the low of July 1915).

Inasmuch as war had been bullish, it seemed to follow that peace would be bearish, and when the German Chancellor, Theobald von

Bethmann-Hollweg, made a conciliatory speech on December 12, 1916, the market slipped. On December 19, the British Prime Minister rebuffed him, but the market declined again. Late the next day, Wednesday, December 20, a rumor circulated that the United States had addressed diplomatic notes to the warring powers. This too sounded bearish, and in the last hour of trading the decline resumed. It came out the next day that the Administration had indeed been in touch with the belligerents in a peaceful vein, but in a separate statement the State Department warned that continued violations of American neutrality had brought the United States to the brink of war. The stock market, fearing both war and peace, was beside itself. More shares of stock changed hands more frenziedly than on any day since the Northern Pacific corner of 1901. The price of Mercantile Marine, measured from its 1916 high to the December 21 low, was cut in half. Bethlehem Steel, which that year had traded as high as 700, closed at 489. ("Prices," sang a reporter on *The Wall Street Journal*, "melted away like the snows of the Pacific Northwest before the Chinook wind.") Although the bottom fell out on the twenty-first, there had been well-informed selling late the day before. To be wiped out in the ordinary way in the stock market is shattering; to be robbed is intolerable. Thomas W. Lawson, the slightly balmy writer and stock trader, crystallized public resentment when he charged that the note had been leaked and that important men had profited from it. "The good old Capitol has been wallowing in Wall Street leak graft for 40 years," he said, "wallowing hale and hearty."

The Lawson charges yielded indignation of an intense, but nonspecific, sort. He himself refused to furnish names, and although the House of Representatives passed a resolution to empower a committee to try to get to the bottom of the matter, no evidence was immediately forthcoming. Lacking facts, the members fell back on rumor, and on January 3, 1917, on the floor of the House, Representative William S. Bennet, Republican of New York, named the first suspect: "I will state . . . what the rumor is. The rumor is that Mr. Barney M. Baruch, a member of the Council of National Defense [*sic*], was the man who was responsible for this information getting to Wall Street, and that thirty minutes before the President's message was made public, he sold, on a rising market, in Steel, by the way, fifteen thousand shares of Steel common short. That is the rumor in New York if the gentleman wants names." There was a round of applause.

Presently more names were bandied, including Joseph P. Tumulty, private secretary to President Wilson; Otto H. Kahn, the Kuhn, Loeb investment banker and friend of Baruch's; and the President's brother-in-law, R. Wilmer Bolling, a Washington stockbroker. Baruch was mentioned a second time in a letter to Representative William R. Wood, an Indiana Republican, which was signed "A. Curtis," of New York.

Curtis, whoever he was, wrote as follows:

> . . . Bernard B. [*sic*] Baruch of this city unquestionably had the news of Secretary Lansing's note as early as Saturday, Dec. 9. The note was dated Dec. 11 and was not dispatched until Dec. 12. [The dates were wrong.]
>
> How Baruch got it I am not prepared to say, but a gentleman of my acquaintance makes the positive statement that he saw Mr. Tumulty and Mr. Baruch breakfasting together at the Biltmore Hotel in this city on two or three occasions coincident with the penning of the note and its secret dispatch.
>
> That Baruch at this juncture smashed the market heavily and in all directions admits of no doubt and can be easily demonstrated in this way:
>
> At his offices, 111 Broadway, he has a system of private telephone lines to various brokerage houses. Before he has an opportunity to remove these wires you must obtain a list of them. If he is compelled to supply you with a list I would check it by obtaining an identical list from the New York Telephone Company and the Western Union Telegraph Company, these being the two companies that supply the wires.
>
> Having obtained this list, you can obtain from all the brokerage houses connected thereby a transcript of all orders executed for his account within the period in question. This investigation should cover not only his personal accounts, but any secret accounts, such as accounts carried by "numbers" or any fictitious names, all of which, as the broker's books will show, are controlled by him or guaranteed by him.
>
> If the brokers refuse this information, Congress has the power to compel it. The Stock Exchange also has the power to enforce its members to produce their books and accounts, and as the rules of the Stock Exchange are sufficiently broad and elastic to cover every departure from ethics in the business methods on the part of its members, an appeal to the Governors of the institution will no

doubt elicit the desired information. Many reputable members of the exchange are anxious to assist you in running to earth this most unsavory scandal.

There is a great deal more in this than you imagine, and if you can once get your machinery in motion I am in a position to say that you will be supplied with all the necessary information. Very truly yours,

A. Curtis

After reading the letter into the record, Representative Wood blandly admitted that he hadn't the faintest idea who Curtis might be. Various Curtises denied authorship (an Allen Curtis was tracked down by a sergeant at arms in Boston on a Sunday morning and was subpoenaed to testify in Washington; he also denied responsibility). A clue suggested that the correspondent might be David Lamar, the "Wolf of Wall Street," then in an Atlanta prison, but the trail went cold. Rumor had it that Baruch's profits in the leak ran to $60 million.

Kahn and Tumulty were outraged by what had happened to them and issued denunciations of Wood. Baruch replied dispassionately, wiring *The New York Times* from Georgetown, South Carolina, on January 5: "I RECEIVED NO ADVANCE INFORMATION OR INFORMATION FROM ANY SOURCE WHATSOEVER REGARDING THE PRESIDENT'S PEACE NOTE NOR DID I HAVE LUNCH [*sic*] OR CONFER WITH MR. TUMULTY AT THE BILTMORE OR AT ANY OTHER PLACE."

Baruch was new to public obloquy, knew that he spoke badly and was frightened by the prospect of a congressional interrogation. Talking it over with Meyer in New York, he mentioned that he was going to retain a lawyer, former U.S. Senator John C. Spooner. Meyer asked him to think twice about it, because Spooner had political influence that an innocent man wouldn't need. (Apparently he wasn't retained.) Meyer made another suggestion. He said that when Baruch was asked the inevitable question about what he did for a living, he should tell the simple truth: "Tell them you're a speculator; that you buy them if you like them and sell them if you don't like them. It doesn't matter whether you [don't] have them when you sell them, and buy them later, or whether you buy them first and sell them later."

When the time came to testify, on January 9 in Washington, Baruch felt haggard from insomnia and loss of weight. His enemies were happy to believe the worst about him, and there was a depressing failure to rally around him by his friends. As Baruch took the stand, the chairman of the

House Rules Committee, Representative Robert L. Henry, of Texas, asked him to state his name, address and occupation. Meyer, who was in the gallery providing moral support, at Baruch's request, held his breath.

"Bernard M. Baruch; my business address 111 Broadway; occupation, investor and speculator. Anything further?" The word "speculator," which to some implied an outright confession of guilt, caused a stir.*

Baruch answered questions without rancor or sarcasm. He testified about his trading at the time of the alleged leak, filling in such details as he could from memory. He made a mild statement denying the gossip about him and said that he didn't know who "A. Curtis" was. Presently the committee steered the conversation to his $50,000 campaign contribution, which prompted some banter with a Republican congressman:

"Our party would be almost willing to adopt him if he promised to keep up his gait of subscription."

"You have got some pretty good givers in your party," said Baruch.

"But the more the merrier."

In response to questions Baruch provided some details about his office paraphernalia. He said that he kept two Dow Jones tickers, one for stock prices and the other for news, and had a number of direct telephone lines to brokerage houses. In that last detail, the "Curtis" letter was correct. (What didn't come out was that the walls of his office were lined with pictures of himself aboard motorboats.) He said that he hadn't executed an order on the Exchange in "a great many years." He testified that he did no brokerage business and did not buy stocks on margin.

He reported that he kept his money in five banks, of which his favorites were the Central Trust and the Guaranty Trust. He had five principal brokers—Fred Edey & Company, Lansburg Brothers, A. A. Housman & Company, Baruch Brothers and H. Content & Company.

"They are licensed brokers, are they?" a congressman asked.

"So they say," Baruch said dryly.

---

*But the word was common enough. In 1916 more taxpayers designated themselves "capitalists: investors and speculators" than any other occupation listed on the income-tax form. In all, 437,036 returns were received by the Internal Revenue Service that year; about 20 percent, or 85,465, were filed by capitalists; fewer than 1 percent, or 2,992, were filed by civil servants. Capitalists accounted for 32 percent of the income-tax take; "dealers and merchants," the next most forthcoming occupational group, provided only 12 percent.

Short selling was in bad odor at the time, not only in Washington but also among the more high-minded type of financier in New York. For his part, Baruch said that he saw nothing wrong with it, and he disagreed with a suggestion of Henry's that it ought to be abolished.

"On the contrary, Mr. Chairman, I believe that if you had a market without short selling, that when the break comes—of course, trees do not grow to heaven overnight—and when securities go up as we see them, and when they start to fall down there might be a crash that would engulf the whole structure, and there is also this, if I may add, that the short seller is the greatest critic of the optimist, who continually calls the attention of the man who is long on securities or the individual who might become long, of the defects, you might say, of these securities, and you might in that way keep people from buying securities at extraordinary high prices."

On another regulatory digression, Henry proposed that every buyer and seller of stock be required to divulge his name along with pertinent financial data in order to discourage the gambling interest. He amended the idea with a deferential "perhaps you may be right, and I may be wrong," to which Baruch cordially replied, "You may be right, and I may be wrong." Several courteous minutes later, Baruch was excused. He was recalled to testify at the end of the month.

Lawson, meanwhile, who had started it all, provided a raft of names, including Paul Warburg, a governor of the Federal Reserve Board; Treasury Secretary McAdoo; and Malcolm McAdoo, the secretary's brother, who said that he hoped the secretary would punch Lawson in the head. The proceedings took on the lunatic gaiety that was Lawson's imprimatur, and when Baruch returned to testify on January 30, he had a lighter heart. On instructions, he brought an audited record of his trading in the days preceding publication of the President's note.

To begin with, on the second appearance, the committee was curious about where Baruch got his financial information.

The committee's counsel, Sherman L. Whipple, asked: "Did you have anything besides the ticker service?"

"No, sir."

"Did you have any representative in Washington?"

"No, sir."

"As to your personal habits of conducting your operations, did you carry them on from your office or by telegraph?"

Baruch had trouble hearing. "Yes, sir."

"Did you avail yourself of means of information that might be in the brokers' offices whom you used?"

"No; I do not pay attention to information that comes [*sic*]."

"I did not quite catch that."

"I say that I do not pay any attention to rumors."

So much for the master speculator's estimate of brokerage-house research. Whipple, consulting the trading records, noted that Baruch had bought 5,000 shares of U.S. Steel on December 11, which was the day before the German Chancellor had mentioned peace. He sold them on December 12 at a loss.

"I know I bought them at 23 and a fraction [meaning 123 and a fraction], and I remember that when I gave the order [to sell] on the tape they were 20½, and I got 19 and a fraction. I have a very distinct recollection of that." In other words Baruch expected to get a higher price than the one his broker got. In an aside he ruefully said his name: "Content."

"That was a loss for that day's operations?"

"Yes, sir. Sometimes it happens that way."

"I am very sorry to bring out that shameful fact, Mr. Baruch, because the world believes you never made a loss."

"That is the only annoying thing about this investigation," said the witness, enjoying himself.

The Chancellor's speech led Baruch to sell his Steel and also Ray Copper, Chile Copper and Cuba Cane Sugar preferred. He testified that he was negotiating to buy a block of railroad securities when he got wind of the speech, and that he broke off talks at once. (He owned no munitions stocks, or "war brides," because he didn't want to run the risk of compromising his position as a spokesman for preparedness.)

At the time the only stock of which he was short—stock he had sold first with the expectation of buying later on, at a lower price—was Canadian Pacific.

"I am speaking of December 12," said Whipple.

"Yes; I was short of that all the time."*

On the twelfth, Baruch sold what he already owned. On Wednes-

---

*What Baruch apparently meant was that he was short of Canadian Pacific during that period. But it was an ambiguous remark, and at least one publication construed it to mean that he was perennially short of the stock. James Warburg, son of the Federal Reserve member, seized on that interpretation, or on a similar one, as evidence of Baruch's financial recklessness.

day, December 13, he sold what he didn't own—23,400 shares of United States Steel Corporation, almost $3 million worth. To put that transaction in perspective, Baruch accounted for 6 percent of the day's trading in Steel and 1 percent of the overall activity on the New York Stock Exchange. He would have sold that on Tuesday too, he explained, but he was out of the office most of the day. He elaborated for the committee:

"But then, when I read of the von Bethmann-Hollweg peace note, so called, to the Reichstag, which was given to the world, and which was, after the greatest war in civilization, a declaration of peace—at least, to my mind—and I think history will record it so, I realized what that meant to all of the great countries, particularly in connection with business and finance, and I realized, or thought, and I do realize still, that people's minds which heretofore had been bent on nothing but war would think of peace, because this was a declaration of peace, and that people would think about what would come with peace, and I thought it would be reflected in our business, trade and financial conditions, and my mind worked to a conclusion that made me believe that men of intelligence ought to act quickly and sell securities."

Something else led him to sell, he said. The Japanese had taken steps to close their stock exchange on news of the German initiative, and there were no "cleverer" people in the world that the Japanese. They had seen peace coming. He added, sorrowfully, that they weren't allowed to sell short in Japan. The dolorous note in his voice raised a laugh.

On Thursday, December 14, he sold another 1,600 shares of Steel short, which brought his line up to 25,000 shares. He had sold at prices of around 119 a share. On Friday, the fifteenth, he began to "cover," that is, to buy back what he had already sold in order to complete the transaction. He bought 14,000 shares at about 110, which netted him something on the order of $126,000. He had been wrong on history but right on the market.

The opening of business on Monday, December 18, found him short of 11,000 shares of Steel. He sold several thousand shares more that day, but he did so as prices were rising, which took some nerve. Whipple asked him why he did it.

"Because," said Baruch, "I wanted to hear the next great thing, and that was the Lloyd George speech; and I felt that his reply would be just about what he did say."

Some of the speech crossed the ticker about noon on Tuesday. Baruch remembered standing in his office, watching the words print.

". . . the first part was just as anyone might have expected, that Lloyd George was not going to listen to peace, and England would not consider it under any conditions, and so on. As the market went up I sold some stock. I kept watching the ticker all the time, and as the message came out, I can see the break in the ticker now—'But he leaves the door open for peace.' I was standing at the ticker, and as soon as I came out I sold stock just as tight and hard and fast as I could."

By the end of the day he was short of another 28,400 shares, raising his short position to 43,400 shares, or some $4.7 million worth. Again Baruch was asked whether he had received any advance word on developments in Washington. None, he said, and submitted as proof his next market move, which was to buy 17,900 shares on Wednesday, December 20. This was the day before the Administration's peace note smashed the market.

"It was a very unfortunate judgment . . . ," Baruch said. "A man who would have known [of the forthcoming note] would have sold all day long. He would not have stopped from 10 o'clock to 3."

On December 21, the day of the collapse, Baruch said that he had covered the rest of his short sales, and bought some other stocks to boot. The low price of Steel was 100 and change, but he said that he hadn't gotten it. "I never get [in at] the bottom or out at the top."

Baruch by now had taken charge of the hearing, and he wondered whether the committee would like to know what he'd bought.

"I do not think the committee would be interested unless—at least nothing occurs to me," said Whipple. "There is no reason for stating them . . . But you did buy other stock?"

"Yes, sir. When the market is very weak I want to buy things which I believe in the most from their intrinsic standpoint, and when the market goes down I try to sell those things which I think will have the least intrinsic merit, or if their technical position is the least valuable as to trading possibilities of any other security."

Whipple, stumbling over a question he had on short selling, marveled at the complexity of that maneuver.

"It is such a simple transaction," said Baruch.

More or less convinced of his innocence, the committee began to satisfy its curiosity.

"Was this a large transaction for you?"

"I have done larger ones."

"So you would speak of it as a major operation but not the largest that you have ever dealt in?"

"It is a pretty fair-sized one; but I have done—do I have to tell here what I have done before?"

"Oh, no."

"If you ask me the question I will answer it."

"The committee will not press it. They appreciate the intrusion into your private affairs."

"I appreciate that, but I am willing to answer every question."

"We are dealing with a public necessity in a private way."

"I will say that I have often been short of this amount of Steel."

"Often?"

"Yes, sir. I have been short a good many times a good many shares of stock, but you see there was only one kind that you could express your activity in and only one that you could get out of." In other words, the market in U.S. Steel provided him the greatest latitude for buying and selling.

There was one more question on everybody's mind, and Whipple respectfully backed into it.

"I do not know whether the committee would think the amount of that profit is material, even if you felt disposed to give it, but it occurs to me that, in certain aspects, and perhaps in an examination of gentlemen alike who did profit by these transactions the question should be put."

Baruch had no objection. He said: $476,168.47. (Jesse Livermore supposedly earned twice as much.)

Before the questioning closed, the committee double back to something that Baruch had mentioned earlier. He had testified that he did, indeed, call two Washington officials, Warburg and McAdoo, but that his calls had nothing to do with the stock market or a peace note. He said that he was passing on a recommendation for a man to fill a directorship at the Federal Reserve Bank of New York. Now the committee asked who had suggested that he telephone.

"Mr. E. M. House," he said, smiling.

The witness exited in triumph and awoke, on the morning of February 1, to an editorial about his work in The New York Times. It was headed: "He needed no Tips or Leaks."

The villain of the peace-note affair turned out also to be its victim.

He was William W. Price, an affable, overweight golf-playing columnist for the Washington *Evening Star*. A pioneer White House correspondent who began hanging around the presidential quarters in the second Cleveland Administration, Price had taken a sideline job as a correspondent for a couple of Chicago brokerage houses at $25 a month. At 11 A.M. on the day the rumors flew in Wall Street, the Washington press corps had been briefed on the American note by the Secretary of State, Robert Lansing, but was held to secrecy until midnight. Price hadn't been present at the briefing, but had heard of the communiqué and had flashed the news to Chicago. (J. Fred Essary, a reporter for the Baltimore *Sun*, had similarly notified E. F. Hutton in New York.) The congressional investigating committee received Price's name in heartbreaking circumstances. A young daughter of his had discovered some unexpected entries in his bankbook and had snitched to a woman who had passed on the information to Lawson. On the witness stand Price said miserably, ". . . The *Star*, a great paper, may misunderstand what I regard as a mere private side matter." It isn't known what the *Star* made of it, but Price, the same year, took a job on the Washington *Times*.

As for Baruch, when he was publicly charged, he had resolved, first, to clear his name, and, second, to have nothing more to do with politics or politicians. So brilliantly did he succeed in the first resolution that he decided to ignore the second.

NINE

Captain of Industry

Just as Baruch reached his financial maturity in the McKinley bull market, so he hit his political stride in the First World War. In both cases his timing was impeccable. In the first instance, he owned stocks in a rising market. In the second, he was present at the creation of the twentieth-century American state.

Having made a fortune in Wall Street under a system of low taxes and limited government, Baruch entered public life to help install a regime of relatively high taxes and intrusive government. When he arrived in Washington the public debt was less than $3 billion, personal income-tax rates were trifling and national economic planning was alien to American experience. On his departure, in 1919, the public debt totaled $25 billion, tax rates in the top bracket had climbed by more than tenfold to 73 percent and federal control of economic life was a firmly established precedent.

War is a dragooning proposition, and in America, as in other belligerent powers, the divergence between the professed liberal aims of the fight and its workaday conduct was ironically wide. In the name of liberty, the United States government conscripted troops, censored the mails, took over the railroads and telegraph lines and fixed the price of wheat. A sign of the times was a questionnaire that arrived in the mail one day at the home of Baruch's father from the *Chronicle Magazine*.

The magazine asked Dr. Baruch whether, as a German immigrant, he would be willing to pledge his allegiance to his adopted country. If not, the editors wanted him to know that his response, or lack of one, would be forwarded to the Justice Department for appropriate action. Dr. Baruch dutifully reaffirmed his loyalty, and his wife, in conversation, began to disown her parental bloodline altogether. "There's not a drop of German blood in my body," she would say, drawing herself up straight. (President Wilson, ignoring genealogy, had a basket of huge chrysanthemums sent to the Baruchs on their fiftieth wedding anniversary in November 1917.) The nation's obsession with the loyalty of immigrants, aliens and political eccentrics led to the formation of a Committee on Public Information, a federal body staffed with leading progressive journalists, which sought to elicit the name of "the man who spreads pessimistic stories . . . , cries for peace or belittles our efforts to win the war."

If it was odd that writers signed on in an agency to control free speech, it was no more or less curious that Baruch, an investor and speculator, should help to suppress free markets. He did so, full time, early in 1917, devoting himself to the transformation of capitalism into a kind of war socialism. This experience he called the greatest of his life.

After his brush with the peace-note leak investigation, Baruch sold his seat on the New York Stock Exchange and most of his common stock (with the exception of his Gulf Sulphur, Alaska Juneau, Cyprus Mines and Atiola, a tungsten mine, the shares of which were unmarketable), and left instructions with Miss Boyle to contribute his residual dividend income to the Red Cross. By this time, his fortune had reached about $10 million, and he invested some three quarters of it in Liberty Bonds. He proceeded to Washington without Annie and the children and took rooms at the Shoreham Hotel. His first job was chairman of the raw materials and minerals committee of the Advisory Commission of the Council of National Defense.

Washington in 1917 was still a small town, and Baruch, who was usually the tallest and best-looking and richest man in any company in which he happened to find himself, naturally made a self-assured raw materials chairman. Unbureaucratically, his first step was to try to organize the commodities side of the defense effort along the lines of supply and demand. The supply side comprised the miners and producers, many of whom Baruch knew personally, and whom he set up in advisory committees, from aluminum to zinc. On the demand side were the various government agencies, which proved harder to organize. As far as the thing could be done, Baruch thus lined up supply to meet the government's vast emergency demand.

In peacetime, supply and demand met automatically, at a price, but in wartime it was Baruch's idea that prices should be controlled in order to reduce civilian hardship and to deprive businessmen of an undeserved profit. The Administration reasoned that if soldiers and sailors were sacrificing their lives, businessmen ought at least to relinquish their dividends. That argument, however, failed to meet the objection that prices convey information, and that the distortion of economic information through price control sows mischief just as the twisting of political and military information does via censorship. Although no comprehensive price and profit controls were installed in World War I, the government inveighed and coerced under a system that Eugene Meyer, Jr., aptly called the "involuntary voluntary" method.

A case study in that technique was described by Baruch in his autobiography. He was, he wrote, attending a White House reception when a military aide approached, saluted and informed him that the President would like to have a word with him. Baruch, wondering what he had done wrong, followed the officer to the President. As the aide saluted again and withdrew, Wilson proceeded to describe a special assignment that he wanted Baruch to tackle. It seemed that a private syndicate had purchased some Austrian ships with the idea of selling them to the United States government in the event of war. The syndicate, perhaps not unreasonably, expected a profit for its trouble—after all, it was risking its capital to conserve scarce vessels until such time as they would be needed most, and if there weren't a war, it stood to lose money—but the element of gain in the matter offended Wilson. Attempts to frustrate the syndicate had so far proved unsuccessful. Now, he told Baruch, "You use all the influence you think the President has, but get those ships." If Baruch savored the irony of one speculator being sent to foil others, he failed to record it. His account continues:

> It was 9:58 P.M. when I left the White House. Arriving at the Shoreham . . . , I began telephoning the people who owned those Austrian

ships. One was in Washington, the others in New York. I roused several of them out of bed that night, and managed to impress upon them the determination of the government to have the ships without profit to the syndicate. I made them see how unwise it would be to oppose the President in this affair.

Next morning I called the President. I had my watch in my hand as the White House phone rang. It was 8:58, eleven hours to the minute since I had left there, when I got Mr. Wilson on the wire. I informed him I had the Austrian ships, without profit to anyone. He was surprised, and complimented me on accomplishing a difficult task with such dispatch.

Although he was out of practice at taking instructions, Baruch turned out to be an ideal subordinate. For one thing, he was irrepressibly cheerful, and the bureaucratic setbacks that would have gnawed at a brooding man—for instance, the loss of coal from his raw materials domain to a separate Coal Administration in 1917—failed to defeat him. (On such occasions, Baruch was prone to quote Bob Fitzsimmons to the effect that a champion has to be able to take it in order to dish it out.) For another, he had a drive for action. Mark Sullivan, the journalist, wrote about this side of Baruch to a friend in the spring of 1917:

> He is always ready to compromise, or change the program, or do something different—only get *something* done. He is a nice fellow, a little naïve, a little overeager, but not at all offending. . . . He is quite on fire with what he is doing, and is so fertile in initiative and so energetic that he is likely to go a long way. It would be a useful thing for his friends to surround him with half a dozen very methodical private secretaries to follow him around and tie up the loose ends, for he is essentially a dashing mind and plunges at it; . . . This very boyish up-and-comingness of his, the obvious pleasure he has in his new game, serves to disarm opposition.

In time one young man, Edward Corcoran, was hired to do the work of the half dozen that Sullivan proposed. Sometimes a document turned up missing at the office—Baruch at first kept no files—and Corcoran would be dispatched to the Shoreham to search the pockets of his boss's suits. Although Baruch suffered the usual drawbacks of being a

Jew from Wall Street, his money was a compensating advantage. When, for example, the Advisory Commission was denied public funds with which to set up offices, Baruch himself rented a floor of the Munsey Building, instructing his secretary that if complications arose to buy the building whole.

One reason that the government was reluctant to furnish space for the Commission was that nobody was exactly sure what it was supposed to do. Its charge was to advise the Army and the Navy in purchasing decisions, to keep watch over business and to help synchronize mobilization. But business was used to free markets, and the Army, which sorely needed advice, was loath to take it from civilians. (The Army supply service, declared General Hugh S. Johnson, who had been a part of it, "was just a cluster of jealous and ancient bureaus.") The Advisory Commission did produce some organizational results—it successfully threw its influence behind the formation of the Shipping Board, Emergency Fleet Corporation and Food Administration, for instance—but industrially speaking it counted for little.

To Baruch this was an unsatisfactory state of affairs, and as early as May 1917 he tried to convince the President of the need to appoint one man to head up an efficient supply bureau. It turned out that the man was Baruch and the bureau was the War Industries Board, but it was in the financial side of things that the future of the home front turned, in which department Baruch, his Wall Street credentials notwithstanding, had little to say.

It developed that the Administration's plan was to raise politically expedient sums in taxes, to inflate the money supply as necessary and to mask the effects of inflation through selective price controls. Broadly speaking, the work of suppressing inflation was given to the War Industries Board. It fell to the new Federal Reserve Board, to the Treasury Department and personally to William G. McAdoo, the Secretary of the Treasury and chairman of the Board, to inflate. The irony of that arrangement was that it was also McAdoo who was instrumental in getting Baruch his job in the anti-inflationary side of the government. Thus the two allies worked cordially at cross-purposes.

Of the two officials, McAdoo had the easier time of it, because inflation had become a tidal force. In 1916, when gold poured into New York in payment for Allied arms and matériel, wholesale prices jumped by no less than 37 percent. After the start of hostilities, the Treasury ran enormous deficits which it borrowed to cover. In fiscal years 1918 and 1919 it spent some $43 million a day, more than any other warring power and enough (as the War Department subsequently observed) to have financed the Revolutionary War for a thousand years at eighteenth-century prices. Part of this money was raised by noninflationary means—via taxation and borrowing from people's savings—but another part the Federal Reserve printed. Thus from 1917 to 1920, the level of credit created by the Federal Reserve grew by $3 billion, to a level unseen again until the 1930s. Whether a given increase in the money supply is inflationary depends on the rigor of business, just as whether a given number of calories is fattening depends on the metabolism of the diner. In the case of America in World War I, the extra money was, on the face of it, inflationary, because civilian production fell. Inasmuch as people had more money to spend on fewer things, the cost of living went up. Thus retail prices, which had risen by 17 percent in 1916, rose by 17 percent again in 1917 and by 15 percent in 1918. Probably the moderation in the rate of rise owed something to the WIB's informal price controls, as did the reduction in the rate of gain in wholesale prices to 12 percent in 1917 and 6 percent in 1918 (from the astronomical 37 percent of 1916). But after controls were relaxed, prices climbed all over again.*

---

*By the close of the war, the War Industries Board (of which Baruch was then in command) was reduced to exhorting the nation at large to bring down the cost of living. Thus a proclamation dated August 1, 1918:

Whereas the high cost of living is daily increasing, which is causing great hardships on the working man and his family and the public generally; and

Whereas the abnormal prices charged the consumer for common necessities is creating a condition that is arousing a spirit of unrest and dissatisfaction which tends to demoralize the unity, harmony and confidence of the public; and

Whereas there is grave danger of continued unrest and labor disturbances which greatly interferes with the National War Program; and

Whereas the determining factor in the winning of the war is that public confidence must be firmly established so that the fullest cooperation be obtained and maintained in support of the national policies: Therefore be it

Resolved by the War Industries Board, That we strongly urge that the prices of commodities be fixed at a fair rate to the consumer, and plans for this purpose will be made to carry out at once the aims and purposes of this resolution.

For reasons more closely related to Baruch's arrival in Washington than to his departure from Wall Street, financial markets suffered a sinking spell in early 1917. Interest rates on long-term, high-grade bonds, for instance, rose from about 4 percent in January to 5 percent in October. It followed that the prices of existing bonds, including the ones that Baruch had just bought, fell. (When Charles G. Dawes, chairman of the Liberty Loan Drive, was informed that some people thought the 4 percent interest rate on Liberty Bonds skimpy, he suggested: "Anybody who declines to subscribe for that reason, knock him down.") That much was only to be expected, since inflation from time immemorial has caused higher interest rates. What was puzzling was the action in stocks. By late 1917, the market was just about where it had been on July 30, 1914, when the New York Stock Exchange was closed against waves of European selling. "Easy money, and industrial activity wholly unparalleled in the country's history," wrote Alexander Dana Noyes, *The New York Times*'s learned financial editor, "were accompanied by financial markets such as in other days would have indicated financial panic."

One cause of the bear market in stocks was the new bull market in government. Although the regulation of business was nothing new, the reach of government was extended in the war, and investors were struck not so much by the volume of trade (so great was the volume and so uncoordinated were the federal agencies that eastern rail traffic by late 1917 was almost at a standstill) as by the way it was being taxed and constricted.

The natural retort to critics was that there was a war on, but after the Armistice the debate was joined, and after the next war, an economist offered a novel alternative to the then customary regime of wartime controls. Ludwig von Mises, a professor of the Austrian school, prescribed a first step of financing as much of the cost of a war as possible out of taxes, thereby reducing civilian consumption and expanding the purchasing power of the Army and the Navy. Since incomes would suffer and the demand for civilian goods would decline, businessmen would spontaneously converge on the growth market of armaments. Baruch had always said that voluntary conversion would be too slow. Von Mises countered that if prices were allowed to run their course, sizable profits would accrue to the firms that converted fastest. For that reason, he maintained, conversion would be lightning fast, and production would soar. Because business would be governed by market forces, no government planning apparatus would have to be built (except to ensure that the government itself knew what it wanted), and if the war were financed by savings and taxes, there would be little or no inflation. The Wilson Administration, however, objecting to the principle of profit in wartime, was led to intervene heavily in the market, deciding (when it could decide) how much ought to be produced, by whom and at what price.

It did so in 1917 in the most basic battlefield commodity, gunpowder. E. I. du Pont de Nemours & Company, the world's leading explosives manufacturer, had been selling to Allied governments at an enormous profit, and in 1916 (while Baruch was still in Wall Street) a munitions tax was passed to recoup some of the windfall for the Treasury. The company condemned the tax as discriminatory and ex post facto, but it nonetheless managed to report a 1916 profit of $82 million, a sum more than three times its gross *sales* in 1914. If the war enriched Du Pont, however, it also worried its management, and as early as 1916 the company petitioned the government for permission to build a hydroelectric plant for the recovery of nitrogen from the air at Muscle Shoals, along the Tennessee River. Nitrogen yields nitrates, which form the basis of explosives and fertilizer. America imported its nitrates from Chile, but the success of German submarines led Du Pont to plan for alternate domestic sources of supply. The atmospheric recovery technique, on which it held patents, required waterpower, a commodity made scarce by federal conservation policy. Hence the company's request of the Administration to build at Muscle Shoals. Congress not only refused, but it also authorized construction of a government-owned nitrogen-from-air works in the same location. Just then Secretary of the Navy Daniels also underscored the importance of public gunpowder plants to compete with private manufacturers, meaning, chiefly, Du Pont.

All this Du Pont baiting preceded the war. After U.S. belligerency, the government was slow to decide how much powder it needed, or how soon. By July 1917 the sum total of contracts let by the Army and Navy to Du Pont was 123 million pounds, an order that could be comfortably filled with the factory capacity already built. But in the fall, following drastic upward revisions of American powder requirements, negotiations were begun with Du Pont for a gearing up of production.

Talks proceeded smoothly, and on October 25 the biggest government contract in American history up until then was signed by the company and by Major General William Crozier, Army chief of ordnance. The contract stipulated a doubling of Du Pont smokeless-powder capacity at a cost of $90 million and an initial order of 450 million pounds of explosives at a cost of about $155 million. The taxpayers would bear all construction costs; Du Pont would earn a building commission, a 5-cent fee on each pound of powder produced and an extra incentive for low-cost production.

Baruch's recollection of General Crozier was of a brilliant but slightly frayed-around-the-edges officer—"Many was the night I sat with him in the War Department, working on production requirement schedules while his wife sat knitting in a corner." The general, in the beginning, hardly thought of Baruch or the War Industries Board at all, and the Board was, indeed, forgettable. It had been formed in July to succeed the Advisory Commission, but its powers, too, were wholly advisory, and its first chairman, Frank Scott, had already resigned in ill health and frustration. Nonetheless, its Committee on Explosives investigated the contract, found fault with it and passed on its criticisms to the Secretary of War, Newton D. Baker. By background and temperament, Baker was inclined to side with Du Pont's critics. As the city solicitor of Cleveland, he had supported the municipal ownership of streetcar lines; and as mayor, the municipal ownership of utilities. In Washington he shared the Wilsonian animus against Du Pont's profits on Allied business, and he was sympathetic to the idea of government-owned munitions plants. Crozier had submitted the contract expecting routine approval, but on October 31 Baker wired instructions to cancel it.

The veto—pending a review of the facts, the Secretary said—started a commotion. The War Industries Board, in particular Robert Brookings, the chief price controller, and Baruch, raw-materials chairman, marshaled points against the contract, while Crozier and Pierre S. du Pont, president of the company, defended it. For the defense it was argued that Du Pont bore substantial costs and risks and that the profit figures under discussion were overstated. Brookings, for the WIB, maintained that the company would gain unconscionably in powder manufacturing. (Once he made a revealing confession: "[I] would rather pay a dollar a pound for powder for the United States in a state of war if there was no profit in it than pay the Du Pont Company 50 cents a pound for powder if they had 10 cents' profit in it," he said.)

Although Baker, for one, and Baruch, for another, were prepared (in Baker's words) to "win this war without Du Pont," if it came to that, Daniel Willard, the current WIB chairman, wasn't so sure. A compromise proposal of his was presented to Pierre du Pont by Baker (who added that, if he had his way, the company would be out of the running altogether); it was relayed to the board and was rejected. There was another counterproposal, this time from the company, but it too got nowhere. Baker's view, which Baruch shared, was that the government should somehow do the work itself. Baruch said that he happened to know just the man to get it done, his mining-engineer friend Daniel Jackling. Calling the candidate long-distance at his suite at the St. Francis Hotel in San Francisco, Baruch said: "I do not know whether they will accept you, but I would like to have you come anyhow." Jackling came to Washington, and when Baker, a few days later, asked Baruch to bring his man in, Baruch could say that he was already there. Jackling got the job.

All that remained was for him to get it done, building a plant, or plants, to produce one million pounds of powder a day without the help of the world's chief explosives manufacturer. When Thompson-Starrett Company, a construction firm that Baker had earlier approached about the work, informed Jackling that it could manage, at best, one half of what he had in mind and even then would require Du Pont's advice, the government's man called on Pierre du Pont; du Pont agreed to help. But Jackling was still in need of a contractor for the other half of the project. Since there was no more logical choice than Du Pont, Jackling asked Baker whether he might not reopen talks with Pierre.

In the months following the cancellation of the original contract, conditions on the home front had deteriorated. There were shortages of ships, coal, railcars, uniforms, small arms and cannon. The coldest and snowiest winter in years froze underclad troops at hastily built wooden camps. In Congress, an investigation was under way into the conduct of the war, and there were appeals for either the creation of a Cabinet-level munitions post to supplant the Secretary of War in the matériel department, the Secretary's head, or both. In the circumstances, Baker had warmed to Du Pont, and the company, reasoning that it would be blamed by the public for a shortage of powder, whether or not it was at fault, decided to let bygones be bygones. A new contract, specifying a tiny construction profit and a commission of 3½ cents a pound of powder, down from a nickel, was signed, and ground for the plant was broken near Nashville, Tennessee, in January 1918, nine months after the declaration of war.

Baruch's advice to Jackling, when he took the powder job, was to stay out of uniform to preserve his freedom of action. But the Du Pont men at the Nashville site, who were also in mufti, found that their freedom of action was being drastically curtailed by Jackling. To start with, the company was told that each man on the job would be treated as a government employee, ". . . subject to all rules and regulations relating to government employees." For another thing, federal agents controlled purchasing decisions and plant design down to such details as the size of steel rails. In an attempt to lift the bureaucratic fog, Pierre du Pont made an offer. Instead of building another plant, as the government asked him to do in March, he proposed that the size of the Tennessee job be expanded. This he offered to do for the sum of $1 if the government would relieve the firm of financial risk and only let it alone. A deal was struck, and in the absence of federal hovering, the foreman reported, "Things began to 'hum.'" By the Armistice, the job was ahead of schedule and the plant had produced 35 million pounds of cannon powder. All told the cost of the work was $129,535,000, for which Du Pont earned the nominal after-tax, all-in profit of $439,000. In this sense—in the satisfactory narrowing between what Du Pont had wanted and what it got—Baruch and his colleagues had won, yet just as clearly the taxpayers had lost. The Thompson-Starrett Company had produced no powder at all, but spent (on the basis of comparative unit costs) some $13.5 million more than Du Pont would have needed for the same work. On the basis of the numbers, the war effort would probably have been better served if the original Army–Du Pont contract had been allowed to stand; that is, if Baruch and the War Industries Board had never become involved.

A day in the life of the chairman of the raw-materials committee of the War Industries Board, as revealed in an office memorandum to Baruch dated February 11, 1918:

Call Colonel McRoberts.

Did you receive an invitation for Dancing Class at the Willard this evening? If not, they would like very much to have you drop in.

Henry Mayer, who came down on the train with you yesterday, would like your assistance in making an appointment with the Secretary of War to take up the subject of a client's contract on the Panama Canal.

Mr. Hibbs phoned to say that Mr. Norwalk, with a letter of introduction to you from Mr. Jake Field, was at his office and would like to know what hour he might call you for an interview. Telephone: M. 545.

Mr. Brand phoned that you said you would see him at any hour he named this afternoon; he stated he would be here at 3 o'clock.

Baruch was chairman of the War Industries Board for the last eight months of the war but labored in the relative obscurity of the commodities and raw-materials committee of the Board and of its predecessor agencies for a full year before that. It was a frustrating apprenticeship, because he was full of advice that wasn't taken, and of plans that weren't followed. Despite his harping on the lack of nitrate of soda, for example, the shortage was allowed to become chronic, and except for some deft work by him it might have become critical. (Not until December 17, 1917, did the WIB get around to withholding licenses for the manufacture of nonmilitary fireworks.) Once, he wrote, he was close to despair over the nitrate situation when a naval intelligence officer walked into his office with some intercepted cables. The cables showed that the Chilean government had some gold in Germany which it was unsuccessfully trying to get out. "This gave me something to work on," he wrote. "When the Chilean Ambassador called on me soon after, and began complaining about the difficulty of controlling inflation in his country, I was prepared to make him an offer. If Chile would seize the 235,000 tons of German-owned nitrate in Chile and sell it to us, we would pay for it in gold." Much to Baruch's relief, the trade was done.*

---

*An uncomfortable fact for the Administration was the rejection of Du Pont's prewar proposal to build an atmospheric recovery plant at Muscle Shoals. The man who had called the company's attention to the strategic significance of American dependence on Chilean nitrates was none other than General Crozier, the Army's negotiator of the repudiated Du Pont powder contract—another uncomfortable fact.

Baruch recorded his disgust in homely intermittent diary entries. For example: "Fiddle while Rome burns," "What is everybody's job is nobody's job" and, apropos of a fruitless meeting to discuss the fixing of nickel prices: "It seems useless to have the whole board meeting and not deciding." (A detached and guarded chronicler of his personal life, he described a Sunday with his family as follows: "Walked with my daughter in the morning [in fact he had two daughters]. . . . Spent afternoon with wife and son.")

By the close of 1917 it was clear that something was fundamentally wrong. "The entire war machine seemed to be grinding slowly to a halt," wrote a historian of the WIB. "General Pershing forecast disaster for the spring offensive, given the present flow of supplies; the railroad snarl along the east coast brought federal control on December 26, . . ." In the Senate an independent-minded Oregon Democrat, George E. Chamberlain, opened hearings into the conduct of the war with the result of embarrassing revelations concerning Army supply. In newspapers there was a hue and cry for a new munitions agency; George Peek, a WIB man, wrote a friend who was about to come east: "By the time you arrive here, there may be no War Industries Board. . . ." Borne along by the tide of disclosure, Baruch incautiously appeared before the Chamberlain committee to call for an improved central supply organization headed by one man, a position he had argued in private for months.

Although Baruch hadn't suggested an executive by name, his own first choice was himself, and he worked to push his candidacy along. Someone who was pushing in the opposite direction was Secretary of War Baker. Baker didn't like Baruch or his Wall Street past, or, for that matter, the War Industries Board, which he correctly viewed as a threat to his supply flank. At the time, however, the Secretary's star was falling while that of McAdoo, Baruch's friend, was rising. (Baruch's name, in fact, had been mentioned by McAdoo to President Wilson for the War Department in case Baker were forced out.) Under White House pressure, Baker was led to endorse a new and fortified WIB along the lines suggested by Baruch. The question was who would run it.

Baruch's name was proposed by, among others, Secretary of the Navy Daniels, whom Baruch had at first taken for a "good, honest, simpleminded jackass." (He revised his opinion, and Daniels and he became friends. So far had their friendship come that in the spring of 1918, when Baruch's older daughter announced that she wanted to join the Navy, his wife, not one to impose on strangers, felt free to take up the matter with Daniels himself.) Baruch was, in truth, politically loyal, financially independent, experienced and decisive—in 1917 Theodore Roosevelt had described him as the "ablest man around the Administration"—but the Baruch boom met with some opposition. Secretary of Agriculture Houston, Secretary of Commerce Redfield and Democratic National Committee Chairman McCormick all questioned his executive capacities. Robert Lovett, a WIB member who had been president of the Union Pacific and Southern Pacific railroads, opposed him. Baker was opposed, as was Interior Secretary Lane. The United States Chamber of Commerce was doubtful. On the other hand, Baruch enjoyed the support of Joe Tumulty, the President's secretary (and a fellow sufferer in the peace-note leak affair); David Lawrence, the newspaperman; Samuel Gompers, president of the American Federation of Labor; and, of course, McAdoo.

Baruch's spirits rose or fell in February according to the latest odds on his candidacy. At a meeting with President Wilson on February 7, he reiterated his ideas on the necessity of one-man control of the Board, but left with the impression that that one man would be Edward Stettinius. Stettinius, however, was a Morgan partner and a Republican, qualifications that (at least to Colonel House) were even less desirable than that of being a Jew. (Baruch himself was uneven on this subject. Shortly after his appointment as chairman, he told Daniels that it would be bad politics to name another Jew to the Board, but later in 1918 he gave $10,000 to the Palestine Restoration Fund, a Zionist cause.) While McAdoo fenced with Baker, who still opposed Baruch, the candidate nervously waited. Meyer advised him not to worry, and Baruch told his friends that if he didn't get the job he would probably join the Railroad Administration. At the same time McAdoo was sizing him up for a job on the War Finance Corporation, and he wrote to ask the President his advice on the matter. Wilson had made other plans, however. "My dear Mac," he wrote back, "I am mighty sorry but I can't let you have Baruch for the Finance Corporation. He has trained now in the War Industries Board until he is thoroughly conversant with the activities of it from top to bottom, and as soon as I can do so without risking new issues on the Hill I am going to appoint him chairman of that board. This is entirely confidential." On Monday, March 4, 1918—a low ebb in Allied fortunes, coming one day after Russia formally withdrew from the fighting and just three weeks before a major German offensive—President Wilson summoned Baruch to the White House to make the news official. Wilson handed him a letter setting out the duties of the chairman of the War Industries Board and of the reconstituted Board itself. Baruch accepted the letter, slipping it into his pocket (and not losing it), and walked out into the cold rain. As he left the White House he said to himself: "Now when you say 'no,' you must mean 'no,' and when you say 'yes,' you must mean 'yes.' Whatever you do, you must make your own decisions and never delay or wobble. You must decide."

Baruch had never been the head, or chairman, of anything before except of his household and office, and Annie managed the household and Mary Boyle, his secretary, supervised the office. Not having built an organization or even worked in one very much, he was unpracticed in the day-to-day style of executive leadership. He was naturally decisive, but the decisions he was used to making on Wall Street usually touched only the market and himself or a few partners. On the Stock Exchange he had been one governor among dozens. Yet so easily and well did he fill the shoes of command that his subordinates respectfully began to call him "Chief." (Daniel Willard, whose resignation as chairman of the WIB created the vacancy that Baruch filled, wrote his successor years later: "Even while I was Chairman of the Advisory Commission . . . and you one of its members, you were at the same time the *most potent member*, not even excepting the Chairman. . . .")

Baruch was an agreeable man, and the hope among businessmen was that his regime at the Board would be an amiable one. *The Wall Street Journal*, for example, favorably compared his record in price disputes with that of the Coal Administration, which had alienated mine owners and caused shortages. "Mr. Baruch's method," the paper said, "was to keep down prices by discussing the problem with the heads of the industries from the standpoint of the Government. His prices have not been liberal but when they were decided upon in conference the industries felt that if a sacrifice was involved it was appreciated." Baruch brought other advantages to the job. As a stock trader, he was accustomed to seeing the economy whole, of seeking the facts and of wondering (after taking action) whether the facts had changed. His fortune invested him with the presumption of wisdom, and his money and looks together cast a spell. When, for example, he brought Leland Summers, an engineer who'd done consulting work for J. P. Morgan, down to Hobcaw to recruit him for a post on the Board, Summers found his host, the surroundings or the proffered job so winning that he volunteered to serve for free.

As chairman, Baruch's powers were as broad as his tenure was brief (from his appointment until the Armistice exactly 253 days). He had been commissioned to know more or less everything about the supply side of the government, to let well enough alone but to intervene when necessary on price or priority questions. To quote from President Wilson's letter:

The duties of the Chairman are:

(1) To act for the joint and several benefit of all the supply departments of the Government.

(2) To let alone what is being successfully done and interfere as little as possible with the present normal processes of purchase and delivery in the several departments.

(3) To guide and assist wherever the need for guidance or assistance may be revealed; for example, in the allocation of contracts, in obtaining access to materials in any way pre-empted, or in the disclosure of sources of supply.

(4) To determine what is to be done when there is any competitive or other conflict of interest between departments in the matter of supplies; for example, when there is not a sufficient immediate supply for all and there must be a decision as to priority of need or delivery, or when there is competition for the same source of manufacture or supply, or when contracts have not been placed in such a way as to get advantage of the full productive capacity of the country.

(5) To see that contracts and deliveries are followed up where such assistance as is indicated under (3) and (4) above has proved to be necessary.

(6) To anticipate the prospective needs of the several supply departments of the Government and their feasible adjustment to the industry of the country as far in advance as possible, in order that as definite an outlook and opportunity for planning as possible may be afforded the business men of the country.

In brief, he should act as the general eye of all supply departments in the field of industry.

At top strength the WIB numbered 750, and it was organized along the industry-committee lines of the first Advisory Commission. In Baruch's day as chairman, there were also departments of price fixing, priorities, conservation and an office of the general counsel, which was occupied by Albert C. Ritchie, a future governor of Maryland. Ritchie issued a riveting first opinion, to wit, that Baruch was operating beyond his legal authority and was personally vulnerable to lawsuit by anyone who suffered losses on account of his decisions. Baruch, who never was one for lawyers or written contracts, chose to ignore that advice (his potential losses in court already exceeded his fortune), but he took the precaution of encouraging the businessmen with whom he dealt on official business to leave their lawyers at home. Mainly they complied, and Baruch emerged from his wartime service litigiously unscathed.

A casual administrator, he was a scrupulous picker of detail men. The men he got usually hadn't reached the top of their professions but were getting there fast when the war began. In the case of Ritchie, the top was almost the Presidency (Franklin D. Roosevelt, the former Navy Department man, beat him for the Democratic nomination in 1932). Alexander Legge, a former cowboy who served Baruch as operations chief, went on to the presidency of the International Harvester Company. Billy Rose, the WIB's ace stenographer, later wrote songs and produced Broadway shows and accumulated 350,000 shares of stock in the American Telephone & Telegraph Company.

Baruch augmented the office of the chairman with a three-man general staff comprising Harrison Williams, the utilities executive; Clarence Dillon, the investment banker; and Herbert Bayard Swope, the newspaperman. Swope and Baruch hit it off famously, and when Baruch was named chairman, Swope obligingly saluted him in the pages of the New York *World*: "That he possesses the President's confidence to a marked degree has been known for some time; that he deserves it is now generally admitted even by those who opposed him." One reason that Swope had written so flatteringly about Baruch was that Baruch, a few days earlier, had written appreciatively to him: "I have often heard repeated your many pleasing and flattering remarks regarding me, and might I be so bold as to say that I think you are prejudiced, as I think you and I understand each other and became friends as soon as we met. I trust that the future will help to ripen our meeting into a lasting friendship." Swope, in fact, became his closest friend.

It was at the WIB that a handful of men conceived a loyalty to Baruch so tenacious that they were long afterward known as "Baruch men." One was John M. Hancock, a deliberate, tobacco-chewing investment banker who would serve Baruch in the next war too, and in the ensuing atomic bomb negotiations. Another was the aforementioned George Peek, a farm implements executive who, with Baruch's moral and financial support, championed the postwar well-being of the American farmer. The most volatile of this inner circle was General Hugh S. Johnson, a West Point graduate who was unwillingly deskbound as the War Department's representative to the WIB. Just before the Armistice, orders arrived liberating him for active service, but he came down with the flu and got no closer to France than a troopship at Hoboken, New Jersey. After resigning his commission, he joined Peek in the implements business, then went on Baruch's payroll as a writer and securities analyst. In 1933 he was elevated to the head of the National Recovery Administration, a New Deal variation on the WIB.

An interesting case of the non-Baruch man was Eugene Meyer, Jr., who had been Baruch's peer on Wall Street, was richer than Baruch and perhaps knew more than he did about raw materials. Early on Meyer had given him the idea that copper producers ought to sell to the Army and the Navy at a concessional price in order to show the public that the European war was not being waged in the interests of the rich. Baruch, then a fledgling Advisory Commissioner, leaped at the idea, but wondered what the copper people would say. To his surprise, John Ryan and Daniel Guggenheim leaped at it too, and a deal was struck at a price of less than half of full freight. In the ensuing exchange of congratulations, Baruch received a warm letter from the Assistant Secretary of the Navy, Franklin D. Roosevelt.

When the United States entered the war in April 1917, Meyer began to look for a job in Washington, and he naturally turned for help to his old Wall Street friend. Baruch, however, was aloof and unhelpful, and the job that Meyer filled was an advisory post in the field of shoes and cotton duck. Dissatisfied (for it was a far cry from his forte of metals), he approached Baruch again, this time frontally. Meyer's biographer wrote of that meeting: "Baruch had not asked him to come and did not invite him to stay; when Meyer stayed anyway, he was not assigned to any particular task."

He made himself useful by answering telephones and organizing papers, from time to time sending Corcoran to the Shoreham to hunt up a missing document in Baruch's closet. Notwithstanding his determination to serve his country, Meyer perhaps reflected on the strange and unsatisfying turn of events that had brought him to Baruch's office in the temporary capacity of file clerk.

"Gene," said Baruch one day, "you're awfully sour. You're always grumbling about things. Why don't you smile more like I do?"

Meyer spoke as evenly as he could. He said that, in view of the production news, there wasn't much to smile about, and that perhaps Baruch would smile less if he knew more. Elaborating, he said: "You've got a big job here. Everybody is telling you you are a wonder and you're blowing up like a balloon. I'm your only friend because I stick a pin in the balloon every once in a while and let out a little of the gas. When things aren't going so well, I'm not going to tell you they are, I'm going to tell you when they're not. If you don't like it, tell me you don't want me around and I'll be glad to find something else to do." Meyer stayed on for a while, eventually heading an advisory unit on nonferrous metals, but he left to take a position on the board of the War Finance Corporation in early 1918. At a Senate hearing to confirm his nomination to that post, Baruch praised him so lavishly that the committee chairman dryly asked whether Meyer was dead. As time passed, Baruch came to view Meyer's wartime career as of his own making, and after the war he circulated the inaccurate, and, to Meyer, infuriating, story that it was he (Baruch) who had brought him to Washington in the first place.

Baruch was always praising his subordinates (and himself for his perspicacity in picking them) and was usually as loyal to them as they were to him. After the war, for instance, he accepted the Distinguished Service Medal but insisted that his chief lieutenants be similarly honored, and in the critical summer of 1918 he urged his overworked division heads and section chiefs to get away for a week or two of vacation. An alumni organization, the War Industries Association, was still going strong at its twentieth anniversary meeting in 1938, when 145 members turned up to hear Baruch speak on current affairs, to see a performance of *Hellzapoppin'* (tickets courtesy of Baruch) and to attend an after-theater party at the Savoy-Plaza Hotel (of which the host was Baruch). For their part, the members presented Baruch with a bust of himself. Howard Ingalls, secretary of the association, reported afterward: "The Chief was deeply moved and I know that probably it is his most prized possession and means more to him than anything else we could possibly have given him."

No doubt Baruch was moved by the sentiment of his wartime

brothers, but he also had an extraordinary attachment to his own likeness. Standing in awe of himself as he did, he naturally tried to explain the phenomenon of Baruch to others. Just after the war, for example, a woman journalist asked him a question, to which he confessed that he didn't know the answer.

> And then [she wrote] he talked to me for two hours about himself. He told me of his start in life as a three-dollar-a-week clerk, how rich he was, his philosophy of life; how you should recognize defeat when it was coming, accept it before it was complete and overwhelming and start out afresh, how liberal and advanced were his social views, how with all his wealth he was ready to accept a capital tax as perhaps the best way out of the bog in which the war had left the world, how democratic he was in his relations with his employees and his servants. It all seemed as amazing to him as if he were describing someone else, or as if it had happened the day before.

Baruch's vanity was so artless that it often evoked wonder rather than scorn, but some people were unsympathetic to it and to him. Robert Brookings, for example, complained of the impression that Baruch managed to leave of having just returned from the White House or of preparing to attend an urgent meeting there. Colonel House, who wrote in his diary in 1917 that "I do not believe the country will take kindly to having a Hebrew Wall Street speculator given so much power," allegedly put a man in the WIB to spy on Baruch. And, according to Alice Roosevelt Longworth, Army intelligence once planted a listening device in the home of a beautiful woman who was thought to be passing information to the enemy. Unsuspecting, Baruch paid a call on the lady one day while the microphone was turned on. Mrs. Longworth, who herself sat listening with the intelligence officers, recalled: "We did hear her ask Bernie how many locomotives were being sent to Rumania, or something like that. In between the sounds of kissing so to speak. 'You are a coward, you don't dare to look' was one of her lines."

Baruch, in any case, was a storehouse of information, and he had the complementary speculator's capacity to act on the basis of what he knew. President Wilson, who called him, in that informational vein, "Dr. Facts," thought of him in the summer of 1918 when there was a demand for a man to get results. At the time the Administration had taken the decision to outfit some Czechoslovakian forces to fight in Russia with the Allies in the expedition against the Bolsheviks. The Secretary of State, Robert Lansing, was trying to arrange the shipment of equipment and warm clothing before the onset of the Siberian winter, but had been frustrated by the War Department. Appealing directly to President Wilson, he urged that one competent man be put in charge of things. Wilson answered him on September 2: "May I not ask you to have a full conference with Mr. Baruch on this matter? He and I were speaking of it the other day, and I found that he was familiar with the available stocks in the hands of the War Department. His information and advice ought to enable us to get final action."*

Fresh evidence of Baruch's high standing was furnished the next day when the President directed the heads of federal agencies to check with the chairman of the WIB before taking it upon themselves to commandeer private property. The decision not only widened Baruch's domain—he was already a member of the President's eight-man War Cabinet and an ex officio member of the Price Fixing Committee—but also simplified his official correspondence. Some months before the order, he had written to Josephus Daniels in acute frustration over a contested utility plant: "Nothing will be gained by the Navy commandeering any particular power plant, because you will come in competition with the commandeering power of the Army and Shipping Board, who are vitally interested in that district as you are vitally interested in other districts that they are similarly interested in."

Despite Baruch's success at uncorking bottlenecks and reducing the level of confusion in federal supply lines, not all of the Administration's wartime economic goals were met. Overall industrial production, for example, hit its peak in May 1917 and gently declined through the war. Although an Expeditionary Force of more than two million men was raised, trained, equipped and shipped to France, only 100 of the 2,250 artillery pieces that they fired in action were actually made in America, and the air corps that was supposed to blacken the skies of Europe essentially amounted to 3,227 De Havilland 4 observation and day-

---

*On Christmas Day 1918, Eduard Beneš, the Czech foreign minister, reported to the American ambassador in Paris that 20,000 U.S. military overcoats were apparently on the way, but he inquired as to the whereabouts of 40,000 shirts, 40,000 pair of boots, 30,000 pair of leggings and 40,000 pair of socks that hadn't turned up.

bombing aircraft, of which only 1,885 ever crossed the Atlantic. The Administration, however, did succeed in slashing corporate profits in 1918, thereby providing an ideological balm to soothe the disappointment of shortages.

Because there was less to go around, the WIB necessarily found itself in the business of telling people what they should do with their own money in the interests of conservation and efficiency. Thus, it successfully encouraged a reduction in the number of automobile tire models to 32 from 287; of steel plows to 76 from 312; of buggy wheels to 4 from 232; and of bathing caps to 1 from 69. It prevailed on traveling salesmen to travel with fewer trunks and on merchants to make fewer deliveries. When only four competing department stores joined in a cooperative delivery scheme, Baruch and the Board reported, the savings amounted to twenty-one drivers, fourteen wagon boys, twenty-nine horses, two stablemen and twenty-one trucks or delivery wagons. In September 1918 Baruch asked the readers of *The Ladies' Home Journal* to do their bit by not insisting that the color of the shoe match the color of the dress: "However harmless such fastidiousness may be in time of peace, in time of war it is inconsistent with serious womanliness."

Just as the draft was portrayed as the selection of willing citizens from a nation that had volunteered en masse, so the WIB was presented as a clearinghouse for the self-regulation of business. There was some truth in that view—the U.S. Steel Corporation, which had protested federal controls at the start of the war, actually opposed their relaxation at the Armistice—but not everyone went along quietly or without a push. When Baruch threatened to seize the property of one independent-minded lumber-mill owner, the man asked him if he thought the government could actually run it. Baruch allowed that it would be difficult, but added: ". . . by the time we commandeer those mills you will be such an object of contempt and scorn in your home town that you will not dare to show your face there. If you should, your fellow citizens would call you a slacker, the boys would hoot at you, and the draft men would likely run you out of town." In a set-to with Judge Gary, chairman of U.S. Steel, there was a similar exchange. Baruch again conceded the shortage of federal executives to manage complex industrial enterprises but added that he could always get a second lieutenant. Gary was a Republican, but the WIB also tackled some prominent Democrats. Mayor John F. Hylan of New York, who wanted to spend $8 million on school construction, was dismayed to receive a letter over Baruch's signature (but which had been drafted by Swope) containing a "civilian order of the day: He serves best who saves most." Building was postponed for the duration.

War or not, the Fords and the Dodges kept building automobiles, tying up steel and labor that the Administration believed could be better used in the war effort. The WIB protested to Detroit, but the pre-Baruch Board was weak and auto demand ran strong. Sparring between government and industry continued into 1918. On March 4, 1918, Baruch's first day as chairman, an agreement was struck to reduce passenger-car output by 30 percent in the 1918–1919 model year. But the accord broke down, and there was another meeting in May, at which John Dodge, president of Dodge Brothers, tactlessly said to the WIB side: "It appears to me that what you want is one big boss to get these departments together and shake them up and get results." As Dodge perhaps realized, Baruch was just that big boss, and at length Baruch threatened: "I know that if we've got to close the automobile industry, you will take your medicine." But nothing came of the threat except more meetings. As the summer rolled around, Edwin Parker, the WIB's priorities chief, argued for cutting off the industry's steel and coal; Baruch advised caution. Then, in August, Detroit proposed a 50 percent cut in production (auto sales were falling anyway). Momentarily good will was restored, but the WIB chose to issue a statement declaring that 100 percent conversion would be necessary by 1919. With that the nation's automotive dealers rose up as one man; next came the Armistice, making the matter moot. A student of the WIB sized up the Board's influence over Detroit as follows: "We have every reason to believe that the industry moved in its own time, according to its own purposes and calculations of market conditions." By chance in 1920, Baruch saw Dodge in the lobby of the hotel in which Dodge was staying in New York. The auto executive, regretting some things that he'd said in the heat of bargaining, walked up to Baruch, shook his hand warmly and invited him up to his room for a drink. Baruch fortunately made excuses. Dodge subsequently fell ill and died of what the papers said was pneumonia but what Baruch had reason to believe was the tainted Prohibition liquor that he drank that day.

If the WIB failed to do all that it might have done, it wasn't for a lack of dedication by its last chairman. After the war a story came to light about a mission that the Board had sent to London to deal with

Allied governments on the subjects of prices and joint purchasing. A twelve-man WIB team was packed and ready to sail in July 1918 when Baruch received a call from the head of the mission, Leland Summers. It seemed, said Summers, that there was no government money for the trip and little or no chance of getting any. Baruch simply referred him to his secretary, Miss Boyle, who wrote a check. The Summers delegation, once financed and settled in London, wangled lower prices from the British for jute and wool. It worked a trade with Spain for mules in exchange for ammonium sulphate (General Pershing needed the animals to haul artillery), and it planned the collective Allied purchase of nitrates, conferring with Great Britain's official in charge of that strategic commodity, Winston Churchill. Baruch's out-of-pocket expenses for the trip amounted to $63,752.25 (for which he refused to be reimbursed); estimated savings to the taxpayers as a result of Summers' work ran to the millions.

Another facet of Baruch's wartime service was also divulged. When the WIB was disbanded after the Armistice, its clerical employees, notably several hundred young single women, were cast adrift in Washington. This worried Baruch, and he hired a matron to interview each woman and to impress on her the desirability of returning home instead of (to quote another chivalrous, or, as it later came to seem, reactionary southerner, James F. Byrnes) "walking the streets of Washington seeking employment." Baruch offered a further inducement for leaving town: a free railroad ticket home (wherever it happened to be), complete with Pullman berth and all expenses paid. The cost of that amounted to $45,000. As the young women climbed aboard the trains, each received a postcard addressed to Baruch with instructions that it was to be mailed when she reached safe harbor. Baruch saved the postcards, and he also saved a loving cup that had been presented to him and inscribed thus: "To Bernard M. Baruch, Chairman of the United States War Industries Board, as a token of confidence and affection, from Members of the organization which, under his leadership, aided in winning the war, Washington, D.C., 25th of November, 1918."

Some twenty years later, a visitor to Baruch's New York home noticed that the only books in his office were the minutes and correspondence of the War Industries Board (and of the subsequent Peace Conference at Versailles), bound in green leather.

TEN

Plainspoken Diplomat

Bernard Baruch, a first-class passenger aboard the S.S. *George Wash-ington*, watched with ambivalence as the ship cast off lines in the fading daylight of New Year's Day 1919. There was the prospect of diplomatic adventure in Paris to contemplate but also the inevitability of a rough winter crossing. Possibly he felt a stab of regret about the mid-level capacity in which he was about to take up new duties. He had been named an adviser to President Wilson in the American delegation to negotiate the peace. Shortly after the Armistice, he had resigned from the War Industries Board, and shortly after that he had refused an invitation to succeed McAdoo as Secretary of the Treasury. He had made the excuses that he was a Jew and a speculator and therefore a po-tential embarrassment to the Administration. Almost certainly the Pres-ident had pointed out that the same alleged stigmata had embarrassed nobody when he chaired the WIB, but Baruch persisted, and the Trea-sury post went to Representative Carter Glass of Virginia.

Also bound to France aboard the *George Washington* were fifty Army clerks bossed by two officers; two thousand sacks of Army mail; $2 mil-lion in gold, also for the Army; Assistant Secretary of the Navy Roosevelt; various Mexican, Chinese and Latin American peace delegates (accompa-nied, in the case of Lu Tsiang of China, by wife, family and servants); and Charles Schwab, the steel titan and wartime shipping official. As the ship steamed out of the harbor and into the gray January swells, Baruch re-

166

tired to be miserable alone. Hearing that he was under the weather, Schwab dropped in to ask what he thought now about the Wilsonian tenet of the freedom of the seas. Baruch had the strength to reply, one millionaire to another, that Schwab could have all his interest in them.

After the ship reached Brest, Baruch went on to Paris by special train to a life of well-appointed idleness. Expecting to bring his wife and a daughter, but then changing plans, he had booked a three-bedroom suite at the Ritz. (Annie and Belle visited Paris in February and sailed home with a maid named Miss Thompson on March 17; Mary Boyle, Baruch's secretary, stayed in New York, and it was her name that he jotted down in the inevitable form in the place marked "Notify in Case of Emergency.") Lacey, his valet, was with him or would soon be sailing, and Baruch himself had let, or was about to engage, a house in the Paris suburb of St.-Cloud for weekend entertaining. In America it was rumored that he was to be the next U.S. ambassador to France, which was untrue, and that he had been appointed to a commission of thirty-six by Governor Al Smith to study postwar problems in the state of New York, which was true. But in Paris no work was assigned. He tried to report to Colonel House, the President's chief of staff, but (as he wrote): "It was not easy to see the Colonel . . . and for some days I sat around wondering why I had been called to Paris. I had the clear impression that my arrival had not occasioned unalloyed enthusiasm in the Colonel's personal entourage." Baruch, however, was not without resources and qualifications—among other things, he was the President's friend, the largest contributor to the Democratic National Committee in 1918 and an experienced traveler in Europe—and soon he won appointment to the Reparations Commission. His American colleagues on that key body were Norman H. Davis, the senior U.S. financial adviser, and Vance McCormick, chairman of the War Trade Board and formerly the Democratic Party's chief fund raiser.

Paris that January was filled with statesmen and their seconds and all manner of staff and miscellaneous persons ostensibly making peace. The most terrible war in history was over, but the Armistice had brought fractiousness, influenza and Bolshevism. Europe was prostrate: Germany hungry, northern France ravaged, everyone war weary. Onto this bare stage strode Woodrow Wilson, speaking to the galleries over the heads of governments to promise "Peace without Victory." The people were thrilled by the President and he by them, so that at first the fact was overlooked that on different sides of the Atlantic peace meant very different things. In Europe there was admiration for Wilson and tolerance for his Fourteen Points and League of Nations but also a deep and un-Wilsonian hunger for booty. As the people cried *"Vive Wilson!"* in Paris, the placards read, *"Que l'Allemagne paye d'abord"*—Let Germany pay first. In the Chamber of Deputies, Louis-Lucien Klotz, the Finance Minister, brushed aside concerns over the financing of the French war debt with assurances that the bill would be paid in reparations instead of in taxes. In Britain, a political slogan was coined: "Squeeze the lemon until you can hear the pips squeak." America, which had entered the war late, suffered relatively few casualties and emerged as Europe's creditor, said that it wanted little or nothing for itself. For its allies it asked a fixed and reasonable sum of reparation (as opposed to the indefinite and unreasonable claims then being heard from the British and the French). It was to advance this line that Baruch, McCormick and Davis took their places on the Reparations Commission.

Baruch accumulated other assignments. He was appointed to the Committee on Form of Payments of Reparation and the Subcommittee on Measures of Control and Guarantee. He was a member of the Supreme Economic Council and of the American Delegation to the Preliminary Peace Conference. He served on the Special Committee on Food, Credit and Raw Materials, the Committee on Economic Clauses, the Committee on Reparations (with respect to Austria, Hungary and Bulgaria) and the Economic Drafting Committee. The drafting work, in particular, promised to be exacting and arduous. Always a believer in having enough technical help, he began to collect staff. The War Industries Board's Paris office placed itself at his disposal. In February, in answer to a call he had issued for reinforcements, five more men booked passage from America to France. On St. Valentine's Day the President handed him $150,000 "for the purpose of creating and maintaining such organization, supplementary to that maintained by the American Commission to Negotiate Peace for the carrying forward of its other activities, as said Bernard M. Baruch may find necessary."*

---

*There is some confusion about who owed what to whom. Chandler P. Anderson, a Republican lawyer, was under the impression that Wilson had borrowed $150,000 from Baruch to defray various ceremonial expenses in Europe until Congress could authorize payment from the Treasury. If so, the $150,000 for Baruch might have been nothing more than a discharge of the presidential debt. Baruch himself reported that he had spent only $24,128.64 of the allotted $150,000 and none of it on his personal expenses.

As an adviser with his own fast-growing advisory staff, Baruch naturally required offices. He arranged for the acquisition of three floors at No. 10 Rue Pauquet, space that had been previously assigned to Herbert Hoover, the dynamic relief commissioner. Inasmuch as the main body of the American delegation was housed at the Hotel Crillon, there was also need of transportation. This demand was filled by the State Department motor pool, which turned over three cars for the exclusive use of Baruch and his staff. (That spring, when his entourage too was consolidated at the Crillon, Baruch received a crisp note from the Department's administrative aide, Joseph C. Grew, asking that he surrender his automobiles.)

He was one of five American economic advisers in Paris, a team that also included Hoover, McCormick, Davis and Henry M. Robinson, a cherub-faced California banker. Thomas W. Lamont—the Morgan partner who would utter the famous Black Thursday understatement, "There has been a little distress selling on the Stock Exchange . . ."— recalled in his memoirs that Baruch had been a kind of roving ambassador, undertaking numerous jobs and enjoying the President's complete trust. It was almost inevitable that the five (or six, counting Lamont) would vie for presidential attention, and that Baruch would prove a resourceful competitor. One day, in unusual circumstances, he pitted himself against Hoover. On the day in question Baruch was riding in an automobile with Rear Admiral Cary T. Grayson, Wilson's naval aide and personal physician, and with Edith Helm, Mrs. Wilson's social secretary. Their car was the fifth or sixth in a caravan that was touring the devastated regions of Belgium with President and Mrs. Wilson and the king and queen of Belgium. Protocol dictated the order of travel, with the royal car first and junior officials bringing up the rear. Just ahead of the Baruch-Grayson car was one in which Hoover was riding. Mrs. Helm related:

We went along at what seemed like breakneck speed—motors did not run smoothly as they do now. As we were dashing along, Mr. Baruch leaned over to the chauffeur, showed him a hundred-franc note and said, "If you can get ahead of that next car and stay ahead, you will have this."

Of course that was enough. We dashed ahead, nearly demolishing a dog on the way, and we stayed ahead. And for some strange reason, Mr. Hoover apparently thought I was responsible, because after the state dinner that night he came up and asked my official rank. I replied that I had none—I had only a clerical position with Mrs. Wilson. He said nothing more. . . . ,

Baruch and Hoover necessarily saw a lot of each other in Paris, but the contact failed to foster a close mutual understanding. At another dinner party Baruch watched as Hoover, flanked by beautiful women, stared distractedly at his plate. Baruch, who was as loath to squander an opportunity to engage the opposite sex as the relief director was to waste food, afterward asked him how he could have ignored such charming companions. Hoover didn't seem to understand the question.

Despite the inevitable clashes of ambition and personality, the Americans were united on the basic economic issues before the conference. Concerning wartime economic controls, they urged a general relaxation and a return to something as close as practicable to free trade. ("The removal, so far as possible, of all economic barriers . . ." was, indeed, the third of Wilson's Fourteen Points.) Baruch, who in wartime had been all for controls, after the Armistice declared himself for free markets. In a memorandum that he handed the President in December, he made the free-trade argument from the point of view of the individual: "A just and continuing peace should include a just and equal access to the raw materials and manufacturing facilities of the world, thus eliminating preferential tariffs. No nation, including neutrals, should be permitted to enter into economic alliance, to the detriment of any other nations. . . . The individual within each nation will thus have an opportunity through ingenuity and application to work out his own salvation."

The longer he sat in committee meetings, the deeper ran his conviction that government policy, especially policy toward Germany, which was still blockaded, was crippling the world. As his frustration rose, an undiplomatic edge crept into his voice. It was audible on April 16, for example, at a meeting of the Raw Materials Section of the Supreme Economic Council, which he happened to chair. The committee was in receipt of a request that had been forwarded from Germany by General Foch for thirty-six tons of wool. Should it be shipped? If so, would an unwanted precedent be set for the movement of other commodities into German hands? "We are all talking about 36 tons of wool," said Baruch. "You can take it and put it in the corner of your eye. What reason is there for discussing the matter of 36 tons of wool[?]" Still the discussion continued. At length, apropos of coal, Baruch said: "I say again that I think the coal and the transportation situation is the gravest one we have in front of us. We have formed committees and we have done nothing. The world will never excuse us for not doing it. It can be done only by mutual self-sacrifices and it cannot be done by everyone holding on to his little pile. This thing has to be done wholeheartedly and I would not give one penny to any nation that would not come through and work the situation out to the mutual benefit of all concerned."

With this a British delegate said he concurred. Later on talk turned to the blockade and to a suggestion that the committee consult another committee about the movement of goods to Germany. Baruch could hardly contain his exasperation, and his words tumbled out:

"The whole subject was brought up and it was suggested that I should be a member of that Committee and I refused to discuss it until we resolve that we will take down the blockade and the frightful unnecessary control of the mails, etc., but it has not been done and I would not sit on a Committee to discuss these things until we do the things which are stopping these things. They have no mail service, no telegraph service and have no way of communicating with the outside world and if they had all the money in the world they could not do so. We have it in our power to stop this and we do nothing toward it."

It was suggested that the Blockade Committee, which was meeting upstairs, would decide. Baruch was not encouraged.

"I have been here for ninety days and we resolve to do something and then turn it over and over. We say we should open up the blockade etc., and then we make it impossible. I say: let us bend our energies in undoing this tangle, rather than discussing it and making resolutions. . . . If you would allow people to communicate freely in these Balkan States the industries would get in touch and would do a great deal better than our Governments. Our Governments have everything so tied up that nobody is able to move."

A few minutes later, a British delegate by the name of Harris needled him:

HARRIS: I wish Mr. Baruch would form himself into a Committee.
BARUCH: If you will give me the authority of all the Governments I will do it and I can assure you it will be done.

HARRIS: There is nobody like a Committee of one.
BARUCH: If there was ever a dictator wanted in the world there is
           one wanted now.

In the war Baruch had been a dictator, albeit a circumscribed one,
and in the peace he felt a sense of letdown. In another meeting there
had been an exchange about nitrate of soda, a commodity over which
he had in fact reigned supreme. Now the problem was that none could
be shipped to Poland until the Finance Section met. "In the happy
times of war we could order these things done but in piping times of
peace we cannot do that," said Baruch. "I would like to take some action."

Sometimes the shoe was on the other foot, with the British or the
French seeking action and Baruch and the Americans favoring a kind of
benign neglect. Thus a scheme to finance postwar reconstruction by the
sale of bonds to governments was proposed by John Maynard Keynes
and opposed by the United States. Presently Keynes, whom Baruch
came to loathe, packed his bags and sailed home to write an acid de-
nunciation of the Peace Conference and of the treaty it finally produced. Another British proposal to retain the various wartime
commodity buying pools in the interest of holding down prices also
met with American opposition. The minutes of a meeting of the Raw
Materials Committee late in June recorded the nut of Baruch's view as
follows: "He stated that the operation of the law of supply and demand,
with as little Governmental control as possible, would be the best solution of the problem."

Although Baruch, probably more than most delegates in Paris, was
accustomed to evening clothes and first-class hotels (to Renée, his
younger daughter, he had written, ". . . remember me to all the servants"), he was untrained in the circumlocutions of diplomacy and
from time to time his plain talk alarmed this diplomat colleagues. A
few weeks after he reported for duty, for example, he announced that
he wanted to see the minutes of some secret meetings that had been
held at the Quai d'Orsay. When the fact of his interest reached the
State Department, Christian Herter, a junior aide in Paris, wrote to
Grew, "I would suggest confidentially that there is liable to be Hell
popping if Mr. Baruch goes to the French for their secret minutes, and
perhaps this could be conveyed to him very discreetly." But the French
were less alarmed than Herter, and Baruch and his associates were

made privy to the documents after all. Baruch had a way with some of the foreign delegates; one told James M. Tuohy of the New York *World* in February that Baruch's was the "ruling mind" of the Reparations Committee. April found him in top nondiplomatic form during an exchange with Lord Robert Cecil at a Raw Materials session:

BARUCH: No. 4 is next on the list. Progress Report of Committee on War Stocks. Has anybody sold anything yet?

LORD ROBERT: Nobody has any money to buy.

BARUCH: All waiting for the Americans to give them the money.*

Baruch thought that the U.S. government should lend to foreign governments sparingly and only on condition that they establish free trade in return. His lifelong approach to economic problems was the fundamental notion that people must work and save. (He preached this doctrine at home as well as in councils of state. From Paris he wrote to his seventeen-year-old son at the Milton Academy about the healing properties of work: "Even after peace is signed we will have great difficulties in getting the world back to work, for the world must get back to work. Work will cure everything, and I would be very unhappy and I know you would be if you did not have some object or ambition which involved study and continuous work.") Although this was never a startling idea, in 1919 it was pertinent because labor was relatively unproductive and governments were meddlesome.

Arthur Krock, a young reporter who was in Paris for the Louisville *Courier-Journal*, sought out the financier for an interview on the economic situation. He arrived at the Ritz one day in the tow of Herbert Bayard Swope, the former WIB man who was back on the New York *World*. The visitors found Baruch in mid-toilet: a manicurist at his nails, a chasseur at his boots, a barber poised at his head and Lacey, his valet, awaiting instructions nearby (or so Krock remembered the scene).

---

*He could also be indirect, as Cecil testified in his diary. Baruch and he had been talking about economic aid to Europe, but Baruch had spoken mainly about himself, Cecil wrote: "There was a long passage about his methods of doing business, which at the time I thought merely one of his usual irrelevancies, but from what I have heard subsequently I think he intended it to be a kind of indication of the way in which he thought the economic problems of Europe should be dealt with."

Baruch graciously rose to greet his guests and listened while Krock posed a question that had been suggested by Swope:

> "Have you any message for the American people now that they have saved democracy in Europe and the world?"
> "Yes," replied Baruch . . . "they must work and save."
> I burst into laughter [wrote Krock] in which Baruch—sensing the incongruity between this platitude and the environment in which it was uttered—quickly joined.*

As one of the richest delegates in Paris, Baruch entertained lavishly, and a particular dinner party that he gave—possibly an affair for forty at the Ritz on May 22, of which Vance McCormick took diarial note—astonished even him. Harold Ickes, Roosevelt's Secretary of the Interior, wrote in *his* diary that Baruch was bragging about it in 1942, twenty-three years after the dishes had been cleared. Baruch had a clear recollection of another party. He was, he said, dancing with a beautiful Englishwoman when his friend Cary Grayson inopportunely cut in, leaving him to dance with a Frenchwoman who shadowed him for the rest of the evening. Presently she moved into a room on his floor of the Ritz and appeared one day in his sitting room bearing a list of securities. Lacey, however, who had been prepared for such a contingency, faithfully clung to his master's side, and the woman walked out, as Baruch told the story, "in disgust."

> Grayson is a very clever practical joker [Baruch wrote]. When he is putting one over, he lies like the old trout at the bottom of the pool and never makes a move or sound. However, one day, he said, "General Pershing and I would like to know about that Frenchwoman with a gold bracelet on her ankle who danced away with you?" and his eyes twinkled just a little. I backed him into a corner and said, "You scoundrel. You put something over on me." And then he confessed. He said that as he was sitting with this woman, she asked who the tall man with the gray hair was and he answered, "Don't you know? That is Mr. Baruch." She said, "Mr. Baruch, the American? Tell me something

---

*Krock took more pleasure in telling this story than Baruch did in listening to it. After Krock had delivered it, or a variation, at Hobcaw one evening, Baruch piped up, "Arthur, you're a dirty liar."

The speculator as toddler. *UPI/ Corbis-Bettmann*

Bernard M. Baruch, age 22, shows the fruits of his patronage of Woods' Gym. *Bernard M. Baruch Papers, Department of Rare Books and Special Collections, Princeton University Library*

Actor, older brother and (to his younger brother) hero: Hartwig N. Baruch, also about 1897. *New York Stock Exchange Archives*

Baruch as a rising young broker, about 1897. *New York Stock Exchange Archives*

Baruch's employer, later
partner, Arthur A. Housman.
*New York Stock Exchange
Archives*

Baruch as his own man—
venture capitalist, "banker"
and millionaire—about 1903.
UPI/Corbis-Bettmann

Baruch's Wall Street: brokers appraise the tape on the floor of the New York Stock Exchange (1899). *New York Stock Exchange Archives*

Crowds and carriages throng Broad Street for opening day of the new New York Stock Exchange, April 22, 1903. *New York Stock Exchange Archives*

Teamsters drive east on Wall Street with Trinity Church in the background (1906).
New York Stock Exchange Archives

Man and the myth: Baruch is rendered larger than life in a newspaper cartoon sometime after the turn of the century. *Bernard M. Baruch Papers, Department of Rare Books and Special Collections, Princeton University Library*

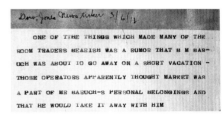

A lighthearted acknowledgment—by, of all media, the Dow Jones news ticker—of Baruch's stock-market might (March 6, 1912). *Bernard M. Baruch Papers, Department of Rare Books and Special Collections, Princeton University Library*

TWENTY MILLION WON BY BARUCH

Daring Speculator, Operating From Little Private Office, "Cleans Up" on Wall Street.

NEW YORK, Sept. 18.—Following the recent active market it was reported in Wall Street to-day that Bernard M. Baruch, a daring speculator, has "cleaned up" $20,000,000.

Word was passed around at the opening of the market Tuesday that the long-delayed activity had come at last, and stocks began to climb at once. Such favorites as Steel, Union Pacific, Amalgamated, Reading and other issues went soaring upward, and the trend of the whole list was toward better prices.

The rise had hardly started before brokers began to believe that Baruch was busy again. Every rise was watched as a barometer of what might be expected, and the floor of the Stock Exchange was again the scene of intense activity after months of comparative quiet.

The Stock Exchange to-day contains no more spectacular character than Bernard M. Baruch. He has two brothers on the exchange, Hartwig N., of Baruch Brothers, and S. W., of A. A. Housman & Co. He was at one time connected with the firm of Baruch Brothers, but for some years has been doing business by himself, and, in a little private office in a building overlooking Trinity Church yard, he sits and does things when the time is ripe.

A fish story of unknown provenance (1912). *Bernard M. Baruch Papers, Department of Rare Books and Special Collections, Princeton University Library*

Every inch the diplomat: Baruch in the year of the Peace Conference (1919). *UPI/Corbis-Bettmann*

Patron of the Democratic Party and friend of American agriculture, Baruch poses with his skimmer (1923). *UPI/ Corbis-Bettmann*

Baruch makes an appearance in *Vanity Fair*'s rendition of the inauguration of Franklin D. Roosevelt (white-haired and bespectacled, he stands in front of a knot of naval officers; March 4, 1933). *Bernard M. Baruch Papers, Department of Rare Books and Special Collections, Princeton University Library*

Baruch, Herbert Bayard Swope and Dwight D. Eisenhower confer after dinner at the Waldorf-Astoria (1947). *UPI/Corbis-Bettmann*

Warhorses take the air:
Baruch and Winston
Churchill out for a walk
at Chartwell Manor
(1949). *UPI/*
Corbis-Bettmann

Baruch's editorial-page
persona: as park-bench
statesman (undated) . . .
Bernard M. Baruch
Papers, Department of
Rare Books and Special
Collections, Princeton
University Library

"Barney Baruch practically lives on a park bench, and you won't let us sit on one for five minutes!"

6-2

. . . as proponent of
statism (1950) . . .
*Bernard M. Baruch
Papers, Department of
Rare Books and Special
Collections, Princeton
University Library*

. . . and as all-around
indispensable citizen
(1955).   *Bernard M.
Baruch Papers,
Department of Rare
Books and Special
Collections, Princeton
University Library*

about him." Grayson asked her what she wanted to know. She said, "Is he clever?" He said, "Well, financially, he is the cleverest man in America. Sometimes he makes millions of dollars in one day and he is very generous with the ladies." He said that she shot over to the middle of the floor, where she insisted upon dancing with me and he said, "And, of course, I had to dance off with your girl."

As rich, outspoken and good-looking people usually are everywhere, Baruch in Paris was the object of gossip. Stories were hatched that he was pro-German and that he favored a return of the city of Fiume (now Rijeka) to Austria instead of to Italy because he held an interest in an Austrian shipping line. It was rumored that he had helped to finance the Russian Revolution; perhaps he provoked that story by declaring that the civilized world, in brooking the tyranny of the czars, had helped to foment Bolshevism. (The year 1919 was a time of labor upheaval and radical politics. Baruch said that he was prepared to give up a substantial portion of his income in taxes in order to stave off confiscation of the rest. As many others did then, he favored the sharing of corporate management with labor.)

A mysterious cable that appears to have been the result of either a gross misunderstanding or of a crude attempt to embarrass him reached the War Department in Washington from Berlin. The message referred to Baruch as the Secretary of the Treasury, which office he was fond of bragging that he had refused. Signed only "Siegmarious," the communiqué said:

PLEASE REQUEST THE AMERICAN AUTHORITIES IN YOUR CITY TO IN-
FORM THE AMERICAN SECRETARY OF THE TREASURY "BARUCH" BY
WIRE THAT THE FORMER REPRESENTATIVE OF HIMSELF AND HIS
BROTHERS, STEINHARDT IN BERLIN URGENTLY REQUESTS AN INTER-
VIEW WITH HIM ALSO IN ORDER TO SUBMIT FINANCIAL PROPOSITIONS
FROM ME. THE SECRETARY OF THE TREASURY "BARUCH" WILL PLEASE
INFORM ME THROUGH YOU AS TO WHEN AND WHERE MR. STEIN-
HARDT MAY SPEAK WITH HIM. MR. STEINHARDT PROPOSES A MEETING
IN THE NEAR FUTURE AT COLOGNE.

The cable was passed from the War Department to the Treasury Department to the State Department, which in June forwarded it to Baruch with an ambiguous covering message: "Treasury suggests you might be interested." Baruch cabled back that he had never heard of Steinhardt or Siegmarious, didn't know anything about his brothers' business dealings and hadn't any interest in meeting the "supposed sender" of the cable whoever he was.

One possible ground for the suspicion of pro-German tendencies in Baruch was that he, along with the other Americans, supported a reparations scheme that was considerably more lenient than either the British or the French program. Baruch's conviction was that Germany ought to pay what she was able and obliged to pay under the Armistice terms, and that the sum should be fixed so that the German taxpayers could see an end to it. He wrote in March or April: "I do not wish in any way to express any sympathy for Germany, nor to lessen her burdens; for she should be made to pay everything she can pay, and brought to a full realization of the crime she has committed against civilization; but it would be a great mistake to be a party to promising the already over-burdened tax-payer of the Associated Governments with the hope of a payment which will never be collected." If the terms were to onerous, Baruch and his American colleagues said, individual Germans would refuse to work, or would emigrate and the victors would get nothing.

An accompanying legal argument was made by John Foster Dulles, thirty-one-year-old nephew to the wife of Secretary of State Lansing. Dulles said that the cease-fire accord was a contract of which the operative part was a phrase of Wilson's, namely, that Germany was bound to make restitution "for all damage done to the civilian population of the Allies and their property by the aggression of Germany by land, by sea, and from the air." It followed that no military costs could be recouped since none had been mentioned in the pre-Armistice language and that the extent of allowable reparations was therefore limited.

The British, French and Australians resisted. France, in fact, denied that there had been a contract at all. Germany, said Klotz, had surrendered, and that was that. To the American proposal that a definite bill be drawn up and presented to Germany—so many houses demolished, civilians maimed, factories dismantled and carted off—Lloyd George objected that to name any one figure would foreclose the possibility of a still higher total and thus would prove a political liability. Baruch guessed that Germany could pay $12 to $15 billion; Keynes thought a little less. Those were conservative, and, as it seemed to some delegates, niggardly, estimates. At one meeting Lord Cunliffe, a former director of the Bank of England, ventured $120 billion, to which Baruch commented: "Let us all take a trip to the moon." The French talked about $200 billion.

No issue put a greater strain on inter-Allied harmony. Where the Americans pressed for a literal interpretation of Wilson's language, the Allies wanted an expansive one. Even when war costs themselves were agreed to be inadmissible, a push began for inclusion of pensions and family allowances on a par with tangible damage. Jan Smuts of South Africa argued that the public expense of sustaining a soldier after he had left the colors, or of supporting his family during the time of his service, in fact represented "compensation for damage done to civilians" and must therefore be paid by Germany. Baruch, Dulles and the other Americans saw the Smuts formula as sophistical and untrue to Wilsonian principle, but Wilson himself found that he rather liked it. On April 1, at the Crillon, the President informed his advisers that he was abandoning them, on this question, for Smuts. But still there was no settlement. So much did Wilson despair of ever coming to terms that on April 7 he ordered the *George Washington* to Brest in case he felt the sudden need to leave the Europeans to their peevish selves.

The compromise that did emerge bore faint resemblance to the Americans' original proposal. A Reparations Commission would be formed to assess what Germany could pay and to see to collecting it. No definite sum would be fixed until 1921. In the end, of course, the Commission failed, and Germany, which careened into hyperinflation and Nazism, wound up paying just $5 billion, of which half was borrowed from America.

Unlike Keynes, who resigned when *his* advice was ignored, Baruch carried on, attending to such business as patents and coal, still seeking (in vain) a definite tallying up of the reparations bill, and from time to time taking in the races at Longchamps with Grayson and Swope. Early in April and again in May, Baruch's father, aged seventy-eight, was near death with double pneumonia and a severe heart attack in New York. Presented with this compelling reason to sail, Baruch nonetheless remained at his post.

On June 28 he donned cutaway, striped pants and top hat to witness the signing of the treaty at the Hall of Mirrors at Versailles. Then, on the twenty-ninth, he reboarded the *George Washington* in the presidential party for the voyage back to New York. On July 5 the weather was so salubrious that he was able to visit the President's salon after lunch to listen to a reading of the treaty speech that Wilson planned to make to Congress. McCormick, Lamont, Davis and others were also on hand. Wilson, after reading the text, asked for comments. Baruch thought it too timid, but characteristically held his tongue until he could tell Wilson so in private. In his autobiography he explained that he hadn't wanted to appear critical in front of the others. That evening, McCormick, Davis, Grayson and Baruch ate splendidly in the captain's cabin. On the morning of the eighth, twenty miles off Sandy Hook, a naval escort consisting of forty destroyers, five battleships, ten seaplanes and a blimp hove into view. Baruch was on the bridge with the President as greetings were exchanged and twenty-one-gun salutes boomed across the water. Late in the afternoon, to the cheering of the crowd along River Street in Hoboken, the *George Washington* warped into berth. The presidential delegation, now landed and augmented by Cabinet officials, was borne across the Hudson by special ferry to West 23rd Street, and then, by a parade of automobiles, to Carnegie Hall for speeches. Although Baruch was assigned to car No. 7, which was to the rear of the President and the Cabinet, he preceded his wartime adversary Judge Gary, who was in car No. 8. Herbert Hoover, with whom there had been the earlier protocolary run-in, had remained in Europe. Baruch literally came ashore campaigning for the treaty—he had prepared a summary of its salient economic points for distribution at dockside—and he defended it three weeks later as the lead-off witness before a hearing of the Senate Foreign Relations Committee. The art in upholding the pro position was to acknowledge with as little forensic damage as possible that the finished product was imperfect and far from what had been sought. The challenge on the reparations matter was especially keen. Instead of a definite sum, there was an indefinite one and the promise of future oversight by a Reparations Commission.

At the hearing Baruch began masterfully by straightening out the senators on a point of French usage in a translation of a worrisome passage of Article 237. He described how the economic work was done and who were the American personnel involved. To Senator Hiram Johnson, a California Republican who asked whether it wasn't true that the entire economic section of the treaty had been drafted by Englishmen, he replied, "It is not, sir; unless you call me an Englishman, sir." He confessed his lack of familiarity with the Central

Rhine Commission and with the reparations liability, if any, attaching to the territories of Memel, Danzig and Schleswig. Having worked until the last minute in Paris to try to get a fixed reparations bill, he now chose to testify that, inasmuch as postwar economic conditions could not be foreseen, there was no way of telling how much Germany could pay and that a fixed bill would have therefore been impossible. In general he said: "The terms are harsh and severe, but I think they are very just, and I would go on record as saying that this commission [the Reparations Commission] is workable. It is a workable arrangement."

Senator Johnson thought he detected a qualm.

"Do you express that with some doubt?"

"No, sir," said Baruch.

"There is much to be left to the future, however, is there not?"

"I have no fear of the future."

In the Republican-controlled Senate, the treaty faced resistance that at first took a passive form under the direction of Henry Cabot Lodge of Massachusetts, chairman of the Foreign Relations Committee. Lodge consumed two weeks by reading the treaty aloud to a sometimes empty committee room, another six weeks in hearings (then an unheard-of accompaniment to a Senate treaty deliberation) and three hours more, on August 19, 1919, in taxing the President himself at a White House audience. Just as Wilson had spoken over the heads of the rulers of Europe, so he felt bound now to appeal to the American people over the head of the Senate. Setting out by rail on September 3, he spoke for twenty-two days before collapsing in Pueblo, Colorado, on the night of September 25. Rushed back to the White House, he suffered a paralytic stroke on October 2. Neither a martyr nor a whole man, he fought for the treaty from his bed, not meeting the Cabinet, breaking with House and Lansing, seeing only a small circle of intimates, among them Baruch. Having bent in Paris, Wilson now refused to compromise. Article 10 of the Covenant, in particular, which bound the members of the League to "undertake to respect and preserve as against external aggression the territorial integrity and existing political independence" of all members, the President held as untouchable. Republicans objected that if the word "preserve" meant anything, it was that members would meet aggression with force, but that under the Constitution only Congress could make war. Former President Taft offered an amendment to state plainly the only constitutional process by which the United States was prepared to enter a foreign war. Carter Glass, who was just stepping down as Treasury Secretary, had tried but failed to persuade Wilson to accept it, or something like it. At Glass's behest, in February 1920, Baruch called on the President with the same conciliatory counsel. He too failed. As Baruch left the room, according to Mrs. Wilson, the President murmured, "And Baruch, too." But presently Wilson had a change of heart and said: "You know, Baruch is true to the bone. He told me what he believed, not what he knew I wanted him to say. Tell the dear fellow that I would like him to be Secretary of the Treasury, and then that will be off my mind."

Since the previous July there had been reports that Baruch was to become Postmaster General, American Reparations Commissioner and Secretary of Commerce. He had already turned down the Treasury portfolio in 1918. But, as he told the story, the second Treasury invitation tempted him, and he went home to try out the idea on his wife. Annie, however, asked him to come back to her and to their children (by then grown or nearly grown); which, he said, he did, although he had never been a homebody even in private life.

He did, however, stay in the thick of the treaty fight. He did the predictable thing of helping to finance the activities of the League to Enforce Peace, a pro-treaty organization, but he also did the unexpected. Early in 1920, as the Senate was preparing to vote on ratification for the third time, a book was published by John Maynard Keynes, the thwarted British adviser in Paris. *The Economic Consequences of the Peace* was a rich polemic that instantly turned sentiment against Wilson and the League of Nations. Wilson was, to Keynes, a "blind and deaf Don Quixote," and a "Nonconformist minister," whose mind was addled and whose very hands lacked "sensitiveness and finesse." His capitulation to the sophistry of the Smuts line on reparations had stripped him of his moral authority. When, near the end of the conference, Lloyd George, the British Prime Minister, suddenly urged moderation toward Germany, "he could not in five days persuade the President of error in what it had taken five months to prove to him to be just and right. After all, it was harder to de-bamboozle this old Presbyterian than it had been to bamboozle him; for the former involved his belief in and respect for himself."

Senator William Borah, one of the treaty's bitter-end foes, delightedly quoted from the book, and the Senate, shortly after its publication, again, and for the last time, failed to ratify. Appalled by the events in the Senate and convinced that Keynes had been a cause of them, Baruch set out to put the record straight with a book of his own. The drawback of his not being a writer was surmounted with $10,000. For that stipend John Foster Dulles agreed to become his principal ghostwriter. The result, in the fall of 1920, was a brief and austerely titled volume, *The Making of the Reparation and Economic Sections of the Treaty.*

At first glance the putative author himself seemed to have had nothing to do with the project. The prose was someone else's, and there were uncharacteristically few allusions to his own career and accomplishments. On closer inspection, however, the book bore a deep Baruch mark. For one thing, there were plenty of facts and documents and also a scene-setting chapter about the "human element" (a favorite phrase of Baruch's) in Paris. The point of that chapter was that wartime emotion so infected the peacemaking that compromise was inevitable, and that, in the circumstances, the Americans did about as well as they could. The narrative was detached, impersonal and, at its best, wise. Although he despised Keynes for his thrust at Wilson, Baruch never named "one of the foremost critics of the treaty and of the President's position on it," or stooped to the ad hominem argument. (Years later, Baruch wrote, with some justice, "Somebody said that 'Kaynes [*sic*] wrote the most interesting book devoid of facts and Baruch wrote the dullest book full of facts.'") In his book, Keynes had praised the President's advisers, but Baruch refused to be flattered, and he stood by Wilson devotedly. A case in point was the pension matter. Along with Keynes, Baruch had opposed the view that pension costs should be folded into the reparations pot. But since the President had chosen to compromise on the question, Baruch loyally put down his own abandoned position as "possibly legalistic." "One must be either ignorant, vicious, or an impractical idealist," wrote Baruch, permitting himself some spleen, "to contend that in the foregoing circumstances it was humanly possible to have found at the Peace Conference a sound, definite solution of the German reparation problem which would have met with ratification." Yet that, of course, was just what he had worked for.

The book was published to a friendly reception on the eve of the 1920 presidential election. *The Nation* hailed it as "an invaluable contribution." Alvin Johnson, a former WIB man, took his former chief to task in *The New Republic* for naïveté on the prospects for a workable reparations outcome, but declared that he had "triumphantly vindicated" the American side in Paris. *The Spectator* of London, describing Baruch as "one of the most impartial men at the Peace Conference," called his book ". . . short and concise, but it is in some respects the most illuminating comment upon the Treaty that we have yet seen."

Among the respectful critics was, unexpectedly, John Maynard Keynes. In *The Manchester Guardian* (and, in New York, in *The Literary Review* of the New York *Evening Post*), he raised an eyebrow at the book's use of what he took to be secret documents, expressed his doubts concerning the Reparations Commission and became gently patronizing in the matter of style. ("If it were written with more art, it would tell less. It powerfully illumines history, and reveals the secret springs of human nature. . . . I wonder if Mr. Baruch is always aware of how much he here discloses.") But he acknowledged the "considerable" part that Baruch had played in Paris and praised his book for its sincerity and truth telling. What Keynes saw brilliantly in his review was that the "human element" thesis of *The Making of the Reparation and Economic Sections of the Treaty* was no mere view of the Peace Conference. It was, in fact, a key to Baruch's outlook on the world. A passage in Baruch's book—"Though the peace delegates individually were able and high-minded, they were bound to the wheel of their national aspirations"—had caught Keynes's eye, and he urged the reader to study it. He wrote: ". . . it is a central doctrine of Mr. Baruch's philosophy of life that 'able and high-minded' persons can, through force of circumstances, become the instruments of misguided and disastrous passions without ceasing to be able and high-minded. Indeed, it may be proof of their ability and high-mindedness that they should so acquiesce, because it may give them an opportunity unobtrusively to moderate their passions."

Baruch did believe essentially that. In the stock market he had learned to cut his losses. So in public life he was usually careful not to cling to a doomed position for the sake of honor or principle. In Paris, again to quote Keynes, he held certain high views which he "did his best to uphold . . . (though not to the death)." A tribute to Baruch's capacity for friendship is the rapport he could feel for a very different kind of man. He continued to see Woodrow Wilson, who, in the end, willingly did go down with the ship. In 1923, a few months before Wilson's death, the two men were talking. Wilson had laid his paralyzed arm on the table beside him, and said deliberately:

"Perhaps it was providential that I was stricken down when I was. Had I kept my health I should have carried the League. Events have shown that the world was not ready for it. It would have been a failure. Countries like France and Italy are unsympathetic with such an organization. Time and sinister happenings may eventually convince them that some such scheme is required. It may not be my scheme. It may be some other. I see now, however, that my plan was premature. The world was not ripe for it."

The pathos of this tied Baruch's tongue. "Well, Mr. Wilson, you did what you thought was for the best!" he said, and regretted not saying more.

Farming, Money, McAdoo

Just before his forty-ninth birthday in the summer of 1919, Baruch took the opportunity of a visit to the White House to discuss his future plans. He tackled the subject by indirection, telling a man from the *Chicago Tribune* what he was not going to do.

I'm through with politics of any sort for good and all. I am through with public life and will assume no occupation which would give anyone the opportunity to say that I was taking advantage of secrets learned while head of the War Industries Board and in charge of war purchases for the Allies.

No, sir, I am not going to give a living soul the opportunity to say that I have profited even in the most remote way because of my war service. The patriotic joy of helping to lick the Huns was reward enough for me.

[He was emphatic about not returning to Wall Street.]

Never again. I was a gambler once, and for many years was a member of the New York Stock Exchange, but I am through.

What exactly Baruch did plan to do with himself was a mystery. That October, at the President's request, he chaired a conference on labor strife, of which the country at the time had too much and from which it continued to suffer after the conference adjourned. Early in

1920 came reports that he was financing a McAdoo-for-President drive, which he denied (the candidate himself denied his candidacy, which, in the event, went nowhere). A Republican congressman accused him of stealing $50 million "in copper alone" from the government in the war. Baruch denied that, and he denied reports that he was secretly running the White House in place of the stricken Wilson. At the same time, Henry Ford's newspaper, the wildly anti-Semitic Dearborn *Independent*, accused him of being the "pro-consul of Judah in America" and a "Jew of Super-Power." Sought out by reporters for comment on the charges, Baruch replied as genially as he could, "Now, boys, you wouldn't expect me to deny them, would you?"

What his enemies might not have imagined was that Baruch at the time was financially depleted. In 1916, his net income had topped $2 million. In the first wartime year of 1917 it amounted to $695,137.57. By 1919 it had fallen to $37,745.34. Not only had he earned less while spending large sums on government business but also he was reduced in capital. Before the war, as a precaution against the appearance of a conflict of interest, he had sold most of his marketable stocks and bought bonds. A list of his holdings, apparently incomplete, for the war period, shows $5.3 million of Liberty Bonds, and more than $1 million each of railroad and tax-exempt securities. (Baruch also liked to keep a lot of cash on hand, which wouldn't have turned up in his bond inventory.) In step with the wartime inflation, however, interest rates had gone up; as rates rose, bond prices fell. In the spring of 1920, when rates made their highs and bond prices their lows, Baruch's losses on paper were sizable. At that moment his fortune probably amounted to little more than $10 million, down from approximately $15 million in 1916. As late as the fall of 1921, he excused himself from making a charitable contribution with the rich man's exaggeration: "I am broke."

It was just at this financial nadir when he came under Ford's attack and when Arthur Krock rose to his defense. Krock, who went home to Louisville to resume duties on the *Courier-Journal* and the Louisville *Times*, had written a pro-Baruch editorial in May 1920. Baruch answered with a warm and (in the circumstances) optimistic letter:

> I "cottoned" to you the first time I saw you [he told the young man]. It is very difficult for me to tell you how much I appreciated

your generous editorial about me. My regard and affection is not lightly bestowed; nor can it be easily removed. I have been through some very severe schools—that of finance and industry, in Wall Street, that of politics, the war and the Peace Conference, and I must say that as I near my fiftieth birthday, which will be in August, that my faith in human nature and my fellow men has been increased.

Another vote of confidence came in the mail that summer. Out of the blue the Kansas State Board of Agriculture asked him to investigate the marketing dilemma of wheat farmers. It was a challenging moment for consulting: a twenty-year period of farm prosperity was ending, business was slumping and the stock market was falling. In the war farmers had planted fence to fence and borrowed to the eyes. Then came peace, a deflation and the shrinking of foreign markets. Land and commodity prices fell and the burden of debt became oppressive. Baruch was unversed in practical farming, but (as the Kansans knew) was thoroughly grounded in the overall economy. His father, who had just turned eighty, had been an amateur agronomist. Delighted by the invitation, he set out for Kansas late in August or early in September.

His visit began at the statehouse in Topeka with a mortification. Meaning well, an official on the greeting committee introduced him to his agricultural audience as the "Wolf of Wall Street." *The* Wolf of Wall Street was in fact David Lamar, the criminal.

Collecting himself, Baruch told his hosts that he would get the facts of the matter and then dispense advice. So far as speculation was concerned, he said, "I was not in any combinations on the market. I played a lone hand, and was just about as popular with Wall Street as I judge Wall Street is with you." For the next week or so he talked to local farmers, grain dealers, bankers, merchants and newspaper editors. He returned to New York, digested what he had heard and wrote to the last Secretary of Agriculture in the Wilson Administration, E. T. Meredith, for more information. (Baruch acknowledged receipt of the Secretary's reply with a politically heady thank-you note: "You can depend on my doing anything that it possible for me to do at the next session of Congress." So much for his boycott of politics.) He pulled together his material and submitted a seventeen-page report a month after the Republican landslide.

Baruch was a believer in the interdependence of world markets, and the report proceeded from the view that prosperity for American farmers depended on the restoration of international trade. The first order of business was therefore to settle accounts with Germany. The next was to build more warehouses and grain elevators so that producers could withhold crops in bad markets and thus bargain on a more even footing with consumers. Private capital should finance that construction if possible, said Baruch, but public funds should be used if necessary. He added that investors might lend to farmers on the collateral of crops in storage. (Although the grain futures markets served precisely the purpose of shifting financial risk from farmers and middlemen to speculators, Baruch, the former professional speculator, made no mention of them.) Despite an occasional populist note—for example, that a "fair share" of the nation's credit should be allocated to agriculture—the report was basically a conservative document. "In closing," Baruch wrote, "let me say that in working for a solution to this most important matter, we shall not find it in Aladdin's lamp or in any form of legerdemain. The only legislation needed will be that which grants the farmer an equal opportunity by opening wide all avenues of marketing, and for cooperative effort."

Reprinted as a pamphlet under the title "Putting Farming on a Modern Business Basis," the report established Baruch as a man with something to say about cooperative farming. Aaron Sapiro, a young California lawyer in the van of the co-op movement, commended him, and the United States Grain Growers offered him a job (which he declined).* He spread his agricultural energies in various directions: in Kentucky by helping to found a tobacco co-op (he was assisted by Krock's boss, Robert W. Bingham, publisher of the Louisville *Times* and the *Courier-Journal*); in South Carolina by subscribing $500,000 to a state cotton finance scheme and by putting up hundreds of thousands more to help shore up country banks that had lent on the collateral of

---

*Baruch and Sapiro made up two-thirds of the trio that *The Outlook* magazine saluted in 1923 in an article headed "Three City-Bred Jews that the Farmer Trusts." The third was Eugene Meyer, Jr., who found the piece so oppressively flattering to Baruch and so patronizing to him that he dashed off an angry note to Baruch.

"I cannot believe that you yourself desire to misrepresent it," wrote Meyer, "but these writers who get their information from you seem to consider it part of their duty in this and other articles to make it appear that everything I do and know is what I get from your inspiration and suggestion. In fact I am made out to be sort of a creature of yours." The note, however, went unmailed.

then-depressed farmland; and in the Midwest by almost, but not quite, bringing off the sale of the Armour Grain Company to farm groups. When Congress in 1923 passed a bill to establish the Intermediate Credit Banks in order to foster commercial-bank lending to agriculture, Gray Silver, chief Washington lobbyist of the American Farm Bureau, wrote Baruch appreciatively. He said that the legislation was nothing that Baruch hadn't talked about in 1920. To toast the new banks, Baruch bought $1.1 million worth of their brand-new notes.

He made another investment sheerly out of agrarian sentiment, some $50,000 worth of the bonds of the state of North Dakota. When he bought, the ruling power of the state was the Nonpartisan League, which preached public ownership and deliverance from Wall Street. In 1919 it set out to build a state bank and a state grain company. A $17 million bond issue was planned to finance those projects, but a taxpayers' organization, maintaining that the state was overreaching itself, filed suit to block the bond issue. At last in 1921 the bonds made their way to market. Wall Street was unreceptive, but Baruch, wishing the League well, bought a bit of the deal for himself.

Baruch was genuinely sympathetic to farmers, would support the occasional eccentric scheme merely because it was agricultural, but ran hot and cold on the most far-reaching farm proposal of the 1920s, the so-called McNary-Haugen Bill for farm equality. The basis of the plan was the unequal working of the tariff. Whereas manufacturers sold in a market that was protected from foreign competition, farmers had to take the unprotected world price for their crops. The McNary-Haugen solution was to broaden the tariff. First the government would decide whether the surplus portion of a given crop, say wheat, had unduly depressed the price of the whole crop. If so, the surplus would be swept up and sold abroad for what it would bring. The price of wheat would rise in the American market; the higher price would be protected by a tariff. The government would do the foreign marketing, but the farmers would finance the program via a special "equalization" tax. From the farmers' point of view, it was thought that the benefits would outweigh the costs.

The rise of the McNary-Haugen idea was a consequence of the agricultural depression of the 1920s and specifically of the troubles of the Moline Plow Company. George Peek, president of that enterprise, had made a successful career at Deere & Company before the war and had served on the War Industries Board in 1918 with General Hugh

Johnson. In 1919 Johnson and he went to Moline together to rejuvenate what they took to be a promising company. But its customers, the farmers, were in no condition to buy its products and the Moline Plow Company, in any case, was dying. Attending to Washington, Peek and Johnson wrote a tract—"Equality for Agriculture"—which, they hoped, would save the situation by lifting the weight of the surplus.

Baruch was uncertain. He endorsed the goal of the legislation and also the equalization tax, by which farmers would be bound to cooperate under the involuntary voluntary method. He respected Peek and Johnson. As a low-tariff Democrat, however, he disagreed with their protectionist thinking. After withholding his support for the bill in 1922, he helped it along in 1924, sent $5,000 to the McNary-Haugen forces and helped to write a plank into the Democratic Party platform that called for the "establishment of an export marketing corporation or commission in order that the exportable surplus may not establish the price of the whole crop." But Calvin Coolidge kept the White House and twice he vetoed McNary-Haugen legislation. Peek's idea was adopted in part by the Hoover Administration and surfaced again in a very different (and, to Baruch, distasteful) form under Franklin D. Roosevelt.

When not looking after the commonweal, Baruch sometimes gave himself up to the pleasures and burdens of wealth. As a rule he summered in Europe, sometimes returning in time for the races at Saratoga, at other times playing the horses vicariously through his partner in breeding, Cary Grayson. He was in New York for the autumn and at Hobcaw over Christmas and intermittently through the close of duck and quail season. In the spring he was back in New York again.

He had definite ideas on traveling. Finding himself increasingly cold-blooded as the years wore on, he liked the sunshine. He wanted plenty of legroom and as much seagoing stability as possible. Thus, aboard ship, he preferred a cabin amidships, where the pitching was minimal, but not the Premier Suite, which was too conspicuous. For the European season of July–September 1924 he lined up a touring automobile and chauffeur with specifications he described to his friend Count René de Rougemont: "I do hope," said Baruch, "it is a cabriolet that can be opened, because for touring one must be in the sunshine. If it is entirely collapsible, it would be perfectly splendid. Would it be too much trouble for you to see that there is not only a trunk for the rear, but trunks at the sides of the running boards, so that we can avoid putting a lot of bags inside the car."

Although castles are conspicuous and notoriously damp, in 1923 he rented one. It was called Fetteresso, and it was on the east coast of Scotland about a mile outside the village of Stonehaven. It had a great hall, dining room, drawing room, smoking room, billiard room, library, fourteen bedrooms, servants' quarters, seven bathrooms and one servants' bathroom. Under the impression (certainly mistaken in Baruch's case) that every vacationing laird wanted instant communications with the outside world, the proprietor had just installed a telephone. The shootings extended to about ten thousand acres, for which the season rental was $15,000. Cost of board and castle ran to an extra $10,000 or so, which Baruch paid gladly. "I have always wanted a season's gunning in Scotland or England," he wrote his London agent, "and have always expected that it would cost quite a little." On August 11, 1923, $2,600 of the cost was instantly defrayed when a horse of Baruch's and Grayson's finished in the money at Saratoga.

As a rich man with time on his hands and few fixed commitments, Baruch sometimes had difficulty finding friends to play with. "I am hooked up with a castle in Scotland," he commanded Senator Joseph T. Robinson of Arkansas, a Hobcaw regular, in 1923, "and you are hooked with me. . . . You are going shooting with me, and you need a No. 12 gauge gun. Make no mistake about this." But Robinson couldn't get away, and Baruch got Governor Albert C. Ritchie of Maryland. All together, between August 13 and September 8, the Baruch party (as subsequently augmented) bagged a roe, 3 capercaillies, 4 plover, 13 partridge, 216 hares and 1,662 grouse. Back in New York, Baruch sent Ritchie a $2,500 contribution to his re-election campaign, "because," as he wrote, ". . . you were a damn good governor and because, as my friend, I love and respect you."

It pleased Baruch that the recipients of his gifts were beholden to him, but for his own protection he did some of his charitable giving anonymously. Sending $25 to an impoverished South Carolina woman via a friend, he asked that the source of the funds not be revealed: "Please do not let her know that I sent it because I have so many requests of this kind that I could use every cent I have, and even as much as people think I have, in this way." He urgently wired Joe Robinson with similar instructions when the senator threatened to divulge that

Baruch was the angel of an Arkansas essay contest (the subject, of course, was agriculture). On the other hand, the newspapermen and politicians who accepted his gifts and hospitality did know whom to thank. In 1920, Garet Garrett, a noted financial journalist; Ralph Pulitzer, publisher of the New York *World*; and Herbert Bayard Swope, also of the *World*, were guests at Hobcaw.* (It was a rare visit for Swope, who had round-the-clock need of a telephone, one of the few conveniences that Hobcaw didn't have to offer.) In 1921 came Senator Byron P. (Pat) Harrison of Mississippi and Robinson; in 1922 there were Garrett, Mark Sullivan, Robinson and Cary Grayson; in 1923, Ralph Pulitzer and his brother, Joseph, publisher of the St. Louis *Post-Dispatch*, Charles Michelson of the *World*, Frank Kent of the Baltimore *Sun* and Governor Ritchie. Not until Franklin D. Roosevelt paid a visit in 1944 did an American President visit Hobcaw during Baruch's time, although freshly killed ducks were shipped in a nonpartisan spirit to the White House under Presidents Wilson, Harding and Coolidge. Twenty-five Hobcaw terrapin were delivered, live, to ex-Premier Georges Clemenceau of France, who said that he found them too amusing to eat. When André Tardieu, a protégé of Clemenceau's, mailed Baruch $19,000 in 1925 with the explanation, "I would like to make them [the dollars] prolific," Baruch graciously ignored his self-imposed rule against managing other people's money. There was a recent precedent for this kindness. Since at least 1923 he had been looking after the affairs of General John J. Pershing.

To newspapermen, who proverbially didn't have enough money to be managed, Baruch's fortune stirred the hope that they might one day work on a Baruch paper. David Lawrence sold him a minority interest in his *United States Daily*, and there was an unsuccessful Baruch bid for the New York *Evening Post* in 1922. In 1923, Arthur Krock moved to New York from Louisville with his wife and small son, took a temporary job at the Motion Picture Producers' Association and began writing ed-

---

*There was a reunion of Hobcaw guests in 1926 at which Pulitzer paid tribute to Baruch with a quatrain in doggerel:

> *Prince of hosts this great agronomist*
> *Is a hunter bold and brave;*
> *This political economist*
> *With his dictum: Work and save!*

itorials part time for the New York *World*. By 1924, he had become assistant to the publisher of the *World* and a publicity adviser to Baruch. Krock needed money, Baruch needed a ghostwriter, each man liked the other, and so their friendship blossomed. In March 1926 Baruch subscribed $1,000 to the *Evening World*'s free-coal fund, because, as he wrote Krock, "you asked me to." That August a friendly profile of Baruch appeared in *The New Yorker* under Krock's signature.

In late 1925 or early 1926 Baruch unwittingly helped Krock into a jam that made his leaving the *World* advisable if not inevitable. At the time Dillon, Read & Company was trying to buy the Dodge Brothers Company, and it had commissioned Charles Schwartz and Morton L. Schwartz, brothers and well-known financial and racing figures, to assist. Baruch knew the Schwartzes (at the Turf & Field Club enclosure at Belmont Charles Schwartz had Box 42, Morton had 43, Swope had 44 and Baruch had 45), and he steered them to Krock for publicity work on the deal, which promised to be controversial. Krock agreed to help (as he wrote in his memoirs) ". . . whenever the request in no way infringed on any professional obligation or involved *The World*." Walter Lippmann, the editor of the editorial page, however, did find what he thought was an infringement. One day he happened to be walking by Krock's office when Krock was on the phone with Charles Schwartz. The conversation that Lippmann thought he overheard concerned an editorial. The piece, which Lippmann himself had written but which (as he recalled) had not yet been published, condemned the Dodge acquisition. Lippmann took his suspicions to Pulitzer, who demanded an explanation of Krock. Krock insisted that there had been a misunderstanding and that Lippmann was mistaken, but the episode was disagreeable all around. In 1927 Baruch mentioned to Krock that Adolph S. Ochs, publisher of *The New York Times*, had an interest in hiring him. Baruch set up a meeting between employer and employee to be, and Krock, on May 1, 1927, joined the *Times*'s editorial board.

Among the New York newspapermen of the day only Swope could pretend to financial equality with Baruch and at that it was a parity mainly on the expense side of the ledger. Swope began as a reporter on the New York *World* in 1909 at $42 a week plus space rates. In 1921, at the age of thirty-nine, he was the paper's executive editor at $1,000 a week plus a 2 percent share of the *World*'s and *Sunday World*'s profits. The salary was large by almost every relevant measure except Swope's standard of living. After his promotion to executive editor, he and his wife moved into a capacious fifth-floor apartment at 135 West 58th Street. Feeling cramped, they annexed the apartment upstairs to create a duplex of twenty-eight rooms, eight baths, a dozen telephones and enough closet space to house the roughly seventy-five suits that Swope usually had in commission. In the summer, when Baruch was off to Europe—Swope once asked that he bring back a dozen pair of white wool socks from Paris for him—the Swopes rented a three-story Victorian mansion in Great Neck, on the North Shore of Long Island, overlooking Manhasset Bay. Ring Lardner lived a hundred yards away, but still within easy earshot.

> It is [he related] almost impossible to work at times and still more difficult to sleep. Mr. Swope of the *World* lives across the way, and he conducts an almost continuous house party. A number of other neighbors do the same; there are guests in large numbers roaming these woods all the time. Apparently they become confused occasionally and forget at whose house they are really stopping, for they wander in at all hours demanding refreshment and entertainment at the place that happens to be nearest at the moment.

Enough found their way to the Swopes to run the editor's grocery bill at high season to $1,000 a week, thereby exactly matching his salary.

Swope's financial requirements were fully proportional to Swope himself, as Peggy Barton, the writer and cartoonist, sketched him:

> Tall, architectural head like a department store, tomato bisque in color, topped by close, well-groomed frills of blond hair. Narrow forehead with square, jutting bones. Steep, pear-shaped nose, pinched in at the bridge, flanked by an inch of eyebrow, a circle of glass, and a wedge of eye. Scornful nostrils snorting with importance. Long upper lip of an early settler, suspending a mouth like a tailored buttonhole and a truculent chin with a slight dribble of flesh beneath. Big swinging stride: style, Lord of Creation. Voice like a dinner gong. Stuck-up, stiffened, starched, easily rumpled. Self-centered as the last dodo. Breathes fire, brimstone, and Big Business. The spirit of old Gotham.

To keep in funds, Swope speculated in the stock market, at first indifferently but later with such brio that his pre-Crash portfolio totaled, on paper, $12 million. He bet extravagantly. One of his gaming companions was Arnold Rothstein, a professional gambler of unsavory reputation who was assassinated in 1928 while carrying $6,500 in his pocket (a not unheard-of amount for Rothstein—at times he had $100,000). In February 1923 Swope got into a two-day poker game in the private railcar of Joshua Cosden, the oilman, in Palm Beach, Florida. Cosden, who could afford it, lost $443,100. Leonard Replogle, Baruch's steel deputy in the War Industries Board, was ahead by a couple of hundred thousand dollars, and Florenz Ziegfeld, owner of the *Follies*, lost a little more than Replogle had won. In advance Swope had allowed himself losses of $150,000. He wound up winning (although not, to the last cent, collecting) $470,300.

Swope continued to see Cosden, whom he took to the Dempsey-Tunney rematch in 1927, and also another oil millionaire, Harry F. Sinclair, who had been Swope's host at the first Dempsey-Tunney bout in 1926. What they told Swope about the market, he passed along to Baruch, and Swope's information in 1923 was that oil stocks were a good thing. Putting their heads together, Baruch and he bought, but the oils went down. That September, Swope reported that Sinclair was still bullish, and that he (Swope) was still holding on: "I have all my Sinclair and Cosden," he wrote Baruch. "I have not bought any more, though I was tempted to. For the purpose of straightening out my account, I have sold my holdings on Atchison, Southern Pacific, Mack Truck, common, Mack Truck, preferred, Detroit Edison and Consolidated Gas. My account, I think, is in fair shape, though of course, it shows a heavy loss."

Writing comprehensively, the editor included a report on the season at Saratoga, news of a mission to Russia by Sinclair to look for oil, "inside dope" on the oil-stock situation, word that Frank Munsey wanted to sell the New York *Herald* ("We might keep our ears to the ground and see what happens"), a guess on the initials of the young lady with whom Baruch had allegedly had a shipboard tiff (B.G., married name H.: "nothing escapes me") and the flattering information that any number of stock-market jobs were Baruch's for the asking, although, Swope added, he felt sure that Baruch would not be interested. Also enclosed was a clipping from the *World* headed "B. M. Baruch Condemns Defiance of League," which contained a statement deploring Mussolini's action against Greece. This Swope had solicited from Baruch at Fetteresso.

There was an undercurrent of dunning in Swope's letter, and Baruch, sensing it, wrote back to offer help. He asked that

the responsibility for the three thousand shares of Sinclair . . . in your account be taken over from yours to mine. There is a loss of some $12,000 in it, and in addition it requires $10,000 or $12,000 more for margin. Thus, it relieves your account to that extent. I am taking the stock over because of what I said at the time, and also because it may teach me a lesson not to go to sleep with even the tip of my finger in anybody's mouth. When it did not materialize at the time the stock was around 22 or 23 [the price had fallen to 18⅝], we should have ducked. This is what I had in mind when I told Miss Boyle to sell the stock, and get rid of a thousand at 24⅞. I do not know enough about oil stocks to do anything in them, but I do know enough to keep out of them.

New losses seven months later brought more assurances from Baruch and additional thanks from Swope.

Inasmuch as Baruch was a friend of the *World*'s publisher and a virtual banker to its executive editor, it was natural to suppose that he enjoyed some special influence over its news columns. E. J. Kahn, Jr., Swope's biographer, however, decided not.

As for Baruch [Kahn wrote], while there was no question in anyone's mind that any public statement he cared to make would find a refuge in the *World*'s columns, Swope extended himself not much beyond sending a memorandum to an assistant in the spring of 1926 that went, "Please tell the Sports Department in referring to Mr. Baruch never to call him 'Barney.' His name is Bernard M. Baruch, and he is to be referred to in that way, or as B. M. Baruch."

When William G. McAdoo, Baruch's candidate for the 1924 Democratic presidential nomination, chafed at the unfriendly treatment he was getting in the *World*, he asked Baruch to intercede on his behalf with Swope. Whatever Baruch may or may not have told Swope (he told Mark Sullivan that there was nothing he could or would do), the *World* never let up on McAdoo.

For not much more than the cost of maintaining Swope, Baruch might have made a down payment on a medium-sized daily, but as Garet Garrett pointed out there was no reason to buy a paper when he could so easily get on the front page of everybody else's. Getting on was easy, but making it seem spontaneous was sometimes a challenge. Prodigious efforts of stage setting were required in 1925, for example, when Baruch gave $250,000 to the Walter Hines Page School of International Relations at Johns Hopkins University to endow research into the idea of "taking the profit out of war." This was, Baruch liked to point out, his idea. He thought that war might be avoided if corporations were denied extraordinary profits for the duration of the emergency. Alternately, if hostilities did erupt, the central ordering of the economy along the lines pioneered by the War Industries Board would help to speed victory. His friend General Pershing agreed to endorse the scheme and Krock was retained for publicity. A letter that was evidently written or edited by Krock but signed by Owen D. Young, president of the school's board of trustees, and addressed to Baruch went as follows:

> My Dear Mr. Baruch:
> In closing Chapter 6 of your report to the President as Chairman of the War Industries Board (March 3, 1921) you said:
>
> > "One is led to the thought that, in a similar emergency, there ought to be not alone a mobilization of manpower, but of things and dollars."
>
> That is the first crystallization in words of the definite system of industrial preparedness and management in time of war which was already in practical operation under the War Industries Board when the great war ended in 1918 and which experience has taught us must necessarily exist in complete form before another war comes, if the nation is to reach its full effectiveness. To this thought you have many times since added these two points:
> (1) That the mobilization of "dollars and things" by an industrial war chief would "take the profit out of war;" and
> (2) That to take the profit out of war would probably prove one of the strongest influences for future peace.
> These suggestions are undoubtedly worthy of study and development from the standpoint of preventing war. The Page School is interested in all such measures. By taking the profit out of war we understand you to mean that you would limit profits through regulation so as to prevent profiteering. Certainly an absence of such profit would tend to repress that jingoism which

encourages war, and, if war were to begin, to shorten, rather than to prolong it.

It seems to the Page School Board that if the plan which you had in practical operation at the end of the war, and have several times since outlined in addresses to the War College, in newspaper articles, in hearings before Congressional committees and in letters to men in public life, could be carefully studied in certain colleges in first-power countries, it would take its place definitely as one of the greatest deterrents to aggressive or causeless war that has yet been devised. For, if profit is eliminated from war everywhere, mercenary incentive to aggressive war will be definitely removed everywhere, and if the mobilization of things and dollars is carried along on the same basis with the mobilization of men in all countries verging on war, there will be less likelihood of joining battle.

As Chairman of the Page School I invite you to center the American study of the problem there. Before coming to this decision the idea was submitted to General Pershing and you will note from his reply, a copy of which I enclose, that he agrees with all that I have said.

Pershing and Young may have agreed but the board of trustees (which included, among other important people, Franklin D. Roosevelt) demurred. Their objection was that publication of the correspondence would leave the mistaken impression with the public that the school, instead of devoting itself to peace, had taken up the administration of war. This wounded Baruch and caused him to withdraw. Then the trustees reconsidered. A reconciliation was effected, and a statement for public release was beamed to Baruch across the Atlantic at the Ritz in Paris. The text included thanks for his "munificent" gift and the stipulation that the correspondence would be given to the newspapers immediately. News of the gift, complete with lengthy excerpts from the Baruch-Young letters, was published on the front page of *The New York Times*.

The proposition that profits were a cause of war was, of course, a socialist evergreen, and it confirmed Baruch's conservative critics in the notion that he was slightly soft in the head. (Whatever the theoretical merits or demerits of the profits from war idea, the Soviet Union, which abolished private property, marched on Finland and Poland in the next war, and Nazi Germany, which severely constricted property rights, marched on nearly everybody.) The fact was that Baruch was neither right nor left but eclectic. General Hugh Johnson described a portrait painter who despaired of capturing Baruch on canvas "because of the infinite variety and shades of expression constantly flitting across that aesthetic mobile face." He was equally changeable in politics. In general he was loyal to men and party rather than to principles, but he was capable of magnificent disregard of personalities. When, for instance, Henry Ford proposed a plan in the early 1920s to develop the hydroelectric potential of Muscle Shoals and Senator George W. Norris of Nebraska countered with a rival scheme for government development, Baruch (who had had extensive wartime experience in the matter) considered the proposals on what he took to be their public merits. He chose Ford, his tormentor. He managed to support both the conservative Ritchie and the ultraliberal William G. McAdoo because he thought both of them were good men. While favoring fewer laws and more liberty, for many years he was also an ardent Prohibitionist.* Notwithstanding his aid to the soak-the-rich Nonpartisan League, he disapproved of the double taxation of corporate dividends and thought that a strict 33⅓ percent limit on income taxes would encourage enterprise.

One of the strangest ideological encounters of his career occurred in the summer of 1925, following the Page School publicity. It happened at a discreet hotel in Versailles where the then commissar of foreign trade of the Soviet Union, Leonid Krassin, had arranged to meet him to make an extraordinary proposition. The Russian told the American that the achievements of the War Industries Board had made a deep impression on the Kremlin. "We have been counting on you, Mr. Baruch," said Krassin, "to do for us in peace what you did for your own country in war." He invited Baruch to become a kind of commissar consultant, and to name his price.

---

*He was not so ardent that he poured out his cellar. In 1926 it contained a case of brandy, 3 of Cognac, 22 of Clos du Cardinal white wine, 34 of vermouth, 51 of gin (Gordon's), 11 of rye, 45 of Scotch, 35 of miscellaneous clarets, 12 of Champagne (including 5 of Pol Roger 1909 and 5 of Dry Monopoles 1907), assorted liqueurs, brandies, sherries and a bottle of Jamaican rum. Evidence is mixed as to whether the 18th Amendment was observed under his roofs. Baruch himself was a light drinker; John Baragwanath remembered that, while the food at Hobcaw was superb, no liquor was served in the 1920s. Guests, he said, brought their own potables and held loud cocktail parties in their rooms before dinner, which Baruch pretended not to notice. However, when the old Hobcaw house burned in 1929, Senator Key Pittman of Nevada, a guest at the time, bravely re-entered it to save a barrel of corn liquor.

Baruch (as he related the episode in his memoirs) agreed, although he said that he wouldn't take any money. He did interpose one condition. It was that the needs of the Russian people in diet, transportation and housing be given priority over heavy industry. This bourgeois sentimentality saddened even Krassin, who had an English wife and was known as a liberal, and the talks went no further. Shortly after this brush with Soviet Communism, Baruch lent some all-American counsel to Cordell Hull, chairman of the Democratic National Committee. "I do hope," said Baruch, "that the Democrats will not ally themselves with these fellows who are either pink or red, or just be against a man because he is a little more successful than the others."*

Through the war years and into the mid-1920s the most important man in Baruch's political life behind Wilson himself was the President's son-in-law, William Gibbs McAdoo. McAdoo wanted to be President and also to be rich, but the latter ambition impeded the former. He was born in Marietta, Georgia, in 1863 and shared the universal poverty of that time and place. In 1877 he moved to Knoxville, Tennessee, with his six brothers and sisters because his father, an ex-Confederate officer, had been appointed adjunct professor of English and history at the University of Tennessee at the annual salary of $1,500. As a young man, McAdoo read the law in Chattanooga, accumulated $25,000 through real-estate speculation but lost that and more in a failed attempt to electrify the Knoxville Street Railroad.

Seeking a theater of operations in which to repay his debts, he moved to New York in 1892. He opened a Wall Street law office, found no clients and tried to sell railroad bonds. To save a dime a day he walked from his home, a furnished fifth-floor walk-up on West 87th Street, to Wall Street and back again, a ten-mile round trip. In 1901, when Baruch, seven years his junior, was already a millionaire, McAdoo conceived a plan to build a railroad tunnel under the Hudson between Manhattan and New Jersey. By 1909, as president of the Hudson & Manhattan Railroad Company, he had built four tunnels ("the McAdoo Tunnels") and coined the corporate slogan "The Public Be Pleased."

---

*Just the same, during the Red Scare in 1920, when the New York *World* set up a Representative Government Fund to defend five duly elected Socialist members of New York State Assembly who had been summarily denied their seats, Baruch contributed $100.

All this brought him prosperity and public esteem but, to his sharp disappointment, not wealth. On the Jersey side of the Hudson he met Governor Woodrow Wilson, joined his campaign in 1912, made himself invaluable and entered the Administration as Treasury Secretary. In the war he kept the Treasury portfolio, shouldered the crushing duties of Director-General of Railroads and chairman of the Federal Reserve Board, headed up the Farm Loan Board, the War Finance Corporation and the International High Commission, and somehow found time to sponsor Baruch within the Administration and to defend his flanks at the War Industries Board. This kindness Baruch never forgot.

McAdoo quit the Treasury in 1918 to replenish his own finances. Probably he would have been the nominee for President in 1920 except that his father-in-law refused to rule out a third term for himself until late in the season. From a new base in Los Angeles, McAdoo busied himself in moneymaking and politics and was off to a fast start in the 1924 race. Baruch fell in with him, raised some $50,000 for him in the early going and in 1923 described him as "head and shoulders above every man who has been talked about."* Then, on January 24, 1924, Edward L. Doheny, a slight and mustachioed oil millionaire, con-

---

*Privately partisan, Baruch in public was circumspect, as the Washington *Star* satirically noted early in January 1924:

Mr. Bernard M. Baruch, noted financier and as genial a sphinx as ever, guarded his tongue, slipped into town yesterday, registered at the Shoreham, and, after calling on his old friend, former President Woodrow Wilson, went over to Annapolis to attend the Jackson day dinner in honor of Gov. Ritchie of Maryland . . .

While graciously consenting to be interviewed, just what Mr. Baruch's opinions are on world conditions and the economic and political situations in America at present must be left to the reader to judge from the following conversation.

"What do you think of the European situation, Mr. Baruch?"

"* * * but, please, don't quote me."

"How are things looking over here?"

"* * *, but I must not be quoted."

"Who do you think the Democrats will nominate?"

"* * *, but for heaven's sake, don't quote me."

"How do you figure the President's chances?"

"* * *, however, that's not for quotation."

"You're certainly looking the picture of health, Mr. Baruch!"

"Well, you may say that I never felt better in my life. Isn't it a wonderful day? I was just—" but right then there was quick shuffling of feet, Barney Baruch was in the elevator, and as the lift shot off all one could hear was, "This is not to be quoted."

fessed to a Senate investigating committee that he had sent $100,000 in bills in a "little black satchel" to Albert B. Fall, Secretary of the Interior under Harding, during negotiations for naval oil reserve leases at Teapot Dome, Wyoming, and at Elk Hills, California. A few days later came another revelation: William G. McAdoo had been Doheny's lawyer.

Thus national politics were turned on their head and stood back up on their feet again. No sooner had the Harding Administration been exposed as corrupt than the leading Democratic presidential contender, McAdoo, was shown to have taken $50,000 in retainers from a presumed Republican malefactor.

When the storm broke, Wilson lay dying. McAdoo and his wife, Wilson's daughter Eleanor, had boarded a train in Los Angeles to be by his side, but he died before they could reach him. In Washington, McAdoo mourned distractedly. He fended off the Doheny insinuations, corralled delegates (which, in the circumstances, struck his mother-in-law as grievously bad form) and demanded the privilege of clearing his name before the Senate committee. This he did, wrote Frank Kent, in his history of the Democratic Party,

> right gallantly . . . He made it clear that he not only had not rendered Mr. Doheny any legal services in connection with the Elk Hills oil lease but had known nothing about these leases. As soon as it had appeared that the breath of suspicion touched these leases he had severed the legal tie that bound him to Doheny and retired from the service. At no time had he ever had any relations with Mr. Doheny that were not clear and aboveboard, or which in any way reflected on him as a lawyer or as a man. It was a clear-cut, manly, convincing statement he made, but it did not in the least diminish the clamor nor lessen the vigor with which he was denounced as "Doheny's attorney."

Baruch had long before advised McAdoo to steer clear of rich clients if he wanted to be President. Now his advice was to take a calculated risk. He urged McAdoo to offer to step down, a maneuver, he thought, that would win the public's sympathy, disarm his enemies and ultimately salvage his candidacy. A resignation statement was drafted— Krock was called in from the *World* to write it—but McAdoo refused to sign. For a while Baruch suspended financial support. Still McAdoo carried on and indeed seemed to gain strength, and presently Baruch was

aboard again. In April he told Senator Harrison: "I am, of course, going to stay along with McAdoo as long as he wants me to and as long as
he desires to run out his string. . . . Whenever a cloud hung over me, no
matter how large or small it was, there was no questioning his faith or
belief or willingness in every possible way."

Either out of personal conviction or out of loyalty to his candidate,
Baruch at the time was in one of his collectivist phases. He stood
foursquare behind Prohibition and spoke in the progressive argot. To
John W. Davis, the conservative corporate lawyer who was to figure unexpectedly in the final outcome of the convention, he offered in-town
quarters and good will. "I should also like to see you very much and
keep in touch with the elbows of my friends," wrote Baruch, "so as to
keep any wet or reactionary from getting the nomination. I think we
will have the nucleus to prevent that in the McAdoo forces."

McAdoo himself was absolutely dry and in harmony with the ideol-
ogy of William Jennings Byran. On the stump he was partial to words
like "reaction," "privilege" and "sinister influences," by which he meant
Wall Street, corporate management, railroads and such hostile eastern
newspapers as the New York *World*. No doubt part of what McAdoo
found sinister about Wall Street was how little money it had yielded to
him (although, unlike Baruch, he had once managed to obtain venture
capital from J. P. Morgan himself). He was tall and thin and had a long
nose, lugubrious eyes and a center-line part in his hair. He was as little
given to self-deprecating humor as most intensely ambitious people are;
to Baruch he once referred to "my restless and adventurous spirit."

McAdoo had been running hard for the Presidency since 1922, had
built a far-flung campaign organization and even after the Doheny ad-
missions was pretty clearly seen as the Democratic front-runner.
Through the unstinting efforts of Swope, his enemy, New York had
been chosen as the site of the 1924 Democratic convention, and on
June 19 McAdoo stepped off a train in Penn Station to the cheers of
men in "Mc'll Do" hatbands. Musicians struck up "Hail to the Chief,"
a cavalcade formed and the candidate made his way by car to the Hotel
Vanderbilt and to a suite that once had been Enrico Caruso's.

Conspicuous among the "reactionaries" who were bound to New
York to oppose him was Senator Oscar W. Underwood of Alabama, formerly of the House, then leader of the Senate, an opponent both of
Prohibition and of women's suffrage and a friend of enterprise. In every
predictable way and in one important surprising one, Underwood's

friends were McAdoo's enemies and vice versa. Paradoxically, the Ku Klux Klan rejected the southern conservative, Underwood; it supported the California progressive, McAdoo.

In those days the Klan was a weighty force in American politics. It naturally had little use for black people, but its agenda was chiefly anti-Catholic, anti-Jew, anti-foreign and anti-beer. In a speech in Houston in the fall of 1923, Underwood had courageously attacked it and so brought down on himself the Klan designation of the "Jew, jug and Jesuit" candidate. McAdoo, holding no brief for the Kluxers but alert to Underwood's subsequent loss of strength in the South and Middle West, held fire. He trimmed on the issue of religious bigotry and refused to condemn the Klan, thereby inviting both the support of that organization and the opposition of its enemies. Baruch was caught in the middle. His friends on the *World* opposed McAdoo. He himself had advised against the tacit courting of Klan support. But when the advice went unheeded he became a silent partner in McAdoo's silence. In May 1924 Swope invited Baruch to submit a brief statement on whether the Democratic and Republican parties should go on record against the Klan. On at least this one occasion, Baruch declined the opportunity to have his views published in the august pages of the *World*.

The convention, which opened at Madison Square Garden on June 24, was the longest (sixteen days), most querulous and most destructive in Democratic annals up to that time. It was the first in which the candidates abandoned the stance of dignified aloofness and generaled their forces on the floor, and it was the first to be broadcast. By radio sets in their parlors, Americans could hear the taunts of Catholics and Kluxers, the baiting chant of "Oil! Oil! Oil!" by McAdoo's enemies and the belated attempts of the convention beadles to restore decorum ("Shut up, you big boob!"). The galleries belonged heart and soul to the governor of New York, Alfred E. Smith, a Catholic, a wet and a product of the Tammany political machine. On all these counts, Smith was anathema to the McAdoo side; the Smith forces loathed McAdoo.

On opening day, flags and bunting were draped festively over the ventilators and the still air bore the scent of some long decamped circus. The tone of the convention was set when Senator Harrison, in his keynote address, innocuously remarked that what America needed was a latter-day Paul Revere. Mistakenly thinking that they had heard the cry "cold beer," the Tammany loyalists sent up a raucous cheer.

After the preliminaries there was a fratricidal platform fight. A pro–League of Nations plank was voted down, and a proposal to denounce the Klan by name lost by one vote. Although nominally a victory for McAdoo, the Klan ballot backfired by steeling the wets and Catholics against him.

On June 30, the first day of presidential balloting, it was clear that, barring a compromise, no candidate had the votes to win. McAdoo had 431½ out of a needed 732. Smith had 241 and Underwood had 42½. By the sixty-ninth ballot on July 4 (a day or two after the delegates were supposed to have amicably disbanded), McAdoo was up to 530 votes while Smith had 335. Hoping to break the deadlock, Baruch and Thomas L. Chadbourne, another moneyed McAdoo man, paid an Independence Day call on Al Smith to ask him to withdraw, but the New Yorker refused. At the eighty-seventh ballot, the oppressed and unpressed Democrats put Smith in front. On July 8, after the hundredth ballot, McAdoo was forced to surrender, but then Smith's support (which had been mainly stop-McAdoo) waned too. At last, on the one hundred and third ballot on July 9, John W. Davis went over the top.

Hardly anyone had really wanted him. A former ambassador to the Court of St. James's and a distinguished advocate, Davis was, in William Jennings Bryan's phrase, "Morgan's lawyer," but The Commoner dropped all objections when the delegates in an exhausted afterthought nominated his amiable younger brother, Charles W. Bryan, governor of Nebraska, as Vice President. Smith and the elder Bryan campaigned faithfully for the ticket. McAdoo issued a perfunctory statement and got on a boat for Europe.

Baruch sailed for his annual vacation on July 9, praising McAdoo in defeat, also lauding Smith and next day sending a wireless message to Davis pledging support. (A news story of his sailing made the Op Ed page of the World, space usually reserved for scintillating commentary.) He held nothing against Davis—McAdoo, he thought, at least had fallen to a good man—but he was put off by the Democratic Party. In 1922, he had said that if he could shake his "desire not to be a leader" and if he weren't a Jew, he might seek the party chairmanship himself in order to prepare for the 1924 season. In 1923 he privately called the then-reigning Democratic chiefs "bums." On reflection at Fetteresso in the summer of 1924 he decided that the quality of leadership had somehow retrogressed. It came to him that the party had spurned him and his ideas and now wanted his money. He resolved to give less than he customarily did and never again to discuss an issue from the stand-point of party. To Krock he waxed uncharacteristically bitter: "Jesse Jones asked me for money—I felt like referring him to all your friends, Mack, Roosevelt, Brennan, Marsh and Cox . . . your friends who read me out of the party—not forgetting Joe Tumulty who does honor me with his friendship and all your other buddies—Not one cent yet. . . ."*

In Vichy Baruch took the baths and in Scotland he helped to kill 1,724 grouse. From the castle he cabled instructions to Mary Boyle to send George C. Jewett, head of the American Wheat Growers Associ-ated, a partisan message, reading: "Davis thoroughly honorable sincere can accept any promises made stop Coolidge adverse." He managed to read the New York *World*. Returning to New York with his wife and son aboard the *Majestic* on September 23, he denied a story that Junior (for so he called his grown son) was engaged to marry the Hollywood film star Lois Wilson. "All I can say is, unfortunately, the rumor is not true," said the father. His son, aged twenty-two, blushed.[†]

The Baruchs had come home to a parlous political situation. The party was riven, and Davis was making so principled a campaign that some of his friends despaired of him. McAdoo sulked, and Baruch hung back, or so it appeared to Jesse Jones, the party's chief fund raiser. A week after Baruch's return, Jones wrote him an extraordinary five-page letter, which began with a review of how much the party had done for him and how little he had reciprocated.

> You have [wrote Jones apropos of what he called Baruch's God-given talent] been permitted to prosper, amass a vast fortune, millions upon millions, and I wonder if you are as [*sic*] much better man for it as you should be. . . . You charge that [Clem L.] Shaver [the national party chairman from Lost Creek, West Virginia] is not a good manager, that you were not consulted in his selection. You question this, that or the other activity, or lack of activity, upon the part of the Committee. You,

---

*Norman E. Mack, head of the New York delegation; Franklin D. Roosevelt; George Brennan, the Illinois boss; and James M. Cox, the 1920 standard-bearer. All had opposed McAdoo.

[†]Intentionally or not, Baruch had a way of patronizing his son. From the Paris Peace Conference he had written him at the Milton Academy: "Lots of people say you look a very nice boy, and want to know if you are clever. I always reply that I am sure of only one thing about my son, that is, he will not lie or do a dishonorable thing."

who should give more, many times more, than any other man in the United States, both in money and effort, rent a castle in England [*sic*] and sail for a pleasant and indulgent summer, leaving scant if any suggestions to the nominee or the National Committee, and after returning still withhold all but your criticism and a miserably small check.

No—You say you are going to spend $120,000 in the interest of our ticket. If your heart is in the election of John W. Davis and the success of our ticket and not in your own glorification, you will ask the Committee in what way can the $120,000 you say you are willing to spend might be used. Why not take counsel of the Committee, of the candidates, not tell them but ask in what way your $120,000 in their opinion might be most helpful? Why not give it, or at least a considerable part of it, to the Committee and let the propaganda you propose be done by the Democratic Party rather than by B. M. Baruch? That would be the part of a great man.

Jones closed with an insulting spiritual suggestion: ". . . you should thank your God every night . . . for your opportunities and privileges, and, further, you should ask Him to give you that humility that goes to make men great."

Baruch was outraged and astonished. He was, in his own estimation, an extraordinary man already, the proof of which was that his ideas had borne fruit in the marketplace. Where had the ideas of Jesse Jones gotten the party? Furthermore, he was certainly one of the top contributors, if not the leading contributor, in the party, and had sustained it through the hard times of the early 1920s. The unspeakably irritating part of Jones's letter was that the party was prepared to ignore him while taking his money, as if it had the right to it (and as if there were as much as it thought). With Krock's help, Baruch got off a hostile reply, stating, among other things, that the string he'd attached to the $120,000 was only that it be spent wisely, which, however, he doubted that Jones was capable of doing. "Your letter was so gratuitously irritating that it disturbed me," said Baruch, "but it was not without value, for it will mark the end of our personal relations and thus relieve us both of personal embarrassment."

On Election Day, Davis suffered an even worse shellacking than he had modestly expected (or than Baruch had apparently foreseen; he lost $3,000 in an election bet that he'd placed through Chadbourne). A few days later Baruch mended fences with McAdoo's blood enemy, Al Smith, with a $5,000 contribution, and within a few years he was corresponding civilly again with Jones. After the election Baruch suffered a temporary reaction against politics, but by the off-year elections of 1926 he was interested again. He contributed $46,500 to the Democratic Senatorial Campaign Fund (including $5,000 earmarked for Alben W. Barkley of Kentucky, future Vice President under Harry S. Truman), raised $20,000 more from Mrs. Thomas F. Ryan and gave $5,000 after the election to help close the senatorial deficit. He gave at least $10,000 to Democratic candidates for the House and looked for an opportunity to bet on Senator James W. Wadsworth, Jr., of New York, a Republican who was pitted against Robert R. Wagner; Wadsworth and Baruch, of course, lost. In the same year he himself was mentioned in the New York papers as possible Senate material. This intelligence was forwarded to him at Fetteresso by Senator Robinson, who observed that it was the kind of thing that ordinarily didn't interest him; nor did it then. The ordeal of Madison Square Garden led Baruch to make, and, for the most part, to keep, another resolution: never to involve himself again in presidential primary elections; henceforth he would have no candidate but the Democratic Party's. In political terms he had renounced speculation for long-term investment.

As for McAdoo, he returned, without much success, to moneymaking. He tried to interest Baruch in a railroad venture late in 1924 and borrowed money from him to pour into Florida real estate in 1925. In 1928, during the fever of the bull market in stocks, Baruch happened to mention that Daniel Roper, another ex-Wilsonian, had lied to him, and that he regretted the fact that he had helped to make him so much money. McAdoo commiserated with this and then redirected the discussion.

> I think [he wrote Baruch] you have been extremely good to Roper in making for him "a great deal of money." It certainly is a good friend who will help another in this way. I wish very much, if you see an opportunity, you would put me in the way of taking on something which would prove profitable. This thing of working one's head off at law, with the small results that can be gotten in this more limited theater of professional and business action, grows very tiresome as I grow older. Think this over and pull an oar for your old friend if you can without too much grief or trouble! You have been most kind to carry me on

TWELVE

"I Would Stand Pat"

October 1, 1928
Pine Bluff, Ark.
Dear Sir:

Knowing that you have had some interest in the fur business, I take the liberty to present to you what seems to me a wonderful proposition, in which you no doubt will take a lively interest, and perhaps wire me the amount of stock you want to subscribe towards the foundation of this company.

The object of this company is to operate a large cat ranch in or near the city of Oakland where land can be purchased cheap for this purpose.

To start with, we will collect say about 100,000 cats. Each cat will average about twelve kittens a year. The skins will run about ten cents each for the white ones to seventy-five cents for the pure black ones. This will give us twelve million skins a year to sell at an average price of thirty cents, making our daily revenue about $10,000 gross.

A man can skin fifty cats per day for $2.00. It will take one hundred men to operate the ranch, and therefore, the net profit will thus be $9,800 per day.

We will feed the cats on rats and will start the rat ranch next door. The rats multiply four times as fast as the cats, and if we start with one million live rats, we will have, therefore, four rats per day for each, which will be plenty.

Now then, we will feed the rats on the carcasses of the cats from which the skins have been taken, giving each rat one fourth of a cat.

It will be seen that this business will be self-supporting and automatic all the way through. The cats will eat the rats, the rats will eat the cats, and we will get the skins.

Awaiting your prompt reply and trusting that you will appreciate the opportunity that I give you, and which will get you rich quick, I remain,

Yours very truly
The Pussy Skin Corporation, Ltd.

—with the compliments of Simon Guggenheim.

The defeat of Davis by Calvin Coolidge brought the consolation of a Republican bull market which Baruch was quick to recognize and capitalize on. The day after the election, a Wednesday otherwise notable for a victory statement by Judge Gary in which Coolidge was compared favorably with Abraham Lincoln, Baruch bought 3,000 shares of Consolidated Gas. On Thursday he bought 8,100 shares of Baltimore & Ohio Railroad, 7,500 of American Smelting & Refining, 8,000 of U.S. Steel, 5,000 of Southern Railway and 5,000 of International Nickel, all told, in two days, almost $1.7 million worth of common stock. Before the month was out, he had paid some $2.1 million for another 31,800 shares, including 3,000 more of Consolidated Gas, 4,900 of Sloss Sheffield, 7,000 of Steel, 4,100 of Gulf States Steel, 12,000 of Northern Ore and 800 of Atlantic Coast Line (not counting 16,000 shares of Reading Railroad, at more than $1 million, which he had begun to accumulate before the election). Such was the strength of the market and the clarity of Baruch's foresight that these operations yielded him a net trading profit in 1925 of $1,424,309.57. His trading losses, while large, were held manageably in proportion to his gains. They were $416,768.50. Both figures dwarfed the sum total of his fee income, $150, which the *Atlantic Monthly* had paid him for an article on taking the profit out of war (which, however, Krock had apparently written).

In his autobiography Baruch left the clear impression that he put the stock market behind him when he took up public service. In a sense that was true. It was true for a time as a matter of geography. After the war he moved his offices from the financial district to 598 Madison

Avenue (before moving downtown again in the bull-market year of 1928). It was also true that his success in the market left him unsatisfied. Still seeking an outlet in the management of a railroad, he made overtures to the Baltimore & Ohio but received no encouragement from the president, Daniel Willard.

"I am 55 years of age," Baruch wrote John R. Morron, a friend and director of the B&O in the summer of 1925, "and I should like nothing better than to take a large interest in the New York Central, which I think is a gold mine and out of which I do not think the stockholders are getting as much as they are entitled to. . . . I really should like to take a very serious interest in the New York Central, and gradually work into a more personal interest in its direction."

Baruch himself, in fact, had recently lost $90,000 in trading the stock of the New York Central. He kept 1,500 shares for investment, but when they showed a small profit in October 1925, he sold them too, thereby relinquishing another railroad hope.

If the stock market was no longer everything for Baruch it still was something. He watched it, traded actively in it (in the process helping to support his brothers in the brokerage business) and took both pleasure and money from it. In 1926, a choppy year, he managed to eke out a net trading profit of $457,597.04 and to take a long-term gain in Texas Gulf Sulphur of no less than $1,936,662.

The seismic bull market that posterity associates with exuberance, credulity and wealth was also a source of disbelief and losses among professional traders who had been given to understand that speculative trees didn't grow to the sky. Between 1906 and 1924 the Dow Jones Industrial Average had shunted roughly between 50 and 100. In the aftermath of Coolidge's election, it pushed through that upper bound; by the close of 1925 it touched 157. In 1926 came a setback to 135, some backing and filling and, as one might have supposed, a return to normalcy. But in 1927 the rise continued; on the nineteenth of December the Dow reached 200. In 1928 the angle of ascent of prices became almost vertical until the average hit 300 on New Year's Eve. By September 3, 1929, when it stopped rising, it had touched 381.17. Then for almost the next three years it fell as steeply as it had risen, not stopping until July 8, 1932. On that day it read 41.22.

The unprecedented extremes of the movement taxed the belief and also, necessarily, the net worth, of even farsighted people. Fred Schwed, Jr., told how this happened:

There was always a scattering of bears, "aginners" by temperament, who spent their business days having their ears knocked off. Many of them, bowing to a force which finally seemed cosmic, switched to being bulls at a sadly late period in the era. The remainder who were still short at the time of the crash covered too soon (as who wouldn't?). Then, after prices had gone inconceivably lower, they took their profits and bought stocks (as who wouldn't?). In due course of time, if they bought on margin, they went to "the Cleaners," that mythical establishment to which their brother speculators had repaired some time earlier. "The Cleaners" was not one of those exclusive clubs; by 1932 everybody who had ever tried speculation had been admitted to membership.

As mentioned, Baruch got in on the ground floor of the bull market in 1924. As will be seen, he was slow to come down from its penthouse in 1929. Sometimes, however, in intervening years, he was seized with doubt. In these moments he decided that the public was too much in the market, that prices had gone too far and that stocks should be sold for the fall. Thus in 1927 he came to sell short General Motors.

In the 1920s GM was as vital and glamorous a business as IBM was to become in the 1960s. From near oblivion in the recession of 1920–1921, it grew to eclipse Ford as the nation's largest auto maker by 1928. Before the Crash, in 1929, the price of its stock had bounded by more than 1,000 percent from the 1925 low, a rise which, to the bears, was literally incredible. In the summer of 1926 Thomas Cochran, a partner of J. P. Morgan & Company, had made the extraordinary statement that "General Motors running at its present rate is cheap at the price, and it should and will sell at least one hundred points higher." This was the kind of thing that personages usually kept to themselves or discussed with reporters only off the record. The sight of the words on the broad tape, attached to the name of a Morgan partner, caused eyes to bulge; naturally (artificially, the bears thought) the price of the stock went up.

This was in August. In October, a mild recession began, and in November Baruch made his first short sale, 3,000 shares through his brother's firm, Sailing W. Baruch & Company, at a price of 150. He sold short another 12,000 shares in January 1927 at prices as high as 155.

As a bear, Baruch hoped for bad news and a drop in the stock, but February brought a rise. Conceding partial defeat, he bought 8,000 shares, paying up to 160¼. He stuck to his guns to the extent of a short position of 7,000 shares.

In March there was more optimism and a new record high for the stock. In midmonth, Baruch resumed buying—covering his shorts, cutting losses—but changed his mind toward the end and began selling again. He got off 26,000 shares at up to 176 per share, but the market went against him again. He bought at higher prices.

This cycle of selling short, hoping for the worst, but buying at rising prices, continued through July until he bought his final share at 213½. The previous November he had sold short his first share 63½ points lower. His losses in the campaign ran to $405,432.50. "I told you some time ago that I was out of step with the market," he confessed to General Pershing in March, "and I have not gotten back in step since; so I can't give you any advice that is worth anything."

In May 1928, as the averages pointed straight up and preparations were being made for the autumn's presidential elections, Baruch moved his office from midtown to downtown. At about the same time he moved his household from West 52nd Street, just off Fifth Avenue, to Fifth Avenue at 86th Street—from midtown, uptown. (He and Annie had been thinking about a move to that block for some time; they bought the first two lots north of 86th Street in 1909, but sold them again in 1915.) His new Wall Street address, which was the thirty-first floor of the Equitable Building, 120 Broadway, gave what he feared was a clear signal of a shift in career from public service to speculation. A public-relations dilemma was presented: Was a man who dealt chiefly in cash, not on margin, who eschewed such razzle-dazzle as large-scale pools, but who traded both on the long and short side and kept accounts at twenty-six separate brokerage houses, as he did—was such a man "in the market"? (Possibly this dispersal of business was intended to protect his confidentiality; at H. Hentz & Company, a firm that Herman Baruch headed and through which his brother channeled considerable business, clerks were discouraged from uttering the name of Bernard Baruch lest they start a market rumor. Back-office functionaries referred to him by account number, which was 19.) Baruch thought not, and he fostered the half-truth that he had moved downtown to cultivate his money but not to speculate. The *Times* ingenuously reported that "he does not intend to do trading in the market."

It was true that Baruch was no longer a visible trader. He had long ago resigned from the New York Stock Exchange, he had made a mark in public life, and, since November 1927, he had been a member of the board of directors of the Baltimore & Ohio Railroad (Willard had, after all, encouraged him). Having taken that directorship, he felt duty-bound to join the board of the American Smelting & Refining Company when Simon Guggenheim asked him to in the spring of 1930.

As Baruch, at the age of fifty-seven, was finally entering corporate life, Herbert Bayard Swope, at forty-six, was leaving it. One day in the fall of 1928, the editor turned to his wife and said, "I don't want to be a hired boy any longer." With that he resigned from the *World*, a very wealthy former newspaperman. The bull market had made him rich, and Swope was not such an ingrate as to cast aspersions on it. When, early in 1929, Thomas Chadbourne expressed some doubts about how high prices had gone, Swope reassuringly told him, "Don't kid yourself. We are going to take a pleasant ride, so climb up in the driver's seat." Trading gregariously, Swope kept a joint brokerage account with John Hertz, the Yellow Cab and car-rental magnate; with Albert D. Lasker, the advertising man; and with Baruch. Swope's principal stock-trading asset was the people he knew, starting with his brother, Gerard, president of General Electric, and including such eminent corporate figures as John J. Raskob, Charles M. Schwab and Walter P. Chrysler. The last-named trio, in fact, good-naturedly cut him into the earnings of a pool in Radio Corporation of America in the spring of 1929 even though Swope hadn't put a cent of his own at risk. In a form of reciprocity, Swope fell into the gay habit of placing large bets in the names of his friends without bothering to tell them until they had won or lost. He bought a thirteen-acre estate in Sands Point, Long Island, complete with a seven-car garage, all-weather tennis court, a quarter mile of beach front (shored up by steel sheet that he had ordered direct from the president of Bethlehem Steel, Eugene Grace) and a salt-water pool. There was a telephone by the pool.

Swope was jobless in 1929, but in the stock market he had an engrossing and, while it lasted, lucrative, avocation. While passing the winter in Palm Beach, he left instructions with his secretary, Helen Millar, to check in with Baruch and Morton Schwartz at noon every day for the latest market news and to pass along anything interesting to him in Florida. In February Baruch wired him that he was, for the moment, uncertain: "UNDERSTAND CORNER PEOPLE [i.e., J. P. Morgan & Company] THINK MARKET IS OVER. PERSONALLY SITTING TIGHT BECAUSE I THINK FEDERAL RESERVE DOES NOT UNDERSTAND CONDITIONS AND STILL

HAVE BELIEF IN MY INDUSTRIAL RENAISSANCE." Sometimes it was Swope who passed along information to Baruch, as in an enthusiastic wire of March 21, 1929: "ACTUAL INSIDERS SAY GOLDMAN SACHS DUE FOR AN-OTHER FIFTY-POINT RISE. THIS COMES SO STRAIGHT I WANTED YOU TO KNOW IT. REGARDS, HERBERT." Although Goldman, Sachs Trading Corporation indeed went higher that day, by 1⅜ to 119, it went lower starting the next day. Seven months later it would strike 32. On March 22, Swope was back again: "FOR YOUR INFORMATION . . . GENERAL ELECTRIC FIRST QUARTER WILL SHOW MORE THAN A FORTY PERCENT INCREASE. UT-TERLY ASTOUNDING. IT SIMPLY FORCED ME TO BUY SOME. LOVE, HER-BERT." Despite the presumptive authority of this tip, Gerard Swope a month later revealed that his brother had been wide of the mark. Profits were up by only 23 percent.

On the day Baruch learned that Swope liked GE, he also read in the papers that the Federal Reserve Bank of New York was worried about excessive credit creation and the possibility of bust following boom. The bank's warning left him cold. For one thing, he believed that the decision to lower the discount rate to 3½ percent from 4 percent in the summer of 1927 (just as he was winding up his campaign in General Motors) was responsible for a good part of the speculative rise, and that it ill behooved the Federal Reserve to deplore what it had so signally helped to foment. A few days later, when Charles E. Mitchell, president of National City Bank, reiterated that the policy of his bank was to lend to stockbrokers, investors and speculators at a price, come what may, Baruch was sympathetic. Writing to Mitchell, he called the 1927 discount-rate reduction "false and unwise" and criticized what he took to be the Anglophile motive of the Federal Reserve:* "I go a little further,

---

*Great Britain, which had returned to a variant of the gold standard in 1925 at what proved an overvalued rate of exchange, had been losing gold and export sales and in 1926 had suffered a general strike. It was faced with the disagreeable choice of deflating—that is, of engineering lower prices at home in order to make its goods more salable abroad—or of refusing to convert pounds sterling to gold on demand. The Federal Reserve action provided an out. With the fall in the discount rate, American interest rates declined. For a time, London became a more attractive place in which to invest than New York. Gold, which had previously been moving westbound, began to be shipped east again.

In effect, the Federal Reserve had embarked on a policy of competitive inflation. In June 1927, a month before the action was taken, it held $398 million worth of Treasury securities. In December it owned $606 million. That is, in six months it had

perhaps, than you would," he told Mitchell, "in saying that I think the Federal Reserve System has no right to enter into agreements with foreign governments for the sale of gold for that is the business of private banks and bankers."

Despite such misgivings and the occasional ill-timed short-selling campaign, however, Baruch was fundamentally bullish on business. Starting in the mid-1920s, he thought he could see the shape of a future "industrial renaissance." There would be huge prosperity, he said, if the reparations dilemma were solved and free trade defended. In the event, reparations were never untangled and protectionism impeded the international flow of goods, but Baruch clung to his idea. Early in 1929, on a visit to Hobcaw, Frank Kent got a full briefing on the renaissance theory, which he distilled into a series of newspaper columns. The immediate basis of Baruch's optimism, as it emerged in Kent's articles, was a forthcoming United States mission to Germany. Headed by Owen D. Young and J. P. Morgan, the delegation would seek a final reckoning of what Germany owed and the mobilization of international capital to aid in its payment. A bond issue would be floated and the proceeds applied to financing German debts to the former Allies. The Allies, in turn, would be able to pay what they owed the United States.

Kent reported that, in the estimation of financial bigwigs, the success of such a scheme would ignite "an industrial boom incomparably greater than any that have preceded it." Indeed, the stock market, he wrote, was merely anticipating it, and he went on to paraphrase Baruch's ideas: "It is the belief of the big boys that Young and Morgan will do this job and that these results will follow. They think the thing is 'all set' now. They believe that unconsciously the market is already discounting the coming 'industrial renaissance,' as one 'man of large af-

---

expanded its portfolio by 52 percent. The proceeds of these purchases provided new funds for the banking system and new loans to brokers. All together, the growth of credit in the second half of the year was in excess of the usual seasonal needs of commerce. Adolph C. Miller, a governor of the Federal Reserve Board at the time, subsequently condemned the policy as ". . . one of the most costly errors committed by it [the Federal Reserve] or any other banking system in the last 75 years! . . ."

Monetary historians disagree on the point, but Milton Friedman and Anna Schwartz are sympathetic with the Baruch position to the extent of observing that ". . . virtually the full increase in bank assets from June 1926 to June 1928 as a result of easy money in 1927 was confined to investments and loans on securities. . . ."

fairs' calls it. What he and others like him see ahead is a prosperity greater than that of the last five years."*

Late in March stock prices (that is, the thirty components of the Dow Jones Industrial Average) stopped going up. There was a break from about 320 to 300 and sideways movement through April and May. It was in June, just as the market began to climb again, that Baruch issued what would prove his least prophetic forecast of the era. Talking with the publicist Bruce Barton, he emphasized the bullish implications of the reparations settlement that he saw clearly in the offing and praised the conduct of monetary policy worldwide.

> For the first time in history [said Baruch], we have sound reason for hope for a long period of peace. For the first time, the business men of all nations are supplied with statistical information, together with some understanding of the laws of economics. For the first time, we have sound centralized banking systems in all the countries and close cooperation between those systems internationally. Because all these factors are favorable, and because of the universal stirring of desire and ambition to which I have already referred, I believe in the "industrial renaissance." We are already seeing something of it in the United States.

When Baruch embarked on his annual European vacation late in June 1929 he was kept current on the market by Swope, who stayed home to speculate for the rise and accumulate a racing stable. In Paris a cable reported on the new yeast and baking-soda company, called Standard Brands, that Morgan was putting together, and to Carlsbad came a message about Armour & Company. In early August (locale uncertain, perhaps Fetteresso), Baruch received assurances that the prior day's boost in the discount rate (to 6 percent from 5½ percent) by the Federal Reserve Bank of New York would do no real harm: "THINK GOOD SECURITIES ALRIGHT. FEDERAL RESERVE TOTALLY INCAPABLE OF UNDERSTANDING PUBLIC PSYCHOLOGY. ACTION WILL RESTRICT VOLUME BUT UNAFFECT REAL VALUES." Sailing home aboard the *Berengaria* in September, it was Baruch who tipped Swope: "LEHAM NEW STOCK A GOOD

---

*Besides counseling Kent, Baruch also managed some of his investments. Just after the column appeared, Baruch apprised him of a $900 trading profit. "This isn't exactly what the 'big boys' do," Baruch wrote, "but . . . what is called a 'little soft money on the inside.'" Kent agreed it was the softest $900 he had ever made.

THING. LOVE MAGGIE BERNIE." Leham meant Lehman Corporation, a mutual fund that the banking firm of the same name was in the process of bringing to market; Maggie was Margaret, Swope's wife.

According to his autobiography, Baruch saw the Crash coming and sold stocks in time to avoid getting caught in it. A biographer who took no position on how, or when, he managed to sell, noted that his presumed investment sagacity in 1929 did perhaps more than anything else to advance his subsequent reputation for wisdom in economic matters.

Certainly he seemed none the worse for wear after the market broke. Early in November 1929, after the first convulsion, he suggested to Senator Joe Robinson that the government should prepare a public-works program in case of serious joblessness, and he was able to precede that advice with a campaign contribution of $1,000. (He mailed the check on October 29, as the Dow slumped by 30 points and many on Wall Street were answering, or refusing to answer, margin calls.) In December he gave $10,000 to the Federation of Jewish Societies of New York City, a large gift except in the relative terms of his own income, which would total $1,986,995.63 in 1929, including stock-trading profits of $615,786.31.

Nor in the sinking years that followed the Crash was he noticeably impaired. He still summered abroad, supported favorite causes and made large political contributions. In the first week of August 1930 he was visiting Winston Churchill in England,* and in the second week of September he was home again (the Dow at 243 and falling; unemployment at 9 percent or so and rising), writing checks for $35.26 to the Riverside Ice Company and $594 to the Metropolitan Opera Company.

---

*Baruch, who had gotten to know Churchill in World War I and at the Versailles Peace Conference, and who liked to keep his friendships on the plane of large events, thanked him for his hospitality in a cable that was couched in geopolitical terms:

THE MEMORY OF MY WEEK VISIT WITH YOU IS A DELIGHTFUL SOUVENIR WHICH I WILL ALWAYS TREASURE STOP I BETTER UNDERSTAND ENGLAND HER PEOPLE AND HER TRADITIONS AND HOPE THAT NEW PROSPERITY AND HAPPINESS WILL COME TO HER IN ORDER THAT SHE MAY CONTINUE FOR THE WORLD WHAT SHE HAS DONE FOR SO LONG STOP I TRUST THAT OUR COUNTRY MAY JOIN WITH YOURS IN THE GREAT RESPONSIBILITY THAT LIES BEFORE US STOP I AGREE WITH GENERAL DAWES THAT IN THE BETTER UNDERSTANDING OF THE ENGLISH SPEAKING NATIONS LIES THE ARK OF THE COVENANT OF CIVILIZATION AND HUMAN FREEDOM STOP MANY MANY THANKS AND AFFECTIONATE REGARDS TO ALL.

He contributed some $40,000 to the Democratic Senatorial Campaign Committee, and he was a principal backer of the Jefferson Islands Club, a Democratic haven in Chesapeake Bay. In 1931 he had an extra $13,000 for the South Carolina Food Research Commission to finance an investigation into the iodine content of his home state's soil and truck crops. He lent handsomely to his friends and relatives, sometimes pressing money on people who hadn't asked for it. He sent his cousin, Virginia Epstein, $100 a month after she came in to ask him for a loan for a friend of hers (she protested that she didn't really need the money for herself, but it kept coming until Mary Boyle put a stop to it), and he contributed £100 to a fund that the friends of Winston Churchill had raised in order to buy the future Prime Minister "the best Rolls-Royce obtainable." With Tom Yawkey, owner of the Boston Red Sox and a South Carolina neighbor, he distributed food to hungry people around Hobcaw. In the presidential election year of 1932 he spent $86,716.07 to maintain his office, which served as an unpaid Democratic research bureau. On July 18, 1932, less than two weeks after the stock market scraped bottom, Annie Baruch made financial preparation for a summer of collecting and touring in Europe by applying for a $25,000 letter of credit from the foreign department of Bankers Trust Company.

All this circumstantial evidence merely points to the conclusion that Baruch was as farsighted as he himself suggested. As he told the story and others repeated it, he was vacationing in Scotland when it dawned on him that not all was well in the market. Sailing early, he returned to America, sold stocks and waited for the inevitable.

It would be interesting to know which stocks he owned late in the summer of 1929 and which he held, month by month, through the long liquidation; what he was worth at the top and bottom of the market and the disposition of his assets throughout the cycle. Not all the answers are at hand. Copies of his income-tax returns are available for 1925, 1926 and 1929, for instance, but not for 1927, 1928 or 1930 and beyond. While extensive and previously untapped, his brokerage-house records for 1929 may or may not be complete. For 1930–1932 they are obviously incomplete.

Even without all the facts, however, one is led to take issue with the man who was there. The weight of the evidence supports the conclusion that he didn't sell out in time. A thoroughgoing industrial-renaissance optimist, he underestimated the gravity of the situation for months following the Crash and sold stocks only belatedly (so belatedly that his 1929 tax return showed a stock-trading profit: he hadn't taken his losses yet). On the other hand, he also managed to say out of "the Cleaners." He was not overextended on margin, and he resisted the temptation to buy stocks heavily before the liquidation had run its course. Before the devaluation of the dollar he had the presence of mind to buy gold and gold-mining shares. He was not the Bernard Baruch of legend, but that was the only standard by which he can be said to have fallen short.

To regain the thread of the story: Late in August 1929 Baruch was in Scotland dressed in sturdy boots, sweater and tweeds, carrying a shotgun and stumping about the moor looking for birds. The shooting was indifferent—where he thought there would be 1,600 brace of grouse, he and his guests killed only 306—and his mind was distracted by financial news. His mood was bullish, however, and he traded, via cable, from the long side. On the sixteenth of August he bought 700 shares of Silica Gel Corporation of Maryland at a shade under 30. He had bought the same stock in March and April at prices as high as 45; for in fact, as he had no doubt noticed, the strength of the averages had masked a weakness in the shares of smaller, less widely traded companies. (Indeed, from the point of view of breadth, or the ratio of advancing to declining issues, the market had been sinking since May 1928.) Feeling out of touch and in need of views of men on the scene, he cabled the chairman of National City Bank, Charles E. Mitchell, for advice.

Baruch had played bridge with Mitchell, had once invited him to Fetteresso for some shooting and thought the world of him as a banker. His esteem was nothing casual. It had withstood a $1 million loss in 1927 when a Cuban sugar property that Mitchell had brought to his attention as a venture-capital investment failed. Mitchell, who himself had a big department-store head and a Lord of Creation manner, had made his career on the securities selling side of the bank, expanding its personnel from 4 to 1,400, setting up branches in fifty cities and successfully instilling the precept that prospective investors should be sought out by salesmen rather than the other way around. People called him Charlie before the Crash, and afterward, derisively, Sunshine Charlie. In his secular faith he was very much like Baruch. Both men believed in the future of America and in the potential for its great prosperity, except that Mitchell was an enthusiast, and he invested accordingly (and honorably if not wisely, for he lost everything in the Crash, refused to declare personal bankruptcy, and at length paid off his debts and built another fortune as the head of Blyth & Company, investment bankers). Thus it could have come as no surprise to Baruch when Mitchell cabled him optimistically in August 21:

GENERAL SITUATION LOOKS EXCEPTIONALLY SOUND WITH VERY FEW BAD SPOTS SUCH AS RUBBER. BELIEVE CREDIT SITUATION PRACTICALLY UNAFFECTED BY DISCOUNT RATE ACTION. MONEY SEASONABLY WEAK. SHOULD STRENGTHEN AS MONTH CLOSES. STRENGTH IN STOCK MARKET CENTERS LARGELY IN SPECIALTIES, WHICH IN MANY CASES SEEM UNDULY HIGH, WHILE THERE ARE MANY STOCKS, SUCH AS COPPER AND MOTORS AND CERTAIN RAILS THAT LOOK UNJUSTIFIABLY LOW. I DOUBT IF ANYTHING THAT WILL NOT AFFECT BUSINESS CAN AFFECT THE MARKET, WHICH IS LIKE A WEATHER-VANE POINTING INTO A GALE OF PROSPERITY. BELIEVE THERE IS LESS PESSIMISM AROUND THAN WHEN YOU LEFT.

Baruch cabled his thanks and apparently asked for particulars, because next day Mitchell reported that the motors were being looked on favorably and that a rise in Anaconda (of which he was a director and in which his bank held a sizable investment interest) was "imminent."

While mulling this information Baruch went for a walk on the moor with General Pershing, who had visited him for some gunning and was about to leave for France. (Next month in New York Alexander Woollcott would broadcast the report that the general had been superficially wounded by an errant shot from the gun of Richard P. Lydon, another guest of Baruch's at Fetteresso; Baruch would say that if such a thing had happened he certainly would have heard about it, but, as he didn't, it hadn't.) As Pershing and he walked, Baruch related later, an uncomfortable feeling came over him. He wrote that he made preparation to leave and set off ahead of schedule for New York. If he turned suddenly bearish at the castle or aboard the *Berengaria* en route, however, there is no record of it. On September 5—two days after the Dow Jones Industrial Average made what would prove its 1929 high and two days before he sailed from Southampton—he bought 5,400 shares of American Radiator, 1,000 of Bethlehem Steel and 1,300 of United Corporation, in round numbers $500,000 worth of common stock.

It is unclear, furthermore, that he left Scotland suddenly or with any sense of alarm. There was a regular board meeting of the B&O on Wednesday, September 18, which he attended; the *Berengaria* docked in New York on Friday the thirteenth. A few days after Baruch landed, Mitchell boarded ship for Europe, and Baruch lightheartedly cabled him bon voyage:

FROM MY WINDOW I CAN HEAR THE REFRAIN OF THE SONG THAT THE LITTLE BANK BOYS ARE SINGING. OH AIN'T WE GLAD CHARLIE IS GONE AND HOPE HE GETS LOST IN A FOG BANK.

Baruch was home for less than two weeks when he bought 5,000 shares of Lehman Corporation and also made a notable short sale. In joint account with Swope, he sold 20,000 shares of Radio Corporation of America, which were worth almost $2 million. Radio was one of the bull market's pillars, but Swope and he thought that the speculative house could stand without it. (Until just then Swope had been tipping the stock to Irving Berlin, but he was considerate enough to drop a broad hint on the eve of his short-selling campaign that the songwriter ought to get out.) The prices of most stocks, however, not just Radio, were falling. On September 27 the Dow declined by 11 points, to 345. This was still, relatively speaking, rarefied, but it was some 9 percent below the September 3 high. Baruch decided to sell some National Acme; he got 33 for 1,300 shares, about 3 points less than he had paid in August.

For the time being that was the full extent of his cautionary selling. On the first day of the fatal month of October, he bought 1,400 shares of a copper-mining outfit on the London exchange called Rhodesian Congo Border and sold short another 3,000 shares of Radio. On October third the Dow suffered a sharp, premonitory setback of more than 14 points, to just below 330. The decline continued on the fourth, but Baruch, trading for the rise, bought 2,600 shares of Anaconda, one of Mitchell's stocks, and 700 shares of American Smelting. By the same logic he also bought 2,700 shares of Radio to begin to cover his and Swope's short position.

On October 8, he nimbly sold his Anaconda for an $8,000 trading profit and took a small loss in American Smelting. He continued to sell Radio short. On the fifteenth, Mitchell, from London, declared that ". . . American markets generally now are in a healthy condition," and on the sixteenth, Irving Fisher, the Yale economist, ventured that soon-to-be-immortal prediction that "stock prices have reached what looks like a permanently high plateau." If Baruch didn't agree with those sentiments, neither did he take violent exception to them. On October 21, the Monday before Black Thursday, Swope and he bought 17,700 shares of Radio, thereby winding up their short-selling operation and netting $100,584.22 each. They had done most of their selling at 93 or so and had bought all the way down to 83. Although Baruch had warned Swope that they would no doubt buy, or "cover," too soon, he could have had no idea how premature they would be. On November 13, Radio would change hands at 28¾. In 1932 it hit bottom at 3⅝.

On Tuesday, October 22, Pershing cabled anxiously from Paris: "CONFIDENTIAL. WHAT DO YOU THINK OF THE GENERAL SITUATION. WOULD YOU HOLD SELL OR BUY ANACONDA. IF SELL WHAT WOULD YOU BUY. PLEASE REPLY." An answer was forthcoming immediately: "I WOULD STAND PAT. BARUCH." Baruch himself bought 1,800 shares of American Smelting and 1,400 of Warner Brothers.

In his previous Wall Street experience, panic had been foreshadowed by monetary trouble or conspicuous bankruptcies. So far there were no such portents. Indeed, as Richard Whitney, then vice president of the Stock Exchange and later president, would observe, an oddity of the Crash was the virtual absence of distress in the money market; and as for nonagricultural bankruptcies, the National City Bank letter, as late as December 1929, could say with all apparent confidence, "There are no great failures, nor are there likely to be."

Baruch had himself changed no less than economic conditions had. Before the war, as a speculator and venture capitalist, he had been more or less his own agent. By 1929, however, he was a full-fledged establishmentarian: corporate director, former high government official, political and public figure; the kind of man to whom Nicholas Murray Butler, president of Columbia University, would naturally turn to fill out a Committee of Five to plot a course for the university's future. In a revealing message to Winston Churchill in December 1929 concerning

some Rhodesian copper properties in which they were both interested, Baruch would say, ". . . it is time somebody led the way in the
development of great enterprises upon which the comforts, benefits
and prosperity of great numbers can be based rather than upon any
selfish motive." The implication was that mere moneymaking was un-
worthy of the enlightened entrepreneur, and that Baruch, as a responsible businessman, was predisposed to a view of constructive
optimism. At all events, he had no inkling that Wednesday, October
23, would be much different from Tuesday; certainly none that the
character of trading on Thursday would deteriorate in such a way as to
constitute a market boundary between what had gone before and
what was to follow.

On that Wednesday the market was shockingly weak. Radio fell 11¾ to
68½, and Telephone gave up 15 to 272. One hundred shares of Adams
Express, an investment trust whose prospects, as far as the public was
aware, hadn't appreciably changed in the prior twenty-four hours,
traded at 440, down 96. The Dow was down by 21, or the equivalent
of a 300-point break from the 5,000 mark. This was, in fact, a sharper
break, opening bell to closing, than occurred next day, the infamous
Black Thursday, but on Thursday all pretense of orderliness gave way
to panic. It was to check this hysteria that a procession of bankers filed
into J. P. Morgan's office at 23 Wall Street shortly after noon to plan a
show of support. A few minutes later the bankers filed out and the
press was ushered in. Thomas Lamont, the former Peace Conference
official and the personification of Morgan mastery, remarked casually
to the newsmen, "There has been a little distress selling on the Stock
Exchange, and we have held a meeting of the heads of several financial
institutions to discuss the situation." Lamont declined to go into details, but at about 1:30 P.M., Richard Whitney, acting in the capacity of
Morgan's chief floor broker (in which he was a successor to Arthur
Housman), strode onto the floor to make large purchases for the account of the bankers. This he did with such panache that the rout was
stemmed. Baruch, operating coolly for himself, bought 2,000 shares of
Anaconda, 400 of Warner Brothers and 1,000 of American Smelting.
(This was his last recorded purchase of Anaconda until December 16,
1931, when its price was 9½; on that Black Thursday he paid 104½.) At
the close the Dow was below 300 but not much below it, and it was

down by fewer than 6 points from Wednesday, which seemed a very long time away.

At the top of the front page of Friday morning's *Wall Street Journal* (adjacent to a report on a surge in earnings at Bethlehem Steel Corporation and directly above a hortatory essay addressed to cotton growers, "Raise Better Cotton") was an editorial on the stock market under the portentous headline, "A Turn in the Tide." The piece explained that weakness in the industrial average on Wednesday had confirmed a drop in the rails on Monday and that, according to the theory of the late Charles H. Dow, a bear market was under way. In the penultimate paragraph, William P. Hamilton, the anonymous editorialist, remarked that "there are people trading in Wall Street and many all over the country who have never seen a real bear market," and who, presumably, would be in for further disagreeable surprises. Baruch, who was hardly one of those tyro optimists, nonetheless chose to buy, and to buy in a company that he knew, American Smelting. On Friday he picked up 5,500 shares, thereby boosting his purchases of that stock in the past week to 8,500 shares, or roughly $835,000 worth.

Prices were up a bit on Friday and off only slightly on Saturday. On Sunday, Broad Street was lined with the double-parked cars of clerks who had gone to the office to send out margin calls. (Thus the New Era was, for the moment, intact; the messengers of bad news could still afford to drive to work.) Faith in the bankers' pool still ran high, and the talk was of a rally on Monday.

Instead there was a catastrophic decline, the Dow plunging by more than 38 points, or 13 percent, to close at a hair above 260. Baruch did some selling—3,000 shares of Standard Brands, 2,500 of American Smelting and $23,000 worth of French government bonds—but also, in counterpoint, some buying of Rhodesian Congo Border in London. At his Fifth Avenue home that evening he gave a dinner party for Winston Churchill, who was visiting America as his guest and losing his own money in the market. Also among the diners were both Swopes, Herbert and Gerard; Mitchell of National City Bank and Albert H. Wiggin, chairman of Chase National Bank; Charles Schwab of Bethlehem Steel and John D. Ryan, president of Anaconda Copper; Eugene Meyer and Thomas Lamont. Evidently absent was another banker friend of Baruch's, George F. Baker, chairman of First National Bank, who, as a result of the day's declines in only three stocks—his bank, Telephone and Steel—was poorer by what the *Times* surmised to be $14,737,000.

Late in the evening, after Mitchell offered a facetious toast to "my fellow former millionaires," talk turned to serious schemes for rescuing the market. The sense of the group was conveyed in a night letter from Herbert Swope to his fellow speculator John Hertz:

THINK I AM ABLE TO SEE CHANGE IN SITUATION FOR BETTER SO AM MAKING DETERMINED EFFORT TO HOLD ON STOCKS BELIEVE YOU SHOULD TOO. CONSENSUS OF OPINION OF MEETINGS AT BARUCH'S . . . WAS THAT THOSE WHO STAND PRESSURE WOULD NOT ALONE BE DISCHARGING PUBLIC DUTY BUT WOULD BE CONFERRING BIG FAVOR UPON THEMSELVES WITH CERTAINTY OF RECOVERY OF STOCKS WHOSE VALUES UNDOUBTEDLY FAR GREATER THAN TODAY'S MARKET REGARDLESS OF HIGH OR LOW QUOTATIONS IN PAST. ARRANGEMENTS MADE FOR BIG POOL TO [O]PERATE. HERE IS SOMETHING IMPORTANT: TOMORROW MAY SEE BEGINNING OF REAL OPERATION IN WESTERN UNION. PLANS BEING MADE TONIGHT OR TOMORROW TO ORGANIZE BUYING POWER. BECAUSE OF ALL THIS AND TAKING ADVANTAGE OF YOUR WILLINGNESS TO DO SO AM LEAVING MY WESTERN UNION INTACT AT HARRIS WINTHROP. I DISCOVERED DISTINCT CHANGE FOR BETTER TONIGHT IN THAT MEN WERE TALKING AGAIN ABOUT MAKING MONEY INSTEAD OF MERELY LOSING MONEY.

Baruch's guests were premature, except, perhaps, for Wiggin, who happened to be heavily short of the shares of his own bank and who therefore had a vested interest in calamity. On unprecedented trading volume next day, Tuesday, October 29, the Dow shed another 30 points. Anaconda lost 8½ points, to 85; American Smelting dropped 6, to 84. On the Curb Exchange, Goldman, Sachs Trading Corporation, which Swope, the previous March, had tipped at 119, plunged by 25 points to close at 35. Sensing that what he saw (or didn't see; the tape was two and a half hours late) must be a selling climax, Baruch bought 1,000 shares of Smelters and 5,000 of U.S. Steel. (No doubt Schwab at Baruch's home had repeated the gist of his remarks to the American Iron & Steel Institute the prior Friday, namely, "In my long association with the steel industry I have never known it to enjoy a greater stability or more promising outlook than it does today.") On Friday, Swope reported to Hertz: "REAL BELIEF WORST IS OVER." Two days later the former editor's net worth had shrunk to *minus* $2,345,000.

Baruch too thought that things were on the mend. About that time he told a director of Lehman Corporation that the market was cheap, and that he, Robert Lehman, had a fiduciary obligation to get out of cash and into common stocks. (Happily for all concerned, Lehman resisted this counsel.) He advised his friend George Armsby, a California businessman, on October 30: "But we have gotten our minds and also prices of stocks down to a level where we can do business with real confidence. Business will probably be bad enough for the next sixty days, but it won't last long in this country. Just long enough for us to get a good investment market and a strong situation."

All the while Pershing was standing pat uncomfortably in Paris. He cabled on November 6 (the Dow had fallen by 29 percent from October 22 when Baruch urged patience), asking that his margin account be guaranteed; Baruch cabled back assurances. Next day, when prices rallied smartly from early losses, Baruch was moved to wire John Morron with a forecast:

LOOKS LIKE ALL TECHNICAL AND FORCED LIQUIDATION ABOUT COM-
PLETED. ONLY THING UNPLEASANT IN SIGHT IS PRESENT AND
PROSPECTIVE DECLINE IN BUSINESS WHICH WILL BE BAD BUT WILL BE
MUCH EXAGGERATED AS THE BULLISHNESS WAS EXAGGERATED SIX
MONTHS AGO. HOW HYSTERICAL BUSINESS MEN WILL NOW BECOME
REGARDING BUSINESS YOU CAN JUDGE AS WELL AS ANYONE BUT BUSI-
NESS CANNOT REMAIN VERY BAD IN THIS COUNTRY LONG.

To Churchill, who had sailed home with heavy losses, Baruch cabled, on November 15: "FINANCIAL STORM DEFINITELY PASSED."

Baruch and his wife and three children and two of his friends, Richard Lydon and Senator Key Pittman, were at Hobcaw in Christmas week 1929 when fire broke out in the main house. The party escaped safely with some valuables, but the old planter's house was destroyed. In 1930 Baruch ordered a new place built of brick and steel, but construction was delayed in November by a second fire. This run of bad luck provides an allegory, although an inexact one, of the financial history of the Depression. Whereas a new house did rise up more or less promptly at Hobcaw (with ten bedrooms, each with its own fireplace and bath, or more plumbing, as the joke went, than in the rest of the state of South Carolina combined), the stock-market fires seemed perpetual. The ashes smoldered, were raked clean and pronounced cold, but still flames broke out. To switch metaphors, in the Crash, prices had fallen like hailstones. In the long ensuing liquidation they floated to earth like leaves. Watching them, people were ruined.

For the short pull, Baruch had been right in his cable to Churchill. Temporarily, in mid-November, the worst was over. But after rising to almost 300 in April 1930, the Dow fell to 212 late that June. About a year later, after the failure of the Kreditanstalt in Austria, with the average at 128, John Morron inquired of Baruch: "WILL YOU USE YOUR INFLUENCE TO SECURE ME AN APPLE STAND IN FRONT OF YOUR BUILDING." As was by then customary, a period of fleeting strength and optimism followed, only to lead to still lower prices. In mid-December 1931 the Dow alighted at 74. At 41.22, on July 8, 1932, it stopped going down. This was 89 percent below the pre-Crash high and the lowest reading since June 5, 1897, when Baruch, not quite twenty-seven, was cleaning up in American Sugar Refining.

Now in his early sixties—richer, wiser, better connected—he had wound up on the wrong side of perhaps the greatest move in American market history. The problem was strategic, not tactical, for he could still bring off the neat trade (he and Meyer, for example, had taken 4 points in 2,200 shares of Southern California Edison in a rally in early 1930). Having the means to hang on, and expecting a better day, he waited; but the days grew worse. In several past crises he had profited by buying what panicky people had thrown overboard. It turned out this time that the alarmists were right.

It must be emphasized that the available trading records for 1930 and beyond are meager. At least they show a sharp curtailment in trading and, contrary to the rumors that were credited at the Hoover White House, little or no short selling.* When, in March 1930, George

---

*In an early draft of his autobiography, Baruch asserted that he *had* sold short—"In my operations, I just about made up on the short side what I lost in the shrinkage of securities which I owned and which I sold"—but that he hadn't begun his selling until the spring of 1930. No records support that claim, however, and Baruch himself contradicted it in other reminiscences. In October 1933, *Fortune* magazine reported that he had been a heavy short seller and that he had channeled his transactions through Mary Boyle's account, but neither do the available records bear out that story.

Armsby wrote to ask for a stock tip, explaining that he needed some money to pay his late mother's doctor bills, Baruch obliged with the confidential information that American Smelting's earnings were running at 60 percent of the 1929 rate, but that if the price of the stock got below 70, he planned to buy some. (That year, it got as low as 37½.) Early in June 1930, he purchased blocks of Radio Keith Orpheum, Public Service Company of New Jersey and Coca-Cola for the account of Cary Grayson. In September Baruch himself sold 1,000 shares of Westinghouse and 2,000 of General Electric. On the other hand, later in 1930 he bought approximately $100,000 (at par value) worth of the bonds of the unsteady Interborough Rapid Transit Company and 3,700 shares of Warren Pipe & Foundry. On October 24, he wrote Churchill that business had reached its nadir. At a B&O directors' meeting on January 21, 1931, he seconded a motion to raise the president's salary.

Baruch bore his losses stoically, confessing only to a few friends that he had suffered at all. "I can tell you," he wrote Senator Joe Robinson, in November 1930, "that the drop in my securities has been very severe, but I can still live in comfort and peace as I have done before. But I may not be able to help out in many of the directions I have heretofore until the ship floats anew on the incoming tide, which, of course, it will do some time."* The tardiness of that tidal movement evidently prompted some introspection. A memo to himself on the basics of investment and speculation, dated only 1930, was found among his papers. It went as follows:

PERSONAL EQUIPMENT

SELF-RELIANCE: Do your own thinking. Don't let your emotions enter into it. Keep out of any environment that may affect your acting on your reason.

JUDGMENT: Consider all the facts—meditate on them. Don't let what you *want* to happen influence your judgment.

COURAGE: Don't overestimate the courage you will have if things go against you.

---

*Not all Baruch's predictions were so definite. In September 1931, for instance, he wrote delphically to a friend, "The fertilizer business appears to be like all other businesses, People have to be fed, clothed and housed and if they find a way to do that, it will make business better."

ALERTNESS: To discover any new facts that change the situation; or which may *affect public opinion.*

PRUDENCE: Be pliable or you won't be prudent. *Become more humble as the market goes your way.* It is not prudent to buy when you think the bottom has been reached. It is better to wait and see, and buy too late. It is not prudent to wait for the top of the market to sell—it is better to sell "too soon." (Never buy so that your margin will be less than 85, or hold if it drops below 80. In a particularly "clear sky" situation with[out] "buts" or "ifs," one can lower these margins to 80–75%.)

PLIABILITY: Consider and reconsider the facts, and your opinions. Stubbornness as to opinions—"cockiness"—must be entirely eliminated. A determination to make a certain amount within a certain time absolutely destroys pliability. When you decide, act promptly—don't wait to see what the market will do.

THE FACTS

(a)   AS INDICATING THE FUTURE

Money market, Bond market, Savings Fund Deposits, Insurance being sold.

Federal Reserve Ratio and operations, Commercial loans.

Yields of stocks including and excluding "rights" compared to bond yields and time money.

Volume of new security offerings.

Ratio stock exchange loans to price of stocks.

Volume of stock transactions.

———

Trend of commodity prices (watch supply of gold and credit facilities).

Crop situation

Political situation; domestic and international.

Bank clearings;

Railway Traffic: —A falling off in tonnage is delayed for considerable time after depression begins; while an increase precedes recovery.

Orders: —Construction permits and contracts awarded.

Steel production orders.

Automobile production orders.

Volume Retail Trade: —Department and chain stores.

Employment
Foreign Trade

(b) HISTORY: —Inventories and instalment purchases.
Production: Volume manufacturing, including electric power.
Volume mining.
Earnings.

(c) INDIVIDUAL COMPANIES:
Is it a growing and standard business (not experimental)
Is competition becoming too keen.
Is it a dominant corporation.
Is it experimenting.

ONE MUST BE THOROUGH AS TO FACTS.

PSYCHOLOGY

Nearly all men are controlled by their emotions: they become alternately over optimistic and over pessimistic. After you have your facts and opinions, wait for the current. Have an opinion on what the market should do, but don't decide what the market will do. The more the public becomes stock minded the greater it's [sic] power. Don't try to go against the mob on the one hand, and don't go with it in it's [sic] excesses. Don't sell short if it is bullish, but don't stay long if there is a chance that it may turn and rend you, and conversely. In a panic the best stocks may not be salable at any reasonable price. Be alert for anything which the public will greet with enthusiasm or fear. When the market is high beware of thinking of things that will make it go higher; think of adverse possibilities, and remember history; and conversely. Watch for the main currents, but be fearful of too much company.

"Stop losses and let profits run."

In general run quickly. If you fail to do so hang on, reducing commitments. Always reduce commitments if doubtful. While you should act promptly when you make up your mind, irrespective of market action, nevertheless, you must at times consider the action of the market, in making your plans.

In comparing any situation with a previous one be sure you have the facts of both, so make allowances in psychology. Over action is always followed by over reaction.

The Unforeseen: —Always make allowances for chance. Keep a financial and mental and physical reserve.

In general run quickly. At first not seeing what one was supposed to be running from, Baruch was slow to make his retreat, but by 1931, at least, he had done some significant selling. Certainly he lacked for no facts concerning the state of the nation. In August 1931 Hugh Johnson returned from a national inspection to report having seen "distinct signs of under-nourishment." He said that real estate was moribund, the farm-implements business was worse than it had been even in 1921, and that prospects for construction, autos and railroads all were nil. Concerning an auto-carpet business in which Baruch and he had invested, Johnson wrote: "It seems a shame to contemplate letting the carpet company go when (speaking relatively with other businesses) its prospects are so good, but I am so firmly convinced of the prolongation of this depression, that I have been unable to make up my mind." In the third week of November Baruch directed Miss Boyle to take financial inventory.*

Millions were out of work, England was off gold, banks were failing and investment-grade bonds were falling along with common stocks. The National Lead Company, which was better off than many, declared an extra 25-cent-per-share "emergency relief" dividend which it asked its stockholders to pass on to the needy. On November 11, 1931, at a reunion of the War Industries Board alumni at which optimism was de rigueur, Baruch could venture not much further than to say, after his old stock-market mentor Middleton Schoolbred Burrill, that ". . . we have disrupted the continuity of pessimism." On November 18 he joined his colleagues at the B&O board in a unanimous resolution to halve their directors' fees.

At this gloomy juncture Miss Boyle counted his stocks and bonds and cash and the loans he had made to his friends, and she copied the details on sheets of legal-sized yellow paper. The totals came out this way:

Stocks: $3,691,874.50
Bonds: $3,067,465.00
Cash: $8,698,000.00 (including $557,000 in his vault; $7,141,000 distributed among seven banks, the largest deposit, $3.4

---

*On November 25, Baruch took out a pistol license, but the timing was apparently dictated by a new gun-registration law rather than by the stock market. If he was worried about his safety in 1931, he had also given the matter some thought in the late bull market. It was reported in 1927 that he was one of only 182 Americans to have insured their lives for $1 million or more.

million, being at the First National; and, by the looks
of it, $1 million in short-term Treasury securities)
Loans: $551,560.00
Total: $16,008,899.50

To have had $8.7 million in cash in 1931 was a rare and wonderful
feat. Somewhere along the line Baruch had obviously shifted large sums
out of stocks. Just as plainly, however, he had borne a loss. At the top in
1929, his financial assets had been worth perhaps $22 to $25 million.*
The list of stocks makes interesting reading. There are the conventional names of going concerns: blocks of Brooklyn Manhattan Transit
Company, Babcox & Wilcox Company, Carrier Engineering Corpora-
tion, Consolidated Cigar Corporation, Consolidated Gas, Cream of
Wheat, McCrory Stores, United Biscuit and Wesson Oil, for example.
But there are also numerous distressed or insolvent companies, includ-
ing Electric Ferries, Mercurbank (of Austria, with branches in Rumania,
Hungary and Poland), Quemont Mining Corporation Limited of
Canada, Revere Copper & Brass, Bahia Corporation, United Artists
Theatre Circuit, Inc., and Mesabi Iron Company (of which Daniel C.
Jackling was president and Herman Baruch and Tom Chadbourne were
directors). All told, Miss Boyle found 114,563 shares of stock for which
the market value was zero. There was a conspicuous absence of blue
chips: no Standard Oil of New Jersey, General Electric, General Motors,
American Can, Sears Roebuck or U.S. Steel. He owned only 200 shares
of American Smelting and 165 of B&O.
   She noticed that his bond portfolio had lost value. From the Crash
through the summer of 1931, interest rates had fallen and bond prices
correspondingly had risen. Following England's departure from gold
on September 21, however, the Federal Reserve raised rates to encourage foreigners not to exchange dollars for gold. At the same time Americans began to withdraw cash from banks; and banks, in order to raise

---

*Derived by inference. In 1929 he reported dividend income of $585,811.81. If he
earned the average dividend yield for the year of 3.47 percent, his portfolio would have
been worth almost $17 million. By the same token, he reported $307,002.26 in interest
income. If he earned an average of 5 percent on his bonds and bank balances, the implied principal value of those holdings would be $4.8 million; if 4½ percent, then $5.3
million. Hence a grand total of roughly $22 million. In 1934 *Time* magazine used $25
million. In 1926 Arthur Krock in *The New Yorker* put his net worth at "somewhere between thirty and fifty millions," which seems high.

money for worried patrons, sold bonds. Railroad bonds, of which Baruch owned about $500,000 worth (at par value), were especially hard hit, and by the summer of 1931 there was talk of having them struck from the list of eligible securities in which banks, insurance companies and trust funds in New York State could legally invest.

At par value Baruch's bond portfolio was worth $4,177,000, but at going prices it was quoted at less than three quarters of that. His largest holding was $811,000 (par value) of subway bonds, the Interborough Rapid Transit Company 5s of 1966. Their price had fallen from 78 in early 1929 to 52 when Miss Boyle checked up. In August 1932, just before the line fell into receivership (and ultimately into municipal ownership), the price was 44. Baruch also owned $148,000 of the bonds of the Manhattan Elevated Company, a money-losing subsidiary of the IRT, and almost $500,000 worth of the obligations of the New York Railway Company, a trolley-and-bus-line successor to the unmourned Metropolitan Street Railway Company. The New York Railway paper was quoted between five cents on the dollar and zero.

Baruch had a director's interest in the creditworthiness of the Baltimore & Ohio Railroad. When he joined the board in 1927, the B&O was profitable but behind the times and in need of physical improvement. Not anticipating the Depression and electing to expand rather than to consolidate, the board—a Wilsonian group that included Newton D. Baker, the former Secretary of War, and Paul M. Warburg, an original director of the Federal Reserve Board, as well as Willard and Baruch, former War Industries Board men—voted in 1929 to spend $20 million on the acquisition of a pair of small railroads to complete a new route between New York and Chicago. Their timing was unhappy. Under the press of the slump and of their own miscalculations, the directors in March 1932 omitted payment of the dividend on the preferred stock for the first time since 1900. To alleviate a cash shortage, they approved a loan application to the Reconstruction Finance Corporation, lately established to check the bankruptcy wave. (Baruch had been asked by the Hoover Administration to join the new agency but had declined.) By August 1932, the B&O had become the RFC's largest railroad borrower, outdistancing sixty-five other depressed roads for that unwanted distinction. Probably only federal aid saved the B&O from bankruptcy. It was at this crisis in the B&O's affairs that Baruch chose to accept an invitation to serve as vice chairman of the National Transportation Committee, a panel that the government convened to propose a solution to the railroad crisis. In time, but without noticeable effect on policy, it recommended that certain competing roads be consolidated and that a national rail system evolve under federal aegis. Baruch, who was laid up with the gout, sent Johnson to deliberate in his place.*

As for herself, Miss Boyle had also made heavy weather of it. In 1929 she reported stock-trading profits of no less than $229,825.06 and received interest and dividend income of $32,883.66. (Her salary amounted to approximately one quarter of her federal income-tax bill, which was $57,028.88.) She was worth perhaps $500,000 to $750,000 at the top, but on November 20, 1931, she had only $120,000 in cash and less than $29,000 worth of securities. However, she was not so discouraged that she stopped wearing diamond jewelry to the office or gave up speculation. On inventory day she had $15,000 tied up in the cotton futures market.

At Baruch's request early in November General Johnson picked out some stocks that looked cheap in the market, but there is no record of Baruch immediately buying them (there were three: American Safety Razor, Canada Dry Ginger Ale and Commercial Credit) or of acting on the idea that the market had bottomed. In mid-December, in fact, as the Dow made new lows, he sold $187,482 worth of stocks and bonds and bought only $13,378 worth. What is recorded is his quickening interest in gold.

Characteristically, Baruch's views on the subject of gold and money—not the mining but the monetary end—were intuitive rather than analytical. He took no known part in discussion of whether the rate of gold convertibility to which Great Britain returned in 1925 might not be (as it later developed) too high; or of whether the newfangled postwar monetary system, called the "gold exchange standard," might not be inflationary in permitting two countries to count the same bar of gold in their separate monetary reserves. On the contrary, he told Bruce

---

*A director's lot was an unsatisfactory one, Baruch reminisced a few years after he resigned. "It took about half my time and then I did not learn much about the railroad. At the board of directors meeting, matters of policy would come up. Large transactions would be reported. Everybody was in a hurry and the man who asked many questions was a nuisance. I cannot see anything in it for a thoughtful or wise man to be a director of a railroad or in fact any large institution of which he does not know all the details. . . . A director becomes more or less a figurehead except in the smaller institutions."

Barton in 1929 that the world's "centralized" central-banking structure was a bulwark of prosperity.

By 1931 everybody knew that it wasn't. Prices had fallen and the purchasing power of money had correspondingly risen. For those in funds the deflation brought a windfall, but for debtors it was ruinous. A mortgage that was manageable in 1929 was in many cases cumbersome or onerous in 1931. Bankruptcies mounted and schemes were devised to make money cheaper and more plentiful. Practically, this meant reducing or eliminating the gold backing of currency. Before Great Britain went off the gold standard in September 1931, Argentina, Austria, Uruguay, Brazil and Germany had already done so; and India, Norway, Sweden, Canada and Japan all shortly followed England. Relative to the world's new paper money, the value of gold was rising.

In the light of the news Baruch decided that a man might prudently lay in some gold for himself. He began with the purchase of gold-mining shares. In the November 1931 inventory, his largest stock holding was Alaska Juneau, then quoted at 15; in 1927 it had traded at 1. (Goldfield Consolidated, however, wasn't stirring; Miss Boyle counted 40,050 shares for which there was a bid of 12½ cents each on the Curb.) The decision to buy gold bullion was a more considered one, because in ordinary circumstances there was every reason not to own it. It paid no dividend or interest, cost money to store and would go nowhere in price if the government kept its solemn monetary promises, which the Hoover Administration and, subsequently, Governor Franklin D. Roosevelt each vowed to do.

When, in the late 1930s, Baruch was officially asked by the then Secretary of the Treasury why he had bought gold, an investment that was outlawed in 1933 and was viewed, even retroactively, with suspicion by the Roosevelt Administration, he answered laconically, ". . . because I was commencing to have doubts about the currency." And indeed in late 1931 and early 1932 there was no shortage of things to doubt. "Money was sick," Malcolm Muggeridge wrote of that time, "and its many friends hurried to its bedside to revive it." In February 1932, an act was passed to authorize the Federal Reserve System to issue greenbacks on the collateral of Treasury securities. Heretofore only gold and commercial paper had constituted eligible collateral, but gold was being drained off to Europe and so little business was being done that some banks had no serviceable paper. The upshot was that the Federal Reserve could issue paper money—

its promissory notes—backed by the Treasury's notes, a case of one debt propping up another. Without further ado the Fed began to create credit by the simple, and soon to become everyday, expedient of "monetizing" Treasury obligations. In March U.S. Steel Corporation suspended dividend payments, and the capitalists Ivar Kreuger and George Eastman killed themselves. In June the federal government closed its books on a $2.7 billion deficit, greatest since the aftermath of the war.

Of all these signs, Baruch was especially alert to the fiscal situation. Since (in his view) a balanced budget was a prerequisite to the return of business and investor confidence, it followed that there could be no end to joblessness and privation unless federal spending were reduced and taxes raised. He elaborated for the New York *Evening Post* on January 11, 1932, about a month after he had sold some securities at distress prices and a month or so before he began to buy gold bullion.

All efforts to bring back prosperity and the employment that will come with it are based on the credit of our Government. All must fail unless the United States moves at once and convincingly in the direction of a balanced budget. While this means less Government spending and heavier taxation, rewards will come in restoration of confidence and resumption of business activity.

Money is at the base of business. It is the Government's promise to pay. It represents the credit of the United States. Its value is measured by the world's faith in that credit. Our money is good beyond peradventure, but as long as our Government permits unbalanced budgets, our public and the world will continue to start at shadows. From the beginning of time, deficits have been the red flags of waning credit. In a world of alarms, our deficits have already impaired credit.

Thousands of people have thrown overboard investments representing their lives' savings in frantic grasping for what they regard as gold. Vast numbers stand with their resources entirely in cash, although sound investment securities are selling at prices lower perhaps than we shall see again.

He closed with a plea for financial orthodoxy:

The sound, effective and quick way to balance budgets is to stop spending. We began our present Federal orgy with war inflation in

1914. For thirteen years [before that] we had spent for Federal Government an average of about six hundred million dollars. Eliminating charges on the public debt, we had increased that to 1.8 billions by 1923 and 2.8 billions—4⅔ times—by 1931. Nearly all economic indices, such as those of commodity prices and production, are back on the pre-war basis. We need no economist to tell us that reduced expenditure is something more than a desideratum, that it is the only road to balanced budgets and that an ax rather than a pruning fork is the necessary implement.

We must have higher prices for our basic commodities but the way to get them is to increase demand by greater activity through fortifying our credit mechanism—not to fool ourselves by reducing the value of money by destroying the basis of public credit.

On April 2, 1932, and from time to time through early 1933, Baruch's vault in New York received shipments of gold. By February 1933, the Alaska Juneau company had sent sixty-six gold bricks (of which Baruch had had three melted down to test the company's assay) while an unknown quantity was received from London. The size of his Alaska Juneau purchases is also unknown, because the bricks were unrefined and irregular. However, based on similar bricks shipped by the company in 1933, the figure is probably close to 72,000 ounces, which at the then-going price of $20.67 an ounce was worth almost $1,500,000. When Philip Bradley, president of the mine, was later asked, in the course of a legal set-to with the government, why Baruch had bought, he replied simply, "In anticipation of a higher price for gold." In the event, the higher price materialized, but Baruch didn't get it. In April 1933, President Roosevelt ordered Americans to surrender their gold at the customary dollar-exchange rate of $20.67 an ounce. Within three months the world price was pushing $29.

When at last the stock market stopped falling, in July 1932, it rebounded with such spring that by September 7 the Dow had come within an ace of doubling from its low. Baruch's timing was better at the bottom than it had been at the top; later in September Churchill cabled his thanks for advice that had gotten him out of the rally at the high. On the sixth of September Baruch did a little selling himself, including 700 shares of Irving Air Chute at 5½. For the same company in the spring of 1929 he had paid 37⅞ a share.

Later that fall Baruch wrote a brief foreword for a new edition of

Extraordinary Popular Delusions and the Madness of Crowds, Charles Mackay's nineteenth-century study of such ill-fated enthusiasms as the South Sea Bubble and the tulip-bulb craze. Baruch praised the book for the light it shed on the psychological element that figures in all great economic movements. "I have always thought that if, in the lamentable era of 'New Economics,' culminating in 1929, even in the very presence of dizzily spiralling prices, we had all continuously repeated 'two and two still make four,' much of the evil might have been averted," he wrote. "Similarly, even in the general moment of gloom in which this foreword is written, when many begin to wonder if declines will never halt, the appropriate abracadabra may be: 'They always did.'" Baruch chose not to mention his industrial renaissance or to indicate, even obliquely, how it might have differed from the "New Economics." He was, however, right on the timing of the decline. From the point of view of stock prices, it was over.

THIRTEEN

Suffering Roosevelt

Hardly a reunion of the War Industries Board passed without Swope retelling the story of the Baruch elephant. This was the animal who would draw suspiciously up to a bamboo bridge, test it with both sets of legs, pronounce it safe, but call to "some other sucker" to cross first. As the cautious venture capitalist in Texas Gulf Sulphur, as the delegate to the Versailles Peace Conference who fought the good fight "though not to the death," as the kingmaker who resolved in 1924 to have no candidate but the party's, as the investor who reminded himself not to try to buy at the bottom but to "wait and see, and buy too late"—as this eminently careful man, Baruch heard the story with the delight of self-recognition.

In the bottom of a depression it was reasonable to suppose that the party out of power would elect the next President, and in early 1932 there was spirited jockeying for position in advance of the Democratic convention in Chicago. One Wall Street man, Joseph P. Kennedy, correctly sensing a change in the trend of the political market, committed his money early to the governor of New York, Franklin D. Roosevelt. Baruch, however, was typically guarded. Though partial to Newton D. Baker, Albert C. Ritchie or Al Smith, and opposed to Roosevelt, he maintained a stance of public neutrality pending the decision of the convention. The delegates having spoken, he reported to the Roosevelt camp for marching orders.

Along with other conservative Democrats, a rare political type which then was common, Baruch saw the electoral issues distinctly: economy in government versus waste, good money versus bad, liberty versus meddling. He was very clear on one point. Roosevelt was the candidate of fiscal and monetary orthodoxy; Hoover, of bizarre and unsound experimentation (as witness, for example, a 1932 budget deficit that would reach $2.7 billion and the unprecedented activism of the Reconstruction Finance Corporation). In 1930 Baruch had recited his political credo.

I am a Democrat for the following reasons: I believe that the Government should mind its own business. I believe that the people who are least governed are best governed. You cannot make people temperate by passing the Prohibition law and you cannot make manufacturers prosperous by putting up a tariff wall which because of reciprocal action will drive our manufacturers into other countries, as General Motors and Ford have been driven employing their labor instead of our own. I do not believe that any makeshift economic measures which attempt to lift out any part of the population by their boot-straps is a part of governmental action. It will fail as the Prohibition law has failed. The people should be free to work out their own problems. The only thing that good government can do is to see that everyone has equally easy access to the door of opportunity. Never in the history of our country have we drifted so far from the principles of good Democracy and good Republicanism as we have under the present administration, where the government is seeking to do everything and accomplishes nothing except disrespect for the law.*

As economic circumstances changed for the worse, free-market views went out of style and collectivist ones came in. Baruch himself in 1931 talked about a "High Court of Commerce" to license cartels when and where desirable in order to check "overproduction and losses due to uneconomic competition." He had, in fact, proposed the idea after the war, but he was willing to go further with it now, as he told the WIB reunion in 1931: "Usually I am frightened by artificial makeshifts

---

*In 1927, in a letter to Frank Kent, Baruch delivered himself of the line "If Christ had been mortal, he would have been a Democrat—certainly not a Republican." He intended no humor.

but I think we might try the experiment of co-ordinating and stabilizing industry. After all, it is only by the trial and error of commission and omission that we can advance along the road to progress."

Baruch was the despair of political taxonomists because he could change his mind as easily on public issues as he could about common stocks. He sincerely espoused some libertarian principles, but if a stray left-wing scheme happened to catch his fancy he saw nothing wrong with advocating that either. (He drew the line at Marx. Later on in the 1930s, when everybody seemed to be reading him, Baruch dutifully made the effort in the incongruous setting of the Paris Ritz. "I don't understand him—I think people who say they do are phonies," he scrawled on a postcard to Swope. "He takes the position in what I have read so far that if you don't understand him and follow his reasoning, it is because you are a vulgar bourgeoisie. Well, maybe I am.") To intellectuals, political ideas lived and breathed. To Baruch, they were not nearly so lifelike as power, party and friendship, and he was usually ready to sacrifice philosophical consistency to any one of those considerations.

Mostly in those days he favored the tried and true. In preinaugural policy sessions he urged a balanced budget, reduced federal spending and the repair of the public credit. He believed that there was plenty of money to finance recovery if government could only coax it out of hiding. In general he stood by the 1932 Democratic platform of which the first plank called for an "immediate and drastic reduction of governmental expenditures and by abolishing useless commissions and offices . . ." and the second for "the maintenance of the national credit by a federal budget annually balanced. . . ."

There was some resentment against him within the Roosevelt inner circle because he had come to the winning side so late. Furthermore, he was rich and independently connected to the press and Congress, which aroused envy. Raymond Moley, the original Brains Trust man, once told him, "Bernie, you're just too luminous a man" (as if he didn't know that already). Baruch cordially reciprocated the New Dealers' suspicions. In December 1932, while in the throes of the gout, he wrote peevishly about the college professors at the President-elect's side: "The horn-rimmed boys are encircling Franklin. . . . You can see that there is no leadership and no idea of any program." As it turned out there was no shortage of leadership and no lack of a program, although it would be a very different program from the one Baruch had imagined.

For a while after the election it seemed that he was back on the inside. Condé Nast cabled from Paris with the instructions that he was to be sure to agree to become Secretary of the Treasury. Kennedy told Walter Lippmann he thought that Baruch was conspiring to become Secretary of State. However, no post was forthcoming. In January 1933, Baruch believed that, while he was out of things politically, he was in the thick of them economically. In February he testified before the Senate Finance Committee on the necessity both of relieving human want and of maintaining the fiscal and monetary integrity of the government. He conferred with Roosevelt and traveled to Baltimore with Annie to receive an honorary degree from Johns Hopkins University (of which Daniel Willard was a trustee and chairman of the board's executive committee). In the encomium that preceded the presentation of the degree and a Commemoration Day address by Baruch, Professor Jacob H. Hollander paid tribute to the honoree's moral, mental and material fiber. (Reference to the material side was delicately vague, no mention being made of stock trading, or of speculating for the fall.) The professor spoke of the highlights of Baruch's public career, noting—significantly, on the eve of a new Administration—that he had been "requisitioned by successive Presidents." Inasmuch as Roosevelt would keep Baruch out of the Cabinet and requisition him only sparingly, this was a small touch of unconscious irony. Baruch answered in kind with a speech on the evils of statism and the inviolability of "natural laws." He titled his remarks "Leaning on Government."

> Thus [said the new Doctor of Laws], bit by bit, we barter away our birthright in such an extension of federal power that the earth, air and water are all, in some sense, regulated by bureaus. Local self-government is a vanishing function. Privacy in business is practically gone. Personal conduct is largely under federal supervision. There is scarcely one of the guarantees of the Bill of Rights that has not been impaired. The cost of all this folly is reflected in a four billion dollar government no better in many respects than the pre-war establishment which spent one-sixth as much. It is the chief threat to federal credit and one of the greatest barriers to economic recovery. We simply cannot afford this sterile luxury.

Interspersed with this talk about freedom was a wistful harking back to the war. Baruch spoke of it fondly—"Government welded the common effort—not by magic, but by breaking down barriers to unified action." There had been sacrifice then, he recalled, also with satisfaction. In closing he urged his audience to support the President-elect in the great burdens he was about to take up. Referring to "our people," he said: "Not for his sake [i.e., Roosevelt's] but for their own sake and that of the whole world, they will demand for him the unwavering loyalty of every man, regardless of prejudice, party, or selfish interest. They will know that anyone who does not accord it in full measure is either dull in his perception of danger or derelict in the most sacred duties of citizenship in an hour of national peril. Public opinion will scourge such a man as it pilloried slackers in the war."

Here was a masterpiece of irony: within weeks Baruch himself—"counselor of statesmen," said Professor Hollander—would fall to deploring a legislative program in which he had hardly been consulted. President Roosevelt was inaugurated on March 4. On the sixth of March, he declared the bank holiday. On the twentieth he signed the Economy Act, by which federal salaries were reduced and other governmental savings effected. It was one of the earliest, and in retrospect the least characteristic but (to Baruch) the most heartening, of New Deal measures. Late that month Charles E. Mitchell was indicted on charges of tax evasion, and Bernard K. Marcus and Saul Singer, respectively president and vice president of the failed Bank of United States, were packed off to Sing Sing. On April 5, an executive order forbade the "hoarding" of gold and directed that bars, coins and gold certificates be surrendered to the nearest Federal Reserve Bank. On April 19 and 20 the President declared a policy of permitting the dollar to deteriorate in terms of foreign currencies as a way of raising American prices. The so-called Thomas Amendment to the Agricultural Adjustment Act was introduced in Congress, granting the President the right to devalue the gold content of the dollar by as much as 50 percent. Next came the Emergency Farm Mortgage Act, the Tennessee Valley Authority Act, the Securities Act, the Home Owners Loan Act and the National Recovery Act, the last named intended to raise domestic prices through a kind of peacetime War Industries Board. On June 5 a resolution was passed to abrogate all contractual clauses, public and private, that specified payment in gold or in money equivalent to the current gold price. Meantime Ferdinand Pecora, Senate committee counsel and a childhood immigrant from Sicily, was interrogating partners of J. P. Morgan and lesser financial personages concerning Wall Street practices in the late boom.

This reforming binge took Baruch's breath away. "There is so much legislation going on and so much of it that I do not agree with," he confided to Senator Key Pittman on April 5, "that I do not want to be put in the position of saying anything to commit sabotage." On the tenth he drafted a congratulatory letter to President Roosevelt (containing, for example, the remark that "people are awakening to the fact that they are witnessing the miracle of an elected candidate keeping his word. . . .") but couldn't bring himself to mail it. For better or worse, as James P. Warburg later observed, the President was well on his way to fulfilling the Socialist platform of 1932, not the Democratic one.

Baruch's response to the unfolding events was revealing mild. Senator Carter Glass of Virginia, a friend of his who had drafted a plank in which the Democratic Party in 1932 had declared for "a sound currency to be preserved at all hazards," publicly condemned the dollar-devaluation bill as repudiation and national dishonor. Baruch himself was disturbed by the gold measures, but he had the stock trader's sense that a change in trend was in the making and a disinclination to quarrel with the tape.* As a citizen, he was concerned by the President's policies. More immediately, however—as would-be adviser to Presidents—he was discomfited by them.

Frances Perkins, Roosevelt's Secretary of Labor, had a hunch concerning Baruch's state of mind. He had, she said later,

> that curious sense of guilt that you have when you don't believe yourself to be guilty. You don't think you did anything wrong, which indeed he had not, and yet you feel guilty. There was nothing wrong in using your best judgment to put your money in gold. But if it was going to be called in, and people who had gold were going to be called hoarders, with penalties, and a bad name attached to them, he began to feel that sense of guilt which was not based on conscious conviction of guilt. It was just, "I'm on the unpopular side of this, and I don't want to be."

---

*His personal financial interests were mixed. As a holder of bullion he would lose by the order to surrender one's gold at the submarket price of $20.67 an ounce. As a holder of gold-mining stock, he stood to gain by the looming formal devaluation. And in the event, Alaska Juneau began to receive $35 an ounce for its gold in 1934.

Probably this was insightful hunch. Perkins went on to relate an exchange that had taken place at a Cabinet meeting concerning the anti-gold-hoarding order. The Vice President, John N. Garner, had been very keen on the policy.

> Then [she said] Garner began to chuckle, his face got red, and he said, "Well, of course, it'll put a lot of people in a very embarrassing position, Mr. President."
> The President looked solemn and said, "Well, I don't think so. I don't think anybody who's doing the right thing by this country will be embarrassed by this at all."
> We had previously talked about the children who had ten-dollar gold pieces given to them by their grandfathers, about whether they had to turn those in.
> Garner then said, "Well, you know, one of our greatest friends has got a hoard of gold."
> Then I, or somebody at the table, piped up and said, "Who's that?"
> "Baruch. I understand Baruch's got a whole bankful of gold bricks."

Although Perkins didn't mention it, an incidental revelation from the Pecora Committee late in May also perhaps nourished the New Dealers' distrust of Baruch. It came to light that J. P. Morgan & Company had kept a "preferred list" of people to whom it had distributed common stock, and that Baruch's name was on it. His companions were a heterogeneously prominent lot, including, among others, John J. Raskob, Charles A. Lindbergh, Calvin Coolidge, Charles E. Mitchell, William G. McAdoo, John J. Pershing and Roosevelt's Treasury Secretary, William Woodin. In 1929 each had been offered stock in one or more newly formed companies. Morgan, which as a rule didn't underwrite new issues, now and then made an exception, and it would find itself with more stock than it wished to hold for its own account. Not caring to sell to the general public—Morgan was not that sort of firm—it offered the overflow to its friends and acquaintances.

One of the issues it distributed was Standard Brands, the yeast and baking-soda consolidation. Baruch happened to be an interested party in that company by dint of his holdings in the Fleischmann Company, one of its corporate components. The proposition before him and the others was that they contract to buy the stock in late June 1929 but pay for it in early September. There was nothing unique in the deal, nor, contrary to the impression left by the committee, was it free of risk to the buyers. If the price of the stock went up, as Pecora strongly implied to be inevitable, there would be a profit, but if it happened to fall, there would be a loss. Baruch took 4,000 shares at 32. His records show that he sold 3,000 shares at 32 as the market was crashing—no profit there—and that a year later he held 300 shares in an account at Morgan at a price of 15¾—no profit there either. (To Baruch, of course, it was absurd to think that the Morgan firm had favored him when, in his opinion, it had consistently opposed him in railroads and sulphur.) When the Pecora headlines struck in May 1933, Swope drafted a long and rambling broadside for use against the committee but wisely concluded that Baruch say nothing.

From time to time in those days the newspapers depicted Baruch as an éminence grise. While not himself the wielder of power, the stories had it, he had planted his right-hand men in office and therefore controlled the government by proxy. Conspicuous among the so-called Baruch men were George N. Peek, administrator of the Agricultural Adjustment Administration; General Hugh Johnson, chief of the National Recovery Administration; and Swope, who filled a visible if subordinate role with the American delegation to the World Monetary and Economic Conference.

Although intriguing and imaginative, the stories were wide of the mark. Before Peek took the AAA job, it had been offered to Baruch. *He* declined it on the ground that the enabling law—which sought to raise prices by paying farmers not to raise crops—was unworkable. Peek accepted with misgivings and was fired seven months later. He took a new job as a special trade adviser from which he resigned in 1935. (On the occasion of his leaving the Administration, the Chicago *Daily News* wondered how gray was Baruch's éminence: "His [Peek's] passing removes the last vestige of the Moline Plow Works from the New Deal, but whether it also indicates that Bernard Baruch, chronic friend of presidents, has also lost his drag remains to be seen.") If anybody was a Baruch acolyte, that man was Johnson, but it was not on Baruch's sayso that the general was given command of the NRA. On the contrary, Baruch had warned Frances Perkins that Johnson was unfit of the job and that someone must impress that fact on the President. Baruch himself was unwilling to bear the message—possibly, Perkins thought, because he was embarrassed at being caught with his gold. At all events,

Johnson joined the New Deal not because of Baruch but in spite of him.

In a way the NRA did owe its commission to Baruch, or at least to the precedent of the involuntary voluntary method of the War Industries Board. In the crisis of 1933, as Johnson saw it, industry abdicated leadership to government. He had a definite theory about the Depression. "It happened," wrote Johnson, "because they [businessmen] were doomed by the law to unchecked and uncontrolled competition—doomed by the law not to take common counsel, not to regard each industry as a unit and not to regard the country as an economic integer in which every citizen had an interest and every employer an obligation."

If, as Johnson thought, the antitrust laws prevented this sensible taking of common counsel—assured frantic competition, overbuilding and the inevitable bust—then the obvious step was to write new laws. In Washington he set to work to help with the drafting of the National Industrial Recovery Act, the charter of what he liked to call industrial self-government. Henceforth, under the law, businessmen would formulate "codes" to regulate maximum hours of work, minimum wages, lawful trade practices and prices, and so on, industry by industry. All this was to be done under federal supervision in the name of the national interest.

Baruch was ambivalent toward this scheme, his free-market side colliding with his war-socialism side. As the Hundred Days wore on, it was the martial Baruch that came to the fore. It was uppermost in a speech at the Brookings Institution on May 20 in honor of the founder of that organization and a WIB alumnus, Robert S. Brookings. Having deplored the loss of "privacy in business," at Johns Hopkins three months earlier, Baruch now urged a regime of "enlightened cooperation" of companies under government control. He likened the current economic crisis to war and held up the record of 1917–1918 ("that high adventure") as an example of what the new National Recovery program might accomplish. Unfortunately, he said, echoing Johnson, the Sherman Act prohibited cooperation among competing firms. What was needed was voluntary action to cooperate supplemented by "the power to discipline." As wages and costs went up—the fruit of rational planning—prices too would rise, which could mean trouble. "Higher prices by agreement constitute a danger signal," said Baruch, "and this brings us face to face with the necessity for governmental provisions. Industrialists who favor this plan must understand clearly that it involves imposition by government of a price limitation, agreed upon by industry to be sure, but always subject to government approval."

There would, of course, be the recalcitrants to deal with, Baruch went on—he suggested a government licensing scheme to trip them up—but the problem would be manageable if the public were prepared. "If it is commonly understood that those who are cooperating are soldiers against the common enemy within, and those who omit to act are on the other side, there will be little hanging back. The insignia of governmental approval on doorways, letterheads and invoices will become a necessity in business. This method was used with success in 1918. It is a short cut to action and to public support, without which no such plan can succeed." Thus the Blue Eagle, the NRA's insignia, was hatched.

As NRA administrator, Johnson worked a revolution in American business practices. Wage and hour laws were written, sweatshops and child labor were abolished, and collective bargaining was instituted. All this was done without subtlety, as Johnson himself promised when he took the job—"It will be red fire at first and dead cats afterward"— and as Baruch had feared. H. L. Mencken described the general truculently presiding over the hearings at which industries formulated codes of operation—"his coat off, perspiration streaming down his face and overshotted mikes bursting all around him," that is, a man as unlike Baruch at the helm of the War Industries Board as could have been imagined.

Baruch felt not so much the paternal pride in the NRA that he might have been expected to feel as disapproval of its regimenting policies. He drew the distinction between an industry that went hat in hand to Washington to seek the right of "self-government" and an industry subdued, and to Johnson he protested in November 1933 that ". . . the whole field of industry is being forced into codes which are really impositions by the Government itself. In other words, the Government is seeking to direct the industrial life of the country even though this was not asked and indeed is not wanted." One of Johnson's bitterest foes was Senator Carter Glass, who happened to publish some newspapers in Virginia and considered the NRA's newspaper code an assault on the freedom of the press. "I just want to tell you, General," said Glass, "that your blue buzzard will not fly from the mastheads of my two newspapers." Testimony to Baruch's charm and political versatility was that as late as the end of 1933, Glass and Johnson each thought that Baruch agreed with *him*. When in the fall of 1934, Johnson was preparing to resign, it was Baruch alone whom he tried to reach for advice and support, just as earlier that year he had gone to him for a $6,000 loan. In 1935, in his book *The Blue Eagle from Egg to Earth*, Johnson called Baruch "the most faithful, kindly, and considerate man I ever knew." He revered him until he died in 1942, attended by nurses whom Baruch had paid for and by Baruch himself keeping vigil at his bedside.

Not inclined to think along ideological lines and reluctant to incur the disfavor of anyone who occupied the White House, Baruch was capable of deft shifts of viewpoint. If he believed anything before the inauguration it was that inflation was evil. He continued to say so in private after the coming of the New Deal, but he was not so incautious as to imperil what access to the White House he continued to enjoy. In the spring of 1933, following the decision to call in gold and the signing of the inflationary Thomas Amendment, he served on a commission to advise the President on issues that would be taken up at the forthcoming World Monetary and Economic Conference in London.

The business of the meeting was to get the gold nations in step with the paper-currency nations, or vice versa, and to try to re-establish fixed values for the world's unsteady currencies. The conference was set for London in June and July; Baruch had been named chief of the American advisory group in February. According to his enemies, he was appointed merely because he hadn't been asked into the Cabinet, and because he was too rich, too smart and too influential in Congress to be alienated. As the conference drew near, what might have seemed a harmless political sop came to alarm (among others) James Warburg, who thought Baruch vain, ill informed and not above turning the sensitive information that was bound to come his way to his own trading advantage. Indeed, there was something of a consensus on this point. Back in January, Roosevelt had told Homer Cummings, the Attorney General to be, that Baruch had earned $1 million profit in the bonds of the Missouri Pacific Railroad, "evidently" after coming into some inside information about a Reconstruction Finance Corporation loan. Furthermore, he had an option on a silver mine, and silver would be on the London agenda.

In May came word that Baruch would not be gong to London but would stay home as a White House liaison. This was a fine joke on Baruch, in Warburg's estimation, because the President would be going away on vacation just as the conference got under way, thus leaving Baruch no one to coordinate with. In June, the President dispatched Moley, then Assistant Secretary of State, to sail to London to look over the shoulder of the regular delegation. Moley, who was getting on well with Baruch, agreed to take Swope.

To those concerned about the abuse of confidential information, the choice of Swope was distressing. It was well known, as one Howard Kiroack, of Portland, Maine, took the trouble to wire the President on June 22, that Swope and Baruch were financially intimate and that Swope, from London, would be in a position to tip Baruch to market-related developments. (Roosevelt, hearing Louis M. Howe, a White House aide, contemptuously describe Swope as a "little brother to the rich," objected, "But I *like* him.") In London, after Swope and Moley landed, there were further insider-trading suspicions predicated on the frequency of telephone communication between Swope and Baruch. Although their calling was, in fact, extensive—the phone bill to Baruch came to $432—Swope was more or less constantly on the phone anyway, and for years he had stayed in touch with Baruch through all known channels of communication. On an especially communicative day in 1931, he had written him four letters. In private life it was quite true that he kept Baruch current on information that a later generation would call privileged. As Baruch's representative on the board of the Brooklyn Manhattan Transit Company, for instance, he regularly divulged earnings and dividend information to him (and to others, including Joseph P. Kennedy) before the rest of the stockholders could read it in the newspapers. It wasn't unthinkable that he sent him investment advice from London. On the other hand, with Baruch's encouragement, Swope before sailing had sold his stock in companies that did a mining or an international business in order to avoid the appearance of a conflict of interest. Moreover, it seems unreasonable that Baruch, after his experience with the peace-note leak investigation and the numerous postwar allegations of self-dealing against him in the War Industries Board, would risk the loss of his reputation for a quick turn in the market at the age of sixty-two.

To Secretary of State Cordell Hull, who headed the U.S. delegation, a more urgent question than to whom Swope was speaking on the telephone was what he and Moley were doing there in the first place. From the start the conference had been a fractious disappointment. The gold-bloc nations, led by France, pressed for an early return to gold convertibility by Great Britain and the United States. The United States, for its part, resisted any immediate currency-stabilization plan and chafed at the repudiation of wartime debts by its former allies. An exchange between James M. Cox, an American delegate, and Georges Bonnet, of France, caught the spirit of the talks:

BONNET: France would not look with favor upon the selection of someone to head the monetary committee who comes from a country that has recently gone off the gold standard.

COX: Nor will the United States look with favor upon the election of a man presented by a country which has repudiated its debts.

The Americans also quarreled intramurally. Senator Key Pittman, one of Hull's delegates, once chased Herbert Feis, a State Department man, down a hall in Claridge's Hotel with a hunting knife. On another occasion, after a dinner party that the Astors gave, the senator got Lady Nancy Astor down on the floor and tickled her. At the conference, Pittman's professional interest was silver, exclusively. Hull was mainly a low-tariff exponent. One thing on which the Americans were generally agreed was the desirability of a return to the international gold standard at some future date.

Before sailing with Swope on June 20, Moley had told reporters that Baruch would be filling in for him at the State Department in his absence and that they could expect to see a lot of him. In the retelling Baruch's role was exaggerated, as it had been throughout the Hundred Days. On June 22, a telegram, addressed to "Bernard M. Baruch, Unofficial President of the United States," was received at the State Department from a well-wisher in Tulsa, Oklahoma, who said, simply, "Congratulations. I know of no better man for the job." As Herbert Feis (who survived the encounter with Pittman) wrote later, it was odd of Moley to have chosen Baruch since gold-standard orthodoxy was just what Roosevelt was veering away from, and indeed, what Moley and Swope had been dispatched to London to guard against.

At the time, however, it wasn't clear to Moley what the President wanted, nor, perhaps, was Roosevelt himself entirely sure. In any case, when Moley called Baruch in New York on June 30 to say that a declaration on gold and the international monetary system had been drafted, that it had gone down well in London and that the President's quick approval was necessary to save the conference, Baruch was enthusiastic. The statement contained some hopeful language about stability in monetary affairs, the general endorsement of an international gold standard and a vague pledge on behalf of the governments to cooperate to limit speculative fluctuations in their currencies. Along with Treasury Secretary Woodin and Under Secretary Dean Acheson, Baruch urged Roosevelt to sign it.

This Roosevelt declined to do. Instead, aboard the U.S.S. *Indianapolis*, in the advisory company of Louis M. Howe and Henry Morgenthau, Jr., he drafted a repudiating statement ever afterward known as the "bombshell." Economically the goal of the New Deal was to raise domestic prices. The AAA and NRA were designed to lift them by law or persuasion, the gold acts through monetary inflation. Talking it over with Morgenthau and Howe, Roosevelt bridled at the idea of relinquishing any domestic freedom of action to an international agreement. To Hull he wrote explosively that "the sound internal economic situation of a nation is a greater factor in its well-being than the price of its currency in changing terms of the currencies of other nations. . . . So, too, old fetishes of so-called international bankers are being replaced by efforts to plan national currencies with the objective of giving those currencies a continuing purchasing power which does not vary greatly in terms of the commodities and needs of modern civilization."

Nothing more was heard of the conference. For the American delegation the political repercussions of the President's turnabout were far-reaching. Moley, who had sponsored the rejected declaration, was out, while Hull, whom Moley had briefly upstaged, was in. The gold-standard advisers were out; and Warburg, for one, promptly resigned, saying, "We are entering upon waters for which I have no charts and in which I therefore feel myself an utterly incompetent pilot."

Being older, wiser and navigationally more agile than Warburg, Baruch made no protest. "I am going along with the new adventures as much as I can," he wrote Josephus Daniels in mid-July, a week before sailing for Europe, where he was to meet Annie and Belle, "but some of it, between old friends, is pretty strong medicine for me to take." He said he was off to Vichy, for the waters, "to take all of the wickedness out of my system, and I hope out of my heart." Swope wired him with a bon voyage wish that his love life should continue to be kept "on an inflated basis." Later the same summer, in Czechoslovakia, Baruch fell in with Carter Glass and Frank Kent, both intransigent old-line Democrats. A Czech count put them up, and they hunted boar and celebrated Baruch's sixty-third birthday. (Krock had been invited too, but couldn't come. In his absence, he observed, Kent would be the "undisputed representative of the Guild of Sourpuss Political Columnists in Europe.") Probably Baruch's good right ear was filled with anti-New Deal ideas, but he returned to New York in a state of political ambivalence.

What to do? He had given unstintingly of money in the campaign— $200,000, he told Moley—and of advice both then and later. A month before the inauguration he had served warning against inflation—a systematic debasement of the currency—before the Senate Finance Committee. Subsequently *The Saturday Evening Post* had invited him to have the testimony boiled down into an article. He said yes. The piece was written, submitted and scheduled to run at the end of November.

Its approaching publication put its author on edge. Although careful to praise Roosevelt's "great labors," Baruch had written that fear of tampering with the dollar was impeding recovery. Some weeks earlier, *Fortune* magazine, in its October issue, had asked the question, "Is this a Baruch Administration?," had answered it in the negative and had quoted Baruch at his most pungently conservative, e.g., "By going off the gold standard we have become a nation of dishonest people in our relations with the bondholders," and "We're raising prices for the benefit of a small proportion—20 percent—of the population, the unemployed, debtor classes—incompetent, unwise people," and, finally, "You don't distribute wealth. You distribute poverty."

Party loyalty and the fear of ostracism worked strongly in Baruch and on November 6, 1933, he set out to explain himself. "About last March," he wrote the President, "I wrote a document against inflation which at the request of many of my friends who read it I finally gave to *The Saturday Evening Post*. . . . Had I been aware that you were going to take the position that you have, I would have not given it for publication because although I disagree with many of the things you are doing, I would not want to be in a position of being publicly opposed to them." Baruch thought better of it. He inserted the qualifying "might" between "I" and "disagree" and changed "many of the things you are doing" to "some." At last he decided to send no letter at all.

The 1930s were filled with issues over which reasonable people argued and drew swords. On the financial scene one of the most acrimonious was the question of how to dispose of contracts in which payment was specified in gold or in the current dollar price of gold. Ever since the inflationist scare of the 1890s it had been common practice for creditors to stipulate payment in dollars of the same gold weight as they had lent. The Treasury's own bonds, as late as May 1933, had been sold with this guarantee. All told, an estimated $100 billion worth of gold-clause bonds and obligations, public and private, were outstanding.

Early on in the New Deal, gold clauses had all been canceled by a Joint Resolution of Congress. Then, on January 31, 1934, the contingency against which clauses had been written occurred: the dollar was devalued. At once the debtor's burden was lightened, but so too the creditor's asset was diminished. Aggrieved bondholders trooped to court, claiming that the cancellation of the gold clauses was unconstitutional and tantamount to theft. One such litigant, a man named Norman, had bought a $1,000 bond of the Baltimore & Ohio Railroad. The railroad had promised to pay 4½ percent a year in semiannual installments in "gold coin of the United States of America of or equal to the standard weight and fineness existing on February 1, 1930." The stated dollar value of the coupon payable on February 1, 1934, was $22.50. However, since the gold value of the dollar had been reduced, the paper-dollar value of the interest payment would go up, as the gold clause provided. Instead of $22.50, Norman wanted the new, devalued dollar rate, $38.10. Invoking the government's abrogation of gold clauses, the B&O refused.

Through 1934 the gold-clause issue was joined. Did the government, in the interest of relieving debtors and raising prices in time of crisis, have the right to cancel contracts? Baruch, of course, had been a director of the B&O—implicitly he had joined in the company's promise to pay Norman in constant gold dollars, come what may—and he therefore had at least a sentimental interest in saving the railroad the extra burden of debt that its creditors demanded. Furthermore, he was a Democrat, and the party necessarily stood behind the Administration and its policies. There was something else. Politics, to Baruch, began with the mass, not the individual, and he was thus disposed to bow to even summary federal laws for the sake of what he took to be the national interest. (The government's lawyers, arguing *in terrorem*, warned that economic calamity would follow restoration of the clauses; the burden of debt would be ruinous.) To *Fortune* in 1933 he had bemoaned the injustice of going off gold—". . . we have become a nation of dishonest people in our relations with the bondholders." In late 1934, as *Norman v. B.&O. Railroad Co.* and other gold-clause cases wound their way to the Supreme Court, he wrote an unsolicited letter of advice to the then Treasury Secretary, Henry Morgenthau, Jr. (Woodin had left office in ill health). In case the government lost and the gold clauses were upheld, Baruch suggested the Treasury should levy a tax on the devaluation premium that Norman and the others were demanding. For a rate of tax he proposed 100 percent, a strange kind of justice for bondholders. In the event the idea was unnecessary. On Monday, February 18, 1935, the Supreme Court, by a vote of 5–4, upheld the government's contention that its sovereign power to define and redefine the value of money counted for more than contracts between individuals. Justice James C. McReynolds, his face flushed with anger and his southern voice pitched high, passionately dissented: "The Constitution as many of us have understood it, the instrument that has meant so much to us, is gone. The guarantees heretofore supposed to protect against arbitrary action have been swept away." The stock market, hailing cheap money and the lightened burden of debt, went up. Baruch wired his congratulations to the President via his secretary, Marguerite LeHand: "PLEASE TELL HIM THIS DELIGHTS ME MORE THAN I CAN EXPRESS."

But there was no predicting just where Baruch would turn up next on the ideological compass, and he continued to espouse a return to a gold-convertible dollar. In 1937 he ventured the prediction to Churchill that all the "managed currency nonsense" would soon disappear and said that for six thousand years the only real money had been based on gold and perhaps silver. A lady who saw a lot of Baruch remembered an evening in London in which Churchill and he were animatedly discussing gold. "All of us were sitting on a divan in front of the fireplace," she said. "Churchill would jump up to make a point, then Baruch would jump up to counter it. Baruch would tower over Churchill. I remember there was a big gilt mirror above the fire, and how often each of the men would lean an elbow on the fireplace and steal a look at himself in the mirror while he was talking."

Herbert Swope, who for years served as a kind of concertmaster in the symphony orchestra of Baruch, once mused of his friend and client: "He has a passion for service and who is to say no to that, even though the service is attended by a fanfare of trumpets. I sometimes wonder whether this reputation is wholly deserved or if he, like most of us, is occasionally synthetic."

It was no easy matter to live up to a reputation that (thanks in no small part to Swope) bordered on the mythical. The Baruch of public mind was rich, wise, avuncular, judicious and powerful. Arthur Krock, who should have known better, startled Baruch by writing in 1932 that he was one of the richest men in the country (he wasn't, even before the Crash), and Roosevelt once supposedly remarked to Rexford G. Tugwell that Baruch "owned" no fewer than sixty congressmen and senators. There was a glimpse of the wise Baruch in a *New Yorker* piece by Heywood Broun about the perfect doctor. "To sum the whole thing up," Broun had written, "the doctor nobody knows is a combination of Baruch, Beecher, Don Juan, Houdini, Mencken and Ed Wynn." (Baruch recalled strolling down the boardwalk in Atlantic City some time before the Crash in the company of Broun, Krock and Alexander Woollcott. He said that when talk turned to the market his advice was to buy bonds.) There was another Baruch of popular imagining, the unredeemed Wall Street Jew conjured by Henry Ford, Senator Huey Long and sundry critics of the Wilson war effort. There was a trace of him in a Broadway version of the Sinclair Lewis novel *Dodsworth*, which played in New York in 1934. In the second act, an "international banker," by name Arnold Israel, is put in his place by Dodsworth, the Midwest automobile man, with the line, "This Israel may be all he says he is internationally and financially but he certainly is no Barney Baruch."

To Baruch, of course, the preferred image was that of the wise and judicious American statesman, and he was at pains to have it projected in newspapers and magazines. He worked at maintaining cordial relations with newsmen, and he often made an impression with simple human kindness. Once the ship-news columnist for the New York *American*, Harry Acton, wrote appreciatively that Baruch had been generous enough to take the time to scan a passenger list to alert him to possible new leads, that he had obliged him in that way before and that he would be welcome in his column any time. It was Baruch's office policy that no friendly editorial should go unanswered by a warm personal letter to the editorialist. To cope with heavy bouts of friendly publicity, he retained a former New York *World* reporter, Charles S. Hand, to write thank-you notes for him.

As a master of the symbolic occurrence later known as the "media event," Baruch in 1928 made news by moving his office downtown. In the summer of 1934, when Wall Street was no longer a fashionable address, he announced a move back uptown. He explained to newsmen that he had given up finance (later in the year he discovered that he would earn a bigger income than ever before but would pay 83 percent of it in taxes) and planned to write three books—*The Autobiography of an American Boy, The Way That Lies Ahead for the Youth of America* and *Man's Conquest of Nature*. Although he had already retained Marquis James, Pulitzer Prize–winning biographer of Andrew Jackson, to write a draft of his autobiography, he said there would be no ghostwriter—an astonishing whopper. "Wall Street will see him less and the public will hear him more," reported *Time* in a story on this ostensible watershed in his career.

His money not only dazzled the press but was also occasionally a source of succor to needy newsmen. Carter Field, a writer on the staff of *Business Week* who went on to publish a flattering biography of Baruch, was in his debt in the Depression, as were David Lawrence, the syndicated columnist George Sokolsky and, of course, Swope. There is no known record of Krock either borrowing money or of entrusting what he did have to Baruch's management. Frank Kent, on the other hand, availed himself freely of Baruch's investment advice. In 1937, for instance, Baruch advised him that Warren Pipe & Foundry was a good thing but that he shouldn't buy too much of it. One thing led to another, and in 1949, weakened by arthritis, Kent asked if Baruch couldn't put him up at his apartment and give him the use of his car when he was next in town for a meeting of the Warren board of directors of which he (Kent) was by then a member. Baruch and the Baltimore columnist traveled together and needled each other in the way of boon companions. One of the Depression waifs to which Baruch had loaned money was Oglethorpe University in Atlanta. In gratitude the university presented the honorary doctor of laws degree to some candidates of his choosing, including Kent and Kennedy. After his investiture Kent received a backhanded letter of congratulation from his sponsor. "I nearly laughed myself sick at the idea of you looking dignified at the time the degree was conferred upon you," Baruch wrote. "Your poor wife! Your poor wife!"

Although Kent was in Baruch's debt for countless favors, the two friends went their own ways in public life, and it can no more be said that Baruch "owned" Kent than the other way around. On most issues they did see eye to eye. Each could deplore the New Deal and each revered the memory of Woodrow Wilson. However, on two matters Baruch was a never-ending source of disappointment to the columnist. Where Kent was forthright and unswerving in his opposition to Roosevelt, Baruch was guarded and wavering. "I suppose," Kent challenged in July 1936, "you are about to play your favorite role of Democratic sap—contributing to a cause in which you do not believe and for the benefit of a man you do not trust or like. What a china egg you are—and Herbert—and all of us. It's a humbug world." The second point of contention was Mrs. Roosevelt.

To Kent the President's wife was the sentimental, meddling, feminine image of the President. Baruch happened to like her, and she liked him. He was a source of cash for her good works and a fatherly counselor; she was a gentle lady, a White House spy and a liaison between him and the President. Once in January 1934 she addressed him as "Barney," but the familiarity rang false. (Baruch in any case preferred "Bernie") and she resumed the formality of "Mr. Baruch." Yet each of them was capable of spontaneous, heartfelt tributes to the other, and Baruch supported her work enthusiastically. In 1934, he gave $25,000 for the Reedsville homestead project; in 1935, $10,000 for the Arthurdale project and $43,500 more for Reedsville. (When, in the same year, Al Smith dunned him for $1,250 on behalf of the Brooklyn Zoo, which needed a pair of black leopards, Baruch pleaded poverty and the press of the New Deal. "If you can show me where I can get the $1,250 which as you know would have to be increased some in order to have this amount when the government finishes with us, I will go and get it and give it to you.") For Reedsville and

Arthurdale together in 1936, he gave more than $57,000. He furnished $200 anonymously to a Florida woman who, sick, pregnant and unable to pay her hospital bills, had had a dream that the First Lady would help her; and in 1937, when Mrs. Roosevelt took an interest in developing a school in New York City, Baruch and his brother Herman promised to buy it for her.

Some of his help was intellectual. He kept a steady stream of ideas on public issues flowing her way with the hope that some would find their way to the Oval Office. Sometimes, in return (she spoke of "our partnership"), she reported what was on the President's mind, or tried to allay Baruch's anxiety over some new policy thrust. In the summer of 1936, as the Administration and its critics were heading for a showdown over the Supreme Court, she wrote him reassuringly, "Franklin feels as keenly as you do about the Constitution."

Even with the coaching or columnar support of Swope, Kent, Krock or Hugh Johnson (who turned to writing after he left the NRA), Baruch was not wholly the master of his own public image. The Depression was a harvesttime of envy and anti-Semitism, and he was vulnerable to attack on either score. Moreover, since he had declared himself openly neither for nor against the New Deal, he was fair game for critics on either side of the political spectrum and for cranks at home and abroad. In the Senate he was regularly assailed by Huey Long as the secret power behind the Administration. As a matter of fact, according to Long, Baruch had run Hoover too—"We thought we were swapping Hoover for Roosevelt, but we were swapping Baruch for Baruch." The Detroit radio priest Father Charles E. Coughlin arraigned him as "Acting President of the United States, the Uncrowned Prince of Wall Street" and insisted that his middle name wasn't Mannes at all but Manasseh, for the wicked king of Judah who dealt in graven images, enchantments, witchcraft and murder. Hate mail arrived uptown, including a handwritten note in 1935 that commanded him, after some vicious anti-Semitic name calling, to "seek a lonely spot and shoot yourself and do the U.S. a favor."

An attack on Baruch often yielded a publicity dividend to the assailant since one or more of Baruch's many prominent friends could be expected to rise to his defense. In a riposte at Long in 1935, for instance, Krock observed that Baruch, far from being the omnipotent being caricatured by the Kingfish, had in fact been frustrated both in Wall Street (he was never permitted to realize his dream of owning a railroad) and more recently in Washington, where his advice went un-heeded. Answering a Paris newspaper that had painted his mentor as "President Roosevelt's great financial adviser and semiofficial chief of Jewish policy in America," Johnson wrote that Baruch in fact deplored the Administration's fiscal policy. Sometimes the best retort was silence, and Swope, for one, insisted in 1936 that nothing be said to provoke Coughlin. (He followed up this shrewd counsel with a prescient report of a small company that made sunglasses but not yet instant cameras and film, Polaroid Corporation. "It looks good," he wrote. "In fact it looks so good I am startled.") Following an allegation by Senator Schall of Minnesota in 1934 that Baruch had unpatriotically channeled invest-ment funds abroad, the accused got in touch with Joe Robinson to frame a reply. So close were he and the senator from Arkansas and so faithfully had the latter taken his side against slander in the past that Baruch couched the proposed rebuttal in an interesting way. Here are the facts, he wrote Robinson, in case "we" should care to answer him.

An attempt in 1935 to prove that Baruch had illicitly profited as chairman of the War Industries Board boomeranged on the accuser and brought the accused his most thumping vindication of the period. The forum was a special Senate committee that Gerald P. Nye had convened in 1934 to investigate the munitions industry. Assisted by an upwardly mobile government lawyer named Alger Hiss, Nye's plan was to expose the scope of corporate profits in the last war, to lay bare the lines of in-fluence between the "merchants of death" and the government and to prevent any such recurrence in a future war. Since (as the reasoning im-plicitly went) capitalism was a cause of aggression, a promising avenue to peace was the suppression of wartime profits. One of the many wit-nesses called by the committee was Baruch.

He was a potentially friendly witness. For years he had advocated "taking the profit out of war," and in December 1934, President Roo-sevelt had appointed him chairman of a high-level federal panel to draft legislation to do just that. Later on, he commended the idea of govern-ment-owned munitions plants to Eleanor Roosevelt. Besides furthering national preparedness, he said, the armories and related manufacturing facilities would yield "great social values."

It was clear from the start, however, that the committee had un-friendly intentions. Although Baruch wasn't called as a witness until March, Senator James F. Byrnes had begun collecting ammunition for use in his defense as early as January. The invitation to testify, when it did arrive, contained the transparently hostile request that Baruch furnish copies of his tax returns for 1916–1919 as well as a list of the securities he owned in that period. Presently word leaked out that the original tax returns had vanished from the Treasury archives (which, in the course of a routine weeding, they had), as if the witness himself had had them spirited away to destroy incriminating evidence.

Nye and Hiss underestimated their man. Not only was Baruch innocent of the wrongdoing they suspected, but he was also well equipped to prove it. In advance of his appearance he sent the committee copies of his tax returns for 1916 and 1917, facsimile reports for 1918 and 1919, lists of securities held (chiefly Liberty Bonds) and of dividends donated in the war to such interdenominational causes as the Knights of Columbus, YMCA, YMHA and the Salvation Army. He coldly promised to furnish further personal details, and also "to further the work of the committee, which I had understood to be an investigation of the munitions industry."

Late in March, Baruch and his party—his valet, Lacey; a secretary, Miss Adele Busch, bearing more documents; and Swope—moved into rooms at the Carlton Hotel in Washington. For two days and two nights Swope and Baruch rehearsed, assembled evidence and planned tactics. Swope reminded him that his Senate friends would be waiting to shake his hand at the committee-room door. He was to draw out this moment of greeting as long as possible. (Swope also advised him to show up a few minutes late, but tardiness, for Swope, was a lifelong policy.) The more time he took with his prepared statement, Swope counseled, the fewer questions would be asked of him and the greater the likelihood that the headlines next day would highlight him, not the committee. On the first day all went according to plan. On the second day, there was no statement to read, but the determined inquisitor, Hiss, had to contend with the stage whispers of Carter Glass in response to his questions—"Never heard such dad bum fool questions in all my bo'n days"—as well as Baruch's forthright answers. Finally Senator Byrnes rose to testify to the generosity and patriotism of Baruch in the war, recounting, among other stories, his distribution of free Pullman tickets to the homebound women of the WIB. "Have you got that down?" Swope whispered loudly to the committee stenographer. The stenographer said yes. Swope then turned to Baruch and said, "Now we got the sons of bitches! From here we just coast in!" They did.

FOURTEEN

"His Métier Was Peril"

Annie Griffen Baruch came down with pneumonia on Tuesday, January 11, 1938, and died the following Sunday afternoon at home in New York. A private funeral was held the next Tuesday. The obituaries described a quiet and motherly woman who had patronized the arts, supported the opera, collected antique silver and furniture and avoided her husband's spotlight. She was sixty-five years old.

"I don't know why he wants me to go to the funeral," Eleanor Roosevelt told a friend when Baruch invited her to attend. "He never paid any attention to her when she was alive." Perhaps he mourned from guilt and old love as much as from anguish, for their marriage had become a formality. His taste ran to young and pretty women, and she was stout and looked her years. She took little interest in power brokerage, stock picking, quail shooting and his other pursuits. Long's and Coughlin's attacks on him horrified her, and the fact that she had no grandchildren saddened her. In the fall of 1936, when a grandson was born to the Swopes, she had wired congratulations wistfully: "YOU HAVE A GRANDSON. I HAVE NOT EVEN A WHIFFEN-POOF."

A month after Annie's death, Cary Grayson, the former White House physician, died. Baruch was genuinely bereaved. Once in the Harding years there had been a spiteful Republican attempt to have the doctor, a Navy man who owed an out-of-line promotion to President

Wilson, shipped off to the Philippines. Hearing of the plot, Baruch intervened. Grayson and he were partners in racing, and a thirteen-thousand-mile separation would have been out of the question. "Through many difficult and also many happy adventures," he once reflected of Grayson, "our friendship has ripened into one of those beautiful relationships that make life worth living." He could have almost said the same thing about Joe Robinson, and he had died, under the burden of Senate work, in July 1937.

The death of a close friend or spouse often serves as a reminder of the inevitability of one's own death, but in Baruch's case the signs were premature. He would carry on to impart advice to President John F. Kennedy, to worry over a world war, two lesser conflicts and the atomic bomb and to exceed by almost a quarter century his Biblically allotted life-span of threescore and ten years. One health-giving force in his life was hypochondria. It never occurred to him, as a rich and egocentric doctor's son, not to take care of himself or to deny himself (or, for that matter, his close friends and relatives) expert medical care. He watched his diet, soaked himself in mineral baths and waved small dumbbells in the air for exercise. After Annie's death he hired a live-in nurse and companion.

Sick or well, he was a model patient. He followed medical instructions to the letter, unquestioningly paid his doctors' bills, and took pills, including vitamins, by the handful. One physician in the Baruch stable billed his famous patient at a premium rate simply because he was expected to make himself available to Baruch at the drop of a hat. "If a doctor said 'go to the moon,'" said the doctor, "he'd go."

Despite conscientious preventive maintenance, however, Baruch's body developed the usual knocks and rattles of old age. The gout, which tortured him in 1932, recurred later in the decade. In 1935 it had him on crutches. In 1936, a year in which he felled an opponent with a single blow during an altercation on East 57th Street (to a policeman who happened on the scene after the fight and asked whether he could be of assistance, Baruch answered, "Yeah! Pick the son of a bitch up so I can hit him again"), he suffered from arthritis. In 1939 he had prostate trouble, a renal attack and a mastoid operation. The hearing in his left ear was gone, but in August 1939 he pronounced himself fitter than he'd been in a decade—his doctors, he said, had discovered a heretofore undiagnosed "low-grade infection."

By that time it was clear that another war was coming, and Baruch wanted to be up and around for it, and to have others believe that he was fit enough to participate, too. He had been predicting war and trying to rouse his countrymen to prepare for it ever since the mid 1930s. As he himself pointed out, he was the living authority on economic mobilization, and he had been lecturing, writing and cajoling on that subject almost since the first Armistice Day.

Baruch, said a perceptive associate of his, loved to be needed when the chips were down—"his métier was peril." Apart from this urge to serve in an hour of crisis, he was a patriot who was willing to put country above everything else, even his own pride. (In the main guest bedroom at Hobcaw there was a picture of Happy Argo, Baruch's champion colt, winning the Parole Handicap at Belmont Park in 1927. The jockey was dressed in the silks of Kershaw Stable, Baruch's *nom de course*. Its colors were red, white and blue.) With the onset of war, he became an unpaid, full-time public servant.

Baruch proceeded in martial affairs in the same ideologically eclectic way as he had operated in political and economic ones. As early as 1935, he had condemned Hitler as the "greatest menace to world safety," and in 1938 he contributed $11,060 to the Abraham Lincoln Battalion, which fought in Spain against Franco, and with the Communists.* Both positions were certifiably progressive. Then, in 1939, he said that Hitler and Stalin were "blood brothers"—a view from the right. In 1941 he pressed for controls on wages, prices and profits, thus siding with the New Deal theorists who were happy to aggrandize the government's power in peace or war. (In 1936 Baruch had gone the New Deal one better by proposing a global minimum wage, and in 1937 he wrote, "I feel that if the businessmen who have to carry into effect the social and economic reforms would place themselves and their lawyers at the disposal of the government instead of against it, we could move much faster and more surely along the paths along which we have already started.") But in quarrels between the civilians and the Army, he usually sided with the Army.

The consistency in Baruch's method was his pushing for more and better defenses. He called for raw-materials stockpiling, expanded armaments production, especially of aircraft, and the revival of something

---

*He said that the money was to bring wounded Americans home.

like the old War Industries Board. President Roosevelt, listening sympathetically to this plea in 1938, on the eve of Baruch's annual summer vacation, agreed that some such conspicuous mobilization planning might worry Hitler, and he agreed to make Baruch the chairman of something they would call the Defense Coordination Board. The Board would meet in September, when Baruch got back, and would make its report in December. In the meantime, Baruch was commissioned to study the European military situation, and he sailed in high spirits. In Great Britain and France he was so appalled by the state of unpreparedness that he placed a transatlantic call to the White House on August 19, his birthday, to suggest that he return at once to get the American program under way. Roosevelt, who had elections to win as well as a country to defend, may or may not have been inclined to agree that such haste was desirable. What he could not abide was the impolitic suggestion, which Baruch had floated in an earlier communiqué, that the new Board include Hugh Johnson and George Peek, two War Industries Board alumni who had had noisy fallings-out with the New Deal. The new Board never met.

Baruch, however, boarded the *Queen Mary* under the impression that he might be taking up where he had left off in 1918. Winston Churchill, then a private citizen with every apparent prospect of remaining one, shared the same impression. He told Baruch as they said goodbye: "Well, the big show is going to be on pretty soon. You'll be in the forefront of it over there, and I'll be on the sidelines here." (Possibly they also talked about stocks. They had gone into Brooklyn Manhattan Transit Company together a few years before, and in October 1937 Baruch had flashed him a general buy signal: "THINK AMERICA ON BARGAIN COUNTER." As he did with his other friends, Baruch was also prone to advise the future Prime Minister not to get in over his head.)

Baruch, said Roosevelt to Jimmy Byrnes in 1938, "was nuts on Army preparation." Certainly he was single-minded. When Louis Johnson, the Assistant Secretary of War, mentioned that for want of a $3 million appropriation, the War Department would be unable to obtain some vital gunpowder facilities, Baruch offered to advance the money himself. Johnson declined. (Early in 1941, however, General George C. Marshall accepted with thanks Baruch's gift of a pair of Zeiss binoculars.) Baruch took a keen, almost proprietary, interest in all phases of military operation, and in officers of all grades. He was a regular lecturer at the Army War College and the Army Industrial College. Once he started an inquiry into the case of a Jewish cadet at West Point who had run afoul of the Academy superintendent just prior to his graduation. Baruch suspected anti-Semitism. He contacted Stephen Early, the President's press secretary, who called the War Department. The superintendent was overruled, and the cadet was duly commissioned a second lieutenant.* The Navy's reassignment of the skipper of the U.S.S. *Panay* to the command of an oil tanker in 1940 prompted a Baruch suggestion to General Edwin "Pa" Watson, the President's secretary, that a more suitable billet for the heroic survivor of a Japanese strafing attack would be a new cruiser or battleship. (Baruch had as much or more faith in battleships than the Navy did. "Has any warship ever been destroyed by an airplane?" he asked Swope rhetorically in 1940. "Has any been put out of commission by an airplane?")

Baruch's stock was usually higher with the military than it was with the President. According to the historian Jordan Schwarz, Roosevelt, concerning Baruch and preparedness policy, had two rules of thumb. First, never share power with him or with a so-called Baruch man; as Moley said, he was too luminous a figure. Second, "never allow even the emergency of war mobilization to become the occasion for erecting power bases that might rival the White House." In other words, deny what Baruch took to be the most obvious and important lesson of the First World War, namely, the necessity of one-man responsibility for the home front.

In August 1939 a War Resources Board was formed to report on the very mobilization question to which Baruch had addressed himself for twenty years; his name was not among the committeemen. Nor was he brought into the Administration's successor war-planning agencies, the Advisory Commission on National Defense and the Office of Production Management (OPM) in 1940 and the Office of Price Adminis-

---

*The young man stayed in the Army and became a hero. In Europe in the Second World War he commanded infantry battalions and was decorated with the Purple Heart and Silver Star. He retired as a colonel in 1955. "In my opinion," he wrote when asked about the incident, "were it not for the efforts of the great Mr. Bernard M. Baruch, I would not have graduated U.S.M.A. . . ." He asked that his name not be divulged; his family knew nothing about the row.

tration and Civilian Supply (OPACS) and the Supply, Priorities and Allocation Board (SPAB) in 1941.

Historians of the period have written that Baruch was more influential in these mobilization alphabet agencies than he appeared to be. Thus, for instance, John Hancock, a longtime confederate of his, was named to the War Resources Board, and one of the first items on the WRB's agenda was to consult with the "Chairman of the old War Industries Board. . . ." Similarly, the industrialist Samuel R. Fuller, Jr., a consultant to OPM, was a friend of Baruch's. Once Fuller had gone to Germany on a mission for the President, had been given an audience with Hitler and had mentioned Baruch's name. Much to Baruch's delight Fuller reported that the Fuehrer had gone off like a rocket. Furthermore (as the historians have also written) Baruch was friendly with Leon Henderson and some of the young New Deal economists with OPACS. In a concession to the value of Baruch's advice, the President, in February 1941, began to eat lunch with him regularly.

What Baruch had to say to the President or to anybody else on the subject was more or less predictable. He advocated all-out federal controls. In the first place, he said, the government ought to be able to direct industrial traffic according to the needs of national defense. Airplanes, for instance, would receive a high government priority and eggbeaters a low one, so that scarce steel would be routed toward vital uses and away from nonessential ones. In the spring of 1941 a salesman had gotten Baruch's patriotic dander up by offering him a new Lockheed Lodestar passenger plane. Under the Baruch priority system he wouldn't have been able to buy a plane even if he'd wanted one; the Army and Navy would have gotten them all. It followed logically that price controls were also essential, he went on, because if prices were free to go up, rich buyers could divert raw materials from defense production merely by paying more for them. He insisted, moreover, that price controls must be all-encompassing, not "piecemeal." (For a man with so much of it, money figured surprisingly little in Baruch's discussion of inflation and of anti-inflationary policies. In a piece in the *Harvard Business Review* in March 1941 he did mention the need to control the supply of money, but the weight of his analysis was on nonmonetary forces. As late as the fall of 1940, the then president of the Brookings Institution, Harold G. Moulton, could find no reference to the banking or monetary side of inflation in any of his published writing or testimony on price controls, which was extensive.) To check excessive consumer spending and to finance as much of the war as possible in the years in which it was fought, Baruch also advocated putting up taxes "as high as a cat's back." The nation that came through with the lowest cost and price structure would be the one to win the peace.

While the Administration kept him at arm's length in 1941, Arthur Krock praised him as the "Socrates of defense," the columnist George Sokolsky called for his reappointment as chairman of a new War Industries Board, and Frank Kent, in *his* column, asserted that "things are in a mess and he [Baruch] is the only man who remotely knows the answers." At the Gridiron Dinner that year the Washington press corps parodied OPM by making out William S. Knudsen and Sidney Hillman, its joint directors, to be Siamese twins and giving them topical lyrics to sing to the tune of "Oh! Susanna":

HILLMAN: *When any problem gets so large*
It might end in a fluke,
We take it straight to F.D.R.—
Who takes it to Baruch!

Both: *OPM, that is the place for me,*

(Slowly and *We'll take our troubles to Baruch*
in harmony) *AND SAVE DEMOCRACY!*

One reason for Baruch's unique success as a freelance critic was that he refused not to be helpful. Another was that so many people were grateful to him. Sokolsky, Kent and Krock, for instance, each saw him through friendly, nonobjective eyes; in March 1941 Kent sent him a copy of an adulatory column he had written about his economic-mobilization ideas with a letter containing equally effusive thanks for his help in wangling some steamship tickets for Frank Kent, Jr., and his fiancée. In his Washington gift-giving, Baruch remembered people of all ranks, from the President and Mrs. Roosevelt to the President's military aide, General Watson, to innumerable senators and congressmen to the office staff of the White House press secretary (who at Christmas 1941 received $50 each in cash). The press secretary himself, Stephen Early, was a bosom friend of Baruch's and a past recipient of his largess. In December 1940 had come a gold dress set; in May 1941, some money that had gone to buy screens for the Early house before the on-slaught of the Washington gnats. Once Baruch had pulled strings after Early had allegedly assaulted a New York City police officer, which prompted an appreciative note. "I am familiar with your quiet but effective methods of 'operation,' during troublous times," the press secretary wrote. "I am grateful."

Because Roosevelt sometimes clashed with Baruch, Early was occasionally pitted for professional reasons on the side of his employer against his benefactor. There was one such run-in in October 1941 after Baruch sent William Randolph Hearst a letter in praise of the publisher's patriotic stand on military preparedness—"How well I remember your efforts to have this country look forward to preparedness and how your papers were among those who advocated this as strongly as I did. Alas our efforts were of no avail." Roosevelt, seeing the letter on page one of the New York *Journal American*, was revolted. He dictated a telegram to Baruch to be sent over Early's name, as follows:

THE PRESIDENT IS AT HYDE PARK BUT SHOULD LIKE TO KNOW IF IT IS REALLY TRUE THAT YOU SENT TO MR. HEARST THE LETTER WHICH APPEARS ON THE FRONT PAGE OF TODAYS NEW YORK JOURNAL AMERI-CAN.

Baruch dashed off a letter to Early, assuring him that it was his letter and that at all hazards he would continue to speak his mind. But he didn't write *that* letter; Swope did, and Early, at least, agreed that it was a fine job.

Not everyone around the President wanted Baruch. Harry Hopkins, perhaps the President's closest adviser, was responsible (or so Baruch thought) for keeping him out of the war effort. A social worker by profession, frail and chronically ill, Hopkins was the head of the Works Progress Administration, later of the Commerce Department, and in the war served at Roosevelt's side as planner and strategist. Baruch ran hot and cold on the New Deal, but he did conceive a relatively fixed opinion of Hopkins' end of it, the federal relief program. He thought that the WPA had reduced personal initiative and had thereby perpetuated joblessness, and he told Hopkins so. Sometimes as he sat on a park bench the sight of pigeon would put him in mind of Hopkins, or the thought of Hopkins would cause him to notice a pigeon, and he would disdainfully call the bird a WPA worker.

However, Baruch was not so artless as to intentionally make enemies of men in high office. As a matter of policy and instinct he cultivated them, and as the war drew near he redoubled his efforts to keep personal animosities out of the nation's business. Moreover, he had the facility of speaking in tongues, and just as he could seem liberal to Eleanor Roosevelt and conservative to Frank Kent, so he could appear pro-Hopkins to Roosevelt and fiercely anti- to Ickes, Hopkins' bureaucratic enemy. On balance, Baruch was probably anti-Hopkins—he blamed him for needless and costly slipups in the conduct of the war—yet when Hopkins' body was borne down the steps of St. Bartholomew's Church in February 1946 Baruch was one of the honorary pallbearers.

In any event, Baruch was characteristically generous to Hopkins in the prewar and early war years. He entertained him at Hobcaw, bought him a lifetime membership in the Jefferson Islands Club and in 1938 helped him with a delicate personal matter. Hopkins, then between wives, had been seeing a lot of Mrs. Dorothy Donovan Hale, a pretty and impecunious widow who danced and acted a little and stayed in debt. Mrs. Hale thought that Hopkins was going to marry her, but he didn't. Compounding her despondency over this failed romance was one of her regular financial crises. Baruch, a friend of hers, advised her not to try to make a career but to land a rich husband, and he gave her a check to apply to sprucing up her wardrobe. One night she came home from a party, sat down at a typewriter, composed instructions for her burial and notes to her friends (to Baruch she wrote that she was sorry she wouldn't be able to take his good advice). Before dawn she jumped to her death from her apartment on the sixteenth floor of the Hampshire House on Central Park South. What happened next is unclear. According to the late Thomas G. Corcoran, Hopkins believed that Baruch had used his influence with the press to see that the story of the suicide was muted.* He related that he had conveyed Hopkins' thanks to Baruch for a job sensitively done.

The New York Times carried it, complete with a reference to her friendship with Hopkins, but without mention of the suicide note to Baruch, on page 34 of the edition of Saturday, October 22, 1938.

When Hopkins did remarry, four years later, Baruch gave his wife and him a buffet supper at the Carlton Hotel and invited sixty of the most prominent people in Washington. There was perfume for the ladies, champagne for all and a menu as long as the host's arm. The gaiety of the evening presented a journalistically exploitable paradox to the wartime austerity being preached by Hopkins, along with others in the Administration, and the anti-Roosevelt press made the most of it. In answer to a hostile report in the Washington *Times-Herald*, Baruch protested to its publisher, Eleanor "Cissy" Patterson, that the food had come from the hotel menu, that he had paid only for what was eaten, that the cost per person had amounted to less than $5, that he had specifically instructed the maître d'hôtel not to serve anything in short supply and that the champagne was some of his own stock, given to him ten years before, that was about to go corky anyway. Hopkins' biographer writes that the event turned into a "first-rate scandal. And oddly enough, Hopkins got more blame than Baruch." The oddity was that Baruch's public-relations sense, or Swope's, had failed even for one night. The lapse was short-lived, however, and a week or so later Baruch was back in the papers in a positive light. He had, he announced, made a $1 million Christmas present to the war-relief agencies of the United States and a half-dozen allied nations.

Baruch suffered another dinnertime embarrassment with Hopkins that Harold Ickes alertly recorded in his diary. The entry was dated February 1, 1942:

> Baruch also told me of a dinner or supper at the White House when Mrs. Roosevelt turned to him and in her penetrating voice said: "Mr. Baruch, I think you are the wisest man in the world." Baruch did not think that this would do him much good in that particular presence, and so he tried to silence her but she became more emphatic. It seemed that Baruch had advised her how to prepare for income taxes that year and she had followed his advice. Bernie said that the president didn't look any too pleased, and that Harry Hopkins' face was very dark.

Baruch could imagine what would happen to him if Hitler won, and after the war, in fact, his name did turn up on a list of the Nazis' most-wanted men. A crude Nazi propaganda broadside of 1940 vintage posed the question "Who profits by war?" and answered that, in large part, Baruch did, he being "one of the richest Jews in the world" and "President Roosevelt's confidential adviseror [*sic*]."

To anyone who made an overture to him on the basis of his being a Jewish-American, Baruch's response was invariably the assertion that he was an American, not a "hyphenate" (Woodrow Wilson's contemptuous designation for ethnic Americans who put the welfare of their former homelands above that of their adopted one). This nomenclatural touchiness was a symptom of the uneasiness that Baruch felt about his own Jewishness. He was not a religious man, and he held some unflattering stereotypes of Jews, particularly East Europeans. On the other hand, there was a strain of "foul weather" Jew in him too, the kind who rallied to Jewry when trouble was brewing.

Some of the trouble touched him personally. He still had relatives in Germany and he did what he could to help them get out safely. (In 1938 a German citizen by the name Bernard Baruch wrote to Treasury Secretary Morgenthau to ask for help; this Baruch claimed to be a relative of Bernard M. Baruch, whom he mistakenly identified, perhaps under the influence of Nazi propaganda, as Morgenthau's predecessor in office.) In December 1939 a German woman credited Baruch with helping her reach England and with saving her husband from a concentration camp. In June 1940, two German aunts of Baruch's, both more than ninety years of age, were making their way to Barcelona thanks to him and the Red Cross.

Late in October 1938 he confronted a financial and moral dilemma. Cyprus Mines Corporation, which owned copper deposits on the Mediterranean island of Cyprus, had been doing a lot of business with the Germans. Baruch had owned stock in the company for twenty-five years. While he would not presume to dictate with whom it could deal, he was sure that he personally wanted no truck with the Third Reich. Inasmuch as there was no public market for the company's shares, he wrote to the president, Harvey S. Mudd (the son of Seeley Mudd, of Texas Gulf days), to offer his stock to him or his family.

Mudd replied that it would be a shame to sell. The company was only just beginning to come into its own, the future looked rich in dividends and it was difficult to say at the moment just what his stock was worth. He explained that there was another practical consideration. The only smelter in Europe that could handle the company's ore was situated in Hamburg.

When Baruch persisted, Mudd, in March 1939, expanded his argument:

> I am very distressed and unhappy over the situation but I do not want to breach our sales contracts and take the consequences, whatever they may be. The company's shareholders may not demur but there are hundreds of workmen in Cyprus who would lose their jobs and they are the ones who would suffer most. I feel as responsible to them as I do to the shareholders. We can decline to ship copper concentrates and pyrites to Germany and Germany will find other sellers but no one is going to find work for the men we lay off.

According to the company history, "This apparently satisfied Mr. Baruch."

When there was a big problem at hand, Baruch like to have a big answer. What he proposed for the plight of European Jewry and of refugees of all religious stripes in the late 1930s was a new nation. He would call it the United States of Africa.

This was no Zionist scheme for the settlement of Palestine. Baruch was no Zionist, and he wanted a catholic, not an exclusively Jewish, solution to the dilemma of homeless people. He thought that a very large mass of central Africa should be appropriated, placed under a British protectorate and settled by pioneers with all the modern implements. Men would go first, with bulldozers, insecticides and construction materials to carve out a foothold. What might have taken generations with an ax and flintlock could be accomplished in relatively short order with up-to-date technology; women and children would follow in due course. Colonization would be financed privately. Jews could tithe themselves, and Baruch, for one, offered to put up $3 million.

At Hobcaw, Baruch put the idea to Representative Hamilton Fish, a New York Republican, and Fish, being sold on it, traveled to Europe in the summer of 1939 to try to drum up interest among the British and the French. In Paris he saw Georges Bonnet, the Minister of Foreign Affairs, and Georges Mandel, Minister of Colonies. He outlined the proposed settlement of an area south and west of Lake Chad, mentioned that he had already seen Lord Edward Halifax, the British Foreign Secretary, on the matter and was trying to see Herr Hitler. Fish identified Baruch as the source of the idea and quoted him to the effect that $100 million might be raised to finance it. All this information came back to Roosevelt from the American embassy in London. Roosevelt forwarded the embassy's report, along with a covering note of his own, to Baruch.

". . . I am quite certain," wrote the President, not being certain at all, "that neither you nor I, who belong to the more practical schools of thought, would ever have commissioned Honorable Ham to represent us or speak for us. I wish this great Pooh-Bah would go back to Harvard and play tackle on the football team. He is qualified for that job." According to Fish, the French were enthusiastic about the idea, but war broke out before anything could be done about it.

Late in May 1941, when Hitler was on his best behavior toward the United States in order to avoid an expanded war, two official directives went out to the German press. The first, dated May 23, was to suspend personal attacks on President Roosevelt. The second, on May 30, was to lay off Bernard Baruch.

Whatever Baruch's standing in the Roosevelt White House happened to be, there were always a number of people, friends and enemies, who assumed it was lofty. Herbert Hoover, who in the main was a friend, valued Baruch not least for his access to Democratic officeholders. Late in November 1941 it was the former President who brought Baruch together with a lawyer named Raoul E. Desvernine. Desvernine's business was most urgent: he was trying to head off a war with Japan.

His client was Saburo Kurusu, Japanese special envoy, who had been engaged in fateful talks with Secretary of State Cordell Hull. Kurusu had found Hull to be hostile, while the American thought Kurusu evasive. Desvernine, who was identified with the Liberty League and was therefore presumably short of high-level Administration contacts, wanted to find a way for Kurusu to reach Roosevelt directly, bypassing Hull. On either December 1 or December 3 (Hoover's notes indicate the former date, Baruch's memoirs the latter) Baruch, Desvernine and Kurusu sat down together at the Mayflower Hotel.

Unlike the Japanese, Baruch had been loath to go outside channels.

He checked with General Watson to get White House clearance. Watson, after checking with Roosevelt, had told him to go ahead with the meeting, and Baruch proceeded. He asked Kurusu what was on his mind.

The envoy explained that the Emperor wanted peace and that a direct appeal to him by Roosevelt might stymie the militarists. He laid out some general proposals, including the withdrawal of most, but not all, Japanese troops from China (the United States had asked for a complete evacuation) and an end to the American trade embargo of the previous July. Unbeknownst to either Baruch, Kurusu or Desvernine, however, it was already too late. The Japanese cabinet council, meeting in the imperial presence on December 1, had elected war.

Like millions of other Americans, Baruch got the news at home while reading the Sunday papers. Unlike the great mass of his countrymen, however, at the time he was dressed in morning clothes, his customary Sunday-morning attire, and he heard the news from a private nurse in the second-floor living room of a Fifth Avenue mansion. (Perhaps he opened his newspaper to the financial section to glance at the price of International Telephone & Telegraph common, which he'd been urging his friends to buy; it had closed Saturday at 2⅜, up from 2¼ on Friday.) The telephone rang. His nurse, Miss Higgins, picked it up, listened a moment and relayed the shocking message that the Japanese had bombed Pearl Harbor. All at once Baruch was out of his chair, saying, "I told them!"—meaning, as she reflected later, that he had predicted war and had told the government exactly what to do to prepare for it. Next he got on the phone to a succession of Washington officials, cursing, advising and encouraging. He was mad at the Administration and at no one more than the President, to whom, however, he apparently did not speak that December 7.

For a long time Baruch worked as a volunteer adviser and a one-man morale officer to the chiefs of the home front. In the first full month of the war he made a reconnaissance of ordnance production in New York and Philadelphia ("I found considerable lethargy and lack of urgency which I think you will now find overcome . . . ," he wrote the President) and submitted a list of five candidates to head the new War Production Board, which was to be the approximate reincarnation of the old War Industries Board. Roosevelt chose not to reappoint Baruch to his old post; nor did he pick one of his men. His choice was Donald

M. Nelson, chief of the unprepossessing outfit called SPAB. As usual in such circumstances, Baruch behaved handsomely. On the evening of Nelson's first day in office he took him out to dinner.

Baruch was a good soldier. Though jobless at a moment of national peril, he took offense at only two things. First, the claim that he was a "Presidential adviser"; and second, the preposterous Nazi propaganda that he was running the American war effort. The latter charge, he told Krock, hurt his professional pride. ("Of course they [the Nazis] put out all this war-mongering, anti-Semitism about me because the do not want to see men like me who understand the job put in charge.") As Baruch devoted himself to his work, he inspired others. He was a constant counselor to Donald Nelson on technical and organizational matters. To Harold Ickes, the Interior Secretary, he offered advice on metals, strategic minerals and self-motivation. He told him to stand in front of a mirror twice a day, draw up his chin and repeat to himself, "Hell, of course I can take it." When Arthur Krock began to feel sorry for himself in the role of Administration critic, Baruch bucked *him* up. Once he jotted a note to General Watson explaining his presence in Washington: "I am here since yesterday holding hands and trying to prop up the weak and faltering."

Baruch often spent part of the week in Washington. Before leaving New York, which he typically did Monday on the four o'clock train (taking a drawing room if he could get one), he would notify any or all of a long list of top officials, by telegraph, of his impending arrival. The list included Robert P. Patterson, Under Secretary of War; James V. Forrestal, Under Secretary of Navy; James F. Byrnes, who was sitting on the Supreme Court; General Levin H. Campbell, Jr., Army Chief of Ordnance; Cordell Hull; General Brehon Somervell of the War Department Service of Supply; Leon Henderson of the Office of Price Administration; Milo Perkins of the Board of Economic Warfare; Professor Luther Gulick of the War Production Board. In Washington at the Carlton he shared a $1,000-a-month suite with Lacey, his valet, one bedroom per man. Baruch told Geoffrey Hellman of *The New Yorker* that he took most of his meals in his room, sometimes with Donald Nelson or other official guests, and that he would eat a beefsteak and a dozen eggs for breakfast if his doctor would let him. "My boy," said Baruch, "I never go out in Washington, because unless I dine at seven-thirty sharp, I get cross and am poor company. I don't drink cocktails, and I hate to sit around till eight o'clock or so watching other people drink. I lock myself in my room, like an animal. I am in bed by eleven."* He told Harold Ickes that he went to bed with a copy of the *Racing Form.*

The job that Baruch finally took up was so perfectly tailored to all his attributes—mental, physical, theatrical—that he might have designed it himself, which, in fact, he did. In 1942 there was a critical rubber shortage. Baruch had seen it coming and for years had urged precautionary stockpiling. He knew the rubber business from the inside as an investor in the rubber-bearing shrub, guayule. The shortage and the political bickering that accompanied it disgusted him. But there was a nobility in his character that made him incapable of recriminating for long it there was work to be done, and in early June he floated an idea with his friend Steve Early. It was that the President should appoint a distinguished citizen to get the facts, make a report on what should be done and clear the way for action.

Action was urgent, because the shortage was acute, and if synthetic rubber were not brought into mass production quickly, the domestic economy would collapse. As Early put the Baruch idea to the President, Congress was devising its own solution. In July it voted to establish a new rubber bureaucracy and to mandate the construction of plants that would derive rubber from grain, one of the two synthetic processes then under development. The competing method was oil-based. Since there were more farmers than oil men, the grain idea had strong political appeal.

Roosevelt, however, would have none of it, and as he considered his veto message he dropped a line to Baruch:

> Dear Bernie:
>   Because you are "an ever present help in time of trouble" will you "do it again"? You would be better than all the Supreme Court put together! Sam [Rosenman] will tell you & I'll see you later.
>
> As ever
FDR

The reference to the Supreme Court was an acknowledgment that Baruch was the President's second choice for the job; Chief Justice

---

*Baruch was distressed to read, or perhaps to be informed, that *The New Yorker* had put his exact words inside quotation marks. At eight in the morning on the day the piece appeared he called Hellman to complain and to threaten to report him to the magazine's publisher, Raoul Fleischmann. "You have quoted me directly," said Baruch, as Hellman subsequently quoted him directly again. "I am never quoted directly."

Harlan Stone had been the first. Baruch nonetheless accepted (it wouldn't have occurred to him to refuse for mere reasons of pride), and the organization of the Baruch Rubber Committee was announced two days later, on August 6.

The chairmanship that Baruch held was an executive and honorific post. His fellow committeemen, Dr. Karl T. Compton, president of the Massachusetts Institute of Technology, and Dr. James B. Conant, president of Harvard University, would weigh the scientific evidence. A technical staff of twenty-five was hurriedly assembled and dispatched around the country to ask questions and make on-site studies. Samuel Lubell, the future political analyst and a wartime aide of Baruch's, was appointed secretary.

The committee's charge was to "get the facts," to investigate the merits of alternative rubber-making processes and to tackle the politically touchy issue of gasoline rationing. It was to decide whether there was sufficient butadiene to sustain the "Buna" rubber program, which was based on petroleum, and to what extent, if any, more Buna rubber would mean less high-octane aviation gasoline.

At first, the committee had no office space. It met at the Carlton, or in Lafayette Park, across from the White House, when the weather was right. "I'm like a lizard," said Baruch in explaining these alfresco quarters. "I get in the sun whenever I can." For a while the group worked at Dumbarton Oaks, indoors or on the lawn, and later in an office in the LaSalle Building, which the government had rented for it. By then its work was almost finished. It was leaning toward (and would soon recommend) the oil-based process for rubber making and was drawing up a program of gasoline rationing and a thirty-five-mile-per-hour speed limit. There was plenty of gasoline; the program was designed to conserve tires.

On technical matters Baruch deferred to the judgment of his scientific colleagues, but he expressed strong views on political and administrative subjects.* Invoking the principle of one-man industrial control in wartime

---

*As the most visible member of the committee, Baruch was the recipient of unsolicited technical suggestions from the public. A man who identified himself as a Rothschild and a former Manhattan neighbor of Baruch's ventured: "Though in rather poor health and not getting about much I have however not very long ago visited several large Hotels and Clubs and everywhere noticed acres of rubber mats on the floors that could be dispensed with." Baruch replied that he was given to understand that there was little scrap value in doormats.

as he had for twenty-five years, he insisted that the new Rubber Administrator should report to Donald Nelson at WPB (which organizational
structure, in fact, the committee suggested). For another thing, he said,
industry, not government, should bring the synthetic-rubber program to
fruition. Once he warned a pair of engineers in the Standard Oil Company
of New Jersey's rubber division about unwanted government meddling.
He said it was up to them to train the bureaucrats to serve them, and he
asked them rather "challengingly" whether they had started to do so. One
of the engineers in Baruch's presence, Frank A. Howard, wrote that he
was relieved to be able to say yes. He vividly recalled Baruch's parting
words: "I know you can do it, and if you can't, I'll take your hides off."

The blunt truth telling of the Baruch Report, as that document inevitably came to be known (Baruch had it distributed to every member
of Congress and every daily newspaper, to 1,800 college and university
libraries, 6,000 public libraries, 1,500 special-subject and business libraries and 230 law libraries), won over the country. Before the committee had its say, only 49 percent of the public favored nationwide
gasoline rationing as a step to conserve tires. After its report appeared,
in mid-September, the proportion in favor jumped to 73 percent. By
the end of the war, as Baruch pointed out, a billion-dollar industry had
been built "from scratch."

Before the occurrence of this industrial miracle and indeed before
the publication of the committee's report, the Baruch appointment
was hailed as a national windfall. Fulton Lewis, Jr., the anti-Roosevelt
radio commentator, praised it, and the Washington *Post* published a
warm editorial on the day after Baruch's seventy-second birthday. Said
the *Post*, in part: "It is curious what a feeling of confidence can be
generated among millions of Americans by the picture of a septuagenarian seated on a park bench. But we dare to say that precisely such a
feeling was created when President Roosevelt asked Bernard M.
Baruch to head a committee of three to report on rubber." (Baruch
jokingly told Eugene Meyer, Jr., the *Post*'s publisher, that the editorial
was of the genre ordinarily reserved for dead men. Meyer might have
recognized that line; a variation on it had once been used on Baruch
by a congressman following an extravagant Baruch testimonial to
Meyer.) A friend of Swope's reported that after the report was released, a movie audience, apparently in New York, had applauded
Baruch in a newsreel.

Because he liked the role of freelance critic and troubleshooter—keeping his own hours, accepting praise but not day-to-day responsibility—and because he was getting on in years, Baruch was understandably picky about the full-time jobs that the Administration offered him in the wake of his rubber triumph. In the case of anti-inflationary posts, he had a specific condition of employment. It was that he receive a voice in the government's fiscal councils. This was denied him, however, not merely because the Administration's tax chief, Secretary of the Treasury Henry Morgenthau, Jr., was unwilling to cede authority, but also because he had no use for Baruch. Baruch had tried to win him over, but Morgenthau remained unwon. When, on the morning of December 15, 1942, Baruch happened to call him on a war-bond subscription matter, each man was in characteristic form with respect to the other:

MORGENTHAU: Hello.
BARUCH: Good morning, Mr. Secretary. B. M. Baruch speaking.
MORGENTHAU: Yes.
BARUCH: I didn't want to—I know how burdened you are—I just . . .
MORGENTHAU: No.
BARUCH: . . . but I didn't want to leave you with the impression that I hadn't done what I said I was going to do about that subscription.
MORGENTHAU: Oh.
BARUCH: And I've done it, but I didn't think it was wise to write a letter that they could publicize because after all the rich man who subscribes money is not doing anything very important, and that's the reason that I did it quietly through the ordinary channels . . .
MORGENTHAU: Yes.
BARUCH: . . . and didn't . . .
MORGENTHAU: Well, it's very kind of you to call me. It wasn't necessary. I know your reputation, and if you say you'll do something, you do it with or without publicity.
BARUCH: Well, I don't like—I think it's—I think it's bad for a man who's supposed to be a little—a rich man to . . .
MORGENTHAU: Yes.

BARUCH: . . . talk about subscribing a million dollars, you know,
                  and they wanted the pub—the publicity people . . .
MORGENTHAU: Oh.
BARUCH: . . . because I thought it was—being so big and be
                  bad for many reasons, if you can understand.
MORGENTHAU: Well, I—I'm sure whatever you decided was right.
BARUCH: And thank you very much, and I'm going to do
                  with the bonds what I said I was going to do . . .
MORGENTHAU: Fine.
BARUCH: . . . in the way of gifts, and that will be done so
                  quietly nobody will know it, at least I hope they
                  won't. I'm sorry to have troubled you so, but I
                  just wanted . . .
MORGENTHAU: No trouble.
BARUCH: Goodbye, sir.
MORGENTHAU: Call me any time.
BARUCH: Thank you.

The first full-time job that Baruch was offered was the top post at the new Office of Economic Stabilization. Samuel Rosenman, the presidential aide who tendered the invitation, in September 1942, called it the "super-duper" job. The head of OES would administer the wage-price laws, rally the public to unpopular rules and regulations and coordinate the Administration's anti-inflation policy. Receiving no assurances about his say in fiscal policy, however, Baruch declined; at his suggestion the job went to James F. Byrnes.

Baruch's second brush with regular work was closer, more dramatic and more irregular than the first. It occurred in February 1943, a time of rising dissatisfaction with the War Production Board and with its chief, Donald Nelson. The Army complained that Nelson was indecisive and incompetent, while Nelson's friends countered that, if perhaps he did tend to err on the side of deliberateness, he at the very least fended off military control of the home front. On the WPB there were pro- and anti-Army factions—the leading anti, of course, being Nelson; the most conspicuous pro being Ferdinand Eberstadt, who had founded Chemical Fund during a brilliant Wall Street career and now supervised (no less brilliantly, his friends thought) the WPB's priorities operation. Baruch was caught in the middle. He admired Eberstadt and was sympathetic to the Army, but he also advised Nelson and wasn't averse to criticizing the Army when he thought it had overreached itself. Early in February Byrnes proposed a solution to the production dilemma. Baruch would replace Nelson.

"You would be taking no chances," wrote Byrnes to Roosevelt concerning Baruch. "He knows that organization better than anybody in it. For the past year he has spent four or five days each week in Washington, and the heads of the various divisions have taken their problems to him. Without any power he has accomplished miracles in straightening out controversies and in securing the cooperation of manufacturers." Byrnes pointed out that Baruch's appointment would be welcomed on Capitol Hill and in the press.* He would disarm critics, and he was unquestionably loyal. "You would be appointing not only the best man for the place, but appointing one of your best friends." Byrnes masterfully added: "Harry Hopkins told me to say to you that he concurs heartily in my suggestion."

Roosevelt gave Byrnes the go-ahead to write a letter for his signature asking Baruch to take the job. Byrnes drafted it, Roosevelt signed it and Byrnes personally delivered it to the Carlton. Baruch opened the letter and read this:

February 5, 1943

Dear Bernie:

For a long time I have been calling upon you for assistance in questions affecting our war production. You have given unsparingly of your time and energy and your advice has been exceedingly valuable. I know that you have preferred to serve in an advisory capacity and have benn [*sic*] disinclined to accept an appointment that would require you to devote all of your time to an administrative position. However, I deem it wise to make a change in the direction of war production and I am coming back to the elder statesman for assistance. I want to appoint you as Chairman of War Production Board with power to direct the activities of the organization.

---

*Turner Catledge of *The New York Times* was offered a public-relations job during the war by Byrnes. When Catledge demurred, pointing out that the government paid only $9,000 a year, which he couldn't afford, Byrnes said not to worry about that. Baruch would provide a supplement. Not wishing to be in anybody's pay but the government's, if he were going to work for the government, Catledge refused.

With your knowledge of the subject and your knowledge of the
organization, I am sure you can arrange so that it will not require
you to work day and night. I would not want you to do that, but I
am confident you will accept because of your willingness to make
any sacrifice you believe will aid in the prosecution of the war.

Sincerely yours,

Franklin D. Roosevelt

What Baruch said in reply wasn't what Byrnes expected to hear. He
did not say yes. He said he needed time to think and to consult with
his doctors. He wanted to make sure that John Hancock of Lehman
Brothers, his old friend and confederate, would be available to serve
with him again. Byrnes was appalled. The man on whom he had just
spent a king's ransom in political capital wasn't sure that he wanted
what he (Byrnes) had contrived to give him. Byrnes argued but Baruch
was obdurate: he announced he was going to New York. (Byrnes had
assured Roosevelt: "Baruch would like the appointment. He has never
told me this, but I know him well enough to know that his heart is in
the production fight. He would rather do that job than anything else
on earth. . . .")

Although Byrnes had moved with stealth, his plans to replace Nelson with Baruch were found out. Someone in the White House had
passed them on to Felix Frankfurter, a Supreme Court justice who liked
to keep a hand in practical politics. Frankfurter was opposed to Baruch
and was therefore in favor of Nelson. (Said Frankfurter of Baruch: "The
war production process cannot be run by intermittent flashes . . . which
is the function that Baruch has been exercising and could only exercise
if he were formally made head of WPB.") The justice alerted a friend at
WPB. The friend called Nelson, who for once took action. The next
morning, February 16, 1943, he fired Eberstadt—whom he thought
to be an Army fifth columnist and also Baruch's man—and announced
the dismissal to the press. That evening he had drinks with the President.

Meantime, en route to New York, Baruch came down with a fever
and went straight to bed in his mansion. There was nothing unusual in
that. Sometimes he really was sick, and sometimes his hypochondriacal
imagination deceived him. In any case, his health was never far from his
mind. From time to time, out walking, he would stop for no particular

reason and take his pulse. Once he declined an invitation to attend an outdoor function by giving the explanation, "I don't like to sit in a big crowd. Everybody comes up to you and they cough in your face." When, in 1945, he flew to Europe on a mission to see Churchill, he tool along his own nurse and doctor. Looking back on the illness that came over him after the invitation from Byrnes, he wrote: "There was a frightening moment when they thought I might have a very serious liver disorder, perhaps even a cancer."

Byrnes recalled that it was days before he heard from him.

Baruch did, of course, return to Washington, and with Hancock in tow, but by then the President had changed his mind.

"Mr. President, I'm here to report for duty," said Baruch as he presented himself to Roosevelt to accept his new duties. The President pretended not to hear.

Baruch had a contempt for psychiatry, amateur or professional, and he would no doubt scorn the following hypothesis, which is offered anyway. Feeling his age but refusing to plead senility, unwilling to exchange his advisory portfolio for a burdensome job, wanting to serve but knowing that Roosevelt would make the decisions—being vexed in this way, he imagined a disease. Whether or not that is true, he walked out of Roosevelt's office a free man and by outward signs a contented one.

In the first spring of the war, a woman from Nashville, Tennessee, fifty-ish, five feet four inches tall, 150 pounds and, she said, "good looking," asked her congressman, Albert Gore, for a favor. She said she would like to marry and that the man she wanted was Bernard Baruch. (Furnishing some additional background material, she said that she had taught piano, edited a cookbook, written ads for department stores in Oklahoma and earned a bachelor of laws degree; she was a regular Democrat and a member of the Order of the Eastern Star.) "I admire him extravagantly," she went on. "He is such a gentleman, refined, educated and a man of means. I am in comfortable circumstances myself. Would you in an indirect manner find out Mr. Baruch['s] views on the subject?"

Baruch's views on matrimony were similar to his views on everyday nine-to-five work. He valued it in the abstract, for other people, but not specifically for himself. Once he told Harry Hopkins that he would cer-

tainly remarry if he could find a bride like the one he had found in
Louise Macy ("you lucky beggar"), but that remark was for chivalry's
sake. Baruch remained a confirmed widower. Before Annie's death he
could tell any woman who wanted to marry him that divorce was out
of the question. After her death he was naked to his mistresses. One of
these, according to Helen Lawrenson, was so persistent that she literally threw herself at his feet on a road in Vichy one summer while he
was taking the cure. (The affair ended badly, Lawrenson wrote: "He
wryly admitted to me that she . . . took him for $25,000 and it turned
out, he said, that she was part of an international blackmail ring and
badger game set-up.") There was one woman, at least, whom he
loved, and probably would have married, but in 1935 she married
Henry Luce. To those who didn't know him very well, his devotion to
Clare Luce and to her theatrical and political careers was evidence of
reactionary tendencies. But Baruch was as nonideological in his choice
of women as he was of men. Luce happened to be conservative;
Lawrenson, with whom he had a fling and a friendship, was all the way
over on the left.

Matriarchy, as opposed to matrimony, was a favorite institution of
Baruch's. Miss Boyle, the petite, elegantly dressed secretary whom
Byrnes addressed as "General," looked after his money, managed his office, aggressively collected overdue debts from his friends and watched
the stock market for him in his absence. At home, Miss Higgins
guarded his health and steered his social life, which became perfunctory. As his deafness worsened, his world closed in. Old friendships
went untended and loneliness weighed on him. (Offering his advisory
services to General Marshall in the summer of 1944, Baruch reported
that he was summering in Port Washington, Long Island, and that he
was all alone.) Swope and he had been seeing less of each other, a situation that Baruch explained had stemmed from his loss of hearing. He
wrote him on Armistice Day 1943:

> My increasing deafness saps my physical and nervous system and it is
> making me more of a recluse—not by wish—but because of the strain
> in carrying on my work. The ordinary amenities, contacts, meals at
> which several persons are present, and evenings at the theatre at which
> large assemblies are present are entirely denied to me. I recognize that
> I can preserve a certain amount of usefulness, but when the evening

comes I am tired. I still am able to function as well, or even better than I ever did, up to the late afternoon.

Even while running on reduced capacity Baruch got an extraordinary amount of work done. After the rubber report he turned to studies of manpower and ordnance production, and he successfully joined in opposing an Administration scheme to conscript labor. Hancock and he surveyed the West Coast labor situation in 1943, and they drafted a report on postwar economic conversion in 1944. Following the postwar report, which took the then-controversial line that peace would bring prosperity, not bust, he contributed $1.1 million for research into rehabilitative medicine and made suggestions for the treatment of returning veterans. Accompanied by physician, nurse and publicist, he flew to London for talks with the British government and to Germany for a fast look at the Third Army early in 1945. General George S. Patton, Jr., pronounced his seventy-four-year-old visitor "just as keen as can be" and amusedly watched him briefing the correspondents, telling them "nothing for a long time."

Consulting is an ethereal business, and it isn't always easy to assess results. Judging by the testimonials of top officials, however, Baruch made a genuine contribution to the war effort by giving advice, making peace among jealous factions and expediting bureaucratic processes. Donald Nelson, for instance, wrote that his advice on priorities was utterly vindicated by events; Rosenman called him "a kind of Mecca for troubled officials." Admiral Emory S. Land, chairman of the Maritime Commission, said that he got him the steel he needed—"The greatest asset I ever had in my maritime career was Mr. Baruch. . . ." In 1945 Under Secretary of War Patterson paid him this tribute:

Dear Chief—

I am thinking of you this Christmas Day, and of the great help you have so freely given me for more than five years, ever since I came to the War Department. I made many mistakes,—mostly when I did not follow your advice or when I acted without getting it. I cannot recall a single case where you gave me a bad steer. The thought that you would give me an approving nod has always been a great source of strength.

Encomia flowed in from private citizens too, and from foreign leaders. When Herman Baruch took up duties as American ambassador to Portugal in 1945, Antonio de Oliveira Salazar, the Portuguese ruler, hastened to express the opinion that Bernard Baruch was one of the "great modern thinkers." Earlier, a listener to Fulton Lewis had responded to some on-the-air praise of Baruch with a telegraphic suggestion:

THIS BARAUCH [*sic*] GUYS OPINION HAS BEEN REQUESTED SEVERAL TIMES AND IN THE LAST PRESENT IMPORTANT OCCASION WARRANTS OR TO ME INDICATES IF HE IS NOT A JESUSCHRIST HE AT LEAST MUST HAVE SOMETHING ON THE BALL AND IF HE HAS IT DARNED GOOD TIME TO PUT HIM IN THE WHITEHOUSE AND PUT THIS MONKEY EX-ASSEMBLYMAN OUT IN THE PARK FEEDING THE SQUIRRELS AND THE BIRDS IF YOU KNOW WHAT I MEAN.

As peace came into view, Baruch made an assortment of statements and predictions on a variety of subjects. Some of his best predictive work was contained in his and Hancock's postwar report, which they wrote for Jimmy Byrnes, then head of the Office of War Mobilization. (This is not to be confused with the Office of Economic Stabilization, which Baruch had declined to direct. On his recommendation, Byrnes was appointed instead; when Byrnes resigned to head OWM, he suggested Baruch to succeed him at OES. Again Baruch refused, but he did agree to serve as Byrne's official adviser at OWM.) In their report, Baruch and Hancock proposed a speedy liquidation of surplus government property at war's end. Interestingly, they warned against sales to "speculators." They put in a good word for capitalism—"There has been too much loose parroting of the slogan, that if individual enterprise fails to provide jobs for everyone, it must be replaced by some one of the other systems that are around"—and they issued a bullish forecast. It was that five to seven years of good times were in the offing despite the parade of returning veterans and the scaling down of government spending. Coming as it did amid numerous predictions of renewed depression, this idea was considered daringly optimistic.

What Baruch hoped most to contribute late in the war was a policy-making voice in the forging of the peace, but it was not to be. He held firm opinions on the diplomatic situation. For instance, he agreed with Henry Morgenthau that Germany should be "deindustrialized" and for a time he endorsed the Secretary's Carthaginian scheme to reduce the enemy to a life of farming and husbandry. Fearing a revival of "sweated labor" and "subsidized exports," he prescribed harsh controls for Japan too. Toward the Soviet Union he asked cooperation and restraint. He had none of his friend Churchill's loathing of Bolsheviks. On the other hand, the advances scored by the British socialists did give him a turn, and he opposed England's application for a large American loan, or gift, on the grounds that the proceeds would merely serve to underwrite the collectivization of British industry. With the exception of his mission to London in March 1945, no important diplomatic assignment was proffered him. He sat out the Yalta Conference at home amidst his collection of documents from Versailles. These he had had bound, indexed and cross-indexed for ease of reference in case he were ever called to service in a time like 1919, but the call didn't come.

Baruch was in London, in his rooms at Claridge's, chatting with his doctor, when he heard the news of Roosevelt's death. The next day, April 13, 1945, he and his party, augmented by Sam Rosenman, boarded a plane for the flight home. Shortly after the Roosevelt funeral, Baruch visited President Truman to report on his talks with the British. He saw Truman intermittently after that—he spent an hour with him on May 8, the President's sixty-first birthday and V-E Day rolled into one—but it was clear that his influence at the White House was on the wane. In the summer of 1945, in a conversation with Henry A. Wallace, Baruch repeatedly mentioned "the President." Interrupting himself, he would say, "By the President, I am referring to Roosevelt, of course."

FIFTEEN

The Atom and All

O n March 16, 1946, following a long interview with his Secretary of State, President Harry S. Truman made a decision about a high-level appointment and jotted a cautionary note to himself about the appointee. The note said, "Asked old man Baruch to act as U.S. representative on U.N.O. Atomic Committee. He wants to run the world, the moon and maybe Jupiter—but we'll see."

Notwithstanding what the President took to be Baruch's extraterrestrial ambition, Baruch himself was disposed to decline the job. When the commission was offered, he was five months away from his seventysixth birthday and was tired from the strains of the war. He was capable of doing some work in the morning and some more in the afternoon, but he was unavailable in the evening. Sometimes he napped after lunch. He wore a hearing aid, with which he fidgeted. Late in 1945 he had suffered a gastric-ulcer attack and had been put on a bland diet. Because he was old, people mistook some of his lifelong eccentricities for senility or balminess. (Treasury Secretary Morgenthau once briefed some subordinates on a baffling conversation he had had with Baruch concerning the postwar world: "I am confused because the man would talk about ten different things, and really wouldn't complete any thought, and the only thought I really got out of him was that reparations is more important and everything else has to wait. Do I leave you people confused?" A voice: "Yes, sir." But Baruch had probably confused his collocutors on the Unlisted Committee of the New York Stock Exchange in the same way forty years earlier.) There was also the problem of the rustiness of his physics, a subject which he had last studied in 1888.

However, there was nothing bigger in the world than the atomic bomb and nothing closer to the dream of Woodrow Wilson than the new United Nations Organization. Baruch, who had been hurt by his omission from postwar planning at Yalta and Potsdam, was moved to accept. Then he almost resigned before he really started.

The broad outline of American atomic policy had been enunciated by Jimmy Byrnes, the Secretary of State, in January 1946. Byrnes declared that so monstrous a weapon as those that were dropped on Hiroshima and Nagasaki should belong to no nation and that the United States was prepared to surrender its bombs and secrets to a properly constituted international authority. The job of working this idea into policy fell to a blue-ribbon committee, which made a report in March. It proposed creation of a new Atomic Development Authority to exercise world control over atomic energy. The Authority would take title to uranium mines, processing works and manufacturing plants, including the only three A-bomb factories in existence, all in the United States. It would disperse atomic stockpiles and laboratories to ensure that no one nation gained a strategic monopoly. The committee, which was headed by Dean Acheson, Under Secretary of State, and David E. Lilienthal, chairman of the Tennessee Valley Authority, put national security in new, atomic-age terms: "The real protection will lie in the fact that if any nation seizes the plants or the stockpiles that are situated in its territory, other nations will have similar facilities and materials situated within their own borders so that the act of seizure need not place them at a disadvantage." The committee acknowledged that its plan might seem utopian, but it anticipated that objection with two points. In the first place the United States was bound to lose its bomb monopoly sooner or later, and it was better to surrender it sooner on advantageous terms. And in the second, no one had proposed a better idea.

Early in March Baruch was in Hobcaw to rest, to plan some congressional testimony he was about to give on inflation, and to escape the begging telephone calls of his relatives, which oppressed him. By the middle of the month he had weighed the atomic-energy invitation and told Byrnes he would take it. Later he had a turn. On the morning of Tuesday, March 26, the newspapers carried a leaked account of the new Acheson-Lilienthal report (as the committee's brief was called). A few days later Baruch was informed by Sir Alexander Cadogan, the British delegate to the United Nations atomic-energy talks, that the report would be offered as a basis of discussion by the United States in the forthcoming session. Baruch, who thought he had a right to learn American policy from his own government first, approached Acheson for an explanation. The Under Secretary replied that Cadogan was right, to which Baruch replied that Acheson would have to find "another messenger boy, because Western Union didn't take anybody at my age."

Next Baruch sought clarification from the White House. To his question of who was to formulate policy on the bomb, the Acheson-Lilienthal group or the representative to the United Nations Atomic Energy Commission, the President genially answered, "Hell, you are!" The crisis was skirted.

Truman thought Baruch was egocentric and devious, but he must have sensed his utility as a political salesman. In March 1946, when the United States proposed to relinquish its secret weapon, the Soviet Union's wartime military strength was largely intact and East European nations were beginning to fall victim to Communist subversion. In February Stalin had charged that the forces of "monopoly capitalism" had made the first two world wars inevitable, and he announced an ambitious new five-year plan to prepare his country for any future struggle.

Baruch was an ideal proponent for a policy as controversial as the Truman A-bomb initiative because what he had said in the past was so often unobjectionable. He was a patriot, an elder statesman and an advocate both of capital and labor. He championed preparedness for war, winning the peace, stable prices, a balanced budget, hard work and humanity in the conduct of affairs. There was something comforting in the sight of him sitting cross-legged on a park bench, one pants leg hiked up to reveal an old-fashioned, high-topped black shoe, which (although the fact had not been publicized) he had bought from Sears. John Francis Neylan, an attorney friend of his from San Francisco, could write Baruch with as much truth as flattery that "the people of this country may disagree with some of your views, but they believe overwhelmingly in your intelligence, your integrity and your courage. . . ."

Almost everybody could agree with him on something. Just before calling on Truman, for instance, he had testified on inflation before the House Banking and Currency Committee. Almost simultaneously he managed to endorse "free enterprise" on the one hand and an extension of wartime wage-price controls, a ukase against strikes and lockouts, and a "High Court of Commerce" on the other. (Once in a feat of concision he distilled this contradiction into a single sentence: "I have unlimited faith in the American people taking care of themselves—if they are told what to do and why.") Coincidentally Baruch testified on the same day as Acheson presented the Acheson-Lilienthal report to an executive session of the joint Senate-House Committee on Atomic Energy. Next day *The New York Times* printed stories of both events on the front page, but it displayed a report of Baruch's testimony more prominently than it did a leaked account of Acheson's.

At a press conference in March the atomic ambassador-designate jokingly reminded newsmen that he never did his own work and that he had already assembled a team of associates to help him with his new job. He introduced Swope and Hancock, his wheelhorses, both of whom he had known since the First World War; Ferdinand Eberstadt, the Wall Streeter whom Donald Nelson had fired from the War Production Board and who had since returned to investment banking; and Fred Searls, Jr., president of Newmont Mining Corporation. The Acheson-Lilienthal committee had had no mining man; the Baruch team as yet had no scientist.

At the beginning there was more friction between the two American groups than there was between either one of them and the Soviets. Acheson, Lilienthal and J. Robert Oppenheimer, the committee's top scientific consultant, all regretted Baruch's appointment. Lilienthal's diarial reaction to the news was, ". . . I was quite sick."

For some time Baruch tried to woo Lilienthal, who described an encounter they had had in April:

I had grimly determined that I would remember that he was the vehicle of our hopes, and that the choice seemed to me fantastic—his age, his unwillingness to work, his terrifying vanity—nevertheless he was the representative of this country. But I was not prepared, even so, for the flow of words about things quite irrelevant. Fully a fourth of the time (he talked almost continuously) he spent saying that it was a shame that the President had insisted on choosing him, that he had tried to get out of it, . . . that it should be a younger man, . . .

Of course, he didn't believe a word of it, and it went on so long because I didn't take my cue and assure him that he was the wisest man in the world, . . .

In the absence of assurances from him, Lilienthal wrote, Baruch furnished them himself, saying that he didn't need to study the facts, that he wasn't senile and that he would "outfox" everybody.

"After about an hour of telling me these things, and urging me (with much palaver and praise put on with a trowel), I spoke up, but I had to fight to keep the floor. . . . I told him he was famous as Dr. Facts, and that without the facts carefully developed, these advisory groups were a menace."

With that, Lilienthal wrote, Baruch seemed to lose his enthusiasm for the job, and for him. The old man "admitted that he was groping and that his impulse had simply been to 'reach out' (this accompanied by gestures) and take in those men who had given so much thought to the subject."

The contribution that Baruch could make was one that seemed dispensable until he did it. This was the tempering of expert technical judgment with the wisdom of the years, and sometimes he performed it brilliantly. Once, after the deliberations began, he was talking with some military men about how long it might take another country to build an A-bomb. Someone said that he knew how long and that the number of years was "predictable." Baruch, who had spent a lifetime on Wall Street seeing prophecies confounded, piped up to object. He said that in his experience it was hard to predict the future of anything, and it would be especially difficult in a field as new as atomic energy. Major General Leslie Groves, who had headed the Manhattan Project and presumably knew what he was talking about, insisted it would take five to seven years. In a report to Truman, Baruch passed on that expert view, said he couldn't vouch for it and guessed that the job might be done in less time than the general expected. The Soviets exploded their first bomb three years later.

In style and substance the Baruch and Acheson-Lilienthal groups were worlds apart. Acheson, a wit, made fun of Baruch's clichés, and Acheson's colleagues disparagingly called Baruch's associates "Wall

Streeters." Once Baruch accused Acheson of secretly tape-recording him on the telephone. (He used to accuse Ickes of the same thing; and Morgenthau, in the Second World War, did produce some of the verbatim transcript quoted above.) Lilienthal, chief of the federally owned TVA, was irritated to hear Hancock say that the government couldn't run a business. Again according to Lilienthal, the Baruch team let his side do all the talking, as if it were laying a trap. There Lilienthal probably did have a point, for Baruch could be a purposeful listener. While talking on the telephone and getting more information than he gave in return, he sometimes caught his secretary's eye and gave her a wink, as if to say that he was winning.

On political issues Baruch and his group were generally to the right of Acheson and Lilienthal and their group. There was less trust of the Soviets on the Baruch side and more concern about property rights. One point of disagreement concerned the ownership of fissionable ore. In its report the Acheson-Lilienthal committee recommended that the international Authority take title to the world's uranium mines. To this the Baruch team raised both philosophical and down-to-earth objections, Baruch, for instance, writing Byrnes in late March: "At least one hundred and twelve uranium-bearing minerals have been described. Some of them occur in at least ten states of the United States, and in twenty foreign countries. Many little prospected regions of Asia and Africa are known to be made up of rock, in which it would be reasonable to expect that uranium ore might occur. Riding herd on the production of these metals will take an 'Authority' of a size to make a bureaucrat beam with pride." Hancock pointed out that the authority would have to buy every mine in the South African Rand since uranium was produced as a by-product of gold. How could such a thing be paid for? What toll would it take on private enterprise? Searls, whose company, Newmont, owned stock in at least twenty nonferrous mining companies, heartily concurred with Hancock. It was Acheson who suggested a compromise solution. Instead of outright ownership by the Authority, why not "dominion"? Each side found the new word satisfactorily ambiguous.

No semantical ingenuity could patch up the weightiest dispute of the spring. This concerned how the parties to the A-bomb treaty should be held to their word, and it went to the heart of Baruch's approach to the problem of national security. He believed that his paramount duty as American representative to the U.N. was to the United States and its defense, not to the world and reformers' hopes for it. Shortly after his confirmation he met with the Joint Chiefs of Staff to sound them out about the bomb. As he subsequently related, he found the military conservative, and he was no less so. Furthermore, he and Swope harked back to Wilson days and to Article X of the Covenant of the League of Nations, which stipulated that an attack on one member of the League should be considered an attack on them all. In their view the logic of that statement was as compelling in 1946 as it had been to Wilson in 1919. In mid-May, at the close of a meeting in Washington between Baruch and his associates and the Acheson-Lilienthal group, the recorded last words were Swope's. He said (as the stenographer paraphrased him): ". . . a law without a penalty was useless." For another thing, Baruch and he were agreed that the penalties for breach of the treaty should be laid out in advance. It would be easy, of course, for a violator to veto the use of United Nations sanctions against it. Baruch proposed to meet this contingency by suspending the right of the veto (available to permanent members of the Security Council) in cases involving the bomb.

The argument against sanctions, which the other side raised, was that they would guarantee Soviet rejection of the plan, nothing more. Baruch did his best to charm the opposition, going so far with Oppenheimer as to disown his own colleagues. ("Don't let these associates of mine worry you," he was quoted as saying. "Hancock is pretty 'Right' but [with a wink] I'll watch him. Searls is smart as a whip, but he sees Reds under every bed.") What he would not abandon was the need of automatic punishment. On May 18, after two days of face-to-face meetings at Blair-Lee House in Washington, the two sides went their separate ways, Baruch's team to develop a policy, the Acheson group to disband; its work was done. Before adjournment, however, there was one last request from Baruch. "Write down what your Report means to you," he told them. "It has been studied by every chancellory in the world, it has been commented on by the press all over the country. Now tell me what it means to you." Lilienthal was dumbfounded. They had talked of almost nothing else for two days.

Alger Hiss, who in 1948 would be accused of conducting Soviet espionage by the former Communist Whittaker Chambers and in 1950 would be convicted of perjury, in that summer of 1946 suggested a program for Baruch in a memo to Acheson. It was an extraordinarily bland proposition. He should, Hiss wrote, base his opening remarks on the Acheson-Lilienthal report, but should offer no fixed position, instead inviting other nations to present their ideas and welcoming an "orderly discussion of such proposals by the Commission."

Baruch declined this policy poached egg (if indeed it was ever presented to him) and developed his own ideas. In the end he accepted the Acheson-Lilienthal report with certain amendments. One was that the United Nations conduct a survey of the world's mineral resources. This had been Searls' idea; he thought it would test the tolerance of the Soviet Union to outside inspection in any circumstances. Another suggestion was that the U.N.'s disarmament inquiry encompass the field of conventional arms too, where the Soviets held the advantage. Baruch also asked for a recasting of the report's language on mine ownership and for a definite statement on veto-proof sanctions. In conference with Byrnes, he lost on the survey and disarmament ideas but prevailed on ownership and sanctions. President Truman approved the finished product, paragraph by paragraph, on June 7.

This was a week before Baruch was scheduled to make his opening speech before the Commission at its temporary quarters at Hunter College in New York. While policy had jelled, the dramatic expression of it hadn't. One day on a bench in Central Park with Swope and Eberstadt, Baruch explained that he wanted to convey the portentousness of the situation in his opening remarks. The next morning Swope was on the phone. "I've got your opening line," he told Baruch. "It comes from the best possible source—the Bible."

On June 14 Lilienthal was thinning carrots in his vegetable garden when his wife called him into the kitchen to listen to Baruch. The voice, reading Swope's words, came over the radio:

"We are here to make a choice between the quick and the dead.

"That is our business.

"Behind the black portent of the new atomic age lies a hope which, seized upon with faith, can work our salvation. If we fail, then we have damned every man to be the slave of Fear. Let us not deceive ourselves: We must elect World Peace or World Destruction.

"Science has torn from nature a secret so vast in its potentialities that our minds cower from the terror it creates. Yet terror is not enough to inhibit the use of the atomic bomb. The terror created by weapons has never stopped man from employing them. For each new weapon a defense has been produced, in time. But now we face a condition in which adequate defense does not exist.

"Science, which gave us this dread power, shows that it *can* be made a giant help to humanity, but science does *not* show us how to prevent its baleful use. So we have been appointed to obviate that peril by finding a meeting of the minds and hearts of our peoples. Only in the will of mankind lies the answer.

"It is to express this will and make it effective that we have been assembled. We must provide the mechanism to assure that atomic energy is used for peaceful purposes and preclude its use in war. To that end, we must provide immediate, swift and sure punishment of those who violate the agreements that are reached by the nations. . . ."

Lilienthal reached for pencil and paper with muddy hands and proceeded to take notes. The familiarity of the speech gratified him—its points were mostly drawn from his and Acheson's report—but the sanctions talk disturbed him. Later Oppenheimer called. The physicist said that he had endorsed Baruch's "Fourteen Points" but that the punishment portion of the talk had unsettled him too. He pointed out that it was a far cry from the "international cooperative development" theme of the Acheson-Lilienthal report and expressed doubt as to Baruch's negotiating faculties. Lilienthal was sympathetic.

Editorial reaction to the speech was enthusiastic—the *Manchester Guardian* declared that in Baruch's (and Swope's and the Bible's) quick-or-dead opening "rhetoric and truth were perfectly fused"—but the Soviet response was cool. Andrei Gromyko, speaking for the U.S.S.R., invited the United States to destroy its A-bombs, to suspend production of new ones and to share its scientific secrets as an earnest of good faith. Although willing to entertain the idea of punishment for an atomic outlaw, he was unyielding on the question of the veto. Gromyko was a guest of Baruch's at the second Joe Louis–Billy Conn fight in mid-June. As the champion was pounding the helpless Conn, the Russian leaned over to his host and said, "Conn must wish he had the veto." Neither then nor later did the Soviet Union consent to open its boundaries to international inspection, to relinquish any real power to an international Authority, or, in general, to hasten the Marxist jubilee of the withering of the state.

Baruch never broke his impasse with the Soviets, but he did make some inroads on unfriendly Americans. One of these was Oppenheimer, who didn't approve of Baruch's diplomacy but agreed to advise the American contingent at the U.N. Once Oppenheimer and Lilienthal shared an inside joke at Baruch's expense. The joke was that Baruch had reported glowing progress to Truman—the vote in the Commission stood at 10–2, he was supposed to have said, with only the Soviet Union and Poland, its satellite, opposed. The point of the story was that the nation most critical to the success of the talks had been alienated—unnecessarily, they thought.

Late in July, Lilienthal agreed to fly up to the Adirondack Mountains to visit Baruch at Camp Uncas, once a retreat of the senior J. P. Morgan's. He went with a heavy heart and only with some urging. An intermediary had brought him the message that Baruch needed help and was hurt that Lilienthal had hung back. At "camp," which was staffed by five servants and a nurse, they talked for two days, Lilienthal this time doing most of the listening. (Apropos of the rustic splendor, Baruch remarked, "If it is good enough for Old Man Morgan, it is good enough for us, I guess.") The transformation in Lilienthal was striking. Before setting out he had dreaded the prospect of Baruch's "confusion and vagueness." In his company he was charmed. An entry from his diary on the second day of his visit, July 29: "He [Baruch] has no illusions, I find, about how little progress there has been made, nor any notion that the 10-to-2 vote means anything. And he knows how terrible the alternative to no agreement will be. I had today by far the most satisfactory talks I have ever had with him—more relaxed, more interesting. . . ." Before his visit Lilienthal had diarially referred to Baruch as "Old Man" or "Baruch." At Camp Uncas he fell into the usage "Mr. Baruch." They returned to New York together on Baruch's chartered DC-3.

What change the course of the arms race might have taken had Stalin visited Baruch at Morgan's lodge is a matter for conjecture. (Baruch in fact wanted to pay a call on the Soviet dictator, but for one reason or another he never got around to it.) Baruch thought that there might be a little more progress if the American plan, which Swope had taken to calling the Baruch plan, got the publicity it deserved. He got after Acheson to distribute it through U.S. embassies and consular offices, and he asked Gromyko why it hadn't been published in full in the Soviet press. Lack of newsprint, the diplomat said. In that case, Baruch said, he would be glad to furnish any amount required; the suggestion fell flat.

Baruch and his colleagues were pessimistic on the outlook for an agreement before the negotiations started. By late summer or early autumn, if not before, Baruch had resigned himself to impasse. In August Charles W. Thayer, a Foreign Service officer with some experience in Moscow, warned him that the Soviets were incapable of trusting American officials: "Repeated efforts over a period of twenty years would seem to prove that the Russians will not trust any foreigner unless he is in jail, dead, or a member of the Communist party." In a meeting on September 10, Swope declared that the problem was the Russians, and Baruch suggested a step-up in American production of atomic bombs. In a report to Truman on September 17, he summarized the divergent positions of the United States and the Soviet Union and concluded that there appeared to be no common ground. The United States, he reminded the President, had proposed international controls on atomic energy and veto-proof punishment of violators. The Soviets declined to relinquish any of the prerogatives of sovereignty. Baruch wound up: "We cannot afford to base national security on the assumption of success in our negotiations."

Henry A. Wallace, the Truman Administration's Secretary of Commerce, agreed that they wouldn't succeed, but he blamed Baruch for that state of affairs, not the Soviets. He thought that Baruch's fixation with the procedural question of the veto and with the hypothetical question of punishment obscured the fundamental business of choosing between the quick and the dead, and he recommended that the United States take steps to destroy its bombs and share its secrets right away. These views he had sent to Truman in a July memorandum. (A sample from it: "Is it any wonder that the Russians did not show any great enthusiasm for our plans? Would we have been enthusiastic if the Russians had a monopoly of atomic energy, and offered to share the information with us at some indefinite time in the future at their discretion if we agreed now not to try to make a bomb and give them information on our secret resources of uranium and thorium?") On September 12, in a speech at Madison Square Garden, Wallace virtually presented a new Administration foreign policy, his own. He said in part, "The tougher we get, the

tougher the Russians will get." On September 18, to Baruch's hor-
ror, the July memorandum was published, including the passages
critical of the Baruch plan. Secretary of State Byrnes, who was in
Paris espousing the official Administration line toward the Soviets,
and Baruch, who was expressing the same policy in New York,
wanted to know what was what. Baruch visited the President and said
courteously that either Wallace must go, he (Baruch) must go, or
Wallace must recant. The next day, September 20, Wallace went, but
Baruch still wanted his apology. He said that the offense to be regretted was not the public row, as unhappy as that was, but the jumbling
of the facts. Wallace refused to apologize, the two men exchanged
charges in the press and there the matter died.

The bluntest foreign charge of the season, hurled in late October by
Vyacheslav M. Molotov, the Soviet Foreign Minister, was that Baruch
was personally the leader of U.S. imperialism. Five months later, in
March 1947, an accusational balance was struck when a woman walked
into the office of the FBI in New York and said that Baruch was the
"main agent for Soviet Russia and had already given the secret of the
atomic bomb to them."

All sides to the bomb negotiations repeated themselves fruitlessly
through the autumn. In November there was some more secret talk
about Baruch going to Moscow to see Stalin, but again no mission resulted. On December 13, Byrnes gave Baruch approval to seek a vote
on the plan he had introduced in June. The day agreed upon was December 30.

The outcome was assumed to be foregone—10–2, with the Soviet
Union and Poland opposed and the United States and its allies in favor.
Just before the polling, however, Sir Alexander Cadogan called Baruch
aside and told him that His Majesty's government would be unable to
support the United States. Baruch threatened him with a public
tongue-lashing if that should happen, and for one reason or another it
didn't. On the surface Baruch remained the epitome of the composed if
ulcerous diplomat. He walked into the United Nations Council chamber with a bottle of milk under his arm and some saltines in his hand.
He spotted Gromyko.

"Here's the atomic bomb I promised you," he said, pointing to the
bottle.

"What, milk?" said the Russian.

"Yes. I expect it will be a long meeting, and I need my milk."

In the event Russia and Poland abstained, and the vote was 10–0. (Not that it made much difference. The Soviet Union exploded its first atomic bomb in September 1949.) On January 4, 1947, Baruch resigned his commission. A week later he declared, again prematurely, that his public career was over.

In the spring of 1942 on the floor of the Senate, Bennett Clark of Missouri, citing the record of the War Industries Board under Baruch and reviewing some of his apposite if unheeded advice in the Second World War, rhetorically put up his name in nomination for the Congressional Medal of Honor. By the close of 1947 that award, the nation's highest (and one for which Baruch as a noncombatant was technically ineligible), was among the few that had not been given to him. In the year that followed his A-bomb work he was honored, cited, awarded or invested by the following entities (among others): South Carolina, the City of New York, the American rubber industry, Jewish Educational Commission Fraternal League, National American Boy Scout Council, Tau Epsilon Rho (the national legal fraternity), U.S. Jewish War Veterans, American Legion of New York County, National Conference of Christians and Jews, College of the City of New York, Columbia University, Princeton University, Rutgers University and Yeshiva University. *The New York Times* subtly conferred its own high praise on Baruch on May 27 by choosing to run the following item, in toto, on page 3:

BARUCH HAS ANKLE INJURY

Bernard M. Baruch turned his ankle yesterday and has been ordered by his physician to "keep off it for a few days." Reached by telephone at his home, the 77-year-old financier and adviser to Presidents declared, however, that he was not bedridden and said, "There's nothing wrong with me."

In June a bust of Baruch was presented to the National War College. George Marshall, then Secretary of State, had heard that some such project was in the wind (Swope had been working on it since at least 1940, even before there was a National War College) and had tried to defeat it. As he had pointed out to Acheson, his Under Secretary, the only other sculptures on the college premises were those of Caesar, Alexander and Napoleon.

One day Marshall handed Acheson a card.

"Read it," he said.

It was an invitation to attend the presentation of the Baruch bust at the National War College.

Acheson dryly remarked that his boss certainly knew how to "handle" Baruch.

"Yes," said Marshall, "and to top it off it seems I am going to make a speech at the unveiling."

Ironically, it was at the height of his public adulation that Baruch reached the nadir of his White House influence. Truman had exasperatedly explained his private position toward Baruch in response to a suggestion in 1947 that he consulted him on a foreign-policy question: "I'm just *not* going to do it. I'm not going to spend hours and hours on that old goat, come what may. If you take his advice, then you have him on your hands for hours and hours, and it is *his* policy. I'm just not going to do it." More or less cordial relations were maintained on both sides until the summer of 1948. Then, on Baruch's seventy-eighth birthday, August 19, Truman asked for a favor. In that election season, Baruch's name had been proposed for a place on the Democratic Party's finance committee. It was exactly the kind of thing that Baruch usually didn't do, as Truman undoubtedly knew, but Thomas E. Dewey was running strong, and Truman needed help. The President asked Baruch to serve.

A week later Baruch replied pleasantly that he had never before served on any party committee, nor, for that matter, had he ever made a political statement, and that his friends, including President Roosevelt, had agreed with him that his policy was the best one. He mistakenly closed by asking a favor of Truman. He said that he hoped the President would feel obliged to send nobody to the coronation ceremony of Princess Juliana of the Netherlands except the U.S. Ambassador to the Netherlands, who happened to be his brother Herman.

Herman had made a successful career in his older brother's shadow, starting with medicine, then Wall Street, then various diplomatic posts, including ambassadorships to Portugal and Holland. He was a humorless septuagenarian who wore precise nose pincers and a white Vandyke. He stood in awe of his brother's poise and self-control, with which he unhappily contrasted his own anxieties. In 1945 he and Truman had chatted for a few minutes, Herman leaving a vivid but unfavorable impression. The President described him in his diary: "Flatterer. Wants to be ambassador to France. Conniver like his Brother."

Baruch's reply to Truman set in motion an unintended chain of events. The first of these was a rocket to Baruch from Truman, who might have suffered either the refusal or the request for a favor, but not both at once. The President wrote on August 31: "I read your letter of the twenty-seventh with much disappointment. A great many honors have been passed your way, both to you and to your family, and it seems that when the going is rough it is a one-way street. I am sorry that this is so." There was a postscript: "I've appointed Mrs. William G. McAdoo and Mr. Thomas J. Watson to be Special Representatives at the coronation of Princess Juliana, along with the Ambassador to the Netherlands."

The dispute smoldered privately until Westbook Pegler disclosed its existence in his syndicated column. The columnist was convalescing in a hospital bed in Brookline, Massachusetts, at the end of October when Joseph P. Kennedy visited and told him of the epistolary row. As Kennedy stood by his bed, Pegler called Baruch in South Carolina to get his version of the story. Baruch came to the phone and roughly confirmed what Kennedy had said. As the call proceeded and Baruch grew madder and more intemperate, Kennedy, listening in at Pegler's end, was seized with laughter. Baruch spoke straight from the heart, charging that Truman was a "rude, uncouth and ignorant man." Just those words appeared in Pegler's column on the eve of the election. Reminding his readers that Baruch was the "number one layman" of the American Jewish community, Pegler claimed that "his language was the strongest that has been directed against any occupant of the White House by any man of comparable prominence and leadership in modern times."

Nothing like this had happened to Baruch before. Jesse Jones had accused him of ingratitude to the party in 1924, but there had been no public airing of charges then. In 1941, when he challenged Roosevelt's defense program by faintly praising the Supply, Priorities and Allocation Board as a "faltering step forward," White House aides were astonished at his candor. His lifelong policy on quotation was to keep partisan, scurrilous and combative matter off the record. He would no more have calculatedly abused a President of the United States to a newspaperman for quotation than a deacon would have uttered a public blasphemy.

According to Baruch, Pegler broke his word by quoting him. This Pegler denied. The accuracy of the "rude, uncouth and ignorant" remark was never denied, however, and Pegler continued to use it, sometimes in ironical praise of Baruch's outspokenness. Krock took the columnist's side in the argument. "The incident reflects one of his worst faults," he wrote Pegler concerning Baruch, "a needless fault as well because he should neither fear a President nor strive so desperately to be 'in' at the White House. It should be the other way around." Despite an attempted reconciliation between them at the home of General Marshall in 1951, the breach between Baruch and Truman was never closed. In 1952, Baruch endorsed the Republican presidential candidacy of Dwight D. Eisenhower.

Swope, who thought Baruch ought to do less conciliating and more punching, tried to foment a public-policy debate with Truman after the President's victory in the 1948 election.

> Let us find a subject in which there is a real margin of disagreement—in which your views are opposed to H.S.T., then publicly disagree [urged Swope]. Let us, first, assure ourselves that we've got certain Senatorial and journalistic support. Do you see what I mean? I am getting tired of the manner in which a childish egotism pervades certain sections of Washington. It may be time to demonstrate that your long devotion to the true Public Interest has brought with it a public confidence and a faith, not to be ignored. This course might be helpful, too, in showing the public that you still have the right of individual assessment and independence of judgment.

When Communist troops swarmed across the 38th parallel into South Korea on Sunday, June 25, 1950, Baruch was propelled into just the kind of controversy that Swope had wanted to invent. The Truman Administration, expecting to fight a limited war, sought correspondingly limited controls on the home front. Baruch rejected that counsel as timid. In July 1950, less than a month before his eightieth birthday, he provided the Senate Banking and Currency Committee with his usual emergency prescription: controls on wages, prices and profits; rationing; a tax boost double the size of the Administration's suggestion.

Swope needn't have worried about Baruch's standing in the nation. Following his testimony there was a giant outpouring of pro-controls sentiment from people who thought that prices were running away. (As they were; in the second half of 1950 the wholesale price index climbed at the annual rate of 22 percent.) With the memory of World War II rationing and money printing still fresh, businessmen and consumers bought things preemptively. As they bought, prices naturally rose, with the result that people demanded the very policies that had inspired the fear that had caused them to bid up the prices in the first place. Thanks in good measure to Baruch's testimony, the Defense Production Act of 1950 contained what the Administration hadn't asked for and said it specifically didn't need, namely, the authority to control wages and prices. Senator Harry Byrd of Virginia paid prompt tribute to the witness: "You performed a miracle in arousing the country in 24 hours to the need for controls."

Albert D. Lasker, a Chicago advertising executive who was Baruch's financial peer but his public-relations inferior, marveled at what he had wrought, and commended it as an object lesson in keeping one's name in the papers. (Once Pegler, observing that Baruch had "scored" in papers all over the country by speaking up for hard work, drew an invidious comparison between the two rich man: "For every paragraph that Albert Lasker gets, BMB gets a page.") Said Lasker to David Lilienthal, who was then leaving public life: "Look at Baruch, our mutual friend. With no actual power or responsibility in his hands, he has just changed a whole Congress—one man."

More and more, Baruch was achieving his archimedean publicity feats without Swope, or with a brooding and unhappy Swope. In June 1947, the month of the installation of Baruch's bust in the National War College, the former editor wrote himself a series of memos on the state of his relations with Baruch. The first was dated June 3: "In March I begged him to duck further publicity. I said he had had too much. Then came comments from General Gruenther [Major General Alfred M. Gruenther, deputy commandant of the War College] and others. What affects me is that I am blamed for it when it's he who wants blood. He even leaks to B. Rose, who plants the stuff for him." Billy Rose, the former WIB stenographer turned showman, was too close to Baruch for the taste of Swope. Baruch had an image to maintain, and Rose, whom a member of the underworld once described as "halfway honest," was jarringly inconsistent with it. Again, on June 10, Swope reflected that he (Swope) was ". . . generally regarded as being B's shadow. . . ." And on June 18, five days after the War College ceremony, there was this: "He gave me no special thanks for the bust presentation, which he wanted very much, nor the speech I wrote for him and which I had to force down his throat. [Mary] Boyle and BMB Jr. both opposed the speech—as usual."

A complicating feature in the Baruch-Swope association was money. Swope's continuing indebtedness to Baruch marred what was otherwise a partnership of equals. Having helped to make Baruch a living legend, Swope was one of the few men who could treat him like an ordinary mortal, interrupting him or shouting him down as the mood struck. Once, catching a glimpse of him in a tattered dressing gown, he shouted pungently, "You son of a bitch, can't you afford a better one?" Baruch could afford it, but chose not to buy (for years he wore a topcoat without its full complement of buttons). Swope, on the other hand, bought a lot of things that he couldn't afford. As debtors and creditors so often do, Swope and Baruch came to resent each other. It irked Baruch that Swope spent as much as he ever had in the face of reduced income, and it seemed to Swope that a greater man than Baruch might have forgiven him his debts for the sake of love and loyal service. In the spring of 1948, having missed a deadline for the payment of $5,000, Swope wrote Baruch emotionally about their career together:

It has been an association of affection; of ambition; of service and of effectiveness. I found my own desire to be helpful answered by what we were able to do together. I was happy in your successes; happier still to be assured by you that I had made contributions to them.

As one grows older, life has few compensations to give. One of the greatest is faith—and friendship. Affection is a major element, and in that pride is always present, aroused by the records of your friends, in whom the bitter; the unpleasant; the disparaging are not to be found.

Life will be less worthwhile if our relationship is to be disturbed. Between us, whatever either does should be—and has been—right. You can do no wrong in my eyes. In this I am merely restating what you have always said: —"You seen him! He drew a knife on me, didn't he?"

You have my love and respect.

E. J. Kahn, Jr., wrote that Swope "thrived on contention. He needed no flaming issue to goad him into action; argument *gratia* argument sufficed." In the early 1950s Swope was still contending with his own feelings toward Baruch. To a good part of the world the two men seemed inseparable (at a sports broadcasters' dinner in 1953 Swope was mistakenly addressed by four people as "Mr. Baruch"), but the truth was that they'd been going their own ways for years. Not wanting to be in Baruch's shadow, yet at the same time wanting to be nowhere else, Swope conceived and nurtured anxieties. He worried about the invitations to his home at Sands Point that Baruch had declined, and he resented Rose. He remembered that when Helen Millar, his secretary, was dying, there had been no flowers from Baruch, and that there had been no gift for Maggie and himself on their fortieth wedding anniversary, although Baruch had hinted at something "substantial." So much did Swope need money that in 1954 he stooped to lend his name, for a price, to harness racing (a drastic step indeed for a former New York State Racing Commissioner). But at the end of that year, it was Baruch who wrote emotionally to Swope: "I have sensed for a long time our drifting apart, but there is nothing either in my heart or mind that should cause that. Sometime[s] people say things to me, as I am sure they say things to you, for the purpose of raising some doubts, but I soon shut them up for there are no doubts in my mind about you, except on one point and that is that you never use, or nobody has ever seen you use, an ability that you have of sensing and expressing public reactions." Baruch said that he had instructed Miss Boyle to write off Swope's debt at the rate of $3,000 a year and to expunge it altogether if he happened to outlive Baruch (he didn't). "I do not want to leave any evidence in my will that you had ever been in my debt. I thought I ought to tell you that for I know at that time it was troubling you."

Even in his intimate personal communications, Baruch was liable to go off on some public-policy tangent (to Swope, between professions of friendship and the forgiveness of his debts, he had briefly digressed on the unhealthy growth of spending by city and state government in New York). As usual it was no easy thing to predict where Baruch would wind up on issues of the day. As he endorsed federal health insurance, conscription, peacetime wage-price controls and a national priorities board (his High Court of Commerce modernized), he issued stinging denunciations of socialism and of the oppression of the individual by the state. Swope in 1946 had used the phrase "cold war" to describe the diplomatic twilight that had fallen over the world, and Baruch believed that so long as the Soviet threat persisted there was nothing to do but put the nation's affairs on a quasi-war footing. He criticized the Eisenhower Administration for letting the price-control law lapse in 1953, and he was regularly on the telephone with free-market newspaper editors, seeking converts. On August 16, 1955, three days before his eighty-fifth birthday,* he conferred his public blessing on the House Un-American Activities Committee by dropping in, unannounced, to a hearing it was conducting at the Federal Court House in Foley Square. Francis E. Walter, Democrat of Pennsylvania, was questioning a folk singer about Communist penetration of the theater when Baruch arrived at the back door of the hearing room. Ushered to a seat behind the court reporter, he directed his hearing aid alternately to the inquisitor and his witness. At a recess, he rebuked unfriendly Fifth-Amendment-pleading witnesses with the remark, "Any person

---

*When Baruch did turn eighty-five, on Friday, the nineteenth of August, the *Herald Tribune* published a "surprise party in print" to which it had asked celebrities, dignitaries and other notables to contribute. There were many and diverse well-wishers, and the variety of Baruch's acquaintances was evident in juxtaposition. Thus, Eleanor Roosevelt and Rocky Marciano; Billy Rose and Clare Luce; Adlai Stevenson, J. Edgar Hoover, Jack Dempsey and Richard Nixon ("To Bernard Mannes Baruch—the sage of our age").

Also: General George C. Marshall, David Sarnoff, Lyndon Johnson (Senate majority leader), Joseph W. Martin (House minority leader), Edgar Faure (Premier of France), Thomas E. Dewey, James F. Byrnes, Omar N. Bradley (General of the Army), Herbert Brownell, Jr. (U.S. Attorney General), Mayor Robert F. Wagner of New York; Governor W. Averell Harriman, C. E. Wilson (Secretary of Defense), Louis St. Laurent (Prime Minister of Canada), Robert Moses, General Curtis LeMay, Lord Beaverbrook, and of course, Swope, who wrote, in part: "You have become the tribune; you are an embodied and vital force in life."

Rose upstaged that with some Broadway doggerel:

> When your buck and luck are
>   both small time,
> And your fake friends pass you by,
> Mr. B's the standing
>   sitting ⸳
>   running
>   jumping all-time
> Champeen stand-up guy.

who hasn't anything to fear can answer anything. In this great country of ours the only thing to fear is guilt." On his way out the door he shook hands with Walter, the chairman, and complimented him on a job well done.

To some people the jump of the stock market in 1954 and 1955 was no less alarming than the threat of the nation's enemies, and Baruch had been called upon for his expert financial judgment by the Senate Banking and Currency Committee a few months before he stopped in to see Walter. In March 1955, when he took his place before the senators (saying that he'd testified before no committee of Congress more frequently than he had theirs), the Dow Jones Industrial Average stood at 415, up 38 percent from the same time a year before, a rate of rise that had prompted some worried analogies of the mid-1950s with the late 1920s. Accompanied by Samuel Lubell, who was along to make sure that he got the questions, Baruch began by saying that nobody could predict the stock market and that he wouldn't try. He sketched some of the bull market's features, including the growing role of financial institutions in it, and he veered off to national economic policies, urging a strong Army and Navy and taxes sufficient to balance the budget. He defended the right of Walter Winchell to tip stocks over the radio and adjured the lawmakers against trying to "legislate against human folly or against the adventurous spirit that helped to make America great." Later on in the hearing, J. William Fulbright of Arkansas, the committee chairman, tried to get Baruch to say something positive about John Kenneth Galbraith, who had testified earlier. This Baruch declined to do, explaining that he hadn't read the gentleman's books and that he didn't pay much attention to economists. "I think economists as a rule—and it is not personal to him—take for granted they know a lot of things," said Baruch. "If they really knew so much, they would have all the money and we would have none."

Still Fulbright persisted, asking whether, in Baruch's opinion, the committee had made a mistake in listening to Galbraith at all.

Baruch answered indirectly.

"It is like the fellow the bartender asked, 'Is Mike good for a drink?'

"He said, 'Has he had it?'

"He said, 'Yes.'

" 'Well,' he said, 'he is good for it.'

"I do not think there is any point in discussing it," he went on. "I do not see any argument. I do not mean to be funny, but like all these things in life, we have got to accept them." (In 1961, after Galbraith had been posted to India as U.S. ambassador, Baruch wrote to confide his fears about the inflationary dangers of the Kennedy Administration's policies. Some sixth sense stayed his hand, however, and the letter went unmailed.)

Inflation worried Baruch as nothing else did in the 1950s and 1960s. He kept his stockbrokers on the phone to talk about it, and he once went on a one-man consumer strike against the price of red meat. He deplored the spinelessness of American institutions, especially colleges, in the face of the danger he saw so clearly. In 1949 he answered a fund-raising letter from the Stanford Medical School with the nonmedical complaint that most colleges were teaching Keynes and other economic faddists. Since he took such an eclectic approach to the cause of inflation—he lumped in greed, profiteering, interest-group politics, unsound money and disregard of the national interest—he equated the creeping rise of prices with the all-around decline of standards. The world had gone bad, and inflation was the name he gave to the corrupting agent. After his death things took the turn he had predicted. For an instant in January 1980, the price of gold, which Alaska Juneau had mined for $20.67 an ounce, touched $875. By that time the purse in the annual Bernard Baruch Stakes at Saratoga was up to $50,000, double its size when the race was given his name in 1959.

The Bernard Baruch Stakes was the second accolade that the sport of kings had presented to the adviser to Presidents within three years. On the eve of his eighty-sixth birthday, in August 1956, Saratoga had named the fifth race after Happy Argo, a ne'er-do-well colt that had been banned from racing in Ireland because of a proneness to "boring," or cutting across a field; had landed in the United States and been bought by Baruch and reformed; and had excelled as a sprinter at Saratoga, Aqueduct, Jamaica and Belmont in the late 1920s. (After he was put out to pasture Mary Boyle was given the job of searching the lists of entries on racing days for the names of his descendants so that Baruch could bet on them.) At Saratoga that August day a reporter had asked the guest of honor about his betting, and Baruch gave this answer: he was ahead of the game over the course of his life but not in 1956 and he had cut back on the size of his wagers. "I used to wait until I was convinced I was right, and then make a good bet," he said. "Now my betting is very small."

In his eighties Baruch sometimes felt the need of more money. The estate he left was valued at $14,076,076.30,* but that was no more than he had before the First World War when prices were lower and income-tax rates nominal. He had given away some money—an estimate, probably a high one, from Robert Ruark in 1952 was $20 million—and since Texas Gulf he had made no more grand financial coups. Once he told his former nurse, Blanche Higgins, who had become Mrs. Jerome Van Ess, that he could no longer get by on his income: "It's a terrible thing, you know, I have to draw into my principal." Sometimes he talked about the money he might have made, saying, "You know, I could have been a really rich man."

In 1946, in the midst of the atomic-bomb negotiations, he sold his mansion at 1055 Fifth Avenue and bought what he described as a "small apartment" at 4 East 66th Street, overlooking Central Park. Baruch was speaking relatively. The mansion had had six stories, an elevator, ten baths and thirty-two rooms, including an oval dining room, ballroom, smoking room lined with Norwegian pine and solarium. The apartment had but a dozen rooms. A visitor in 1951 noticed that it contained a pair of exquisite Chinese Chippendale cabinets, two large oils by Chandor—one of Churchill, and the other of Baruch—a "eulogistic framed citation" from the Daughters of the Confederacy, a vase filled with yellow chrysanthemums, miscellaneous photographs of himself and an inscribed photograph of Cardinal Spellman, who had been snapped in red vestments. In the bedroom there was a night table lined with bottles of pills.

If he cut back at the racetrack (in 1948 a retired New York City fireman returned a roll of twenty-two $100 bills he had lost at the Turf & Field Club enclosure at Belmont) he was still capable in his eighties and nineties of buying and selling 10,000 shares in a single stock-market session. He talked to his best broker three or four times a day, and he could spend hours by the ticker in Miss Boyle's office, feeding the tape

---

*Mary Boyle, who kept a live-in butler and cook and who generally spent money as if she had more of it than her wealthy employer (it amused Baruch to say that she did), died in 1973 with $1,115,200.81.

through his hands. He read the papers as closely as he ever had—Swope, in 1955, called him the best newspaper reader of his acquaintance—and he knew where the market was.* If his broker reported offhandedly that such and such common had closed at 50¼, Baruch would be able to correct him emphatically—"It was an eighth."

When people asked him for money, an associate of Baruch's remembered, "his eyes got very blue." Annie Malone, his cook, was exposed to both the generous and the tightfisted sides of his personality. She was a friendly woman, and after the move to 4 East 66th Street she fell into the habit of giving leftover food to the elevator operator. Baruch, who had once or twice bailed her out of stock-market losses, was told of her generosity with his larder, and he asked her what she thought she was doing. She made the excuse that the food would only have gone to waste if she hadn't given it away. Baruch said let it go to waste. For a while she followed orders, but then she resumed her old ways. One day Baruch inquired of the elevator man whether Annie was taking good care of him. He said that she certainly was—she'd just brought him his dinner. With that she was fired.

The dismissal raised the question of what would become of a trust fund that Baruch had set up in her name. He consulted his lawyer, and together they decided that she could have the money if she really needed it. They asked Annie to come by to discuss the situation. She arrived, impeccably dressed. They told her that in order to receive the money, she would have to disclose her income. This she refused to do, and she flounced out of the office.

Time passed, and Annie invited some friends to visit her in her new apartment. They arrived at a handsome building on West 72nd Street, off Central Park West, and announced to the doorman that they had come to see Miss Malone.

"Oh," he said, *"Annie."*

---

*Baruch kept his eye on foreign markets too, and in September 1957 he saw something that he thought was fishy on the London Metal Exchange. He called an FBI man to his office, and the G-man filed the following report to *his* office: "Mr. Baruch stated that he is very much concerned about the 'wide gyrations' in the price of copper that have been occurring on the London exchange. He said these exaggerated fluctuations could have an unsettling effect on the world economy and he felt they could be occurring through sinister manipulations, possibly by persons under Communist direction or affiliation." Baruch admitted that the information was vague and probably outside the purview of the FBI, but he said that someone might want to look into it.

There was a cruel streak in Baruch that money could bring out. In the appraisal of his wife's jewelry that was taken after her death, a sapphire ring for which she had paid the equivalent of $16,000 in London was valued at only $4,000. Baruch said it was impossible, but a second appraisal yielded that same result. This time the jeweler said that the sapphire was one of the finest synthetic cabochon stones he had ever seen. Annie had been duped.

Some time after this discovery, Baruch happened to be sitting in his mansion with a secretary. On a nearby table was the ring, which he picked up and studied. For a moment, the secretary thought that he might give it to her.

"You know," he said finally, "Mrs. Baruch could wear an artificial stone and everybody would think it was real. You could wear a real one and everybody would think it was fake."

Yet when he did choose to be generous, Baruch could be forthcoming not only with money but also with extraordinary and spontaneous declarations of affection. E. D. Coblentz, editor of the San Francisco *Call-Bulletin*, and his wife heard from him out of the blue in March 1955—"You may wonder why I write you now. I don't know. I was just thinking of you and what happy times we have had and what a wonderful tender friend you have been and that I love you both very much."

In November 1950 Baruch was the victim of an extortion attempt. An FBI agent who dropped by his apartment to investigate returned with a message from Baruch for the director of the Bureau in Washington: "Tell Mr. Hoover that the Old Man is not afraid."

Devoted to his father in all things, Baruch had decided to die as well as he had. Simon Baruch had exacted a promise from his sons that no rabbi would be called to his deathbed, because "there is no use trying to fool God at this late date." As he lay dying in 1921, at the age of eighty-one, his sons kept their word. Their mother, who thought it was never too late, and who was sick in her own bed, turned on her side and wept.

Baruch suffered every common affliction of the long-lived male, from arthritis to loneliness. His feet hurt him, he slept badly, he had prostate trouble, his deafness embarrassed him and he quarreled with his grown son. In 1957, the year in which the first volume of his autobiography, *My Own Story*, appeared (and became an instant best seller), he suffered a loss of weight and feared for his life.* In 1958, blaming doctors' orders, he declined to travel to Chicago to accept the American Legion's Distinguished Service Medal. In the spring of the same year, within ten weeks of each other, Swope and Kent died.

With so many unhappy and disagreeable things happening to him, Baruch leaned for support on Elizabeth Navarro, his nurse and companion. She was by his side in the daytime and was up to make him comfortable at night, when he couldn't sleep. When he entertained she was his hostess, which was no easy job because of the imperfections of his hearing aid. If another couple came to dinner, it was up to her to keep the woman quiet so that he could hear the man. Although forbearing in matters of statesmanship, Baruch could be peevish about little things. He demanded his lunch at 12:30 and his dinner at 7:30 sharp, and he could wolf down a meal in minutes. One night at dinner there was a lady who was immobilized by the artichoke on her plate. "Elizabeth," said Baruch impatiently, "show her how to eat that thing so we can get it off the table." At his death, in 1965, he owed Miss Navarro (on paper) $400,000 in canasta stakes, a legacy of the uncounted days and nights she had beaten him at one-tenth of a cent a point. But he disapproved of her gambling even for small sums of real money. "When Mr. Baruch found out I was playing cards for a quarter, he just about preached my funeral," she said.

While stoical about death, Baruch was in no hurry to get on with it, and he conscientiously continued to look after his health. He got a daily cream message from Miss Navarro. For exercise he waved his dumbbells and swam in a pool, although about the age of ninety he stopped entering the water headfirst. He hunted quail until his early nineties, when

---

*Baruch had a narrow escape that he never knew about. In the late 1950s—the memory of the police is unclear on the date—the South Carolina Law Enforcement Division discovered a plot to assassinate him. The lawmen thought that the Ku Klux Klan was behind it, and they took their information to Governor George Bell Timmerman, Jr., who passed it on to former Governor James F. Byrnes. Byrnes feared that if Baruch were told the shock would kill him. The police, not having enough evidence to put anyone in jail, paid a call on their prime suspect, a farmer, to try to scare him off. They confronted the man with what they knew, or suspected, and he, who was wearing a pistol stuck upside down in his back pocket, gave an unconvincing denial. He said he hadn't planned to kill Baruch himself, but added, "It would be a pretty good idea if somebody did kill the old Jew son of a bitch." One of the policemen said years later: "There's no question in our mind that it was planned."

he found that he hadn't the strength. "I can't keep up with the birds," he said, "and I can't keep up with the people." As heart-transplant surgery first made news, he asked a doctor to go to South Africa to investigate the technique in case he ever had need of it. While vacationing in Europe he patronized the clinic of Dr. Paul Niehans, a Swiss exponent of "cellular therapy." Niehans reasoned that the essence of the liver of a pregnant sheep would restore the human liver, and that a bouillon of cow heart would restore the human heart, and so on, and he injected his patients with huge syringes of animal organ extracts. For whatever reason (Baruch himself doubted that the Niehans cure did him any good), Baruch's heart lasted until 9:25 P.M. on June 20, 1965, fifty-nine days before his ninety-fifth birthday.

Mentally, he kept going. To the end he made up his mind on issues and let people know what he thought. He endorsed the Kennedy Administration's essay in price controls and the fifth and final war of his lifetime, in Vietnam. Reports that Canada was preparing to sell wheat to Communist China in 1961 pushed him into correspondence with Secretary of State Dean Rusk. Baruch wrote that the sale was wrong because it would help the Chinese "live and be strong to destroy us. I am sure that you are taking steps to stop this now." At the age of ninety-one Baruch was still a sufficiently formidable figure that Rusk felt obliged to answer with a fourteen-page memorandum.

Once Harold Epstein, the coauthor, along with Samuel Lubell, of the second volume of Baruch's autobiography, *The Public Years*, found him engrossed with some reading over breakfast. The printed matter turned out to be a speech that Epstein had written for him. "That's the best thing I ever read," said Baruch, who sometimes quoted back lines to Epstein that Epstein had picked out of Stevenson's *Home Book of Quotations*. (After Swope was gone, Baruch one day was worrying about a speech that somebody had written for him and that he thought should be getting more attention. "God damn it," he said, "If Swope were alive he'd needle these guys and get this thing in the papers for me!") Baruch continued to flower in the company of military officers, and he repeated his ideas on wartime priorities and price control as if they had only just occurred to him. Even world-weariness, when it came over him, had a robustness about it. In about his ninetieth year he received a call from Clare Luce, whom he had never stopped loving. To Epstein, who was within earshot of Baruch's side of the conversation, it was obvious that she was unhappy in her marriage and that Baruch was trying to comfort her.

Baruch advised her against hasty action, reminded her of what she had and mentioned her "well-feathered nest." At last the conversation ended and Baruch put down the phone. There was a pause. Then he said, "Ah, who the hell cares."

On June 23, 1965, three days after his death, there was a memorial service at the old West End Synagogue, East 79th Street and Second Avenue. In his lifetime Baruch had been an irregular worshiper there, and he had asked for a simple funeral. He wanted to die as a Jew—"He wanted to make that statement," Epstein said—but not to try to fool God. His body was cremated, in keeping with instructions, and there was also an unplanned event. Twenty minutes before the service began the temple's air conditioning gave out, but this too might have pleased Baruch, who was always cold.

Inside and outside the temple, the mourners, some seven hundred strong, were representative of all walks of his work and life. There were his two surviving children, Bernard M. Baruch, Jr., and Mrs. Renée Samstag (Belle had died, at the age of sixty-four, in 1964); his confidante and secretary, Miss Boyle; and his companion and nurse, Miss Navarro. Ferdinand Eberstadt, of atomic-bomb days, was there, along with Mayor Wagner, Billy Rose, Senator Jacob Javits, Henry and Clare Luce, Dr. Buell Gallagher, president of City College, and Sir Patrick Dean, British Ambassador to the United States. Ernest Stresser, an eighty-two-year-old Austrian who lived on East 79th Street, had come to pay his respects to the man who had made it possible for him to reach America twenty-five years before. There were Governor Byrnes, who had been with Baruch when he died, and Adlai Stevenson, the Democrat whom he had not supported in 1952. Cardinal Spellman, with whom there had been a recent disagreement, was also on hand. A few months before his death, Baruch and Spellman had suffered a mutual mortification. The Cardinal, dropping by Baruch's apartment for a visit, had come across his host napping. Jumping to conclusions, Spellman hurriedly began to administer last rites. Baruch awakened to the hubbub. He swore mightily and kicked the Cardinal out. But Baruch was never one for losing a friend, and somehow the two of them had patched it up. As usual, all was forgiven.

Notes

One A Doctor's Son

PAGE

1   "I guess . . .": James Myers, a partner of Stillman, Maynard & Co., to author, May 12, 1980.

3   "My first recollection . . .": Mrs. Rebecca R. Stewart to Baruch, May 2, 1938; Baruch papers.

3   "The bearer of this . . .": Bernard M. Baruch, *Baruch: My Own Story* (New York, 1957), p. 21.

3   "Grandfather also claimed . . .": Ibid., p. 3.

4   Sailing Wolfe's birthplace: Bureau of the Census, 1850 and 1860, County of Fairfield, S.C., Post Office, Winnsboro.

4   "God grant her . . .": Baruch, *My Own Story*, p. 19.

5   "Now say something . . .": Ibid., p. 25.

5   "Now, Doctor, don't . . .": Ibid., p. 30.

6   "I have the most distinct . . .": Baruch to Mark Sullivan, Jan. 21, 1927; Baruch papers.

7   "There is one recourse . . .": Claude Bowers, *The Tragic Era* (New York, 1929), p. 359.

7   "She told Harty . . .": Baruch, *My Own Story*, pp. 34–35.

9   "You see . . .": *New York Times*, Nov. 11, 1881.

10   "sheenie": Baruch, *My Own Story*, p. 49.

10   "body of land . . .": Ibid., p. 47.

10   "The method of . . .": Department of the Interior, Census Office, *Social Statistics of the Cities*, Part I (Washington, D.C., 1886), p. 582.

11   "I consider . . .": Marilyn Thornton Williams, "New York City's Public Baths: A Case Study in Urban Progressive Reform." *Journal of Urban History*, Vol. 7, No. 1 (Nov. 1980), p. 60.

11 Club memberships: Virginia Epstein to author, June 24, 1980, and *New York Times,* July 12, 1914.
12 "Yes, and you're not . . .": Virginia Epstein to author, Feb. 16, 1981.
12 "Not long ago . . .": *New York Times,* July 12, 1914.
13 "Now, Doctor . . .": Virginia Epstein to author, Feb. 16, 1981.
13 "When we first . . .": "The Secret Fraternities and Literary Societies of the College of the City of New York," *Microcosm,* Vol. XXX (1889), p. 71.
13 "under our noble flag . . .": Ibid., p. 163.
13 "cribology": Ibid., pp. 164–165.
14 "nonsense": S. Willis Rudy, *The College of the City of New York: A History, 1847–1947* (New York, 1949), p. 162.
14 Baruch's grades: CCNY class records.
14 "When prices go up . . .": Baruch, *My Own Story,* p. 55.
14 "[T]he economic end . . .": George B. Newcomb, "Political Economy in Its Relation to Ethics." A lecture delivered before the American Institute of Christian Philosophy, Asbury Park, N.J., July 25, 1885.
15 "It arises solely . . .": Francis A. Walker, *Political Economy* (New York, 1888), p. 66.
15 "Baruch is greatly . . .": *The College Journal,* May 16, 1889, p. 175.
15 "a vile name": Baruch, *My Own Story,* p. 63.
16 "As an evidence . . .": *The College Journal,* June 21, 1889, p. 210.

Two Three Dollars a Week

17 "I am thinking . . .": Bernard M. Baruch, *Baruch: My Own Story* (New York, 1957), p. 71.
18 "Son, when you are ready . . .": Ibid., p. 75.
18 "To think that at my age . . .": Ibid., p. 76.
18 Forty years later: Baruch reminiscences, Unit XV, Box 272, pp. 71–72; Baruch papers. (Hereafter referred to as Baruch reminiscences.)
19 "I am so glad . . .": Baruch, *My Own Story,* p. 76.
19 "My son, Bernard.": Ibid., p. 77.
20 "I felt a slap . . .": Ibid., p. 65.
21 "It seems to me . . .": *New York Times,* July 24, 1898.
21 "While Housman never said . . .": Ibid., Aug. 22, 1907.
22 "I was paid . . .": Baruch reminiscences, p. 83.
22 Brooklyn Union Gas story: Baruch, *My Own Story,* p. 27.
22 "symphony of gamble": Thomas W. Lawson in *The New York Times,* Jan. 4, 1913; Lawson also said of Keene, ". . . it was a greater pleasure to lose to him than to win from a bungler. We often wrangled, but my admiration for his ability was excelled only by my wonder at his nerve."
23 "Why does a dog . . .": Baruch, *My Own Story,* p. 157.
23 "Uneasy lies the head . . .": Baruch reminiscences, p. 92.
23 "You don't see . . .": Baruch, *My Own Story,* p. 157.
23 "He had the most . . .": Baruch reminiscences, p. 87.
24 "Keene's horse won . . .": Baruch, *My Own Story,* p. 89.
24 "free ride": James Myers to author, Oct. 25, 1980.

25 Lytton story: Baruch reminiscences, p. 102.
25 "Perhaps the actors . . .": Baruch, *My Own Story*, pp. 69–70.
27 "Raising my hat . . .": Ibid., p. 99.
27 "Being a junior partner . . .": Baruch reminiscences, p. 97.
28 Sugar speculation: The arithmetic raises some questions. In the reminiscences, Baruch said he put down $300 (p. 102); and in his autobiography, he said that he bought 100 shares (p. 100). But at a price of $115 a share, and at the standard margin rate of 10 percent, his $300 down payment would have controlled only 26 shares. Either he put down more than $300, or he got away with a margin requirement of less than 10 percent, or he bought fewer than 100 shares.
29 "You'll lose it . . .": Baruch, *My Own Story*, p. 102.
29 "Yes, and you . . .": Ibid., p. 102.
30 Gift to his father: Baruch reminiscences, p. 108.

Three Baruch's Wall Street

PAGE
31 "In a year . . .": *New York Times*, Feb. 7, 1884.
32 "Everybody was making . . .": Edwin Lefèvre, *Reminiscences of a Stock Operator* (Larchmont, N.Y., 1964), p. 34.
34 "strange scene . . .": Karl Baedeker, ed., *The United States: With an Excursion into Mexico* (New York, 1971), p. 27.
34 Amount of commission income: Unidentified newspaper clipping in NYSE archives, dated July 31, 1892.
34 Visiting Christians: New York *Herald*, July 12, 1892.
34 Hazing: For example, resolution of Jan. 15, 1900, of the Committee of Arrangements; Box No. 1, NYSE, 1880–1899, Officers Governing Committee.
34 Gambling: Minute Book No. 5 of the Governing Committee, Nov. 10, 1897.
35 Gratuity Fund: For details on this and other antiquarian topics, see Moses King, ed., *King's Views of the New York Stock Exchange, 1897–98* (New York, 1897).
35 "detrimental to the interest . . .": NYSE Constitution, Art. XVIII, Sec. 8, 1902.
36 Quotations from Granberry: Minutes of the Committee on Unlisted Securities of the NYSE, Apr. 4, 1906.
37 "Accessibility to the street . . .": Percy C. Stuart, "The New York Stock Exchange." *Architectural Record*, Vol. 11 (July 1901), p. 540.
37 "The silver is Thine . . ." and ". . . but one of the many . . .": Edmund Clarence Stedman and Alexander N. Easton, eds., *The New York Stock Exchange* (New York, 1905), p. 413; also *New York Times*, Apr. 23, 1903. Bellwether trading issue: *Wall Street Journal*, Apr. 20, 1900.
38 "Every conceivable line . . .": Arthur Stone Dewing, *The Financial Policy of Corporations*, Vol. IV (New York, 1920), p. 36.
38 Trust study: Ralph L. Nelson, *Merger Movements in American Industry, 1895–1956* (Princeton, N.J., 1959), pp. 96–100.
39 "This, as a record . . .": E. G. Campbell, *The Reorganization of the American Railroad System, 1893–1900* (New York, 1938), p. 27.
40 "absorbed in various ways": Quoted in W. Z. Ripley, *Railroads: Finance & Organization* (New York, 1915), p. 461.

40   "At the beginning . . .": Campbell, pp. 331–332.

40   "Rembrandts": Quoted in Julius Grodinsky, *Jay Gould: His Business Career, 1867–1892* (Philadelphia, 1957), p. 491.

44   "Amalgamated Copper Co. . . .": Thomas W. Lawson, *Frenzied Finance* (New York, 1905), p. 338.

44   Insider trading survey: H. L. Wilgus, "Purchase of Shares of Corporation by a Director from a Shareholder." *Michigan Law Review*, Vol. VIII, No. 4 (Feb. 1910), pp. 267–297.

44   "It has been . . .": King, p. 82.

45   "except in the regular course . . .": Application for listing of Sears, Roebuck & Co., dated Nov. 12, 1906; NYSE archives.

45   "to deal . . .": W. H. Granberry, Apr. 4, 1906; minutes of the Committee on Unlisted Securities, p. 22.

45   Weird dress: Robert Sobel, *The Curbstone Brokers* (New York, 1970), p. 103.

46   ". . . because I do not . . .": Apr. 4, 1906; minutes of the Committee on Unlisted Securities, p. 27.

46   "Quotations frequently represent . . .": Report of Gov. Hughes' Committee on Speculation in Securities and Commodities, June 7, 1909, quoted in U.S. House of Representatives, 62nd Cong., 3rd Sess., Report of the Committee Appointed . . . to Investigate the Concentration of Money and Credit (Washington, 1913), p. 2195. (Hereafter cited as Money Trust Investigation, Report.)

46   "In other words . . .": Ibid., p. 116.

46   Bucket shops: Concerning Pittsburgh, transcript of meeting between a contingent of visiting brokers and George W. Ely, secretary of the NYSE, July 17, 1905, in Box No. 1, NYSE, 1900–1919, Governing Committee, Admissions-Arrangements; re Milwaukee, statement of George B. Post, Jr., to the Law Committee, June 28, 1905, in Box No. 3, NYSE, 1900–1919, Governing Committee, External Relations, Law, Special.

47   "I stood . . .": *Wall Street Journal*, Sept. 20, 1899.

48   "I cannot describe . . .": Money Trust Investigation, Report, p. 869.

48   Gould's trading failure: Grodinsky, p. 514.

Four   "Wealth Commenced to Pour In on Me"

PAGE
49   Loving son: Mrs. Virginia Epstein to author, Feb. 16, 1981.

49   "the recognized representative . . .": *New York Times*, Jan. 3, 1898.

50   "Great American victory . . .": Bernard M. Baruch, *Baruch: My Own Story* (New York, 1957), p. 108.

51   $6,000 a year: Baruch to Harold Epstein, Dec. 17, 1953; Baruch papers.

52   "The stock . . .": *Wall Street Journal*, Apr. 19, 1898.

52   "Their conversation . . .": Baruch, *My Own Story*, pp. 111–112.

52   Minority stockholder: *St. Louis Republic*, Feb. 2, 1899.

52   Wetmore's control: Ibid., Feb. 3, 1899.

53   "hang on the flank" and Lavino and Tobey: Memo on Liggett & Myers; Baruch papers.

53   "I want you . . .": Baruch, *My Own Story*, p. 115.

54   Conspiracy: *St. Louis Republic*, Feb. 3, 1899; *Wall Street Journal*, Feb. 21, 1899;

John Wilber Jenkins, *James B. Duke, Master Builder* (New York, 1927), p. 105; Baruch, *My Own Story*, p. 116.

54 $10,000 offer to Page: Page to Baruch, Dec. 10, 1930; no rebutting letter was found in Baruch's papers, which suggests that Page's recollection, albeit more than thirty years old, was accurate.

54 "ridiculously small": Liggett & Myers memo.

54 Published tips: *Wall Street Journal,* June 12, 1899; also, June 21 and June 23.

55 "Whitney syndicate": Ibid., June 24, 1899.

55 "You will be . . .": Baruch, *My Own Story*, p. 72.

55 "Rather sheepishly . . .": Ibid., p. 122.

55 "I have come back . . .": *Wall Street Journal,* June 13, 1899.

56 "I am a believer . . .": *New York Times,* May 13, 1899.

56 "The ex-governor . . .": Henry Clews, *Fifty Years in Wall Street* (New York, 1908), p. 705.

57 "To hold the price . . .": Baruch, *My Own Story*, p. 126.

57 "As you get older . . .": Yousuf Karsh, *Faces of Destiny: Portraits by Karsh* (Chicago and New York, 1946), p. 22.

58 Weil episodes: Arthur Pound and Samuel Taylor Moore, eds., *They Told Barron: Conversations and Revelations of an American Pepys in Wall Street* (New York, 1930), p. 221.

59 "Probably 1901 . . .": Alexander Dana Noyes, *The Market Place* (Boston, 1938), p. 195.

59 "gambling purposes": George Kennan, *E. H. Harriman, A Biography*, Vol. 1 (Boston, 1922), p. 315.

60 "Who's that damn fellow . . .": Typescript in File No. 1, Box 273, Unit XV, p. 17a; Baruch papers.

61 "'Bernie,' he said . . .": Baruch, *My Own Story*, pp. 141–142.

62 Hill's statement on speculation: Albro Martin, *James J. Hill and the Opening of the Northwest* (New York, 1976), p. 503.

63 "Only the stoutest . . .": Baruch, *My Own Story*, p. 147.

63 Housman and Bache stories: *Wall Street Journal,* May 10, 1901; "A broker . . .": Ibid., May 11, 1901.

64 London purchases at $112–$115: Memo on Northern Pacific corner in the Baruch papers, dated May 27, 1935, pp. 11–12.

64 Biggest day's profit: Baruch, *My Own Story*, p. 145.

64 Short of stocks against calls: Northern Pacific memo, p. 5; Baruch papers.

65 "Mr. Baruch . . .": New York *Herald*, July 2, 1901.

65 "Bernie . . .": Baruch, *My Own Story*, p. 128.

65 "I became . . ." and ff.: Baruch dictation in Unit XV, Box 272; Baruch papers.

67 Baruch's prowess: Ibid.

67 "The substantial . . .": Unidentified newspaper clipping; Baruch scrapbook.

Five His Own Man

PAGE

69 "knees from shock.": Bernard M. Baruch, *Baruch: My Own Story* (New York, 1957), p. 188.

69 "luxurious sanitary quarters": New York *Tribune,* Aug. 22, 1907.

69 Official notice of the Stock Exchange: No mention of the firm appears in the minutes of the Committee on Insolvencies for this period.

69 Housman evolution: "We the People" (the Merrill Lynch house organ), Jan.–Feb. 1959.

69 "After a particularly . . .": Baruch, *My Own Story*, p. 184.

70 "Let unswerving integrity . . .": Ibid., p. 189.

70 "funny looking": Marcia Kendrick McCue to author, May 6, 1980.

71 "born in iniquity": *New York Times*, Mar. 22, 1902.

71 Prag complaint: *Motz Prag v. Bernard M. Baruch*, New York State Supreme Court, Sept. 28, 1903.

71 "as a matter . . .": *Answers of Defendant Bernard M. Baruch in the action titled Frank G. Turner and Barreda Turner v. Bernard M. Baruch and Motz Prag*, New York State Supreme Court (6406-13), Apr. 17, 1913.

72 The record shows . . . : Minutes of the Committee on Unlisted Securities, Jan. 24, 1906, p. 319.

73 "Shall a separate . . .": Agenda attached to the minutes of the Unlisted Committee, Apr. 4, 1906.

73 "I am like Mr. Thomas . . .": Minutes of the Unlisted Committee, Mar. 29, 1906, p. 7.

74 "Mining Corporations . . .": Ibid., Jan. 10, 1907.

74 "It's in Bingham . . .": T. A. Rickard, *Utah Copper Enterprise* (San Francisco, 1917), p. 26.

74 "a good many shares": Baruch, *My Own Story*, p. 222.

74 "damn figures": Rickard, *Utah Copper Enterprise*, p. 28.

75 "He's a big man . . .": Isaac F. Marcosson, *Metal Magic: The Story of American Smelting and Refining Co.* (New York, 1949), p. 76.

76 ". . . I told Mr. Untermeyer . . .": Baruch, *My Own Story*, p. 199.

77 Baruch's bull pool: *Wall Street Journal*, Apr. 14–15, 1905.

77 Solomon Guggenheim's apology: Baruch, *My Own Story*, pp. 202–203.

77 "My self-confidence . . .": Memo titled "Notes on Coffee" in Baruch papers, Unit XV, Box 273.

78 Sielcken's coffee role: See U.S. House of Representatives, 62nd Cong., 3rd Sess., Report of the Committee Appointed . . . to Investigate the Concentration of Money and Credit (Washington, 1913), p. 36ff.

78 "Nixon," said Crocker . . . : Baruch, *My Own Story*, p. 249.

79 "I haven't a closer friend . . .": *Nevada Mining News*, June 29, 1907.

79 Psychological element: Baruch, *My Own Story*, p. 250.

80 "confused and inconsistent": *Mining & Scientific Journal*, Dec. 21, 1907.

80 "the unlawful dynamiting . . .": New York *Tribune*, Dec. 7, 1907.

80 "It being . . .": Baruch memoir; Baruch papers.

80 Baruch as evil genius: See, for example, *Nevada Mining News*, June 13, 1907.

80 "There is a rumor . . .": Ibid., May 18, 1907.

80 Stockholder attitudes and settlement: *New York Times*, Sept. 21, 1907.

81 Baruch's reported holdings: *The New York Commercial*, Jan. 21, 1908.

81 Baruch sold stocks in advance: Baruch, *My Own Story*, p. 192.

81 "Like many other people . . .": Ibid., p. 226.

81 "At the height . . .": Boston News Bureau, June 6, 1911.

81 Utah Copper financial information: Utah Copper Co. Third Annual Report, 1908.

82 Baruch's 6 percent loan: Baruch, *My Own Story*, p. 227.

84 "pulled us off the suit": Ibid., p. 214.

84 "The wisdom of Bernard . . .": Boston News Bureau, Apr. 4, 1912.

84 "[Baruch] didn't do the work . . .": Columbia University Oral History Collection, Meyer interview, pp. 114–115.

85 "as a knowledge . . .": Meyer to Baruch, July 27, 1909; Meyer papers.

85 Meyer's report: Merlo J. Pusey, *Eugene Meyer* (New York, 1974), pp. 71–72.

85 "AFRAID IMPOSSIBLE . . .": Baruch to Meyer, Aug. 4, 1909; Meyer papers.

85 Meyer's bullish wire: Meyer to Baruch, undated; Meyer papers.

85 "BARUCH LENDS YOU . . .": Baruch to Meyer, July 30, 1909; Meyer papers.

85 "Under no conditions": Baruch to Meyer, Aug. 23, 1909; Meyer papers.

86 One of the most lucrative: Baruch memoir; Baruch papers, Unit XV, Box 272.

86 Baruch's letter to Ryan: Nov. 27, 1915.

87 "Dear Mr. Baruch": R. Lancaster Williams to Baruch, Mar. 26, 1915.

87 "unique" demand: *Wall Street Journal*, Mar. 23 and 25, 1915.

87 "serious blunder": T. A. Rickard, *A History of American Mining* (New York, 1932), pp. 76–77.

87 "My relation to Juneau": Meyer to Bradley, Apr. 19, 1920; Meyer papers.

Six The Baron of Hobcaw

PAGE

89 "You be off . . .": Appellate Division Reports, New York Supreme Court, V. 103, pp. 577–580.

90 "If your chauffeur . . .": *New York Times*, Dec. 9, 1913.

90 "ardent convivialist": Quoted in Alberta M. Lachiotte, *Georgetown Rice Plantations* (Columbia, S.C., 1955), p. 9.

90 "Sightwood Pitchings . . .": Grant to John Roberts, Oct. 8, 1736, p. 9; Special Grants (Royal), Vol. 43, p. 114, South Carolina archives.

91 "of fine address": *The Carolina Field* (Georgetown, S.C.), May 24, 1905.

91 Details of property transfer: Various deed books from the Office of the Clerk of Court and the Auditor's Office, Georgetown County, S.C.

92 "How I miss . . .": Hobcaw guest book, entry dated Feb. 21, 1916; Unit XVIII, Box 287, Baruch papers.

92 "I love my ducks . . .": Ibid., entry dated Nov. 22, 1913.

92 New York *Herald* report: Dec. 30, 1911.

92 "I do my hunting . . .": Bernard M. Baruch, *Baruch: My Own Story* (New York, 1957), p. 277.

92 Baruch's visit to church: Elizabeth Navarro to author, Feb. 21, 1980.

93 "Jesse, keep quiet . . .": Ibid., pp. 282–283.

93 Annie as guest: Baruch to William Glasgow, Jr., June 10, 1926. Baruch wrote: "Mrs. Baruch has written a letter to Mrs. Glasgow, but I want to clear up the diplomatic side of your invitation. Seriously, and as a matter of fact, Mrs. Baruch never issues an invitation either for Hobcaw or Fetteresso [the Scottish castle].

She is only a guest and not the hostess. This is not bragging behind her back; if you want me to, I will say so in front of her."

93   "level headed": Baruch to Herbert Hoover, Aug. 27, 1921.

93   Not his type: Dorothy Schiff to author, July 14, 1980.

93   Lousy lover: Helen Lawrenson, *Stranger at the Party* (New York, 1975), pp. 135–136.

94   "That really was the bitterest . . .": Baruch reminiscences, Unit XV, Box 272, pp. 194–195. (Hereafter referred to as Baruch reminiscences.) Brearley wasn't literally out of bounds to Jews at the turn of the century—Jacob Schiff's first child, Frieda, was a student there—but to Baruch's mind, at least, it did apply a quota system. The school can only confirm that Belle applied but did not enroll.

95   City College trustee: Sherry Gorelick, *City College and the Jewish Poor: Education in New York, 1880–1924* (New Brunswick, N.J., 1981), p. 137.

95   Perkins' perceptions: Frances Perkins interview, Columbia University Oral History Collection, Book 5, p. 118 and p. 131.

95   Oakland Golf Club affair: Baruch reminiscences, pp. 192–193.

96   "above the turf": Baruch reminiscences, pp. 631–632.

96   "The belief prevailed . . .": Boston News Bureau, June 23, 1911.

96   "One of the things . . .": Dow Jones ticker, Mar. 6, 1912.

96   "The Stock Exchange . . .": Charleston *Post*, Sept. 24, 1912.

97   "The good features . . .": Boston News Bureau, Oct. 8, 1912.

97   "Barney" Baruch has gone . . . : *Morning Telegraph*, Aug. 8, 1913.

98   Jacob Schiff's suspicion: Dorothy Schiff to author, July 14, 1980.

98   chronically short: James P. Warburg interview, Columbia University Oral History Collection, p. 41.

98   "It doesn't affect me . . .": Garet Garrett, "The Wall Street Boys," *Collier's* (Jan. 27, 1912), p. 22.

99   "Baruch is something . . .": Boston News Bureau, May 30, 1911.

99   Laimbeer gift: New York *Sun*, Sept. 7, 1913.

99   Baruch's book: *Short Sales and Manipulation of Securities* (New York, 1913), 67 pages, privately printed.

100   "by far the ablest . . .": Quoted in Mortimer Smith, *William Jay Gaynor: Mayor of New York* (Chicago, 1951), p. 157.

100   Baruch's voting: Bernard M. Baruch, *Baruch: The Public Years* (New York, 1960), p. 5; and Jordan A. Schwarz, *The Speculator: Bernard M. Baruch in Washington, 1917–1965* (Chapel Hill, N.C., 1981), p. 35.

100   "Resolved, . . .": Frank R. Kent, *The Democratic Party: A History* (New York, 1928), p. 399.

100   ". . . Bernard Baruch ought to have . . .": Boston News Bureau, Aug. 13, 1912.

101   "three wealthy Democrats": Arthur S. Link, *Wilson, The Road to the White House* (Princeton, N.J., 1947), p. 484.

102   "Baruch interests": For example, New York *Globe*, Dec. 14, 1911; the *Globe* also reported, under a story plainly headed "Gossip," that Baruch was making a market in U.S. Steel for none other than J. P. Morgan.

102   Reports of a Baruch pool: E.g., Boston News Bureau, June 20, 1911.

103   "Some of the keenest . . .": Ibid., July 18, 1911.

103   "Both B. M. Baruch . . .": Ibid., May 14, 1912.

103   "Conservative Wall Street . . .": *Wall Street Journal*, Jan. 4, 1913.

104 "It's always been a great relief . . .": quoted in Jacob Alexis Friedman, *Impeachment of Governor William Sulzer* (New York, 1939), pp. 17–19.
105 Baruch's attitude toward Stock Exchange incorporation: Autobiographical typescript by Marquis James, Unit XV, Box 273, pp. 163–164.
105 "Bernard M. Baruch, who now . . .": New York *World*, Aug. 8, 1913.
106 Baruch's contribution to Sulzer defense: Baruch, *The Public Years*, p. 3.
106 "It is not true . . .": New York *World*, Aug. 8, 1913.

Seven Striking It Rich Reluctantly

108 "president of various railroad corporations": Translation of an article from *Der Angriff* (Aug. 15, 1935); General Correspondence.
108 Besides the standard reference sources (*Moody's, Poor's, Commercial & Financial Chronicle*, etc.), the following were especially helpful on the history of the Terminal Co.: Committee on Interstate and Foreign Commerce, House of Representatives; Investigation of the Wabash-Pittsburgh Terminal Co., Washington, 1914; Albro Martin, *Enterprise Denied: Origins of the Decline of American Railroads, 1897–1917* (New York, 1971); William Z. Ripley, *Railroads: Finance & Organization* (New York, 1915).
108 Hope and bafflement: See, for instance, New York *Sun* and *Financial America*, Mar. 31, 1911.
110 "Thoroughly disgusted . . .": House Investigation, p. 36.
111 "Speaking in general terms . . .": Twenty-second Annual Report of the Directors of the Wabash Railroad Co. for the Fiscal Year Ending June 30, 1911, p. 4, p. 6.
112 Hearst prediction: New York *American*, May 4, 1912.
112 "Those who know . . .": New York *Herald*, May 18, 1912.
112 "The announcement . . .": *Wall Street Journal*, Apr. 5, 1912.
113 "Though we have . . .": Cyrus Adler, *Jacob H. Schiff: His Life and Letters* (New York, 1928), pp. 128–129.
113 "The reorganization plan . . .": *New York Times*, Apr. 22, 1914.
114 "Passenger rates have been broken . . .": *Commercial & Financial Chronicle*, Vol. XCIX, p. 1132, 1914.
114 "You know I am with you . . .": Baruch reminiscences, Unit XV, Box 272, p. 100.
115 "gross misrepresentation": Quoted in Jordan Schwarz, *The Speculator: Bernard M. Baruch in Washington, 1917–1965* (Chapel Hill, N.C., 1981), p. 31.
116 "no one was able": Baruch to Frank Kent, Mar. 18, 1936. Different men saw Baruch as a different animal. Both James P. Warburg and Henry Morgenthau unflatteringly likened him to a fox, and Drew Pearson, another detractor, wrote that he had an elephant's memory for people who crossed him. Hamilton Fish, in praise, compared him to an owl, and on Wall Street he was sometimes heroically called a "Lone Eagle." Baruch himself, remarking on his fondness for the sun, used the analogy of a lizard.
116 "the Asiatic elephant . . .": E. J. Kahn, Jr., *The World of Swope* (New York, 1965), p. 206.
116 At length, the Baruch party: Texas Gulf history is based on the following: Dr.

Charles F. Fogarty, *The Story of Texasgulf: A Story of Natural Resources Essential to a Higher Standard of Living for Everyone*, The Newcomen Society of North America, 1976; Williams Haynes, *The Stone That Burns: The Story of the American Sulphur Industry* (New York, 1942); David Lavender, *The Story of Cyprus Mines Corporation* (San Marino, Cal., 1962).

117 "gamble": Bernard M. Baruch, *Baruch: My Own Story* (New York, 1957), p. 235.
117 "at or near . . .": Application for charter of Gulf Sulphur Co., Dec. 23, 1909. This and other documents and correspondence that follow, unless otherwise noted, are drawn from the archives of Texasgulf Inc., Stamford, Conn.
118 "worthy of further work": Baruch to Alfred C. Einstein, Mar. 24, 1911.
118 "entirely out of the question": Baruch to Einstein, June 23, 1911.
119 "Personally and frankly . . .": Einstein to Baruch, Jan. 6 and 15, 1912.
119 "The man supposed . . .": Baruch to Einstein, Jan. 9, 1913.
119 "All these men . . .": Baruch to Einstein, Apr. 11, 1912.
120 "I am willing . . .": Baruch to Einstein, May 27, 1913.
120 "I am becoming . . .": Einstein to Baruch, June 28, 1913.
121 "I don't believe . . .": J. M. Allen to Einstein, Feb. 9, 1914.
122 "Mr. Baruch said to me . . .": Einstein to Harrison, Mar. 10, 1915.
123 "squeeze them out": Einstein to Baruch, June 1, 1915.
123 "I wish . . .": Baruch to Einstein, Jan. 26, 1916.
124 "NO MORE OPTIONS . . .": Allen to Einstein, Feb. 7, 1916.
124 "ALL CASH IMPOSSIBLE . . .": Einstein to Allen, Feb. 8, 1916.
124 "IN VIEW OF . . .": Baruch to Einstein, Mar. 2, 1916.
125 Baruch turning to Morgan: Baruch, *My Own Story*, p. 238.
125 "Three and one half . . .": Arthur Pound and Samuel Taylor Moore, eds., *They Told Barron: Conversations and Revelations of an American Pepys in Wall Street* (New York, 1930), p. 238.

Eight   Poison-Pen Letter

PAGE
128 Favors from and for Murphy: Baruch reminiscences, Unit XV, Box 272, p. 910.
128 "on Mezes' account.": Quoted in Jordan A. Schwarz, *The Speculator: Bernard M. Baruch in Washington, 1917–1965* (Chapel Hall, N.C., 1981), p. 43.
128 "He had been . . .": S. Willis Rudy, *The College of the City of New York: A History (1847–1947)* (New York, 1949), p. 342.
129 "The only thing . . .": *Journal of Commerce*, July 8, 1915.
129 "Boiled down . . .": New York *Call*, July 9, 1915.
129 Baruch accident: Ibid., Dec. 1, 1914.
129 White House visit: New York *Herald*, Sept. 9, 1915.
129 "Mr. Baruch happens . . .": Einstein to Allen, Sept. 18, 1916 (Texasgulf archives, Stamford, Conn.).
130 "Mr. House has handed . . .": Bernard M. Baruch, *Baruch: The Public Years* (New York, 1960), p. 24.
130 "somewhat vain": E. David Cronon, ed., *The Cabinet Diaries of Josephus Daniels, 1913–1921* (Lincoln, Neb., 1963), p. 131.

131 "the New York banker": *New York Times*, Oct. 12, 1916.
131 "I doubt his sorrow . . .": Quoted in Schwarz, p. 46.
131 "All the women . . .": House of Representatives, 64th Cong., 2nd Sess., Committee on Rules, Investigation Relating to Alleged Advance Knowledge of the President's Note of December 20, 1916, Washington, D.C., 1917, p. 1495. (Hereafter cited as Investigation.)
132 "Prices melted away . . .": *Wall Street Journal*, Dec. 22, 1916.
132 "The good old . . .": Investigation, p. 274; Lawson tarred a number of prominent people in connection with the alleged leak but he testified that "Bernie Baruch is a reputable character" (p. 303).
132 "I will state . . .": *New York Times*, Jan. 4, 1917.
133 Curtis letter: Ibid., Jan. 6, 1917.
134 "Tell them . . .": Eugene Meyer, Jr., interview, Columbia University Oral History Collection, p. 217.
134 Abandonment of Baruch by his friends: Ibid., p. 220.
135 "Bernard M. Baruch; my business . . .": Investigation, p. 187.
135 "Our party . . .": Ibid., p. 194.
135 "a great many years": Ibid., p. 198.
135 "They are licensed . . .": Ibid., p. 206.
136 "On the contrary . . .": Ibid., p. 212.
136 "perhaps you may be right . . .": Ibid., p. 213.
136 "Did you have . . .": Ibid., p. 553.
137 "I know I bought . . ." and ff.: Ibid., pp. 556–557.
137 He owned no munitions stocks: Boston News Bureau, Jan. 9, 1917.
137 "I am speaking . . .": Investigation, p. 557.
137 Canadian Pacific understanding: Boston News Bureau, Jan. 31, 1917.
138 "But then . . .": Investigation, p. 558.
138 "Because, I wanted . . ." and ff.: Ibid., pp. 563–564.
139 "It was a very unfortunate . . .": Ibid., p. 564.
139 "I never get . . ." and ff.: Ibid., pp. 565–566.
139 "Was this a large . . ." and ff.: Ibid., pp. 564–565.
140 "I do not know . . .": Ibid., p. 569.
      Suspicion about the affair lingered long afterward. In 1953 one Arthur Mefford, who claimed to have been a Wall Street telegrapher at the time of the leak, wrote the columnist Westbrook Pegler with what he said was the true inside story of Baruch's culpability. Mefford wrote that he had personally "handled" the leak on the wires of S. B. Chapin & Company, that the information had been given to Baruch and that the speculator had made at least $3 million and undoubtedly more. Furthermore, Mefford was paid $15,000 in "hush money" by a man whom he (Mefford) presumed to be Baruch. But (and here the story came unraveled) by the time the congressional investigation got under way, Mefford had been called up from the reserves to active service in France. Pegler, who had no use for Baruch, evidently doubted his informant—for one thing the investigation was finished months before the United States entered the war—but if nothing else the charge is revealing of the kind of myth that clung to Baruch (Mefford to Pegler, Aug. 5, 1953; Westbrook Pegler Papers, Herbert Hoover Presidential Library).

Nine   Captain of Industry

142   *Chronicle Magazine* episode: *New York Times,* Oct. 1, 1917.
143   "There's not a drop . . .": Virginia Epstein to author, Feb. 6, 1981.
143   President Wilson's flowers: *New York Times,* Nov. 28, 1917. The ballroom at
       Sherry's was filled with chrysanthemums and with more than a thousand people,
       including Dr. and Mrs. Baruch's four sons, their wives and eight of their nine
       grandchildren. For his founding of the Rivington Street public baths, the doctor
       was presented with a gold tablet; and for his gift of the Charity Hospital to the
       city of Camden, S.C. (which our Baruch financed), with a gold loving cup. Mrs.
       Baruch, the *Times* reported, wore "a trailing gown of white and gold brocaded
       satin and chiffon, with diamond ornaments." Her clubs deluged her with flow-
       ers.
143   "the man who spreads . . .": Quoted in David M. Kennedy, *Over Here: The First
       World War and American Society* (New York, 1980), p. 62.
143   Wartime financial details: Baruch to Senator Gerald P. Nye, Mar. 22, 1935;
       quoted in the report of the Special Committee to Investigate the Munitions In-
       dustry, U.S. Senate, 73rd–74th Cong., Washington, 1935, pp. 6260–6262.
       (Hereafter cited as Nye hearings.)
144   "involuntary voluntary" method: Merlo J. Pusey, *Eugene Meyer* (New York,
       1974), p. 143.
144   Austrian ships affair: Bernard M. Baruch, *Baruch: The Public Years* (New York,
       1960), pp. 40–41.
145   "He is always ready . . .": Quoted in *Collier's* (Jan. 31, 1920).
145   Corcoran story: Eugene Meyer, Jr., Columbia University Oral History Collec-
       tion, p. 256.
146   Buying the building: *Collier's* (Jan. 31, 1920).
146   "was just a cluster . . .": Hugh S. Johnson, *The Blue Eagle from Egg to Earth*
       (Garden City, N.Y., 1935), p. 93.
147   "Whereas the high cost . . .": Quoted in Nye hearings, p. 392.
148   "Anybody who declines . . .": Quoted in Sidney Homer, *A History of Interest
       Rates: 2000 B.C. to the Present* (New Brunswick, N.J., 1977), p. 346.
148   "Easy money . . .": Alexander D. Noyes, *The War Period of American Finance,
       1908–1925* (New York, 1926), p. 225.
148   Von Mises' ideas: Ludwig von Mises, *Human Action* (New Haven, Conn.,
       1949).
149   Du Pont story: Unless otherwise noted, Alfred D. Chandler, Jr., and Stephen
       Salsbury, *Pierre S. du Pont and the Making of the Modern Corporation* (New York,
       1971), chapters 14–15.
150   "Many was the night . . .": Baruch, *The Public Years,* p. 57.
151   "I do not know . . .": Bernard M. Baruch, *Baruch: My Own Story* (New York,
       1957), p. 228.
153   "This gave me something . . .": Baruch, *The Public Years,* p. 45.
154   "Fiddle while Rome burns": Ibid., p. 46.
154   "Walked with my . . .": Baruch diary, Feb. 24, 1918; War Industries Board Pa-
       pers.
154   "The entire war machine . . .": Robert D. Cuff, *The War Industries Board: Busi-
       ness-Government Relations During World War I* (Baltimore, 1973), p. 135.

154 "By the time . . .": Ibid., p. 136.
154 Baker's dislike of Baruch's Wall Street past: Daniel R. Beaver, *Newton D. Baker and the American War Effort, 1917–1919* (Lincoln, Neb., 1966), p. 106.
154 "good, honest, simpleminded . . .": Quoted in Jordan A. Schwarz, *The Speculator: Bernard M. Baruch in Washington, 1917–1965* (Chapel Hill, N.C., 1981), p. 70.
155 "ablest man . . .": Theodore Roosevelt to Moe Gunst, Aug. 14, 1917, General Correspondence.
155 "My dear Mac . . .": Quoted in Baruch, *The Public Years*, p. 50.
156 "Now when you . . .": Ibid., p. 52.
156 "Even while I . . .": Willard to Baruch, Jan. 28, 1936.
156 "Mr. Baruch's method . . .": *Wall Street Journal*, Mar. 8, 1918.
157 Wilson letter: Quoted in Margaret L. Coit, *Mr. Baruch* (Boston, 1957), p. 698.
158 "That he possesses . . ." and ff.: E. J. Kahn, Jr., *The World of Swope* (New York, 1965), p. 200.
159 Copper episode: The copper episode later became a source of contention between Baruch and Roosevelt. According to Henry A. Wallace, Secretary of Agriculture under Roosevelt, who quoted Rexford Tugwell (Columbia University Oral History Collection), Roosevelt "had his fingers very much crossed about Baruch as a result of Baruch's manipulations of the regulations on behalf of high copper prices in World War I." In the 1930s, Baruch heard the same story from his White House sources and once, in a joking way, from F.D.R. himself. Sensing that the President wasn't joking, Baruch tried to set the facts straight in a letter (July 8, 1937): how he, personally (he made no mention of Meyer), was the "father" of the $16\frac{2}{3}$-cent concessionary price, but how, after this initial coup, he had had no decisive voice in the fixing of any price.

Roosevelt was still suspicious, and he asked the Navy Department to investigate. On July 21, 1937, the Bureau of Supplies and Accounts answered with a seven-page memorandum that concluded that F.D.R. and Baruch each had a point, but that they had in mind different episodes. Baruch was, indeed, responsible for thee $16\frac{2}{3}$-cent price, the memo said, but it added that the WIB, on presidential authority, had subsequently allowed a higher price: a point for F.D.R. The memo continued that when Baruch and the Guggenheims and others came forward with their proposal to sell to the Navy at a very low price, the nation was at peace. The offer was intended to cover a year's supply, and it was left up to the Navy to decide what the amount might be. The estimate given was 20 million pounds, which turned out to be less than one fifth of actual wartime demand. Nevertheless, the 20 million pounds was said by Baruch and the War Industries Board to have discharged thee $16\frac{2}{3}$-cent obligation, and a new, higher price was decided on.

Something that apparently escaped both Baruch and Roosevelt was the fact that copper-smelter output under the wartime price regime actually declined by 1 percent from the 1916 prewar level.
159 "Baruch had not . . .": Pusey, p. 139.
160 "Gene," said Baruch . . . : Ibid., pp. 148–149.
160 "The Chief . . .": Memo to members of the War Industries Association from Howard P. Ingalls, Dec. 6, 1938; General Correspondence.
161 "And then [she wrote] . . .": Anonymous, *The Mirrors of Washington* (New York, 1921), pp. 145–146.

161   Brookings' attitude: Schwarz, p. 56.
161   "I do not believe . . .": Ibid., pp. 58–59.
161   Spy for House: Baruch interview with Harold Epstein, Dec. 19, 1953, p. 166.
161   "We did hear . . .": Michael Teague, ed., *Mrs. L.: Conversations with Alice Roosevelt Longworth* (Garden City, N.Y., 1981), p. 162. Mrs. Longworth said that Franklin D. Roosevelt, her cousin and then Assistant Secretary of the Navy, had provided false "official" documents that were laid in the suspect's path and that she allegedly forwarded them to an uncle in Bucharest. Mrs. Longworth continued: "Eleanor [Roosevelt] apparently knew about what was going on—as a great many people did—and years afterwards when Franklin was at the White House, we were both chuckling about the incident one time and Eleanor said, 'You know, Alice, I have always disapproved of what you and Franklin were doing.' Oh, we had a hilarious time! He really could be the greatest fun.

"I think Bernie enjoyed the whole thing too. Once much later he said that he had heard I was involved in the matter and I said, 'Yes, I was, and all I can tell you is I hope you got what you wanted.' "

What, if any, espionage information the eavesdropping yielded and whether there was any attempt at blackmail, unfortunately, are questions without answers.

In his interview with Harold Epstein (p. 90), Baruch alluded to what might have been the same incident, saying: "Like in World War I they came to me with a story of how I was going to divorce my wife and my three children and marry a girl. And they had it all on the dictograph but it was another fellow. And he did divorce his wife. But the gang was trying to get me."
162   "May I not . . .": Wilson to Lansing, Sept. 2, 1918, State Department No. 860F. 24/9-2.
162   "Nothing will be gained . . .": Baruch to Daniels, June 26, 1918, Daniels papers.
163   "However harmless . . .": *The Ladies' Home Journal* (Sept. 1918), p. 29.
163   ". . . by the time . . .": Quoted in Grosvenor B. Clarkson, *Industrial America in the World War: The Strategy Behind the Line (1917–1918)* (Boston, 1923), p. 99.
164   "civilian order of the day": Kahn, p. 206.
164   "It appears . . ." and ff.: Quoted in Cuff, p. 209.
164   "We have every . . .": Ibid., p. 218.
165   "walking the streets . . .": Nye hearings, p. 6296.
165   "To Bernard M. Baruch . . .": Ibid., p. 519.
165   Baruch's library: The visitor was David E. Lilienthal, *The Journals of David E. Lilienthal*, Vol. I, *The TVA Years, 1939–1945* (New York, 1964), p. 226.

Ten   Plainspoken Diplomat

167   Plans to bring family: On Dec. 24, 1918, the American delegation in Paris had cabled Washington that Baruch was "anxious" to bring his wife and his nineteen-year-old daughter and that "in view of his position assume these passports should be granted." For undisclosed reasons, however, the Baruch women sailed later. Baruch's State Department personnel file, document no. 184.1.
167   "Notify in Case . . .": Ibid.
167   "It was not easy . . .": Bernard M. Baruch, *Baruch: The Public Years* (New York, 1960), p. 95.

167 Largest contributor: He gave $25,000 and participated in a $150,000 loan, *New York Times*, Oct. 29, 1918; his gift represented 16 percent of the total funds raised by the Democratic National Committee.
168 "Squeeze the lemon . . .": and other diplomatic background: Howard Elcock, *Portrait of a Decision: The Council of Four and the Treaty of Paris* (London, 1972).
168 "for the purpose . . .": *New York Times*, Mar. 19, 1919.
168 $150,000 loan: Anderson diary quoted in Jordan A. Schwarz, *The Speculator: Bernard M. Baruch in Washington, 1917–1965* (Chapel Hill, N.C., 1981), pp. 110–111; also, Baruch to Senator William S. Kenyon, May 23, 1921.
169 Office space and automobiles: Various State Department documents, including 184.13/134, May 14, 1919.
169 "There has been . . .": Quoted in John Brooks, *Once in Golconda: A True Drama of Wall Street 1920–1938* (New York, 1969), p. 124.
169 Complete trust: William Boyce Thompson, the mining entrepreneur, however, told Clarence Barron in 1920 that Lamont "was more relied upon abroad in financial matters than was Barney Baruch. In fact Baruch, I hear, did not see much of Wilson in Europe." Arthur Pound and Samuel Taylor Moore, eds., *They Told Barron: Conversations and Revelations of an American Pepys in Wall Street* (New York, 1930), p. 328.
169 "We went along . . .": Edith Benham Helm, *The Captains and the Kings* (New York, 1954), pp. 131–132.
170 Hoover flanked by women: Baruch reminiscences, Unit XV, Box 274, p. 362; Baruch papers.
170 "A just and continuing . . .": Quoted in Arthur Walworth, *America's Moment: 1918—American Diplomacy at the End of World War I* (New York, 1977), p. 251.
170 "We are all . . .": Raw Materials Section, Supreme Economic Council, Sixth Meeting, Apr. 16, 1919; State Department No. 0064-0089, p. 3.
171 "I say again . . .": Ibid., p. 8.
171 "The whole subject . . .": Ibid., p. 12.
171 "I have been . . .": Ibid., p. 12.
171 Harris episode: Ibid., p. 14.
172 "In the happy . . .": State Department document FW 180.05301/8, p. 2.
172 "He stated . . .": State Department document 180.05301/15, Minutes of an Informal Meeting of the Raw Materials Section Held in Mr. Baruch's Room on the 21st of June.
172 ". . . remember me . . .": Baruch to Renée Baruch, Mar. 13, 1919, American Commission to Negotiate Peace Papers (Baruch). (Hereafter cited as American Commission papers.)
172 "I would suggest . . .": Herter to Grew, Feb. 4, 1919, and related documents; State Department No. 184.00101/4.
173 "ruling mind": New York *World*, Feb. 10, 1919. The unnamed foreign delegate also said of Baruch: "He is, in my impression, one of the most remarkable men we have met at the Peace Conference. His knowledge, his quickness of mind and of decision and his business acumen have made a great impression on every one."
173 Cecil exchange: Raw Materials Section, Minutes of Seventh Meeting, Apr. 24, 1919, State Department No. 180.05301/7, p. 5.

173 "There was a long . . .": Quoted in Schwarz, p. 123.
173 "Even after peace . . .": Baruch to BMB, Jr., Mar. 13, 1919; American Commission papers.
174 "Have you any . . .": Arthur Krock, *Memoirs: Sixty Years on the Firing Line* (New York, 1968), p. 53.
174 "Arthur, you're . . .": John Baragwanath, *A Good Time Was Had* (New York, 1962), p. 158.
174 "in disgust" and ff.: Baruch reminiscences on Grayson, p. 647.
175 Baruch's views on taxes and labor: Quoted in Schwarz, p. 149.
175 "Siegmarious" cable and ff.: State Department Nos. 862.51/1202 and 862.51/1199.
176 "I do not wish . . .": Quoted in Schwarz, pp. 128–129.
176 "for all damage . . .": Quoted in Bernard M. Baruch, *The Making of the Reparations and Economic Sections of the Treaty* (New York, 1920; reprinted by Howard Fertig, Inc., 1970), p. 291.
177 "Let us all take . . .": Baruch, *The Public Years*, p. 107.
177 Illness of Dr. Baruch: Herman Baruch, the family's other doctor who went into Wall Street, wired his brother in Paris on Apr. 2, 1919: "Father has double pneumonia and severe heart attack. Greatly improved today and personally feel now chance excellent for complete recovery. Please don't consider returning to New York under any circumstances . . ."; American Commission papers.
178 "It is not . . .": Senate Foreign Relations Committee, hearings on the treaty, Washington, 1919, p. 45.
179 "The terms . . .": Ibid., pp. 69–70.
180 "And Baruch, too.": Baruch, *The Public Years*, pp. 138–139.
180 Rumors of Baruch's career: *New York Times*, July 17, July 22 and Sept. 6, 1919.
180 "blind and deaf . . ." and ff.: John Maynard Keynes, *The Economic Consequences of the Peace* (New York, 1920), pp. 40, 41, 42, 52–53, 54–55.
181 John Foster Dulles as ghostwriter: Schwarz, p. 158.
181 "Somebody said . . .": Baruch to David Lawrence, Sept 6, 1927.
181 "possibly legalistic": Baruch, *Making of the . . . Treaty*, p. 28.
181 "One must be . . .": Ibid., p. 54.
181 *The Nation*'s review, Nov. 3, 1920; *The New Republic*'s, Dec. 1, 1920; *The Spectator*'s, Dec. 11, 1920.
182 Keynes's review: *The Literary Review* of the New York *Evening Post*, Dec. 4, 1920.
182 "Though the peace . . .": Baruch, *Making of the . . . Treaty*, p. 5.
183 "Perhaps it was . . .": George Allardice Riddell, *Lord Riddell's Intimate Diary of the Peace Conference and After, 1918–1923* (London, 1933), p. 409.

Eleven   Farming, Money, McAdoo

PAGE
184 "I'm through with politics . . .": *New York Times*, July 19, 1919.
185 "in copper alone": Ibid., May 28, 1920.
185 "pro-consul of Judah . . .": Bernard M. Baruch, *Baruch: The Public Years* (New

York, 1960), p. 162. For a time Baruch apparently weighed legal action against Ford. His papers contain a five-page document that describes some causes of libel in the *Independent* articles (In re *Baruch* v. *Ford*, General Correspondence, Vol. III). On Jan. 4, 1921, Baruch wrote Josephus Daniels, "Thus far I have not taken any notice of his action. I may decide to go after him, and if I do somebody is going to get his head cracked." But nobody did.

185   Bond holdings: General Correspondence, Vol. III; in general, on Baruch's post-war finances, see Baruch to Senator William S. Kenyon, May 23, 1921.

185   "I 'cottoned' . . .": Baruch to Krock, May 28, 1920; Krock papers.

186   Baruch in Topeka: Kansas City *Post*, Sept. 4, 1920.

186   "You can depend . . .": Baruch to Meredith, Oct. 8, 1920.

187   "In closing . . .": Baruch to J. C. Mohlen, Dec. 3, 1920; Selected Correspondence.

187   Agricultural background: Baruch, *The Public Years*, pp. 149–170, and Jordan A. Schwarz, *The Speculator: Bernard M. Baruch in Washington, 1917–1965* (Chapel Hill, N.C., 1981), pp. 227–241.

187   *The Outlook*: Aug. 8, 1923; Meyer to Baruch, Aug. 9, 1923; Meyer papers.

188   Baruch notes and bond holdings: Securities inventory; General Correspondence, Vol. III.

189   "establishment of an export . . .": Quoted in Gilbert C. Fite, *George N. Peek and the Fight for Farm Parity* (Norman, Okla., 1954), p. 96.

189   "I do hope . . .": Baruch to Rougemont, May 13, 1924.

190   "I have always . . .": Baruch to F. G. Bonham-Carter, Apr. 16, 1923.

190   "I am hooked . . .": Baruch to Robinson, June 26, 1923.

190   Fetteresso bag: Game book, Unit XVIII, Box 287.

190   "because . . .": Baruch to Ritchie, Dec. 4, 1923.

190   "Please do not . . .": Baruch to Richard Manning, Oct. 15, 1925.

190   Robinson wire: Baruch to Robinson, May 19, 1924.

191   Pulitzer doggerel: Pulitzer to Baruch, Jan. 20, 1926.

191   "I would like . . .": Tardieu to Baruch, Dec. 7, 1925.

192   "you asked me to": Baruch to Krock, Mar. 26, 1926.

192   *New Yorker* profile: "Ulysses Ashore—For a While," Aug. 7, 1926.

192   ". . . whenever the request . . .": Arthur Krock, *Memoirs: Sixty Years on the Firing Line* (New York, 1968), p. 62.

192   Not yet published: Ronald Steel, *Walter Lippmann and the American Century* (New York, 1980), pp. 200–201.

193   "It is . . .": Quoted in E. J. Kahn, Jr., *The World of Swope* (New York, 1965), pp. 291–292.

193   "Tall, architectural head . . .": Ibid., p. 23.

194   "I have all . . .": Swope to Baruch, Sept. 12, 1923.

195   "the responsibility . . .": Baruch to Swope, Oct. 19, 1923.

195   Swope's subsequent losses: Baruch to Swope, May 24, 1924.

195   "As for Baruch . . .": Kahn, p. 276.

195   McAdoo's complaint: Baruch wrote Sullivan (Feb. 8, 1923): ". . . you know that nobody can control the news columns through Herbert Swope. . . . I hope you cannot too strongly refute anybody who says I am controlling *The World* or any other publication."

196   Young letter: Young to Baruch, June 27, 1925.

197 "munificent" gift: Radiogram from Young to Baruch, July 9, 1925.

198 "because of the infinite . . .": Hugh S. Johnson, *The Blue Eagle from Egg to Earth* (Garden City, N.Y., 1935), p. 111.

198 Muscle Shoals matter: Preston J. Hubbard, *Origins of the TVA: The Muscle Shoals Controversy, 1920–1932* (Nashville, Tenn., 1961), p. 82.

198 Tax views: Baruch to Joseph T. Robinson, May 16, 1924.

198 "We have been . . .": Baruch, *The Public Years*, p. 197.

198 Baruch's wine list: Vol. XIV, General Correspondence, 1926; Baragwanath's recollections in John Baragwanath, *A Good Time Was Had* (New York, 1962), p. 157.

199 "I do hope . . .": Baruch to Hull, Oct. 29, 1925.

200 "head and shoulders . . .": Quoted in Robert K. Murray, *The 103rd Ballot: Democrats and the Disaster in Madison Square Garden* (New York, 1976), pp. 42–43; for additional information on the politics of the day, Herbert A. Gelbart, *The Anti-McAdoo Movement of 1924*; unpublished doctoral dissertation (New York University), 1978.

200 *Star* clipping: Joseph T. Robinson to Baruch, Jan. 12, 1924.

201 "right gallantly . . .": Frank R. Kent, *The Democratic Party: A History* (New York, 1928), p. 482.

202 "I am, of course . . .": Baruch to Pat Harrison, Apr. 16, 1924.

202 "I should also . . .": Baruch to Davis, Mar. 24, 1924.

202 "my restless . . .": McAdoo to Baruch, Nov. 21, 1928.

203 "Shut up . . .": *New York Times*, July 5, 1924.

204 "desire not to . . .": Baruch to Mark Sullivan, Sept. 22, 1922.

204 "bums": Baruch to Daniel Roper, Apr. 21, 1923.

205 "Jesse Jones asked . . .": Baruch to Krock, Aug. 29, 1924; Krock papers.

205 "All I can say . . .": New York *American*, Sept. 24, 1924.

205 "You have . . .": Jones to Baruch, Oct. 1, 1924.

205 "Lots of people . . .": Baruch to BMB, Jr., Feb. 27, 1919; American Commission to Negotiate Peace Papers (Baruch).

206 "Your letter . . .": Baruch to Jones, Oct. 9, 1924.

207 "I think . . .": McAdoo to Baruch, Nov. 21, 1928; McAdoo papers.

208 "I got 500 . . .": McAdoo to Baruch, Nov. 30, 1928.

208 "Is it not . . .": Baruch to Daniels, Mar. 21, 1941; Daniels papers.

Twelve "I Would Stand Pat"

PAGE

210 Financial data and stock transactions: Unless otherwise noted, information is drawn from Baruch papers, Unit XVIII, Memorabilia, Miscellany: Financial Records.

211 "I am 55 . . .": Baruch to Morron, July 1, 1925.

212 "There was always . . .": Fred Schwed, Jr., *Where Are the Customers' Yachts? or, A Good Hard Look at Wall Street* (New York, 1940), p. 28.

212 "General Motors . . .": Quoted in John Brooks, *Once in Golconda: A True Drama of Wall Street, 1920–1938* (New York, 1969), p. 87.

213 "I told you . . .": Baruch to Pershing, Mar. 3, 1927.

213 Baruch's twenty-six brokerage firms: They were: Appenzellar, Allen & Hill; Sailing W. Baruch & Co.; Benjamin, Hill & Co.; Campbell, Starring & Co.; H. Content & Co.; Edey & Gibson; Foster, McConnell & Co.; Goldman, Sachs & Co.; Hallgarten & Co.; Harriman & Co.; Harris Winthrop & Co.; Hayden, Stone & Co.; H. Hentz & Co.

    Also: Herrick, Berg & Co.; Hibernia Securities Co., Inc.; F. B. Keech & Co.; Lehman Brothers; Mabon & Co.; Peter P. McDermott & Co.; Otis & Co.; Pynchon & Co.; Redmond & Co.; Salomon Brothers & Hutzler; E. H. H. Simmons & Co.; Tucker, Anthony & Co.; Winthrop, Mitchell & Co.

213 Account number 19: Source of the story is a former Hentz clerk who asked that his name not be divulged.

213 "he does not . . .": *New York Times*, May 25, 1928. About this time, in response to a story in the London *Daily Express* that described Baruch as "the stock market operator," Arthur Krock drafted a letter to be sent over Baruch's signature to the editor of the offending newspaper. "It has been, I think, many years since that could be called descriptive," wrote Krock rather pompously. "I am disposed to believe that, if you asked for a description of my activities from any five of the men with whom I have been associated in war and peace during the last ten or twelve years you would not be told that I am a 'stock market operator.' More generally I am referred to as a financier or economist, or as former chairman of the War Industries Board and member of the Economic Commission of the Peace Conference." Whether this was ever sent to anybody is unclear. Krock papers, undated.

214 "I don't want . . .": Quoted in E. J. Kahn, Jr., *The World of Swope* (New York, 1965), p. 308.

214 "Don't kid yourself.": Ibid., p. 315.

214 "UNDERSTAND CORNER . . .": Baruch to Swope, Feb. 8, 1929.

215 "ACTUAL INSIDERS . . ." and ff.: Swope to Baruch, Mar. 21–22, 1929; Swope papers.

215 "false and unwise": Baruch to Mitchell, Mar. 27, 1929.

216 ". . . one of the most . . .": Quoted in Lionel Robbins, *The Great Depression* (New York, 1936), p. 53.

216 ". . . virtually the full . . .": Milton Friedman and Anna Schwartz, *A Monetary History of the United States, 1867–1960* (Princeton, N.J., 1963), p. 291*n.*

216 "industrial renaissance": For example, Baruch to Cordell Hull, Oct. 29, 1925. Wrote Baruch of the next spring, ". . . there may be what might be properly called an 'industrial renaissance,' if nothing unforeseen happens."

216 "an industrial boom . . .": Baltimore *Sun*, Feb. 5, 1929.

217 "This isn't . . .": Baruch to Kent, Feb. 13, 1929.

217 "For the first time . . .": Bruce Barton, "Bernard M. Baruch Discusses the Future of American Business," *American Magazine* (June 1929).

217 "THINK GOOD SECURITIES . . .": Swope to Baruch, Aug. 9, 1929; Swope papers.

217 "LEHAM NEW STOCK . . .": Baruch to Swope, Sept. 12, 1929; Swope papers.

218 A biographer: Jordan A. Schwarz, *The Speculator: Bernard M. Baruch in Washington, 1917–1965* (Chapel Hill, N.C., 1981), p. 252.

218 "THE MEMORY . . .": Baruch to Churchill, Aug. 29, 1930.

219 Virginia Epstein gift: Mrs. Epstein to author, June 24, 1980.
219 "the best Rolls-Royce . . .": Brendan Bracken to Baruch, Jan. 14, 1932.
221 "imminent": Mitchell to Baruch, Aug. 22, 1929.
221 Baruch account of Crash: Bernard M. Baruch, *Baruch: The Public Years* (New York, 1960), pp. 224–229.
222 Baruch's market confidence: However, he canceled an open order to buy 12,000 shares of Bethlehem Steel on Sept. 6 and another open order to buy 17,400 shares of Alaska Juneau on Sept. 16.
222 Board meeting: Minutes of Directors, Baltimore & Ohio Railroad Corp., Vol. "S," Feb. 24, 1927–Nov. 21, 1934.
222 "FROM MY WINDOW . . .": Baruch to Mitchell, Sept. 23, 1929.
223 ". . . American markets generally . . .": *New York Times*, Oct. 16, 1929.
223 "stock prices . . .": Quoted in Edward Angly, *Oh Yeah?* (New York, 1932), p. 38.
223 Baruch's warning to Swope: Mentioned in Swope to Baruch, Oct. 21, 1929; Swope papers.
223 "There are no . . .": Quoted in Angly, p. 14.
224 ". . . it is time . . .": Baruch to Churchill, Dec. 17, 1929.
224 "There has been . . .": Quoted in Brooks, p. 124.
226 "my fellow former . . .": Baruch reminiscences, Unit XV, Box 275, p. 70.
226 "THINK I AM ABLE . . .": Swope to Hertz, Oct. 28, 1929; Swope papers.
226 "In my long . . .": Quoted in Angly, p. 27.
227 "REAL BELIEF . . .": Quoted in Kahn, p. 324.
227 Baruch remark to Robert Lehman: Robert G. Merrick, Sr., to author, Aug. 18, 1981.
228 "WILL YOU USE . . .": Morron to Baruch, May 31, 1931.
229 "I can tell you . . .": Baruch to Robinson, Nov. 10, 1930.
229 "The fertilizer business . . .": Baruch to Charles MacDowell, Sept. 23, 1931.
229 "Personal Equipment": Memo initialed "BMB," Unit VI, Vol. XXIV.
232 "distinct signs . . .": Johnson memo to Baruch, Aug. 3, 1931.
232 ". . . we have disrupted . . .": *New York Times*, Nov. 12, 1931.
233 *Time*'s estimate published July 2, 1934; Krock's, in *The New Yorker*, Aug. 7, 1926. Said *Time*: "Back of Baruch's success was his own shrewd economic judgment, of which the ultimate triumph was foreseeing the debacle of 1929. He got out in advance—liquidated a large part of his investments."
234 B&O dilemma: See especially Herbert H. Harwood, Jr., "Nothing at the End of the Rainbow: The B&O's Adventures in Western Pennsylvania," *Railroad History* (The Bulletin of the Railway and Locomotive Historical Society), 129, pp. 56–70; also *Moody's Manual of Investments: American and Foreign Railroad Securities*, 1932, p. lxxxix.
235 "It took about half . . .": Baruch reminiscences, p. 601.
236 ". . . because I was . . .": Baruch to Henry Morgenthau, Jr., Dec. 30, 1937.
236 "Money was sick . . .": Malcolm Muggeridge, *The Thirties* (London, 1940), p. 121.
238 "In anticipation . . .": Quoted in Henry Morgenthau, Jr., to Baruch, Dec. 23, 1937.
238 Churchill's thanks: Churchill to Baruch, Oct. 7, 1932.

239 "I have always . . .": Charles Mackay, *Extraordinary Popular Delusions and the Madness of Crowds*, with a foreword by Bernard M. Baruch (New York, 1932). The writing was probably Hugh Johnson's. Compare, for instance, p. xiii of the foreword to p. 100 of Johnson's own *The Blue Eagle from Egg to Earth* (Garden City, N.Y., 1935).

Thirteen Suffering Roosevelt

PAGE

241 "I am a Democrat . . .": Baruch to Albert C. Ritchie, Sept. 14, 1930.

241 "If Christ . . .": Baruch to Frank Kent, Oct. 17, 1927.

241 "Usually I am . . .": *New York Times*, Nov. 12, 1931.

242 "I don't understand . . .": Baruch to Swope; postcard in Swope papers, c. 1937.

242 "Bernie, you're . . .": Margaret Coit, *Mr. Baruch* (Boston, 1957), p. 449.

242 "The horn-rimmed . . .": Baruch to Krock, Dec. 19, 1932.

243 Johns Hopkins speech: *The Johns Hopkins Alumni Magazine* (June 1933), pp. 370–380.

245 Glass's views: Rixey Smith and Norman Beasley, *Carter Glass: A Biography* (New York, 1939), p. 354.

245 "that curious sense . . .": Perkins interview, Columbia University Oral History Collection, pp. 103–105.

247 Swope telegram: Swope to Baruch, May 27, 1933. Swope had written for Baruch to say: "No favors were shown me. I make it a rule to accept none."

247 "His [Peek's] passing . . .": Chicago *Daily News*, Dec. 4, 1935.

248 "It happened . . .": Hugh S. Johnson, *The Blue Eagle from Egg to Earth* (Garden City, N.Y., 1935), p. 187.

248 Brookings speech: Baruch papers.

249 "It will be . . .": Johnson, p. 208.

249 "his coat off . . .": Baltimore *Evening Sun*, Oct. 1, 1934.

249 ". . . the whole field . . .": Baruch to Johnson, Nov. 1, 1933.

249 "I just want . . .": Quoted in Smith and Beasley, pp. 361 and 364.

250 "the most faithful . . .": Johnson, p. 111.

250 Missouri Pacific suspicion: Quoted in Jordan A. Schwarz, *The Speculator: Bernard M. Baruch in Washington, 1917–1965* (Chapel Hill, N.C., 1981), p. 275. In *F.D.R.: My Exploited Father-in-Law* (Tulsa, Okla., 1968), Curtis B. Dall wrote of an encounter he had had with Baruch just prior to Roosevelt's first inauguration. Baruch, said Dall, bragged that he owned $5/16$ths of the world's visible supply of silver. The subsequent rise in the price of the metal confirmed the author in the view that Baruch was a participant in a worldwide conspiracy; clearly (or so Dall believed) Baruch had been tipped off in advance. Dall was married to Anna Roosevelt.

250 Warburg views: Warburg interview, Columbia University Oral History Collection, p. 819 and pp. 90–91.

251 "little brother . . .": E. J. Kahn, Jr., *The World of Swope* (New York, 1965), p. 382.

251 Swope's stocks: On Jan. 9, 1935, Swope wrote Baruch that the London trip had cost him $4,000 out of pocket and that the forgone profits on his investments amounted to another $125,000.

252   "France would not look . . .": Quoted in Herbert Feis, *1933: Characters in Crisis* (Boston, 1966), p. 180.
253   "the sound . . .": Ibid., pp. 231–232.
253   "We are entering . . .": Quoted in John Brooks, *Once in Golconda: A True Drama of Wall Street, 1920–1938* (New York, 1969), pp. 159–160.
253   "I am going . . .": Baruch to Daniels, July 14, 1933.
254   "on an inflated . . .": Swope to Baruch, July 20, 1933; Swope papers.
254   "undisputed representative . . .": Krock to Baruch, Aug. 7, 1933.
255   Gold-clause controversy: Basic reference source is Henry Mark Holzer, *The Gold Clause: What It Is and How To Use It Profitably* (New York, 1980).
256   Suggestion for Morgenthau: Baruch to Morgenthau, Nov. 26, 1934.
256   "PLEASE TELL HIM . . .": Baruch to LeHand, Feb. 18, 1935. Baruch went on: "BECAUSE OF THE REMOVAL OF THIS UNCERTAINTY, I EXPECT TO SEE BUSINESS RESUME ITS ADVANCE. I JOIN YOU IN THE HAPPINESS WHICH YOU MUST ALL FEEL."
256   "managed currency . . .": Baruch to Churchill, May 22, 1937.
256   "All of us . . .": The lady asked that her name not be divulged.
257   "He has a . . .": Swope to Kent, Nov. 1953 (unmailed); Swope papers.
257   "To sum . . .": *New Yorker* (Nov. 12, 1927), p. 30.
258   Harry Acton: New York *American*, Jan. 7, 1929.
258   "Wall Street . . .": *Time*, July 2, 1934, p. 45.
259   "I nearly laughed . . .": Baruch to Kent, June 3, 1938.
259   "I suppose . . .": Kent to Baruch, July 16, 1936.
259   "If you can . . .": Baruch to Smith, May 31, 1935.
260   "Franklin feels . . .": Mrs. Roosevelt to Baruch, July 12, 1936.
260   "We thought . . .": *New York Times*, Mar. 6, 1935.
260   "Acting President . . .": Ibid., Mar. 13, 1935.
260   "seek a lonely . . .": Anonymous note; General Correspodnence, 1935.
261   "It looks good . . .": Swope to Baruch, July 15, 1936. On Jan. 24, 1947, in the wake of the atomic-bomb negotiations, Swope wrote as emphatically about the same company: "The processes deal with the mysteries of Nature which are illimitable. A group of scientists under the headship of Land (President of the Company) are making such great strides as to justify almost a comparison with nuclear fission." Swope papers.
261   "great social values.": Baruch to Mrs. Roosevelt, Feb. 7, 1937.
262   "to further . . .": Baruch to Nye, Mar. 22, 1935.
262   Nye strategy: Adele Busch to author, Jan. 7, 1983.
262   "Never heard . . .": Bernard M. Baruch, *The Public Years* (New York, 1960), p. 269.
262   "Have you got . . .": Kahn, p. 398. Swope declined a $25,000 check for his week's work but later accepted a $37,500 credit against his debt.

Fourteen   "His Métier Was Peril"

PAGE
263   "I don't know . . .": Dorothy Rosenman to author, Nov. 15, 1979.
263   "YOU HAVE A . . .": Annie Baruch to Swope, Sept. 23, 1936.
264   "Through many . . .": Baruch reminiscences, Unit XV, Box 272.
264   "If a doctor . . .": A physician of Baruch's who asked not to be identified.

264 "Yeah! Pick . . .": Robert Ruark, "Prophet without Portfolio," *Esquire* (Oct. 1952).
264 "low-grade infection": Baruch to Swope, Aug. 30, 1939.
265 "his métier . . .": Harold Epstein to author, Apr. 15, 1980.
265 "greatest menace . . .": Bernard M. Baruch, *Baruch: The Public Years* (New York, 1960), p. 263.
265 Abraham Lincoln Battalion contribution: Jordan A. Schwarz, *The Speculator: Bernard M. Baruch in Washington, 1917–1965* (Chapel Hill, N.C., 1981), p. 348.
265 "I feel . . .": Baruch to Marriner Eccles, Jan. 21, 1937.
266 "Well, the big . . .": Baruch, *The Public Years*, p. 273.
266 "THINK AMERICA ON . . .": Baruch to Churchill, Oct. 19, 1937. On that date the Dow Jones Industrial Average stood at 127; six months later it was 116. However, one year after the bullish cable it was up to 150.
266 "was nuts on Army . . .": Quoted in Schwarz, p. 363.
267 "Has any warship . . .": Baruch to Swope, Apr. 21, 1940.
267 "never allow even . . .": Schwarz, p. 360.
268 "Chairman of the . . .": Eliot Janeway, *The Struggle for Survival: A Chronicle of Economic Mobilization in World War II* (New Haven, 1951), p. 63.
268 Baruch's mobilization views: See, for instance, "Priorities: The Synchronizing Force." In the *Harvard Business Review* (Spring 1941), pp. 261–270.
269 "Socrates of defense": Krock in *Town and Country* (Sept. 1941), p. 61.
269 "things are in . . .": Baltimore *Sun*, Mar. 15, 1941.
269 "*When any problem* . . .": Carter Field to Baruch, Apr. 3, 1941.
269 Kent thanks: Kent to Baruch, Mar. 8, 1941. On Oct. 29, 1941, Baruch asked the columnist to mention him less frequently.
270 "I am familiar . . .": Early to Baruch, Dec. 5, 1940.
270 "How well I . . .": New York *Journal American*, Oct. 5, 1941.
270 "THE PRESIDENT . . .": William D. Hassett to Early, Oct. 5, 1941; Roosevelt papers. Hassett, who was Roosevelt's, and subsequently Truman's, correspondence secretary, loathed Baruch, as he vituperated in the privacy of his diary following the President's return from vacation at Hobcaw in the spring of 1944. "The Boss," wrote Hassett, "paid a heavy penalty in accepting Bernie Baruch's hospitality. Bernie added himself to the household and so was there for most of the month F.D.R. spent in South Carolina. That will make Bernie an important personage when the newspaper stories are released. He planned it that way—the punishment the President takes. In another country, after the circumcision, they throw the Jew away." (Vol. III, p. 47, May 7, 1944.)
271 Hopkins-Hale story: Corcoran to author, Aug. 20, 1981; Adele Busch to author, Mar. 9, 1980; and an interview with a lady who asked for anonymity. According to Ickes, who said that he got the information from Baruch, Baruch "was one of a group that kept Harry [Hopkins] going financially for a time." (Ickes diary, Aug. 1, 1943, p. 8043.)
272 "first-rate scandal.": Henry H. Adams, *Harry Hopkins: A Biography* (New York, 1977), p. 303; and Baruch to Patterson, Jan. 7, 1943.
272 Christmas gift to war relief: Asked why he had chosen that moment to give, Baruch replied (*New York Times*, Dec. 24, 1942), "Because I wanted to." The British embassy, and no doubt other observers too, suspected that the announce-

ment was timed to get him back into the public's good graces following the Hopkins contretemps. (See H. G. Nicholas, ed., *Washington Despatches, 1941–1945: Weekly Political Reports from the British Embassy* [Chicago, 1981], pp. 128–129). The suspicion is reasonable. Before the Hopkins dinner Baruch had intended that the gifts should be kept secret. Afterward, he changed his mind.

272 "Baruch also told . . .": Ickes diary, Feb. 1, 1942, p. 6285.

272 Nazi wanted list: William L. Shirer, *The Rise and Fall of the Third Reich: A History of Nazi Germany* (New York, 1960), p. 784.

273 "Who profits . . .": Two-page document, published in English, in Hamburg; Swope papers. "Baruch himself," the sheet said, reviewing his career in the First World War, "who is today one of the richest Jews in the world, saw to it that his co-racialists took a prominent part in the war-supplies trade. Statistics prove that 70% of the new war millionaires in the City of New York were Jews. . . . Subsequently Baruch became President Roosevelt's confidential adviseror [*sic*]."

273 Baruch's stereotypes: Harold Epstein to author, Apr. 15, 1980. Another stereotype of Baruch's was that Jews are smarter than other people. He would tap his temple, Epstein recalled, and say, "We've got it up here." Sephardic Jews, however, he called "dumb."

273 Baruch relative's letter: "Baruch" to Morgenthau, June 27, 1938. In making his case for emigration, the German Baruch added, "I would like to mention that both of us [his wife and he] present a good appearance; we do not look Jewish." Morgenthau papers.

274 "I am very . . .": David Lavender, *The Story of Cyprus Mines Corporation* (San Marino, Cal., 1962), p. 266.

275 ". . . I am quite . . .": Roosevelt to Baruch, Nov. 1, 1939; Fish to author, May 9, 1983.

275 German press directives: Quoted in John Lukacs, *The Last European War, September 1939/December 1941* (Garden City, N.Y., 1976), p. 508.

276 "I told them!": Blanche Higgins Van Ess to author, June 5, 1982.

276 "I found considerable . . .": Baruch to Roosevelt, Jan. 16, 1942.

277 "Of course they . . .": Baruch to Krock, Mar. 9, 1942.

277 "I am here . . .": Baruch to Watson; Samuel Rosenman papers (President's personal file), April 8, 1940.

277 "My boy . . .": *The New Yorker* (Oct. 3, 1942).

278 "You have quoted . . .": Geoffrey T. Hellman, *Mrs. de Peyster's Parties, and Other Lively Studies from the New Yorker* (New York, 1963), p. xi.

278 "Dear Bernie": Baruch, *The Public Years*, p. 304.

279 "I'm like a lizard . . .": *The New Yorker* (Oct. 3, 1942).

279 "Though in rather . . .": Alfred Redgis to Baruch, Sept. 25, 1942.

280 "I know you . . .": Frank A. Howard, *Buna Rubber: The Birth of an Industry* (New York, 1947), p. 222.

280 "It is curious . . .": Washington *Post*, Aug. 20, 1942.

281 "Hello.": Morgenthau Diaries, 20, Dec. 15, 1942, pp. 179–180. Baruch was evidently discussing his $1 million Christmas present.

283 "You would be . . .": Quoted in Schwarz, p. 437.

283 Catledge story: Turner Catledge, *My Life and Times* (New York, 1971), p. 148.

283 "Dear Bernie": Baruch, *The Public Years*, p. 314.

284 "Baruch would like . . .": Quoted in Schwarz, p. 437.

284 "The war production . . .": Ibid., p. 440.
285 "I don't like . . .": Morgenthau Diaries, 28, Oct. 18, 1944, p. 12.
285 "There was a . . .": Baruch, *The Public Years*, p. 317.
285 "Mr. President . . .": Ibid.
286 "He wryly admitted . . .": Helen Lawrenson, *Stranger at the Party: A Memoir* (New York, 1975), p. 135.
287 "just as keen . . .": Martin Blumenson, ed., *The Patton Papers*, Vol. II, *1940–1945* (Boston, 1974), p. 682. The high quality of Baruch's publicity-staff work is indicated by a note that Lubell wrote him on Apr. 25, 1945, following the return of the Baruch party to the United States: "Here are the addresses and the information on the two soldiers who were wounded and whom you saw in the hospital. I have drafted a possible letter that you may want to send. I'm checking on the photographs as to when they will be ready."
287 "a kind of Mecca . . .": Quoted in Schwarz, p. 426.
287 "The greatest asset . . .": Ibid., p. 425.
287 "Dear Chief": Ibid., p. 468.
288 "great modern thinkers.": Herman Baruch to Secretary of State, Apr. 12, 1945. (State Department document.)
288 "THIS BARAUCH . . .": Fred Jenny to Fulton Lewis, c. Sept. 1943; Baruch General Correspondence.
288 "There has been . . .": Baruch and Hancock, "War and Postwar Adjustment Policies," Feb. 15, 1944, p. 7; Baruch papers. As late as Dec. 23, 1943 (Baruch to Garet Garrett), Baruch himself was worried about a postwar deflation, but his revised bullish opinion was correct.
288 Baruch attitude toward Germany: See, for instance, Morgenthau Diaries, 45, Apr. 21, 1945, p. 106, in which Baruch was quoted as saying: "That is all I have to live for now is to see that Germany is deindustrialized and that it's done the right way, and I won't let anybody get in my way." Morgenthau said that he spoke with tears in his eyes.
289 "the President.": Wallace interview, Columbia University Oral History Collection, p. 4012.

Fifteen   The Atom and All

PAGE
290 "Asked old man . . .": Robert H. Ferrell, ed., *Off the Record: The Private Papers of Harry S. Truman* (New York, 1980), p. 87.
290 "I am confused . . .": Morgenthau Diaries, Franklin D. Roosevelt Library, 44, p. 164; memorandum dated Mar. 13, 1945.
291 "The real protection . . .": *New York Times*, Mar. 29, 1946.
291 Begging calls: Baruch wrote to Swope on Mar. 2, 1946: "There are so many friends and relatives who continually harass me for help of all kinds, that what with being bothered by them on the telephone, I would go mad." Swope papers.
292 "another messenger boy . . .": Bernard M. Baruch, *Baruch: The Public Years* (New York, 1960), p. 361.
292 "Hell, you are!": Ibid., p. 363.
292 "monopoly capitalism": *New York Times*, Feb. 10, 1946.
293 Baruch's House Banking Committee testimony: Ibid., Mar. 26, 1946.

293 "I have unlimited . . .": Baruch to Senator Joseph Guffey, Feb. 24, 1945.
293 ". . . I was quite sick.": David E. Lilienthal, *The Journals of David E. Lilienthal*, Vol. II, *The Atomic Energy Years, 1945–1950* (New York, 1964), p. 30.
293 "I had grimly . . .": Ibid., pp. 39–40.
294 "predictable": Informal Notes of a Meeting with the American Members of the Military Staff Committee, 10:30 A.M.—Sept. 12, 1946, p. 4 (State Department document).
294 "Wall Streeters": John M. Hancock, "Memorandum for Atomic Energy File" (State Department document), Apr. 19, 1946, p. 2. Hancock wrote as an aside: "I wonder as a matter of personal curiosity whether more generally abusive terms were not used."
295 Baruch's accusation of Acheson: Acheson to Baruch, Aug. 23, 1946 (State Department document).
295 Lilienthal suspicions: Lilienthal *Journals*, Vol. II, p. 42; wink of the eye: Adele Busch to author, May 4, 1983.
295 "At least one hundred . . .": Draft Memorandum to the Secretary of State, Mar. 31, 1946 (State Department document).
295 "dominion": Minutes of a meeting at Blair-Lee House, Washington, D.C., Friday, May 17, 1946, p. 6 (State Department document). (Cited hereafter as Blair-Lee minutes.)
296 Baruch's Joint Chiefs meeting: Mentioned in Blair-Lee minutes, May 18, 1946, p. 37.
296 Article X: Lilienthal *Journals*, Vol. II, pp. 130–132 (dated Jan. 11, 1947).
296 ". . . a law without . . .": Blair-Lee minutes, May 17, p. 18.
296 "Don't let these": Lilienthal *Journals*, Vol. II, pp. 42–43.
296 "Write down . . .": Ibid., p. 53.
296 Hiss memo: Hiss to Acheson, May 8, 1946 (State Department document).
297 "I've got . . .": Baruch, *The Public Years*, p. 369.
297 "We are here . . .": Quoted in E. J. Kahn, Jr., *The World of Swope* (New York, 1965), pp. 400–401.
298 Lilienthal-Oppenheimer reaction: Lilienthal *Journals*, Vol. II, pp. 60–61.
298 "rhetoric and truth . . .": Quoted in Kahn, p. 401.
298 "Conn must wish . . .": Baruch, *The Public Years*, p. 379.
299 10–2 vote: Lilienthal *Journals*, Vol. II, p. 69.
299 "If it is good . . ." and ff.: Ibid., pp. 75–76.
299 Newsprint story: Baruch, *The Public Years*, p. 378.
300 Baruch's resigned attitude: In a meeting on Aug. 1, a stenographer wrote: "Mr. Baruch stated that there has been a tremendous change in public attitude toward Russia. We must do everything we can to reach an agreement: nevertheless, ultimately, we must face the facts. If we have made every effort to reach an agreement, we can then face a break with a clear conscience." (Notes on conference with General McNaughton and Mr. Ignatieff, Aug. 1, 1946, State Department document.)
300 "Repeated efforts . . .": Observations Concerning the Attitude of the Soviet Representatives on the Atomic Energy Commission, Aug. 12, 1946, p. 1.
300 Baruch's bomb suggestion: A minute-taker quoted him: "In strengthening our military potential against the day that negotiations may break down, efforts should be redoubled to accumulate stockpiles with raw materials and atomic

bombs." (Informal notes of staff meeting, 11 A.M.—Sept. 10, 1946, State Department document.)

300 "We cannot afford . . .": Memorandum for the President, Sept. 17, 1946, p. 21 (State Department document).

300 "Is it any wonder . . .": *New York Times*, Sept. 18, 1946.

300 "The tougher . . .": Ibid., Sept. 13, 1946.

301 "main agent . . .": Memo to the director of the FBI, Mar. 22, 1947; FBI document 62-45288-143.

301 "Here's the atomic . . .": *New York Times*, Dec. 31, 1946.

302 War College anecdote: Quoted in Lilienthal *Journals*, Vol. II, p. 258.

303 "I'm just *not* . . .": Ibid., p. 163.

304 "Flatterer. . . .": Ferrell, p. 64.

304 "rude, uncouth and ignorant . . .": New York *Journal American*, Oct. 31, 1948. Just those words appear in Pegler's notes of the conversation; Pegler papers.

305 "The incident reflects . . .": Krock to Pegler, Dec. 8, 1951; Pegler papers.

305 "Let us . . .": Quoted in Kahn, p. 403.

306 "You performed . . .": Quoted in Jordan A. Schwarz, *The Speculator: Bernard M. Baruch in Washington, 1917–1965* (Chapel Hill, N.C., 1981), p. 530.

306 "For every paragraph . . .": Pegler column (Pittsburgh *Sun Telegraph*), May 29, 1947.

306 "Look at . . .": Lilienthal *Journals*, Vol. III, *Venturesome Years: 1950–1955*, p. 31.

306 Swope memos: Swope papers.

307 "You son . . .": Quoted in Kahn, p. 395.

307 "It has been . . .": Swope to Baruch, Apr. 30, 1948; Swope papers.

308 "thrived on contention. . . .": Kahn, p. 440.

308 "Mr. Baruch": Swope to Baruch, Apr. 14, 1953.

308 "substantial": Swope note to himself, Dec. 28, 1953; Swope papers.

308 "I have sensed . . .": Baruch to Swope, Nov. 26, 1954.

309 "Any person . . .": *New York Times*, Aug. 17, 1955. On Aug. 10, 1953, in a letter to E. D. Coblentz, Baruch offered this view on internal security: "Whether they [the Soviets] have the hydrogen bomb through spies I do not know but they certainly got the atomic bomb through spies. What else they got, we do not know but we do know that no one has the right to be a communist or a fellow-traveler while we face an antagonistic enemy—imperialistic communism."

310 Stock-market testimony: Stock Market Study; Hearings before the Committee on Banking and Currency, United States Senate, Washington, D.C., 1955.

312 "I used to wait . . .": *New York Times*, Aug. 19, 1956.

312 Baruch's estate: According to probate documents, he left $115,801.84 in cash, $8.4 million in bonds, $5.5 million in stocks, with the balance in miscellaneous accounts.

312 "It's a terrible thing . . .": Van Ess to author, June 5, 1982.

312 "You know . . .": Harold Epstein to author, July 9, 1980.

312 Description of Baruch's apartment: Dorothy Schiff in the New York *Post*, Oct. 21, 1951.

312 Stock-market details: James Myers to author.

313 "Mr. Baruch stated . . .": E. J. Powers to J. Edgar Hoover, Sept. 25, 1957 (FBI document).

313 "his eyes . . .": Harold Epstein to author, July 9, 1980.

313 Malone story: Adele Busch to author, Feb. 12, 1980.

314 Sapphire story: The source asked for anonymity.

314 "You may wonder . . .": Baruch to Coblentz, Mar. 5, 1955.

314 "Tell Mr. Hoover . . .": Edward Scheidt to J. Edgar Hoover, Nov. 15, 1950 (FBI document).

314 "there is no use . . .": Bernard M. Baruch, *Baruch: My Own Story* (New York, 1957), p. 50.

315 "It would be a pretty . . .": J. Leon Gasque, Jr., in oral history interview with the South Carolina Department of Archives and History, Mar.–Apr. 1979.

315 "Elizabeth, show her . . ." and ff.: Navarro to author, Feb. 21, 1980.

316 "I can't keep up . . .": *New York Times*, Aug. 19, 1964.

316 Niehans story: Helen Lawrenson, *Stranger at the Party: A Memoir* (New York, 1975), p. 161; and an interview with a doctor of Baruch's who asked not to be identified.

316 "live and be strong . . .": Baruch to Rusk, Oct. 11, 1961.

316 "That's the best . . .": Epstein to author, Apr. 15, 1980.

316 "God damn it . . .": Quoted in Kahn, p. 410.

317 "Ah, who the hell . . .": Epstein to author, July 9, 1980.

317 Spellman story: Navarro to author, Feb. 21, 1980.

Index

347